ARMENIAN CHRISTIANITY TODAY

Armenian Christianity Today

Identity Politics and Popular Practice

Edited by

ALEXANDER AGADJANIAN
Russian State University for the Humanities, Russia

ASHGATE

© Alexander Agadjanian 2014

All rights reserved. No part of this publication may be reproduced, stored in a retrieval system or transmitted in any form or by any means, electronic, mechanical, photocopying, recording or otherwise without the prior permission of the publisher.

Alexander Agadjanian has asserted his right under the Copyright, Designs and Patents Act, 1988, to be identified as the editor of this work.

Published by
Ashgate Publishing Limited
Wey Court East
Union Road
Farnham
Surrey, GU9 7PT
England

Ashgate Publishing Company
110 Cherry Street
Suite 3-1
Burlington, VT 05401-3818
USA

www.ashgate.com

British Library Cataloguing in Publication Data
A catalogue record for this book is available from the British Library

The Library of Congress has cataloged the printed edition as follows:
Armenian Christianity today : identity politics and popular practice / edited by Alexander Agadjanian.
    pages cm
  Includes bibliographical references and index.
  ISBN 978-1-4724-1271-3 (hardcover) -- ISBN 978-1-4724-1272-0 (ebook) -- ISBN 978-1-4724-1273-7 (ePUB) 1. Armenians--Ethnic identity. 2. Armenia (Republic)--Religion. 3. Christianity--Armenia (Republic) 4. Armenian Church. 5. Protestants--Armenia (Republic) 6. Armenians--Foreign countries. I. Agadjanian, Alexander, 1958- editor.
  DK683.3.A664 2014
  281'.62--dc23

2014016694

ISBN 9781472412713 (hbk)
ISBN 9781472412720 (ebk – PDF)
ISBN 9781472412737 (ebk – ePUB)

Printed in the United Kingdom by Henry Ling Limited, at the Dorset Press, Dorchester, DT1 1HD

Contents

	Introduction *Alexander Agadjanian*	1

PART I THE REPUBLIC OF ARMENIA: RELIGIOUS REVIVAL AND RENEWAL

1	"One Nation, One Faith, One Church": The Armenian Apostolic Church and the Ethno-Religion in Post-Soviet Armenia *Konrad Siekierski*	9
2	Church, God and Society: Toward the Anthropology of Church Construction in Armenia *Yulia Antonyan*	35
3	Where Did We Come From? Creationism versus Evolution in Armenian Public Schools *Satenik Mkrtchyan*	57
4	The Religious Modernity of the Brotherhood: A New Face of Armenian Grassroots Christianity *Alexander Agadjanian*	71
5	Evangelical and Pentecostal Communities in Armenia: Negotiating Identity and Accommodation *Anna Ohanjanyan*	91

PART II ARMENIAN DIASPORAS: PUZZLES OF IDENTITY

6	Identity, Borders and Religious Belonging: Armenians between Two Spiritual Centers, Etchmiadzin and Cilicia *Hovhannes Hovhannisyan*	125

7	Venerating the Saints, Remembering the City: Armenian Memorial Practices and Community Formation in Contemporary Istanbul *Christopher Sheklian*	145
8	The Three Religions of Armenians in Lebanon *Irina Papkova*	171
9	The Chronotopes of the Armenian Diaspora in Romania: Religious Feasts and Shrines in the Making of Community *Konrad Siekierski*	197
10	Armenians in St. Petersburg: Belonging to the Church as a Key Marker of Ethnic Identity *Anatolii Tokmantcev*	215
11	Finger on the Pulse: Armenian Identity and Religiosity in Southern California *Dyron Daughrity and Nicholas Cumming*	233
12	Sanctuary, Community or Museum? The Apostolic Church in the Life-Worlds of a Sample of American Armenians *Sara Kärkkäinen Terian*	253

Index 273

Introduction

Alexander Agadjanian

The vast majority of Armenians living in the world today belongs, in multiple forms and with varying intensity, to the Christian religion. Among the denominations currently associated with Armenians, the Armenian Apostolic Church is seen overwhelmingly as *the* national Church, the endemic tradition that almost all Armenians are born into. This unique Church tradition, with its special liturgical language and order, esthetics, texts and practices, claims a great and uninterrupted antiquity and is often considered the main pillar of Armenian identity.

In fact, however, this tradition, as so many others, went through a long historical journey: it was initially tightly linked to emerging Syriac and Greek Christianities in the first centuries of Christian era; then split, gradually and slowly, from the early imperial Church after rejecting the rulings of the ecumenical Council of Chalcedon; then went under the millennial impact of both a predominantly Muslim environment and alternative Christian agencies of Roman Catholicism and Byzantine Orthodoxy; then continued seeking difficult accommodation under the rule of Ottoman, Russian and Soviet empires, resisting both physical and ideological pressures from rulers, mobs, other religious agents or strong secular forces of the nineteenth and twentieth centuries.

It is true that, despite all these pressures and influences, the Armenian Apostolic Church remained a significant reference point and a powerful institutional player in the lives and thoughts of Armenians both in today's Republic and in the diasporas worldwide. However, precisely because they have had such a long history, the Armenian communities and individuals could not remain religiously monochromic. The relatively small groups of Armenian Catholics and Armenian Protestants of various denominations have become visible actors within the overall picture, both in the Republic and elsewhere. These Catholic and Protestant Armenians pose inevitable problems of identity. The Armenian Eastern Orthodox is even a less plausible combination, because

Eastern Orthodox churches are also tightly linked to particular ethnies (Russian, Greek, Georgian, etc.), and conversion to them requires a clear sacrifice of identity. In any case, those Armenians who have converted to Russian Orthodoxy or American Protestantism (to refer only to the two largest diasporas in Russia and the United States) are struggling between affirming their Armenianness or becoming assimilated. There are also groups of Islamized Armenians, such as Hemshins (Hemşins), but they are very unlikely to be counted as bearers of the Armenian identity: the combination of an Armenian with Islam, or another non-Christian religion, for that matter, seems to be not common at all, although in this global world of postmodern spirituality certain Armenian individuals may choose to convert to Buddhism, the Bahai faith or any blend of the New Age.

What, however, *is* real and hugely widespread among the Armenians, as among many other nations, is religious indifference, secularism or even atheism; such an outcome was also caused by long historical trends experienced in the two last centuries. It goes without saying that the modern nationalism of the Armenians developed mostly within the Ottoman and the Russian empires, under the auspices of mostly secular, at least non-clerical, ideals of European Enlightenment and Romantic provenance, and although the Church certainly played a role in this national formation, it also went through a secularization and evolved into a quasi-secular institution as one of the political players. Partly this new role drew upon the legacy of earlier times, when the Church hierarchy was a political leader of the Ottoman Armenian *millet*, but the later secularism, from the nineteenth century onward, was certainly a product of Western "disenchantment." The blow of the Ottoman genocide during the World War I further shattered the religious tradition in what was called "Western Armenia." Afterwards, the Soviet rule in "Eastern Armenia" served as the latest assault against religion and formed a few generations of non-religious Armenians who grasped for other sources of identity.

And yet, in the last Soviet decades, the Armenian Christian tradition gradually acquired tremendous symbolic authority, tightly linked with ethnic revival, which was galvanized by the independence movement and new nation-building objectives in the aftermath of the Soviet Union. All this led to a certain revival of public and private religiosity, translated into both patronizing state politics of the de facto "national Church" and the grassroots search for a symbolic and spiritual renewal. However, Armenians continue to be seen as largely secular people, with predominantly relatively "cool" forms of religiosity and a "consumerist" massive interest to only life-cycle rituals. In this sense, the Republic of Armenia and the self-proclaimed Republic of Nagorno-Karabagh

(Artsakh) seem to represent a median type of low European religiosity. This does not prevent, however, some particular groups, movements or individuals from being religiously passionate and creative; much of this creativity springs from a new visibility of the vernacular (folk) forms of religion, mostly in the Republic, and partly exported to the diasporas by the new post-Soviet migrants.

Therefore, overall, we have a rather variegated picture, which this volume seeks to illuminate at least in part. We seek to show that the Armenian Christian tradition continues to be distinct, being deeply and even intimately "national"; at the same time, it is undergoing some experiences that are typical of current global mutations, with their contradictions: desecularizing impulses clashing with the deepening spread of secularity; growing transnationalism opposed to strongly articulated ethno-centrism.

* * *

This multiple reality of Armenian religiosity is presented in the two parts of the volume, one dedicated to the Republic of Armenia and the second to the diasporas.[1] In the first part, Konrad Siekierski's chapter sets the overall political frame of the current situation—a powerful symbolic mythology of oneness and uniqueness of the Armenian ethno-Christianity, so much promoted by both the Church hierarchy and the state. Drawing upon Danièle Hervieu-Léger's view of religion as a "chain of memory," Siekierski shows the six building blocks of this great narrative of the unique link of the Armenian culture and its particular brand of Christianity. Yulia Antonyan takes up the officially promoted revival, as manifested in the exuberant scale of church construction (similar to Russia and other post-Soviet lands); but Antonyan looks at the process "from the bottom up," drawing upon popular narratives of the private investors and donors, rich and poor, who are translating the power of Christian symbolism into social benefits.

Satenik Mkrtchyan explores another evidence of current desecularization— the impact of the officially promoted narrative of Christian Armenian identity in public schools. After mapping the overall encroachment of this discourse into public education and, therefore, on to the formation of dominant cultural codes, Mkrtychyan looks at one particular facet of this phenomenon—a "latent culture war," as she calls it, within the curriculum, namely, the debate between

---

[1] The preparation of this volume was partly supported by a grant from Melikian Center of Russian, Eurasian and East European Studies at Arizona State University.

creationism and evolution—a century-old debate which has now reached the Armenian textbooks, in the aftermath of the tradition of strict Soviet atheism.

My own chapter looks again at the grassroots religiosity that exploded after the end of the Soviet ideological domination; here the focus is on a religious group turned into a whole movement with its *tour de force* in the early 1990s, the fateful time of the nation-building, suffering and war. This particular movement, the "Brotherhood," emerged paradoxically both within the Armenian Apostolic tradition and outside it, and this border identity created an unusual space for unfettered spiritual seeking and experiments, but also a precarious sense of otherness. Anna Ohanjanyan, in her chapter, moves a few steps further away from the endemic, mainline Armenian Christianity—to the Protestant spectrum of churches operating in the Republic: she gives a detailed overview and then shows how intricate and fragile are the negotiations they lead to assure the place of religious minorities, and how they try, in the course of this enculturation, to animate the "hidden scripts" of the old popular sectarian tradition within the Armenian Christian memory.

The second part of the book deals with a few examples of the Armenian diaspora, whose numbers, especially after a new post-Soviet emigration, perhaps, exceeds the population of the Republic (exact figures are almost impossible to count). It starts with an essay in ecclesiastic politics by Hovhannes Hovhannisyan who traces the history of relationships between the two main administrative centers of the Armenian Church—the Holy See of Etchmiadzin, outside Yerevan, and the so-called Catholicosate of Cilicia, now located in Antelias, Lebanon. Hovhannisyan shows how their strained relations were interwoven with politics in Soviet times, as well as how they improved after the independence, but only temporarily: besides politics, they represented a deeper difference between Eastern and Western Armenian memories, and also, between two different ecclesiastic styles.

Christopher Sheklian's chapter comes next and explores the current Armenian religiosity in Istanbul, once the capital of the Western Armenian culture; around 60,000–70,000 Armenians who remain in the city maintain a communal memory, broken by the turbulences of the twentieth century, through the liturgical observances and especially through the veneration of saints, old and new. For Sheklian, communal *memory* is the key word, and analyzing it he refers to the model Mary Carruthers used for the study of the Western medieval culture. In the next chapter, Irina Papkova provides a detailed mapping of a major Middle Eastern Armenian diaspora, in Lebanon (where the above-mentioned "Cilician" Catholicos dwells), showing how the Apostolic Orthodox, Catholic and Protestant groups interact and share—although in various degrees—the sense of ethnic belonging, fastened by and anchored in the common memory of the early twentieth-century genocide.

We then move west and north, to Romania and Russia, where the traces of the Armenian community are indeed very old, just as they are in other Eastern European lands such as Bulgaria, Hungary, Poland or Ukraine. Both Konrad Siekierski and Anatolii Tokmantcev present recent field research, and in both cases the issue of identity is predictably the key issue. Siekierski, using Mikhail Bakhtin's theoretical model of chronotope, illustrates with the examples of Armenian church feasts in Romania how the liturgical calendar organizes the life of the community—similar to what we saw in Istanbul. Siekierski then refers to his account of the Armenian ethno-religion in the first chapter in this volume and shows how this notion is manifested in Romania and how the "preservation of Armenianness" through religious belonging remains the ultimate goal of the community. We find the same situation in the city of St. Petersburg, where Armenians stick to their church life and where drifting toward the dominant Russian Orthodoxy threatens Armenianness, perhaps, even more than being only a formal member of the Mother Church—lest it be on terms of "belonging without believing."

And finally, with the two last chapters, we are moving far west, to the United States, the place of the second largest Armenian diaspora. Dyron Daughrity and Nicholas Cumming use recent quantitative survey data to explore the Christian "pulse" of the Californian Armenians, and they a show a picture quite different from what we saw in the old world and especially in the Republic. It looks like the American melting pot mentality—reinforced by the plurality of origins among the local Armenian immigrants themselves—dissolves the great narrative of the ethno-religion and makes Armenian religiosity more and more in line with the mainstream as recorded by the pan-American Pew Research data, with only a slightly stronger family commitment. Sara Terian's chapter, based upon the qualitative survey, provides an analysis with the use of David Carr's rendering of the Husserlian *life-world* concept. For different Armenians, coming from various backgrounds (including not only Apostolic, but also Catholic and Evangelicals), the church is either a sanctuary, or a community with shared culture and memory, or a museum of cultural heritage. It may be either of the three or all the three together. These are facets of what the Armenian Christianity continues to be in today's world—the world whose condition of either secular or desecularizing continues to be under heated debates.

PART I
The Republic of Armenia: Religious Revival and Renewal

Chapter 1
"One Nation, One Faith, One Church": The Armenian Apostolic Church and the Ethno-Religion in Post-Soviet Armenia

Konrad Siekierski

This chapter discusses the historical foundations and the modern manifestations and implications of the Armenian-Christian ethno-religion, as maintained and promoted by the Armenian Apostolic Church (AAC) in the post-Soviet Republic of Armenia. First, it examines a number of symbolic events and figures that constitute the Armenian-Christian "chain of memory" from the biblical Deluge to the Armenian genocide. Second, it presents and analyzes selected examples of the modern discourse of the AAC, taken from the Church's publications or collected during the author's interviews with members of the clergy. The chapter concludes by locating the ethno-religion of the Armenian Apostolic Church within the wider frame of the current socio-religious situation in Armenia.

The Armenian-Christian Chain of Memory: Origins and Reformulations

French sociologist Danièle Hervieu-Léger devoted a chapter of her seminal book *Religion as a Chain of Memory* to the phenomenon of "ethno-religion." As she states, both religious and ethnic belonging create social ties on the basis of a postulated genealogy, which is, on the one hand, naturalized, since it appeals to blood and earth, and, on the other hand, symbolized, since it is established through invoking and praising the myth of origin. Hence religious and ethnic identities, in sharing a common essence, often strengthen each other, or even fuse together, and are perceived as inseparable.[1]

---

[1] Danièle Hervieu-Léger, *Religion as a Chain of Memory* (New Brunswick, 2000), pp. 157–62.

Although Hervieu-Léger writes about ethno-religion in a section entitled "The Chain Reinvented" and concentrates on examining modern cases of nationalisms that emerged as a fusion of ethnic and religious elements, she acknowledges two exceptional groups in which this paradigm of inseparability goes back deep into history and precedes the modern era, namely, the Jews and the Armenians. The view that the "Armenian case" is exceptional can be found not only in Hervieu-Léger's work: it is supported by a number of historians and anthropologists, including Anthony Smith, Anne Elizabeth Redgate, Razmik Panossian, Abraham Terian and Levon Abrahamian. What leads all these authors to such a conclusion is their shared view that the Christianization of Armenia at the beginning of the fourth century and the subsequent creation of a separate literary tradition were watershed events that resulted in establishing and fixing a distinctive Armenian identity. More specifically, Smith, in his book devoted to the religious sources of national identity, states that by the act of adopting Christianity Armenians started to consider themselves as "Peoples of the Covenant."[2] According to Redgate, the "creation of the Armenian alphabet made possible a truly national sense of Armenian identity."[3] Panossian claims that "through ... religious conversion church leaders were also producing a unique form of literary tradition ... In this crucial respect they were 'creating' Armenians."[4] Finally, Terian speaks about the Armenian "blend of patriotism and piety"[5] that occurred in the fourth and fifth centuries, while Abrahamian uses the term "early constructivism" to describe the unification project undertaken in that period by the state and the Church.[6]

However, the fusion of the ethnic and religious components of Armenian identity, as it exists today and is eagerly promoted by the Armenian Apostolic Church, should not be seen as a straightforward continuation of this "early constructivism" and "blend of patriotism and piety." Even if the Armenian ethno-religious chain of memory was indeed "forged" centuries earlier than most other ethno-religious chains, it was undoubtedly reshaped by the grand

---

[2] Anthony Smith, *Chosen Peoples: Sacred Sources of National Identity* (Oxford, 2003), pp. 66–73.

[3] Anna Elizabeth Redgate, "National Letters, Vernacular Christianity and National Identity in Early Medieval Armenia," in Vladimir Barchurdarian (ed.), *Armenian Letters: International Conference Dedicated to the 1600th Anniversary of the Armenian Letters Creation*, Collection of Papers (Yerevan, 2006), p. 176.

[4] Razmik Panossian, *The Armenians: From Kings and Priests to Merchants and Commissars* (New York, 2006), pp. 44–5.

[5] Abraham Terian, *Patriotism and Piety in Armenian Christianity: The Early Panegyrics on Saint Gregory* (New York, 2005), p. 7.

[6] Personal conversation with Levon Abrahamian, Yerevan, 2010.

narrative of modern nationalism, introduced to Armenians in the nineteenth century by the first Armenian political parties,[7] and further developed in Soviet Armenia and in the post-genocide Armenian diaspora.

In the mid-nineteenth century the leaders of the emerging Armenian national movement blamed the AAC for the fall of the Armenian state and Armenians' powerlessness in the face of perpetual invasions and persecutions. This anticlericalism was famously expressed by Raffi, one of the most influential Armenian writers of that time:

> O fathers! O fore-fathers! ... Had you built fortresses, instead of monasteries with which our country is full; had you guns and ammunition, instead of squandering fortunes on Holy urns, had you burned gunpowder instead of perfumery incense at the Holy altars, our country would have been more fortunate ... From these very monasteries the doom of our country was sealed.[8]

In a few decades, however, this stance was eased and the authority of the Church became perceived as an important factor in cementing ethno-national identity. The AAC itself also employed the national discourse in order to strengthen its position among the people. As a result:

> the priests were educated as national workers, as another party. The Church was subordinated to nationalistic feelings, and the churchmen themselves became the missionaries of nationality rather than religion.[9]

In post-World War II Soviet Armenia, with the emergence of a new secular "blend of patriotism and socialism,"[10] the Armenian Apostolic Church was saved from the pre-war policies of annihilation. Its activities, however, took

---

[7] In this period legal regulations implemented in the Russian and Ottoman empires—the Polozhenie of 1836 and the National Constitutions of 1863—also contributed to the process of secularization in the AAC.

[8] As quoted in Vigen Guroian, *Ethics after Christendom: Towards an Ecclesial Christian Ethic* (Grand Rapids, 1994), p. 118.

[9] Author's interview with an AAC clergyman, Etchmiadzin, 2010.

[10] As Panossian describes it, "a view that is quite widely accepted in postindependence Armenia [is] that the Soviet Armenian leadership used communism to build the nation and that most Armenian intellectuals, political leaders, and even some party apparatchiks—especially after Stalin's death—pursued nationalist goals within the confines of the USSR." Razmik Panossian, "Post-Soviet Armenia: Nationalism and its (Dis)contents," in Lowell W. Barrington (ed.), *After Independence: Making and Protecting the Nation in Postcolonial and Postcommunist States* (Ann Arbor, 2006), p. 226.

place predominantly in the context of the preservation of national identity and heritage. The Church was largely deprived of its spiritual functions, and reduced to a minimum in its structures. Meanwhile, selected elements of the Armenian-Christian heritage, such as the creation of the Armenian alphabet at the beginning of the fifth century, were recalled in a secular context and promoted thanks to official propaganda and compulsory education.[11]

Summarizing the impact of modern nationalism on the Armenian Apostolic Church over the last hundred years, Vigen Guroian offers the following assessment:

> As it entered the twentieth century, the Armenian Church ... embraced [the] role of safeguarding Armenian identity prescribed by secular Armenian nationalism ... In the eighty years since the genocide, the Armenian Church hierarchy and clergy have constructed a religio-national myth ... The myth traces the origins of the present secularized nationalistic church back to the founding acts of the Armenian Church in the fourth and fifth centuries. It is preached and argued in all sorts of public forums that the religionized nationalism that the church promotes is the self-same faith of the Church's founders and its martyred defenders through the centuries.[12]

Six Elements of the Armenian Ethno-Religious Genealogy

The Armenian ethno-religious genealogy postulated by the Armenian Apostolic Church consists of a number of symbolic events and figures. Six of them,

---

[11] For more on the situation of the AAC in Soviet Armenia see: Edward Alexander, "The Armenian Church in Soviet Policy," *Russian Review* 14, no. 4 (1955); Felix Corley, "The Armenian Church under the Soviet Regime, Part 1: The Leadership of Kevork," *Religion, State & Society* 24, no. 1 (1996); Felix Corley, "The Armenian Church under the Soviet Regime, Part 2: The Leadership of Vazgen," *Religion, State & Society* 24, no. 2 (1996); Felix Corley, "The Armenian Church under the Soviet and Independent Regimes, Part 3: The Leadership of Vazgen," *Religion, State & Society* 26, no. 3/4 (1998); Vahakn Dadrian, "Nationalism in Soviet Armenia—a Case Study of Ethnocentrism," in George W. Simmonds (ed.), *Nationalism in the USSR and Eastern Europe in the Era of Brezhnev and Kosygin* (Detroit, 1977), pp. 216–44; Claire Mouradian, "The Armenian Apostolic Church," in Pedro Ramet (ed.), *Eastern Christianity and Politics in the Twentieth Century* (Durham, NC, 1988); Konrad Siekierski, "The Armenian Apostolic Church and Vernacular Christianity in Soviet Armenia," *Keston Newsletter* 18 (2013).

[12] Vigen Guroian, *Faith, Church, Mission: Essays for Renewal in the Armenian Church* (New York, 1995), pp. 124–5.

arguably the most important, widely known and continually recalled elements of this genealogy will be discussed here.

Chronologically the first element is the biblical story of the Deluge, Noah's landing on Mount Ararat, and his settlement in the Ararat Valley from where life returned to earth.[13] The city of Nakhchivan (the capital of the Nakhchivan Autonomous Republic, part of Azerbaijan), a name which in Armenian (Nakhijevan) means "the first place of resettlement," is considered to be the eternal resting place of Noah, and his tomb used to be an important destination for Armenian pilgrims.[14] Today, on the official website of the AAC one can find the following information: "When Noah emerged from the Ark, he prepared a sacrifice in the Araratian Valley and built an altar for the sacrifice in the place where Holy Etchmiadzin[15] is now located."[16] Furthermore, ever since Movses Khorenatsi wrote his "Hayots Patmut'yun" (The History of Armenia)[17] the story of Noah has been supplemented in the Armenian tradition by the story

---

[13] Sometimes this chain is lengthened even further by the supposition that the biblical Gardens of Eden were located on the territory of historic Armenia. As Hamlet Petrosyan shows, already in the fifth century Armenian authors were comparing the Ararat valley to Paradise, and "by the 14th century, Armenians were identifying the river Araks, which flows through Ararat plain, with the Bible's Gihon River ... There were also attempts to locate Eden's fourth river, Pison, in Armenia, even though there was no other large river there. Together the legends and beliefs gave rise to widespread speculations—full-blown by the 18th century—that Armenia might, indeed, be the land of the Lost Paradise." Hamlet Petrosyan, "The World as a Garden," in Levon Abrahamian and Nancy Sweezy (eds), *Armenian Folk Arts, Culture, and Identity* (Bloomington, 2001), pp. 28–9. This idea was taken even further by the eighteenth-century Armenian-Catholic monk Michael Chamchian, who suggested that Adam communicated with God in Armenian. Razmik Panossian, "The Past as Nation: Three Dimensions of Armenian Identity," *Geopolitics* 7, no. 2 (2002), pp. 127–8.

[14] K.A. Nikitin, "Gorod Nakhichevan i Nakhichevanskiĭ uiezd," in *Sbornik Materialov dlia Opisaniia Miestnosteĭ i Plemen' Kavkaza, Vypusk Vtoroĭ* (Tiflis, 1882), pp. 111–13. [The city of Nakhichevan and Nakhichevan district, in the Materials of the regions and tribes of the Caucasus].

[15] The Mother See of Holy Etchmiadzin, located in the town of Vagharshapat some 20 kilometers from Armenia's capital city of Yerevan, is the spiritual and administrative center of the Etchmiadzin Catholicosate of the Armenian Apostolic Church. The AAC is currently divided into two Catholicosates (the one in Etchmiadzin and the Catholicosate of the Great House of Cilicia, located in Antelias, Lebanon), and two Patriarchates (in Jerusalem, Israel and in Istanbul, Turkey).

[16] History, The Armenian Church, Mother See of Holy Etchmiadzin, www.armenianchurch.org/index.jsp?sid=1&id=2361&pid=2360&lng=en, accessed October 18, 2013.

[17] Movses Khorenatsi himself claims to be the disciple of Mesrop Mashtots', the creator of the Armenian alphabet, and is conventionally referred to in Armenian historiography as an author of the fifth century. An alternative dating of Khorenatsi's work was proposed by

of Hayk, the son of Noah's great-grandson, who is claimed as the forefather of the Armenians.[18]

It is worth noting that, contrary to Armenian Apostolic Church discourse and popular knowledge, it was probably as late as the beginning of the second millennium AD when the localization of the biblical Mount Ararat was permanently moved from the highlands hemming upper Mesopotamia to Mount Masis in the heart of historical Armenian territory.[19] Mount Masis was a sacred mountain even before its identification with Ararat, and afterwards its symbolic importance for the "Armenian Issue"[20] has made Masis-Ararat crucial in the formation of modern Armenian identity. At the same time, just as in the case of the AAC, the modern "nationalization" of Masis-Ararat has also led to its partial secularization. Although less than 200 years ago high-ranking Armenian clergyman commented that to climb the sacred mountain was "to tire the womb of the mother of all mankind in a dragonish mode,"[21] nowadays to ascend Ararat is the most highly valued goal of some of the patriotic pilgrimages that are organized in growing number from Armenia and the Armenian diaspora.

The second set of traditions included in the Armenian-Christian chain of memory traces back to apostolic times. First, two disciples of Christ—Saint Jude Thaddeus and Saint Bartholomew—are believed to have been martyred during their evangelical mission to Armenia in the middle of the first century. The Armenian Church considers itself to be the direct successor to their mission,

---

Robert Thomson in his English translation of Hayots Patmut'yun [History of Armenia], who stated that it was written in the eighth century.

[18] Movses Khorenatsi, *Istoriia Armenii* (Erevan, 1990), pp. 18–25 [History of Armenia]. In the Armenian language Armenia is known as Hayastan, and Armenians refer to themselves as Hayer (plural; the singular form is Hay).

[19] Armen Petrosian, "Dva Ararata: Gora Kordueny i Masis" [The two Ararats: Kordueny and Masis], in Ruth Büttner and Judith Peltz (eds), *Mythical Landscapes Then and Now: The Mystification of Landscapes in Search for National Identity* (Yerevan, 2006); Hamlet Petrosyan, "The Sacred Mountain," in Levon Abrahamian and Nancy Sweezy (eds), *Armenian Folk Arts, Culture, and Identity* (Bloomington, 2001), p. 36.

[20] As Harutyun Marutyan explains: "The concepts of 'the Armenian Cause' or in a broader sense 'the Armenian Issue,' are used today to indicate the struggle for the survival of Armenians, the liberation of the territories of Western Armenia and Eastern Armenia that are outside the Republic of Armenia, and the restoration of a united Armenian state. This is a complex cause which, apart from the already mentioned political and territorial dimensions, also carries moral, socio-economic and legal aspects." Harutyun Marutyan, *Iconography of Armenian Identity: The Memory of Genocide and the Karabagh Movement* (Yerevan, 2009), p. 66.

[21] Quoted in Petrosyan, "The Sacred Mountain," p. 37. This statement was made after Friedrich Parrot and Khachatur Abovian reached the peak of Ararat in 1829 (p. 35).

and thus has the word "Apostolic" in its official name. Second, the apocryphal story of King Abgar of Edessa, "armenianized" by Movses Khorenatsi, establishes an Armenian history of conversion that precedes by almost three centuries the official adoption of Christianity by the Armenian kingdom.[22] According to this apocryphon, Abgar, who suffered from an incurable sickness, "believed without seeing" in Christ's divinity, asked him for healing, and offered him asylum in his palace. In reply, Christ sent to Abgar one of his Seventy Disciples, St. Thaddeus, equipped with the Mandylion—a cloth on which the image of Christ's face had been miraculously imprinted. King Abgar, healed and baptized by St. Thaddeus, became the world's first Christian ruler.

The third element of the mythological genealogy is the story of the Armenian conversion to Christianity at the beginning of the fourth century. This story, as handed down by the fifth-century historian Agat'angeghos, includes an account of the 13 torments of St. Gregory the Illuminator, including his imprisonment in a Khor Virap pit; the martyrdom of St. Hrip'simē, St. Gayanē, and their companions; and the divine punishment of King Trdat III, turned into a boar for his atrocities, his subsequent healing by St. Gregory followed by the baptism of the king and his subjects. Agat'angeghos also describes a vision in which Christ appeared to St. Gregory pointing to the place where the spiritual center of the new religion should be built as well as King Trdat's ascent of Ararat, from where he brought eight stones to be placed in the foundations of the cathedral.[23] This cathedral, built on the site of a pagan temple (and of Noah's first altar, according to the first element in the tradition), received the name Etchmiadzin, meaning the place where "The Only Begotten Descended." Accordingly, in the AAC's tradition Etchmiadzin is also referred to as the "Armenian Bethlehem."

It is worth noting that the exact date of adopting Christianity—the year 301—was actually introduced only at the end of eighteenth century,[24] and was glorified even more recently: the 1,700th anniversary of the conversion held in 2001 was the first to be celebrated with great pomp and the mobilization of people and resources.[25] Nevertheless, the date 301, which establishes Armenian

---

[22] Khorenats'i, *Istoriia Armenii*, pp. 85–6.
[23] Agatangelos, *Istoriia Armenii* (Erevan 2004), pp. 56–85, 216–26, 242–4.
[24] Panossian, "The Past as Nation," pp. 127–8.
[25] Mesrob Ashjian, "Introduction," in Mesrob Ashjian (ed.), *The Etchmiadzin Chronicles* (Armenia, 2003), p. 34. In 1903 the anniversary (the 1,600th) of the erection of Etchmiadzin Cathedral was held for the first time, despite the unfavorable political conditions in which the AAC was operating at that time. In the decree on this occasion, Catholicos Mkrtich' I wrote: "And what a joy that [we] will have had a chance to celebrate this jubilee, which for sixteen centuries had remained without remembrance" (quoted in Ashjian, "Introduction," p. 36). In

precedence among the peoples who accepted Christianity as a state religion, is absolutely central today for Armenian-Christian identity. Every academic attempt to challenge this "canonical" dating by suggesting that the conversion took place around 314–315[26] is dismissed by the Church. Even when the year 305 was cited as a possible alternative to 301 in the footnotes of the "History of Armenia" school textbook a few years ago, the Church protested, and the whole edition was removed from print.[27]

The celebration of the 1,700th anniversary of Armenia's conversion to Christianity in 2001 began in the Khor Virap monastery, built on the site of St. Gregory's imprisonment. During the celebration, the head of the AAC, Catholicos Garegin II, climbed down into the pit and emerged with a lighted torch, symbolically "re-illuminating Armenia" and recreating the mythical past.[28] This light was then carried to Armenian churches around the world. On the occasion of the anniversary, a new Yerevan cathedral with 1,700 seats was built and named after St. Gregory the Illuminator. Mass baptisms, pilgrimages and various evangelizing activities took place, a number of exhibitions and publications were prepared, ecumenical events were held, trees were planted, and prisoners were granted amnesty. However, as one of the AAC hierarchs admitted:

> this 1700th anniversary was somehow a secular project, suggested by our national mood, stressing the national image of the Armenian Church. We know that our forebears were more faithful to the primary mystery of the Church.[29]

The fourth tradition within the Armenian-Christian genealogy, dating back to the fifth century, is the creation of the Armenian alphabet by Saint Mesrop

---

2003 the 1,700th anniversary of the erection of Etchmiadzin Cathedral was celebrated with pilgrimages from Armenia, Karabagh, and the worldwide Armenian diaspora.

[26] Panossian, "The Past as Nation," p. 126; Anna Elizabeth Redgate, *The Armenians* (Oxford, 1998), pp. 115–16; Ronald Grigor Suny, *Looking toward Ararat: Armenia in Modern History* (Bloomington, 1993), p. 8.

[27] Author's interview with lecturers in the Faculty of Theology, Yerevan State University (Yerevan, 2010). Interestingly, the AAC seems to be so firmly opposed only when the date of conversion is "postponed," but is not so decisive about claims that this act took place even before 301. For example, Torkom Postajian, once a staff bearer for Catholicos Garegin I (of Cilicia), states in one of his books, readily available today in Armenia, that the proper date of Armenia's baptism is 279. See Torkom Postajian, *The Armenian Church and the Others* (n.p., 2005), pp. 1–3.

[28] Panossian, "The Past as Nation," p. 129.

[29] Ashjian, "Introduction," p. 34.

Mashtots' in 406. First recorded by Koriun,[30] one of the disciples of Mashtots', this tradition was later strengthened by Movses Khorenatsi, who introduced the idea that the letters were given to the saint by God in a vision.[31] The work of Mesrop Mashtots', endowed with sacral status, also "sanctified" the old Armenian language, *grabar*, for which the alphabet was introduced and which still serves today as the liturgical language of the AAC.[32] The fifth-century monks who translated Holy Scripture from Syriac and Greek into *grabar* were collectively included in the ranks of the saints of the Armenian Apostolic Church, and the feast of Surb Tarkmanchats' (the Holy Translators) is celebrated each year with a pilgrimage to the grave of St. Mesrop Mashtots' in the village of Oshakan. Next to the church, where the saint's tomb is located, stands a monument dedicated to the Armenian alphabet, with each letter separately carved out of tuff and combined with Armenian *khachkars*, or cross-stones.[33]

This combination is not accidental, since religious books and texts (especially manuscripts) written in the Armenian alphabet are, next to images of the Cross, the most worshipped objects in official as well as in vernacular[34] Armenian Christianity. The Bible is venerated by believers during church services, and many old gospels and prayer books are kept in Armenian families as "home

---

[30] Koriun, *Zhitie Mashtotsa* (Erevan, 1962), pp. 91–2.

[31] Khorenats'i, *Istoriia*, p. 193.

[32] Nowadays, *grabar*, although hardly comprehensible to contemporary Armenians, is seen by the ecclesiastic institution as the warrant for the connection between the present time and the sacred past, and the AAC rejects the idea of reforms in the liturgical language.

[33] As Petrosyan explains: "The khachkar, or cross-stone, is a memorial stone unique to Armenia. It is a free-standing, upright, rectangular stone slab that is elaborately carved in a deep bas-relief on the side facing west. A cross is carved in the center of the stone against a background of vegetal and interlaced geometric motifs ... [Khachkars] are found in various sizes and designs ... in ancient settlements and cemeteries ... at crossroads, on mountain ledges, by springs and bridges, and near monasteries ... Cross-stones first appeared in the 9th century AD and were continuously produced until late in the 18th century ... Following a hiatus during the last two hundred years, they have begun to reappear late in the 20th century." Hamlet Petrosyan, "The Khachkar or Cross-Stone," in Levon Abrahamian and Nancy Sweezy (eds), *Armenian Folk Arts, Culture, and Identity* (Bloomington, 2001), p. 60.

[34] Following Joyce Burkhalter Flueckiger, I use the word "vernacular" (Christianity) instead of the more widespread (but also contested) terms "folk" and "popular" (Christianity) to describe local beliefs, traditions and practices that are not under the immediate control or subject to the teachings of the official ecclesiastical institutions. See Joyce Burkhalter Flueckiger, *In Amma's Healing Room: Gender and Vernacular Islam in South India* (Bloomington, 2006), p. 2.

saints."³⁵ However, hundreds of such books were "nationalized" and collected in the Matenadaran in Yerevan—a state archive, museum, and research center established in 1959, and named after Mesrop Mashtots'.³⁶ Today, two of these manuscripts—the Shurishkani gospel and the Shukhonts' gospel—peregrinate each year to the churches of Mughni and Oshakan, where they are venerated by those gathered there, while many other manuscripts are visited in Matenadaran by their previous owners for prayers. The third manuscript that is regularly allowed to leave the Matenadaran is the Vehamor gospel, on which each Armenian president-elect has given his oath since the inauguration of Levon Ter-Petrosyan in 1991. This special attitude toward the literary tradition has also been marked recently by celebrations of the 1,600th anniversary of the creation of the Armenian alphabet in 2005 and of the 500th anniversary of Armenian printing in 2012, when Yerevan was declared the World Book Capital.

The fifth element in the ethno-religious narrative is the fifth-century story of the battle of Avarayr, fought against the Persians in 451.³⁷ Although the battle was militarily lost by the Armenian army, it is still presented as the greatest Armenian "moral victory" and the very first armed defense of the faith in the history of Christianity. The Armenian military commander, Vardan Mamikonyan, who lost his life in the battle, was canonized along with his 1,036 companions and became the highest exemplar of the true patriot and true believer. The story of Avarayr also gave Armenian culture the archetype of the true priest—St. Ghevond, who blessed Vardan's army, as well as the archetype of the traitor—Vasak Syuni, who is blamed for siding with the Persians.

Nowadays, on the Feast of Surb Vardanants' (The Feast of St. Vartan and His Companions)³⁸ a person representing St. Vardan appears in Yerevan on a white horse to lead the solemn procession. After him follow representatives of the clergy, state officials, politicians (especially right before election time) and representatives of the army. Soldiers carry banners, on which one can read such slogans as "Vardan and his companions marked out the sacred path of our duties."³⁹

---

[35] Harutyun Marutyan, "'Tan surb' erevuyt'ě: akunk'neri hartsě ev merorja drsevorumnerě," in Sargis Harut'yunyan and Aram K'alant'aryan (eds), *Hajoc srberě ev srbavajrerě: akunk'nerě, tiperě, pashtamunk'ě* (Erevan, 2001). [The Phenomenon of "Home saint": The question of origins and contemporary manifestations, in: Armenian saints and sacred places: origins, types, veneration].

[36] In pre-Soviet times, the central Matenadaran (meaning "depository of manuscripts") was located in Etchmiadzin and maintained by the AAC.

[37] Eghishe, *History of Vardan and the Armenian War* (Cambridge, MA, 1982).

[38] It is celebrated on the last Thursday before Great Lent.

[39] For an analysis of St. Vardan Mamikonyan's role in today's Armenian ethno-religion see Konrad Siekierski, "Vstrecha u dereva: dub polkovodca Vardana i politika simvolov v

The last major element of the ethno-religious genealogy is the Armenian genocide that took place in the Ottoman Empire in 1915 and the following years. This element is by no means comparable to the other events discussed here in terms of the role of the Armenian Apostolic Church in its canonization and symbolization. In fact, the memory of the genocide and the lost homeland is perceived by some authors as the basis for a distinctive form of modern Armenian nationalism,[40] or even interpreted as a religion-like phenomenon in its own right.[41] What is important for this discussion is that the AAC is engaged in the cultivation of this memory, from erecting Armenia's first monument dedicated to the victims of the genocide next to Etchmiadzin Cathedral in 1965 to hosting the Armenian Genocide 100th Anniversary Planning Commission (the centennial anniversary will be commemorated in 2015). The Church's prayers always accompany commemorative ceremonies, khachkars are erected around the world in memory of the victims, while Komitas, the monk and composer (1869–1935), is often perceived as a personification of the Armenian tragedy. However, despite these facts, almost a century has passed since 1915 and the AAC has not yet endeavored to provide a theological response to the questions raised by the sufferings and losses experienced during the genocide.[42] The idea of canonizing the victims of the Armenian genocide—already expressed on the occasion of the 1,700th anniversary of Christianity in Armenia in 2001, and later re-announced as part of the commemoration of the 100th

---

sovremennoĭ Armenii," in Levon Abrahamian and Pavel Avetisian (eds), *Avandakanĕ ev ardiakanĕ hayots' mshakuyt'um* (Erevan, 2010) ["The meeting by the tree: The oak of Vartan, the military leader, and the politics of symbols in today's Armenia," in *Tradition and modernity in Armenian culture*].

[40] Panossian, "The Past as Nation," pp. 136–9.

[41] As Christian Garbis observes: "Recognition of the Genocide ... long ago became a political movement uniting Armenians around the world in a common struggle, indeed as a way to maintain a sense of identity in environments that invite assimilation, even more so a vehicle than the Armenian Church. Monuments can be found in Armenian communities most everywhere by now. The pilgrimage to the Tsitsernakaberd Armenian Genocide Memorial every year on April 24 can be compared to that made by thousands of Muslims making their way to the Mecca ... Thus the acceptance of the Armenian Genocide has become a kind of religion, worshiped by attesters and deniers alike. Its acceptance is worshiped in the sense that people still struggle in coming to terms with the understanding that a tragedy occurred of some magnitude and search for limitless knowledge to prove that it did or did not exist." Christian Garbis, "Living in the Past," Notes From Hairenik: A Journal of One Man's Observances and Experiences in Armenia, April 13, 2006, http://noteshairenik.blogspot.com/2006/04/living-in-past.html, accessed September 5, 2013.

[42] Vigen Guroian, "Armenian Genocide and Christian Existence," *Cross Currents* 41, no. 3 (1991).

anniversary of the genocide—has been raised by the Church as a step towards filling this void.[43] Work on this project was still in its initial phase at the time of writing this chapter. The decision of the 2013 Synod of the AAC to adopt the principle of the collective canonization of the victims, however, has already raised certain concerns,[44] due to the immense number of those who perished.[45] Another fundamental question is whether such a canonization would be yet another element in the Armenian national martyrology and the sacralization of the nation—or whether it would reach beyond that.

The events and figures described above constitute the Armenian-Christian "postulated genealogy," as defined by Hervieu-Léger. In line with her argument, this genealogy is, on the one hand, naturalized by providing a shared line of great ancestors (Noah, King Abgar, St. Gregory the Illuminator, St. Mesrop Mashtots', St. Vardan Mamikonyan, etc.) and by establishing ties with special territories where watershed events and miraculous occurrences took place (Etchmiadzin, Masis-Ararat, Ararat Valley, etc.). On the other hand, it is symbolized by invoking a number of myths—of origin, of the golden age, and of decay—which are additionally strengthened by also being myths of precedence[46]—the one of the Deluge and first settlement, the one of adopting Christianity, the one of defending the Christian faith, and even the one of being the victims of the first genocide of the twentieth century.

---

[43] In practice, the victims of the genocide are often referred to by the clergy as "martyrs," and a few years ago the church of the village of T'eghenik (in Kotayk province) was named after Surb Nahatakner (the Holy Martyrs) particularly in memory of the Armenians killed during the genocide.

[44] In this context it is important to note that the tradition of the canonization of saints has been abandoned by the AAC for centuries. The last saint of the church was Grigor Tat'evats'i, who lived in the fourteenth to fifteenth centuries. In earlier ages the principle of collective canonization was employed by the AAC a number of times, including the already mentioned Vardan Mamikonyan and his 1,036 companions (Surb Vardanants') as well as the Armenian translators of the Bible (Surb Tarkmanchats').

[45] In Armenian historiography and popular discourse it is customary to reckon the number of victims of the genocide at one and a half million.

[46] On the Armenian "pioneer complex" see Levon Abrahamian, *Armenian Identity in a Changing World* (Costa Mesa, 2006), pp. 113–14.

"One Nation, One Faith, One Church":
The Current Discourse of the Armenian Apostolic Church in Armenia

As constituents of the Armenian-Christian "postulated genealogy," all these events and figures provide powerful symbolic resources on which the current ethno-religious discourse of the Armenian Apostolic Church draws extensively. Time and again, they are explicitly invoked or implicitly included in Church representatives' statements, both in commenting on contemporary Armenian issues and for the sake of recalling and reinforcing the general notion of the "inseparable ties between the Apostolic Church and the Armenian nation."[47] As Kimitaka Matsuzato and Stepan Danielyan observe: "Specialists on religion are often surprised by the ... tone of sermons and addresses by AAC hierarchs and priests: these normally contain few references to Christian ideas such as love, salvation and doomsday but constantly speak of nation, tradition and patriotism."[48]

This phenomenon is perhaps best illustrated by a modern "creed" of the Armenian Apostolic Church, formulated by the Catholicos Garegin II in one of his speeches: "In Armenian life, we are one and united, always and forever—one nation, one faith, one church."[49] Further amplification and explanation of this "creed" can be found in the following quotations:

> For us, there is no Christianity without our national identity, and no Armenian nationality without Christianity. You cannot say: 'This is Christian and that is national,' because they are the same. Our Christianity is like the color of our skin and we cannot change it. Christianity is embodied into this culture and is present everywhere—in our literature, in our history, in the water that we drink, and in the bread that we eat. To be Armenian is to be Christian and that means to be a member of the Armenian Apostolic Church.[50]

---

[47] Author's interview with an AAC clergyman (Yerevan, 2006).

[48] Kimitaka Matsuzato and Stepan Danielyan, "Faith or Tradition: The Armenian Apostolic Church and Community-Building in Armenia and Nagorny Karabakh," *Religion, State & Society* 41, no. 1 (2013), p. 18.

[49] The Message of His Holiness Karekin II Supreme Patriarch and Catholicos of All Armenians on the Occasion of the Blessing of the Holy Muron, Mother See of Holy Etchmiadzin, September 28, 2008, www.armenianchurch.org. At the beginning of the 1990s, right after Armenia gained its independence, the Catholicos Vazgen I proclaimed a similar, although more "politically oriented" creed: "One free nation, one free government, one free national Church" (Guroian, Ethics after Christendom, p. 107).

[50] Author's interview with an AAC clergyman (Etchmiadzin, 2005).

> If there was no Armenian Church, I doubt if during the last, let's say, 650 years we could have maintained our faith, language, and traditions. This would have been impossible. And this is the main role of the Church—to protect everything that belongs to us. So we can't look at the Church as a purely religious organization; the Church leads us and helps us also in the secular life. Redemption has come from the Church so that our nation did not vanish. There were many powerful nations in history that disappeared. But we have endured everything because of the conviction that we should rely on our Church.[51]

On some occasions the last part of the above "creed" is narrowed down: in some official statements one sees "one Catholicosate" instead of "one Church."[52] In the words of Catholicos Garegin II:

> On the level plain at the foot of Masis, through Holy Etchmiadzin, the Will of God and the will of the Armenians became one. Across from the Ark of Noah rested the ark of salvation of the Armenian people—the Only-Begotten Descended Mother See of the Armenian Church ... Our Christ-sealed faith became one with our identity. Holy Etchmiadzin became the spiritual Motherland of the Armenians, and kept alive the love and vision in Armenian life for the reestablishment of lost independent statehood ... The light radiating from the Holy Altar of Descent became more visible and kept us warmer the farther we were dispersed ... Holy Etchmiadzin is a singular, unconditional sanctity for every Armenian, the vessel to be an Armenian and a Christian.[53]

In the same vein, speaking to a group of pilgrims visiting Etchmiadzin, a high prelate of the Church reiterated:

---

[51] Author's interview with an AAC clergyman (Shushi, 2005).

[52] One of the sources of such a formulation can be policies of "centralization," introduced by the current Catholicos Garegin II (elected in 1999), which are, on the one hand, directed towards the internal structures of the Catholicosate and, on the other hand, include Etchmiadzin's claims to supremacy over the Catholicosate of the Great House of Cilicia. For more on this issue see Hratch Tchilingirian, "In Search of Relevance: Church and Religion in Armenia since Independence," in Bayram Balci and Raoul Motika (eds), *Religion et politique dans le Caucase post-soviétique* (Paris, 2007), p. 302; Chapter 6, this volume.

[53] Pontifical Encyclical of His Holiness Karekin II given on January 30, in the Year of Our Lord 2003, and in the date of the Armenians 1452, at the Mother Monastery of Holy Etchmiadzin, Number 124, Press Release, Mother See of Holy Etchmiadzin, Information Services.

Etchmiadzin is our mother, our glory and our conscience. All that we have to present to the civilized world, we have obtained through Holy Etchmiadzin. To weaken Holy Etchmiadzin, is to weaken the soul of the people. Etchmiadzin is, and will always be, the most beloved and sacred site of our people.[54]

In the Church's discourse one can also find a clearly expressed notion of the "innate Christianity of Armenians," which is presented as a contrast to the Soviet atheistic ideology, and which is believed to prevail over the current threats posed by competing religious denominations. According to this notion, an Armenian, even if he or she was not baptized and has not even the most basic knowledge of the Church's doctrines, is still considered "a bearer of Christianity," as if this were a part of the person's biological or genetic character. Consequently, the "Christian blood" that flows through the veins of Armenians is often viewed as precluding the possibility that their minds could have been fully secularized in Soviet times, or that they can nowadays be irretrievably "brainwashed" or "bribed"[55] by some other religious group. In the words of one priest:

In our nation—no matter what will happen—the roots, something in our blood, will stay faithful. Only now it sleeps. Armenians always gathered around the Church. Whether you want it or not, he who is an atheist or a Jehovah's Witness, deep in his heart loves the Armenian Church.[56]

Furthermore, the struggle between the "natural Christianity" of Armenians and alien influences is a struggle not only for beliefs but also for one's Armenianness, and for the well-being of the Armenian nation as a whole. As one can read in the AAC's communiqués:

The activities of totalitarian religious organizations, including Jehovah's Witnesses, run counter to our national and state interests and aspirations.[57]

---

[54] "Pilgrims from the Dioceses of Romania and Bulgaria in Holy Etchmiadzin," June 16, 2003, Press Release, Mother See of Holy Etchmiadzin, Information Services.

[55] According to a view expressed by many AAC clergymen, religious denominations that were established or re-established in Armenia after the fall of the USSR obtain new members by offering them financial help or by brainwashing them, not by virtue of their spiritual message.

[56] Author's interview with an AAC clergyman (Yerevan, 2005).

[57] As quoted in Ani Sarkissian, "Religion in Postsoviet Armenia: Pluralism and Identity Formation in Transition," *Religion, State & Society* 36, no. 2 (2008), p. 171.

We find incomprehensible, unjustifiable, and unacceptable such activities that are being carried out ... by para-church, Christian and non-Christian organizations, sects and movements ... which consider Armenia as fertile land for their preaching. For the love of Christ and of our nation and country, we cannot let such movements ... 'preach Christianity' to our people who are already devoted followers of Christ. We believe and expect that our own people of Armenia ... will reject such persons and actions which sow weeds and thorns in our 'small orchard' as our country was described by Movses Khorenatsi ... Such 'preachers' should become aware that the seeds of Christianity have been sown here by the two Apostles of Christ (St. Thaddeus and St. Bartholomew), that this 'orchard' of the Lord has been irrigated by the tears of St. Gregory and cultivated by the sacred alphabet of St. Mesrob Mashtots. The custodian and the laborer of this 'vineyard planted by God' has for centuries continuously been ... the Armenian Apostolic Church. And it remains the same laborer today, with renewed awareness of its mission ... All such people, who have the thirst and the need for inner spiritual awakening, should turn to their Church, to their own mother and receive the genuine milk, and should not turn and look for such milk and food, which is distorted and which affects the unity of the nation and the country.[58]

These quotations offer a good insight into the current situation in Armenia regarding religious plurality, which is generally perceived and discussed as a national issue rather than a matter of religious teaching and/or individual freedom of conscience. This approach allows the AAC to defend its right to a special status among the religious organizations operating in Armenia by claiming its "most national character."[59] The AAC's status as "more equal than others" is

---

[58] *The Mother Church and Roman Catholic Missionary Activity in a Reborn Armenia. Documents Pertaining to the Armenian Uniate Patriarchate's Design to Proselytize in Armenia* (New York, 1993), pp. 13–14.

[59] Other religious organizations operating in Armenia are trying to use the same nation-oriented strategy (Konrad Siekierski, "Religious and National Identities in Post-Soviet Armenia," in Irena Borowik and Małgorzata Zawiła (eds), *Religions and Identities in Transition* (Kraków, 2010), pp. 158–62). Thus, the Armenian Catholic Church stresses the important role played by the Armenian Catholic Mekhitarist order in Armenian culture since the eighteenth century, and sometimes claims that it follows in the line of succession from medieval Chalcedonian Armenians. Evangelical Protestants present themselves as being an integral part of the Armenian heritage for more than 150 years, and even claim to originate from Armenian "indigenous Protestants"—the medieval sectarian movements of Paulicians and Tondrakians (Vahram Hovyan, "The Protestant Armenians," March 16, 2010, www.noravank.am/eng/articles/detail.php?ELEMENT_ID=4480). Finally, the Armenian neo-pagans (Arordiner) claim that they are descendants of the only true Armenian ethno-

backed by its constitutional recognition as the "National Church," its separate agreement with the state signed in 2007,[60] and its sole right to teach in schools and have chaplains in the army. As reported by human rights organizations, the nationalization of the discourse on religious plurality in Armenia is the main source of popular intolerance—and, at times, hostility—toward representatives of non-traditional religious groups, particularly Jehovah's Witnesses.[61] However, as Ani Sarkissian demonstrates, it is the AAC that, despite its privileged position, often pictures itself as the victim of the missionary denominations that entered Armenia after the fall of the USSR.[62]

References to the events and figures discussed earlier in this chapter also appear in AAC representatives' statements regarding various aspects of the socio-political situation in Armenia. In some cases, they express in their specific language general national concerns and desires, as in the two following quotations that, respectively, evoke the unresolved "Armenian Issue" and address the current uneasy situation in the country:

> Armenian people are united by their Church, by Holy Echmiatsin, April 24, Sardarapat, the Sacred Mount Ararat, and the unique and unreserved dream that there will be a day when all Armenians will gather around Mount Ararat. Maybe it would seem a miracle to many people, and it would be a miracle indeed, but we believe in miracles ... Those who don't believe in the miracles of Armenian history do not admit the reality.[63]

> His Holiness delivered his pontifical message, in which he reflected on the sacredness of the day and the victory of the Armenian people witnessed not only at Avarayr, but also at Sartarapat and Karabagh. The Armenian Pontiff

---

religious tradition that preceded Christian times, and picture the AAC as alien and harmful to this tradition (Yulia Antonyan and Konrad Siekierski, "A Neopagan Movement in Armenia: The Children of Ara," in Kaarina Aitamurto and Scott Simpson (eds), *Modern Pagan and Faith Movements in Central and Eastern Europe* (Durham, 2013), pp. 267–8).

[60] The Law of the Republic of Armenia Regarding the Relationships between the Republic of Armenia and the Holy Apostolic Church, 2007, www.armenien.am/forum/index.php?page=Thread&threadID=7477, accessed September 29, 2009.

[61] See Meri Yeranosyan, Vahan Ishkhanyan, and Avetik Ishkhanyan, *Freedom of Religion in Armenia: A Study* (Yerevan, 2010) and Stepan Danielyan, Vladimir Vardanyan, and Artur Avtandilyan, "Religious Tolerance in Armenia," www.osce.org/documents/oy/2010/04/43497_en.pdf, accessed June 29, 2009.

[62] Sarkissian, "Religion in Postsoviet Armenia," pp. 171–2.

[63] As quoted in Sen Hovhannisian, *Armenia Ararat* (Yerevan, 2008).

encouraged all to face life's temptations and dangers with the same resilient spirit [as was demonstrated] in the Battle of Avarayr and the bravery of St. Vartan.⁶⁴

In other cases the Church leaders express their direct engagement in current politics. In this respect, the message of the Catholicos Garegin II to the nation, on the day Serzh Sargsyan was inaugurated as the president of the Republic of Armenia in 2008, speaks volumes:

> The experience you have gained from previous high state positions; your will and devotion to strengthen our country; your plans and your proposed methods and prerequisites; inspire us with confidence that under your leadership, through ongoing and consistent efforts, the challenges and obstacles which confront our lives will be overcome now, as well as in the coming years. Thus, our country will be greater, reinforced in the spheres of peace, justice and human rights, and with the desire to further strengthen our freedom. Our Holy Church will assist you on these paths blessed by God, and will always support our native state as it has done for centuries. Through its unity, our people have achieved victories, and today as well, together we shall secure the welfare of our homeland. Incidents which endanger the unity of our people must not find a place in our lives. Through unity, we shall ensure an enduring blessed life, keep vibrant the Armenian Diaspora, and transform our dispersion throughout the world into strength for the homeland. Through unity we shall be able to find the peaceful solution to the Nagorno Karabagh conflict, and see our just claims for recognition of the Genocide of the Armenians prevail.⁶⁵

This statement was made soon after mass protests against the alleged falsification of the election results were bloodily broken up by police and army. It reflects the modern continuation of the traditional politics of the Armenian Apostolic Church, which, during centuries of existence under the domination of alien powers, be they Turkish sultans, Russian tsars, or Soviet commissars, developed effective mechanisms of accommodation and subordination. These mechanisms were steadily internalized and today, as in the past, the Church is not able to act independently and keep its distance from the center of political power. Instead, in exchange for its loyal support, the AAC looks for state

---

⁶⁴ Vardanants Celebrated in the Mother See of Holy Etchmiadzin, February 20, 2009, www.armenianchurch.org.
⁶⁵ The Message of His Holiness Karekin II Supreme Patriarch and Catholicos of All Armenians on the Inauguration of Serzh Sargsian, President of the Republic of Armenia, April 9, 2008, www.armenianchurch.org.

protection of its privileges and exclusive rights. In the words of Guroian, whose summary of this phenomenon is brief and to the point: "What came of necessity grew into habit."[66]

Conclusion: The Forces and Frailties of Ethno-Religion

In the mid-1990s Guroian described the post-Soviet development of the ethno-religious tradition of the Armenian Apostolic Church in the following way:

> The unmistakable mark of expediency in the church's shift from cooperation with the Communist regime to sacralizer of the new nationalism was worrisome; its neglect of the spiritual needs of the people was conspicuous and unforgivable … The hierarchy and clergy seemed more comfortable wearing ethnic pride under gold filigreed ecclesiastical robes.[67]

As the excerpts from the Church's official statements and the quotations from interviews with AAC clergymen presented in this chapter show, during the two decades since Guroian drew this conclusion, the general line of the Church has not changed significantly. The results of the continuing dominance of the ethno-religious paradigm promoted by the Armenian Apostolic Church are manifold today.

There is no doubt that the Church was able to mobilize in its favor significant financial resources and that the structures of the AAC in Armenia have been greatly strengthened in the period under discussion: the number of churches opened has multiplied, the number of priests ordained each year has increased from a few to several dozens, and there has been no shortage of applications to the Etchmiadzin seminary. The Church also strengthened its role and visibility in many spheres of ceremonial life—from national festivals to individual rites of passage. At the same time, the AAC largely failed to direct the post-Soviet "spiritual hunger" toward Church-oriented religiosity, and the attempt to renew the Church "from below" undertaken in the 1990s by the *Yekhpairakts'ut'yun* (Brotherhood) movement lost its impetus.[68] Today parish

---

[66] Vigen Guroian, "Faith, Church and Nationalism in Armenia," *Nationalities Papers* 20, no. 1 (1992), p. 36.

[67] Vigen Guroian, "The New Nationalism and the Gospel Witness: Western Tolerance vs. Christian Repentance," *Commonweal* 122 (July 1995), p. 11.

[68] For more on the Yekhpairakts'ut'yun movement see Chapter 4 in this volume.

life in Armenia remains underdeveloped[69] and personal religiosity is still only weakly influenced by the Church. Instead, it rather follows the model inherited from Soviet times, when it was vernacular Christianity that remained vital in family circles and local communities. The ethno-religious paradigm, however, has quite successfully limited Armenians' redirection toward new, more zealous religious denominations, and the Church's hostility toward these non-traditional denominations is shared by most of society. For example, the number of Protestants in Armenia only grew from 0.53 percent of the population in 1990 to about 2 percent in 2005,[70] and two out of three Armenians disagree with the idea that "It is a good thing for any society to be made up of people from different religions."[71]

The yearly Caucasus Barometer survey provides interesting data for assessing the forces and frailties of the Armenian ethno-religion. According to the results of the 2013 survey, 92 percent of Armenians consider themselves as religious which, in terms of self-reporting, made Armenia one of the most religious countries in the world. At the same time only one out of 10 Armenian respondents declares that he or she attends religious services once a week or more, and one out of two states that he or she participates in such services only on special occasions. These numbers locate Armenia well below the average frequency of church attendance in 28 countries of the "secular continent" (Europe). Armenia is also reported to have a very high index of social regulation in the religious sphere (9.1/10), which indicates the extent of the socio-cultural pressure to belong to the dominant religious tradition and the lack of acceptance

---

[69] In the capital city of Yerevan active churchgoers usually follow the priest(s) of their choice rather than attending services in their nominal parish church. Actually, many of such people choose churches located in villages on the outskirts of the city. In the rural regions of Armenia, where one priest usually serves a number of villages, the attendance at Sunday masses is generally very low, and contacts between clergy and most of their nominal parishioners are limited. A 2009 initiative of the Diocesan Representative Assembly of the AAC to create parish councils in every rural community in Armenia has met with mixed reactions, and proved to be impossible to implement in the scheduled time (end of 2012) (Matsuzato and Danielyan, "Faith or Tradition," pp. 23–30).

[70] According to World Christian Database as cited in Sarkissian, "Religion in Postsoviet Armenia," pp. 170–71. The Armenia-based specialist in the country's modern religious situation, Stepan Danielyan, recently gave a figure of 120,000 for the number of members of "'sectarian' denominations" in Armenia—around 4 percent of the population (Matsuzato and Danielyan, "Faith or Tradition," p. 23).

[71] According to the Survey of Armenian Public Opinion of July 5–12, 2007, conducted by the International Republican Institute, Baltic Survey Ltd/The Gallup Organization, and the Armenian Sociological Organization, cited in Sarkissian, "Religion in Postsoviet Armenia," p. 173.

of alternative religious commitments.[72] All these data point to the conflation of ethnic and religious identity in Armenia, combined with a low observance of "religion as prescribed."[73]

The results of the Caucasus Barometer survey also show a relatively high level of trust in religious institutions in Armenia (76 percent). However, these data may point to the high esteem in which the AAC is held as a national symbol rather than to a high level of satisfaction with the current policies and representatives of the Church, skepticism toward which can be traced in private conversations, and, at times, in public discourse. One factor that contributes to this situation is the growing differentiation of Armenian society, exposed much more than in Soviet times to various cultural influences. This trend goes against the Church's tendency to downplay the diversity of Armenian culture and identity and to oppose the very idea that diversity could be treated as a virtue and a positive trait rather than a threat or an obstacle. Another factor is the popular conviction that many Church representatives do not follow the moral standards they preach and are preoccupied with earthly affairs. Furthermore, some initiatives undertaken by the AAC in the last few years have triggered counteractions and protests. For example, the AAC's plan to replace one of the culturally and architecturally important buildings in the center of Yerevan with a new church was met with long-running public protests that forced the withdrawal of the proposal.[74] With respect to this critical attitude, the ethno-religious paradigm sometimes reveals its reverse side. While participating in a local religious feast attended by a number of clergymen, the author observed that, after the priests had left the place, a gathering of men started to discuss their misbehavior. As one of them concluded, "We could make all this celebration without them, it is our feast and they have nothing to do with that. Always in Armenia it was the people who kept our faith and traditions."[75]

This chapter surely does not reflect all dimensions of the ethno-religious paradigm of the Armenian Apostolic Church and its implications for the position of this Church in Armenian society and for the religious situation in

---

[72] "Religiosity in the South Caucasus," September 1, 2013, Caucasus Research Resource Center.
[73] Ellen Badone, "Introduction," in Ellen Badone (ed.), *Religious Orthodoxy & Popular Faith in European Society* (Princeton, 1990), p. 6.
[74] Levon Abrahamian, "Yerevan Sacra: Old and New Sacred Centers in the Urban Space," in Tsypylma Darieva, Wolfgang Kashuba and Melanie Krebs (eds), *Urban Spaces after Socialism: Ethnographies of Public Places in Eurasian Cities* (Frankfurt/Main, 2012), pp. 147–51.
[75] Author's interview (Vardenik, 2013).

Armenia in general. It may be concluded, however, that this paradigm is eagerly promoted now by the AAC and it continues to dominate in modern Armenian socio-cultural reality. Appropriating Armenian history and transforming it into an ethno-religious myth allows the AAC to keep its privileges in society and in the state. A number of phenomena outlined above, however, point to a weak side in the current situation of the AAC, some of which have their source in the very same ethno-religious paradigm.

References

Abrahamian, Levon, *Armenian Identity in a Changing World* (Costa Mesa: Mazda Publishers, 2006).

Abrahamian, Levon, "Yerevan Sacra: Old and New Sacred Centers in the Urban Space," in Tsypylma Darieva, Wolfgang Kashuba and Melanie Krebs (eds), *Urban Spaces after Socialism: Ethnographies of Public Places in Eurasian Cities* (Frankfurt/Main: Campus Verlag, 2012), 131–51.

Agatangelos, *Istoriia Armenii* (Erevan: Nairi, 2004).

Alexander, Edward, "The Armenian Church in Soviet Policy," *Russian Review* 14, no. 4 (1955): 357–62.

Antonyan, Yulia and Konrad Siekierski, "A Neopagan Movement in Armenia: The Children of Ara," in Kaarina Aitamurto and Scott Simpson (eds), *Modern Pagan and Faith Movements in Central and Eastern Europe* (Durham: Acumen, 2013), 266–82.

Ashjian, Mesrob, "Introduction," in Mesrob Ashjian (ed.), *The Etchmiadzin Chronicles* (Armenia: Moughni Publishers, 2003), 31–94.

Badone, Ellen, "Introduction," in Ellen Badone (ed.), *Religious Orthodoxy & Popular Faith in European Society* (Princeton: Princeton University Press, 1990), 3–23.

Corley, Felix, "The Armenian Church under the Soviet Regime, Part 1: The Leadership of Kevork," *Religion, State & Society* 24, no. 1 (1996): 9–53.

Corley, Felix, "The Armenian Church under the Soviet Regime, Part 2: The Leadership of Vazgen," *Religion, State & Society* 24, no. 2 (1996): 281–343.

Corley, Felix, "The Armenian Church under the Soviet and Independent Regimes, Part 3: The Leadership of Vazgen," *Religion, State & Society* 26, no. 3/4 (1998): 291–355.

Dadrian, Vahakn, "Nationalism in Soviet Armenia—a Case Study of Ethnocentrism," in George W. Simmonds (ed.), *Nationalism in the USSR and*

Eastern Europe in the Era of Brezhnev and Kosygin (Detroit: The University of Detroit Press, 1977), 201–58.

Danielyan, Stepan, Vladimir Vardanyan and Artur Avtandilyan, "Religious Tolerance in Armenia," www.osce.org/documents/oy/2010/04/43497_en.pdf, accessed June 29, 2009.

Eghishe, *History of Vardan and the Armenian War* (Cambridge, MA: Harvard University Press, 1982).

Flueckiger, Joyce Burkhalter, *In Amma's Healing Room: Gender and Vernacular Islam in South India* (Bloomington: Indiana University Press, 2006).

Garbis, Christian, "Living in the Past," *Notes From Hairenik: A Journal of One Man's Observances and Experiences in Armenia*, April 13, 2006, http://noteshairenik.blogspot.com/2006/04/living-in-past.html, accessed September 5, 2013.

Guroian, Vigen, "Armenian Genocide and Christian Existence," *Cross Currents* 41, no. 3 (1991): 322–42.

Guroian, Vigen, *Ethics after Christendom: Towards an Ecclesial Christian Ethic* (Grand Rapids: William B. Eerdmans Publishing Company, 1994).

Guroian, Vigen, *Faith, Church, Mission: Essays for Renewal in the Armenian Church* (New York: The Armenian Prelacy, 1995).

Guroian, Vigen, "Faith, Church and Nationalism in Armenia," *Nationalities Papers* 20, no. 1 (1992): 31–40.

Guroian, Vigen, "The New Nationalism and the Gospel Witness: Western Tolerance vs. Christian Repentance," *Commonweal* 122 (July 1995): 11–14.

Hervieu-Léger, Danièle, *Religion as a Chain of Memory* (New Brunswick: Rutgers University Press, 2000).

Hovhannisian, Sen, *Armenia Ararat* (Yerevan: Nahapet, 2008).

Hovyan, Vahram, "The Protestant Armenians," March 3, 2010, www.noravank.am/eng/articles/detail.php?ELEMENT_ID=4480, accessed October 16, 2013.

Khorenatsi, Movses, *Istoriia Armenii* (Erevan: Aïastan, 1990). [A history of Armenia].

Koriun, *Zhitie Mashtotsa* (Erevan: Aïpetrat, 1962).

The Law of the Republic of Armenia Regarding the Relationships between the Republic of Armenia and the Holy Apostolic Church, 2007, www.armenien.am/forum/index.php?page=Thread&threadID=7477, accessed September 29, 2009.

Marutyan, Harutyun, "'Tan surb' erevuyt'ĕ: akunk'neri hartsĕ ev merorja drsevorumnerĕ," in Sargis Harutyunyan and Aram Kalantaryan (eds), *Hajoc srberĕ ev srbavajrerĕ: akunk'nerĕ, tiperĕ, pashtamunk'ĕ* (Erevan: Hayastan

2001), 337–46. [The Phenomenon of "Home saint": The question of origins and contemporary manifestations, in: Armenian saints and sacred places: origins, types, veneration].

Marutyan, Harutyun, *Iconography of Armenian Identity: The Memory of Genocide and the Karabagh Movement* (Yerevan: Gitutyun, 2009).

Matsuzato, Kimitaka and Stepan Danielyan, "Faith or Tradition: The Armenian Apostolic Church and Community Building in Armenian and Nagorny Karabakh," *Religion, State & Society* 41, no. 1 (2013): 18–34.

The Message of His Holiness Karekin II Supreme Patriarch and Catholicos of All Armenians on the Inauguration of Serzh Sargsian, President of the Republic of Armenia, Yerevan, April 9, 2008, www.armenianchurch.org, accessed on October 12, 2008.

The Message of His Holiness Karekin II Supreme Patriarch and Catholicos of All Armenians on the Occasion of the Blessing of the Holy Muron, Mother See of Holy Etchmiadzin, September 28, 2008, www.armenianchurch.org, accessed on October 12, 2008.

The Mother Church and Roman Catholic Missionary Activity in a Reborn Armenia. Documents Pertaining to the Armenian Uniate Patriarchate's Design to Proselytize in Armenia (New York, 1993).

Mouradian, Claire, "The Armenian Apostolic Church," in Pedro Ramet (ed.), *Eastern Christianity and Politics in the Twentieth Century* (Durham, NC: Duce University Press, 1988), 353–74.

Nikitin, K.A., "Gorod Nakhichevan i Nakhichevanskiĭ uiezd," in *Sbornik Materialov dlia Opisaniia Miestnosteĭ i Plemen' Kavkaza, Vypusk Vtoroĭ* (Tiflis: Tipogr. Glavn. Upravl. Glavnonaczal'stvuyushago Grazhd. Chastīiu na Kavkazie, 1882), 109–42. [The city of Nakhichevan and Nakhichevan district, in: Materials of the regions and tribes of the Caucasus].

Panossian, Razmik, "The Past as Nation: Three Dimensions of Armenian Identity," *Geopolitics* 7, no. 2 (2002): 121–46.

Panossian, Razmik, *The Armenians: From Kings and Priests to Merchants and Commissars* (New York: Columbia University Press, 2006).

Panossian, Razmik, "Post Soviet Armenia: Nationalism and its (Dis)contents," in Lowell W. Barrington (ed.), *After Independence: Making and Protecting the Nation in Postcolonial and Postcommunist States* (Ann Arbor: The University of Michigan Press, 2006), 225–47.

Petrosian, Armen, "Dva Ararata: Gora Kordueny i Masis," in Ruth Büttner and Judith Peltz (eds), *Mythical Landscapes Then and Now: The Mystification of Landscapes in Search for National Identity* (Yerevan: Antares, 2006), 261–74.

Petrosyan, Hamlet, "The Khachkar or Cross-Stone," in Levon Abrahamian and Nancy Sweezy (eds), *Armenian Folk Arts, Culture, and Identity* (Bloomington: Indiana University Press, 2001), 60–70.

Petrosyan, Hamlet, "The Sacred Mountain," in Levon Abrahamian and Nancy Sweezy (eds), *Armenian Folk Arts, Culture, and Identity* (Bloomington: Indiana University Press, 2001), 33–9.

Petrosyan, Hamlet, "The World as a Garden," in Levon Abrahamian and Nancy Sweezy (eds), *Armenian Folk Arts, Culture, and Identity* (Bloomington: Indiana University Press, 2001), 25–32.

"Pilgrims from the Dioceses of Romania and Bulgaria in Holy Etchmiadzin," June 16, 2003, Press Release, Mother See of Holy Etchmiadzin, Information Services.

Pontifical Encyclical of His Holiness Karekin II given on the 30th of January, in the Year of Our Lord 2003, and in the date of the Armenians 1452, at the Mother Monastery of Holy Etchmiadzin, Number 124, Press Release, Mother See of Holy Etchmiadzin, Information Services.

Postajian, Torkom, *The Armenian Church and the Others* (n.p., 2005).

Redgate, Anna Elizabeth, *The Armenians* (Oxford: Blackwell, 1998).

Redgate, Anna Elizabeth, "National Letters, Vernacular Christianity and National Identity in Early Medieval Armenia," in Vladimir Barchurdarian (ed.), *Armenian Letters: International Conference Dedicated to the 1600th Anniversary of the Armenian Letters Creation, Collection of Papers* (Yerevan: Gitutiun, 2006), 168–76.

"Religiosity in the South Caucasus, September 1 2013," Caucasus Research Resource Center.

Sarkissian, Ani, "Religion in Postsoviet Armenia: Pluralism and Identity Formation in Transition," *Religion, State & Society* 36, no. 2 (2008): 163–80.

Siekierski, Konrad, "The Armenian Apostolic Church and Vernacular Christianity in Soviet Armenia," *Keston Newsletter* 18 (2013): 15–20.

Siekierski, Konrad, "Religious and National Identities in Post-Soviet Armenia," in Irena Borowik and Małgorzata Zawiła (eds), *Religions and Identities in Transition* (Kraków: Nomos, 2010), 149–62.

Siekierski, Konrad, "Vstrecha u dereva: dub polkovodca Vardana i politika simvolov v sovremennoĭ Armenii," in Levon Abrahamian and Pavel Avetisyan (eds), *Avandakanĕ ev ardiakanĕ hayotsʻ mshakuytʻum* (Erevan: "Gitutʻyun," 2010), 273–87. [A meeting by the tree: The oak of Vardan the warrior and the politics of symbols in today's Armenia, in: Tradition and modernity in Armenian culture].

Smith, Anthony, *Chosen Peoples: Sacred Sources of National Identity* (Oxford: Oxford University Press, 2003).

Suny, Ronald Grigor, *Looking toward Ararat: Armenia in Modern History* (Bloomington: Indiana University Press, 1993).

Tchilingirian, Hratch, "In Search of Relevance: Church and Religion in Armenia since Independence," in Bayram Balci and Raoul Motika (eds), *Religion et politique dans le Caucase post-soviétique* (Paris: Maisonneuve & Larose, 2007), 277–311.

Terian, Abraham, *Patriotism and Piety in Armenian Christianity: The Early Panegyrics on Saint Gregory* (New York: St. Vladimir's Seminary Press, 2005).

Yeranosyan, Meri, Vahan Ishkhanyan and Avetik Ishkhanyan, *Freedom of Religion in Armenia: A Study* (Yerevan: Helsinki Committee of Armenia, 2010).

Chapter 2
Church, God and Society: Toward the Anthropology of Church Construction in Armenia

Yulia Antonyan

The anthropology of church construction is a relatively underdeveloped subfield in the current anthropology of religion. It has traditionally bordered on themes that were the preserve of architectural historians, who were generally interested in the cultural, social or ritualistic and symbolic context of architectural forms,[1] or historians of religion.[2] However, if the architect's approach focuses on the cultural and social context of architectural forms, anthropologists bring to the fore the socially and culturally constructed meanings, communities, institutions, identities and practices that develop in relation to churches as objects and spaces.[3]

Despite the large number of works on the history and specifics of Armenian religious architecture, only a few aspects relating to the construction of Armenian temples have been explored anthropologically. Levon Abrahamyan, for example, has discussed the mythological roots and motifs associated with the construction

---

[1] Jeanne Halgren Kilde, *Sacred Power, Sacred Space: An Introduction to Christian Architecture and Worship* (New York, 2008); Douglas R. Hoffman, *Seeking the Sacred in Contemporary Religious Architecture* (Kent, OH, 2010).

[2] Jonathan Z. Smith, *To Take Place: Toward Theory in Ritual* (Chicago, 1987).

[3] Tobias Köllner, "Built with God or Tears? Moral Discourses on Church Construction and the Role of the Entrepreneurial Donations," in Jarrett Zigon (ed.), *Multiple Moralities and Religions and Post-Soviet Russia* (New York, 2011), pp. 191–213; Tobias Köllner, "Businessmen, Priests and Parishes: Religious Individualization and Privatization in Russia," *Archives des sciences sociales de religions* 162 (April–June 2013), pp. 37–53; D. Tocheva, "Ot vosstanovleniia khrama k sozdaniiu obshchiny: samoogranichenie i material'nye trudnosti kak istochniki prikhodskoi identichnosti" [Rebuilding a church, creating a community: Self-restraint and material scarcity as markers of parish identity], in Alexander Agadjanian and Kathy Rousselet (eds), *Prikhod i obshchina v sovremennom pravoslavii: kornevaia sistema rossiiskoi religioznosti* [Parish and community in contemporary Orthodoxy: The grassroots system of Russian religiosity], (Moscow: Ves' mir, 2011).

of the first Christian churches in early medieval Armenia.[4] Scholars of Armenian identity argue that the image of a temple or a destroyed temple[5] is one of the most dominant identity symbols for Armenians. In texts and discourses, a church or monastery appears as a sign of the "Armenianness" of the landscape, as a marker of the religious and ethnic identities of the social group to which it belongs, and as an objectified and materialized landscape memory of past historical periods and metaphoric cultural model of the "ideal" past to be used in the present and future.[6] Yet none of these works has problematized the church as an instrument for and of particular social and cultural processes: the building of community, relationships, links, hierarchies, meanings and values; the empowerment of social groups or individuals; and the reconfigurations of power and influence. In this chapter I will be focusing on social and cultural meanings that are shaped by the process of church construction, on the reconfigurations of social structures this process produces in the community, and its translation into the "languages" of religiosity and morality.

The whole idea of a Christian church as a sacred space where communication with God is legitimized, "true" and effective has evolved throughout history. Initially, a "church" was simply a place for the meetings and joint prayers of early Christian communities. The ordinary houses of community members served as such places.[7] These "house churches" were ritual places (as is true for most Protestant churches today), but not necessarily sacred ones. Later on they became formal constructions closely linked to the cult of martyrs and thus acquired "sacredness."[8] The difference between the ritual and the sacred is best seen in the attitudes to temples in different religious cultures. Not every religion has

---

[4] L. Abrahamian, "Zohi marmnits achogh erknayin tachary" [A heavenly temple raised of the body of a victim], in *Hayots srbery ev srbavairery* [Armenian saints and sanctuaries] (Yerevan, 2001).

[5] One of the widespread iconographic motifs at the beginning of the twentieth century was the "Ruins of Ani" or "Mother Armenia," picturing a woman leaning over the debris of temples, each bearing the name of one of the 12 historical capitals of Armenia. This motif was drawn, embroidered or carved and was part of the interior of many Armenian houses in the South Caucasus. Another identity symbol often used as a metaphoric symbol of the Armenian nation is the destroyed temple of Zvartnots. See Levon Abrahamian, *Armenian Identity in a Changing World* (Costa Mesa, 2006), pp. 131–2.

[6] Hamlet Petrosyan, "The Temple," in Levon Abrahamian and Nancy Sweezy (eds), *Armenian Folk Arts, Culture, and Identity* (Bloomington, 2001), p. 50; Abrahamian, *Armenian Identity*, pp. 28–133.

[7] Kilde, *Sacred Power*, pp. 16–29.

[8] Kilde, *Sacred Power*, pp. 33–7; Peter Brown, *The Cult of the Saints* (Chicago, 1981), pp. 7–9, 40–41.

developed the idea of a church as an architectural building which serves ritual purposes and is simultaneously perceived as a space where the sacred makes its presence felt. Some religious cultures place little value on a physical space, seeing the community itself as the source of the sacredness (for example, Protestant cultures); others avoid the confinement of the space and the "enchurchment" of ritual altogether; while some religions, on the contrary, expend much effort and direct a significant part of their religious practices toward the creation and re-creation of sacred places and constructions.[9] This last is true for Armenian Apostolic Christianity.

The Traditional and the Modern: The Debate over Sacredness and Identity

The recent large-scale construction and re-construction of churches in Armenia pursues, among other things, the post-secular restitution and development of the institutional structure of the Armenian Apostolic Church. The re-establishment of the canonical ritual functions of churches was given priority. Hence newly constructed churches became better organized and more prepared for such ritual processes as the liturgy and ritual services than the semi-destroyed medieval churches that were even unable to accommodate large numbers of people. However, functional changes such as modernized church spaces, better interior organization of the ritual space (strict division into parts with different ritual functions, for instance), modern utilities like chairs, and highly formalized and canonized ritual requirements, provoked negative reactions and even protests among the secularized layers of the population. "I am not religious, but earlier I liked going to a church, it made me calm and reflective, but now when they [the clergy] forcibly impose upon me with their requirements, their excessive piety, endless signing of the cross, sermons, and prayers, I lost any willingness to go there"—as one of my informants, a highly educated old woman, said.

This attitude stems from the secular understanding of "spirituality" that dominated in Soviet times and which was closely intertwined with the image of "(destroyed) churches" as a cultural heritage, evoking one's "lost culture," the memory of a glorious past, and a spirituality that was assumed to be specific to the oppressed Christian culture, persecuted first by the Muslims and then by the Soviet authorities. In the Armenian religious vocabulary, a destroyed church is called *khonarhvats*, the "bowed down." However, unlike the institutional Church, which does not recognize "bowed" churches as ritual places unless they

---

[9] Hoffman, *Seeking the Sacred*, pp. 2–3.

are reconstructed and blessed anew, people—especially members of communities nearby—have always believed in the sacredness of destroyed churches and monasteries and actively recurred to them in their everyday religiosity.

The special status of ancient churches has become meaningful in the discourse on newly constructed churches, involving the issues of church construction and reconstruction, by the professional society of architects as well as by the general public. Old, "traditional" forms are perceived as markers of stability and continuity: "The image of a church was not created in one day nor by one person to be changed so abruptly," as the architect Artak Ghulyan has written in a post on his Facebook page. "Personally I don't want a modernized church, I want a traditional one"—echoed one of the participants of an architectural forum, organized in Yerevan in April 2013. "Traditional" architectural forms (meaning the classical medieval ones) are seen by many as perfectly functional markers of the presence of sacredness and "spirituality": "My friend and I, we once visited Gandzasar [a thirteenth-century monastery] and after a while we made a visit to the Grigor Lusavorich church [constructed in 2001]. My friend is not an architect, but he said: I don't find God here. In Gandzasar, He came down directly to me." The construction and opening of Grigor Lusavorich Cathedral was in fact accompanied by a lot of negative feedback, mostly due to disapproval of its modernized forms and spatial organization.

If secular discourse is focused on the idea of "traditional" and "modern" forms and symbols, then vernacular religious discourse emphasizes the "sacred" legitimacy of newly constructed churches, which must be proved in a number of ways, such as miracles, dreams or visions: "I don't accept some newly constructed churches like the one in Alaverdi [a small town in the northwestern Armenia], built by Vallex [a mining company]. But I accept, for example, the church in Malatya [a district of Yerevan]. Its builder comes from our village and he saw this church in a dream. I accept churches that come through dreams" (quoted from an interview with an elderly woman from the village of Akori). Dreams and visions are the main "conductors" of miracles.

Another typical story was told by a colleague of mine, the ethnographer Hripsime Pikichyan, about a painter who had emigrated long ago to the United States.

> During a fieldtrip to the village of Martiros, she was told a story about their reconstructed church. Previously, the villagers had an old destroyed church, worshipped as a 'shrine.' One day a woman had a dream in which one of the stones of the church cried out and asked her to come and take it out of the earth. 'Very soon,' this stone added, 'a person sent by me will come and build a church here.'

The dream was repeated twice or thrice but the woman paid no attention to it. After that, she had an accident and the saint came to her in a dream and said: 'Didn't you hear what I said to you? Come and look after me, call the people, and keep my place in safety.' She called her relatives and neighbors together and they cleaned up the place. After a while an Armenian painter from America came to the village. He, in turn, had also had a dream in which he was told to go and find that village and rebuild a church there.

The concept of a miracle did not disappear in the secular environment of Soviet times, but transformed and came to mean the "human-made miracle" brought about by unbelievable human mental and physical efforts. Building, creating a miracle with one's own hands, goes in concert with the secular approach to the Armenian religious heritage adopted in Soviet times. One illustration of such a miracle is the underground "temple" built by Levon Arakelyan, discussed later in this chapter. The newest transformations of this concept include totally secular, rationalized tools and criteria for "measuring" the miracle. Thus, Levon Arakelyan's temple is said to have been evaluated by architects, geologists and other professionals, who confirmed it as an unusual phenomenon. Post-Soviet modernity has offered other, Westernized and globalized measurement tools for a "miracle"—such as the *Guinness Book of World Records*. Thus, the newly erected Church of Saint Hovhannes in the city of Abovyan has a huge image of Christ under the dome, and people proudly say that this image should be registered in the *Guinness Book of World Records* as the largest image of Christ in the world.

The modern secular concept of a "human-made miracle" is also connected to the changed image and role of the architect that developed in Soviet times, when he became the main and true author of a building. During the opening of the Saint Hovhannes Church in May 2013, the donor Gagik Tsarukyan, a businessman and politician (a so-called oligarch[10]), "accidently" did not mention the names of the architect or the builders in his opening speech. This became grounds for resentment and heated public discussions. The architect Artak Ghulyan bitterly wrote on his Facebook page: "I have endured sleepless nights for seven years. For seven years I have spent days under the sun and rain in the building yard, with builders, professionals, and sculptors, and celebrated every new arch and sculpture. And as it has turned out I do not deserve even a mentioning of my name." Most of the comforting comments in response to

---

[10] An "oligarch" in Armenia is a person who, due to money, property and personal connections, wields economic, social and political power on the country or community level. Sometimes, in vernacular usage, the term is extended to cover any rich and influential person, or one holding a high administrative position.

this post referred to historical eras when "no architects were mentioned, but their creations survived for centuries." Other comments emphasized the human superiority of the architects and the moral inferiority of the oligarchs: "they think if they have money they are above everything"; "After I saw the miracle you had created, I asked myself: who are the architect and builders of this church, which has been constructed with money stolen from the people?" Here we encounter both the concept of a "miracle made by hands" and morality-based utterances, two specifics that are markers of the discourse on church construction in contemporary Armenia.

Church Building: Personal Motives and Social Reasons

In his paper devoted to church construction in post-Soviet Russia, the German anthropologist Tobias Köllner problematized the moral side of donations for the construction or reconstruction of Orthodox churches, as interpreted by priests or the devout. He found that "there are conflicting public discourses pertaining to both types of church-building activities: churches built with gold and churches built with tears."[11] This division is not relevant for Armenia, because public volunteering for church construction is not a common practice. Even if it does takes place (as in the case mentioned below of diaspora youth voluntarily renovating churches), nobody would describe it as a case of religious devotion, sacrifice or repentance, but rather as an act of patriotism and cultural self-identification. However, interpretations of church-building in terms of morality and social and religious values are certainly part of public discourse.

Of course, at first glance all donations seem to have very concrete, individual motivations that would hardly be considered immoral. For instance, donators in Movses (Tavush region) and Sarukhan (Gegharkunik region) villages were driven by a mystic dream in which they were told to build a church, and a donator in Koghb (Tavush region) was realizing his late father's dream. In Abovyan, according to actively circulating gossip, the "oligarch" Gagik Tsarukyan built one church to realize his desire to have a son and was now going to build another to help his wife recover from a serious illness. One widespread motivation is to perpetuate the memory of someone, usually a relative, friend or a respected community member. In Karabagh, for instance, a number of churches were built in memory of fallen soldiers, but every initiator or donator emphasized the names of those whom he knew personally. Thus, according to a

---

[11] Köllner, "Built with God or Tears?" pp. 191–2.

local inhabitant, T. Kyureghyan, the famous politician Paruir Hayrikyan built a church in Berdzor in memory of his co-partisans. Another church in the same place is said to be consecrated to the memory of a politician of the early 1990s, Hambardzum Galstyan, a close friend of the donator, and therefore called Saint Hambardzum (Resurrection).[12]

Yet some part of individual motivations remains unknown to the wider public and even to the clergy. Priests I talked with did not know (or claimed not to have known) about most of these motivations. Unlike Orthodox priests, who tend to moralize motivations and come forward as mediators between a businessman and God,[13] Armenian priests usually avoid such close connections[14] and take the autonomy of the relationships between a businessman and God for granted. The community, however, is more curious about those "relationships," and in most cases people are ready to tell a "legend" about how and why a certain temple was built. This "legend" becomes part of the vernacular biography of a church and a community.

Yet, even when motivated by very personal or family purposes, a donator sends a certain message to the community: he demonstrates his power, wealth, social connections and position in relation to the community. A newly constructed church becomes a reified and visible marker of a donator's improved financial and social status. A. Stepanyan, a young architect and builder, who has participated in the construction of a number of churches throughout Armenia, said: "In the villages people say: one becomes a labor migrant, then a billionaire, and then builds a church. Therefore, his acquaintances and his power are enhanced, one of his relatives becomes a mayor, the other runs a shop." Not in every case does a community accept such a sudden change in the social status of one of its members. Such situations engender social conflicts, accompanied by a lot of moralizing discourses, in which donators are accused of using religion as an easy way to repentance. "They construct two churches in our village, both are rich, both build churches to repent their sins," as Syuneh, a young student from the village of Koghb, said. Her father was a representative of the educated village elite in Soviet times, and the recent changes in the local status hierarchy has affected him personally. He has not been able to reconcile himself with the fact that people who used to be much lower in status than he was now claim that

---

[12] Sometimes the person called the "donator" here does not input his own personal funds, but asks for them from multiple sponsors, most of whom remain unknown. People give money to a very particular person for a particular purpose, mostly a socially important one.

[13] Köllner, "Businessmen, Priests and Parishes," pp. 45, 49.

[14] The role/institution of priests as "spiritual teachers" is poorly developed in Armenia.

they are at the top of the social hierarchy and make this visible by constructing a church, a marker of the new religiosity, also alien to the father's secular worldview.

Almost the same opinions sounded at the architectural forum devoted to "Contemporary Church Construction" in Yerevan in April 2013. "These are 'money churches,' not even 'power' ones," as one of the participants said—meaning that those churches were built by the nouveau riche to demonstrate their affluence.

Every construction of a church must be approved by the Armenian Apostolic Church and the ultimate decision-maker is the Catholicos himself. Formally, the official orderer of any church is always the Armenian Apostolic Church itself, although after the church has been ritually founded, the clergy rarely intervene in the process. Construction may be initiated by a community and its spiritual leaders. In this case, if the AAC approves the request and the architectural project for the church, the community itself then searches for sponsors. In the cases discussed below, one person is simultaneously the initiator and the sponsor/donator.

"Social" Typologies of Newly Built Churches

In terms of the social characteristics of their donators, all newly constructed churches could be provisionally divided into three categories: those sponsored by the "oligarchs," by the "migrants," and by the diaspora. For each of these categories, the social and cultural context of the construction as well as expectations and outcomes are quite different.

Churches constructed by the so-called oligarchs have gone through a kind of evolution. Most early churches (the end of the 1990s and beginning of the 2000s) were small, even tiny, and built in close proximity to the oligarch's house. They seem to have served as a marker of "his" territory (for example, churches in the Avan district of Yerevan built by Samvel Aleksanyan, in the Davitashen district by Ruben Gevorgyan, or in the village of Arinj by the aforementioned Gagik Tsarukyan). These churches are usually open to visitors, but there may be some limitations: I was told that people were not allowed to enter Gaguk Tsarukyan's church in Arinj during one of the local holidays. The next stage is the construction of bigger churches. As time passes, small churches for "personal" use, perceived as demonstrating the wealth and power and ostentatious religiosity of a nouveau riche, are succeeded by much larger churches, located at the center of a community and promoted as a big charity project, a donation for the benefit of everyone in a community. Such churches are meant to reflect the moral qualities of the donators, such as generosity, self-sacrifice, solidarity and integrity with the community, and are supposed to help improve the oligarch's image—to make it more positive and thus neutralize the negative feedback that accompanies them since they have become far richer than their neighbors.[15] A good example of such a church may be the one in Artashat, which is being built by the head of the Armenian parliament, Hovik Abrahamyan (Prime Minister since 2014), who is originally from this town and known there as a big businessman. In the eyes of the majority, the church is a proof not only of his power and expanded influence, but also of his generosity and humanistic aspirations ("he is making something for the people"), although those opposed may mock such efforts at looking "good." "He is building a church for his own glory," as one of the elderly and respected citizens of Artashat, a journalist and a writer, says with a hint of irony in his voice.

The construction of "community" churches can also show the successful convergence of the spheres of power and influence of both the "oligarchs" and the Armenian Apostolic Church. A striking example here is a "community" church in Askeran, a town in Karabagh. The church was built by an oligarch who made his fortune in the oil business. I was told that he originally wanted to build a church in his home village, but the Catholicos persuaded him to invest his money in a bigger church in the urban community of Askeran in order to combat the Protestant churches actively expanding there. Most of the town's population belongs to Protestant communities, however, and they don't need this church. When I was there, only a few people attended the Sunday liturgy, and most of them, as I found out, were the priest's relatives, who had made a special trip for the purpose from Stepanakert (the capital and the biggest city in Karabagh) where they live. The church occupies a rather large territory. It is well-made, and surrounded by old and new khachkars (cross-carved tombstones). Signs and posters indicating its location can be seen everywhere in the town. Obviously, the church is playing a symbolic role, signaling the presence and the superiority of the AAC.

To fight the multiple Protestant movements that have become rooted in Armenia since the early 1990s, the AAC, among other things, encourages the church construction process. The moral image of the donators, so actively discussed by ordinary people, seems to matter little to the clergy. They even try to smooth over people's reactions: "If by constructing a small church they

---

[15] In fact, none of the current Armenian oligarchs made their fortune in a legal way. Every one is known for some kind of illegal activity (corruption, theft of communal property, racketeering, etc.). That is why their social projects are perceived as attempts to improve their public image.

were not able to repent their sins, how would they do it by constructing a bigger one? Thank God, they construct churches and donate them to people. Why do people endlessly gossip about them?" (from an interview with Father Avetis).

The social meaning of building a church is different for labor migrants who became affluent in other countries and now want to make an investment in their homeland. This is not just an issue of empowerment. This is the symbolic regaining of a social status, which is frequently lost (even temporarily) in emigration. Labor migrants, especially men, usually suffer from a loss of status even if they have succeeded in making a good or even average income.[16] As strangers they never fully integrate into the local hierarchies of their host countries and always remain outsiders. In some cases, people try to fill this gap with a symbolic demonstration of wealth and power in their homeland. One way of doing this is to fund charity or social projects in their home villages or towns. Surprisingly, out of all possible projects, the construction of a church is thought to be the easiest one. As Father Avetis said:

> That's because constructing a church is easy. It's enough to inform a priest about such a decision and he would discuss the issue in Etchmiadzin [the Catholicosate]. The Church would coordinate the architectural project and the construction process. But if anyone wants to invest money in a school or a hospital, he has to coordinate this issue with the ministries, prepare hundreds of documents, pay taxes, and waste a lot of time and money.

That is why "socializing capital"—turning one's capital into social power and prestige—is much more effective and easier through a church.

The construction of a church, among its other advantages, reserves more freedom for personal motivations of a religious or social nature. One of these motivations for the donator is to perpetuate his own name or the names of his children or relatives in the name of the church, concomitantly acquiring a patronizing saint: "An Armenian migrant in Stavropol (Russia) wanted to construct a church and asked me if he could name it after Saint Kristineh,

---

[16] Surveys on migration point out the fact of the decline of immigrants' social status in their host countries: see, for example, A. Minasyan, A. Poghosyan, T. Hakobyan, and B. Hancilova, *Labor Migration from Armenia in 2005–2007: A Survey* (Yerevan, 2007), p. 47. Labor migrants often start out at the kind of low-ranking jobs they would never have taken in the homeland. They would feel ashamed if someone knew what they were forced to do. See N. Shahnazaryan, "Transgranichnye migratsii iz Armenii i Nagornogo Karabakha skvoz' prizmu konflikta i gendernykh otnoshenii" [Transborder migrations from Armenia and Nagorno-Karabagh through the lens of conflict and gender], *Diaspory* 1 (2013), p. 10.

because that was the name of his daughter. I promised him that I would check to make sure and found the day dedicated to Saint Kristineh in the Armenian religious calendar. So my answer was: 'Yes, you can'" (from the interview with Father Avetis). Gagik Tsarukyan, the oligarch, constructed five churches devoted to Saint Hovhannes, after the name of his eldest son.

Some dedicate churches to their parents, thus implying the patriarchal character of family and power relationships in Armenia. One architect, A. Danielyan, when telling about a project he participated in, recalled: "He [a donator] was not religious at all, but he wanted his father's wish to have a church in the village to come true." Similarly, one of churches in the town of Sevan is being built by an affluent migrant near the cemetery where his father is buried, thus dedicating the church to the memory of his father.

The migrants who construct churches do not claim to take on any real power in the village, unless they are going to relocate there. In most cases, they have no plans for an immediate or final return, but they do intend to come back from time to time, for summer vacations or winter holidays, and they like to experience the feeling of being high-ranking persons, respected and influential for at least some part of their sojourn in the homeland. In some cases, relatives of theirs who have remained in the village may benefit from this influence in many direct or indirect ways.

The third category covers the involvement of the Armenian diaspora[17] in the construction and renovation of churches in Armenia and Karabagh. Several factors may really matter in these cases: the symbolic "homeland" with which people in the diaspora want to establish a bond,[18] the social/political dispositions in an Armenian community in their home country, and the political or economic advantages of social projects.

Diaspora donors prefer to finance huge churches of national importance, preferably those in big cities, or national cathedrals. The biggest cathedral in Armenia, that of Grigor the Illuminator, built to commemorate 1,700 years of Christianity in Armenia, was funded jointly by several huge diaspora donors. A large Saint Trinity church in Malatya, one of the districts of Yerevan, was funded by one of the richest diaspora donors, Louise Manoogian Simone, famous for her charity projects. The current construction of a residence for the Catholicos

---

[17] I mean here the "traditional" diaspora that emerged after the Genocide of 1915 and not the post-Soviet migrant communities.

[18] On the diaspora symbolically uniting with its "homeland," see Abrahamian, *Armenian Identity*, pp. 335–41; and Tsypyima Darieva, "Bringing the Soil back to the Homeland: Reconfigurations of Representation of Loss in Armenia," *Comparativ* 16 (2006), Heft 3, pp. 87–101.

in Yerevan and the Saint Anna Church are funded by Hrayr Hovnanyan, another influential benefactor. Some projects are combined with personal or family motives (in honor of one's late parents or husband), such as the church of Saint Trdat in Vayk built by the Soghoyan family from Detroit in the United States. Different parts of this church are consecrated to the late husband, son and family friend. It turns into a symbolic "burial" in a symbolic "homeland." It is easy to notice that churches built by the diaspora representatives are not linked to particular local networks, they tend to belong to everyone. Even the Saint Trdat church, which formally belongs to the Vayk community, is located on the main road almost outside the city, and is usually visited by the inhabitants of the whole region and by numerous passing tourists.

But arguing that donors from the diaspora are not seeking social benefits is not fully relevant. In order to understand the social motives of these diaspora representatives, it is important to have some idea about the particular nature of Armenian communities in the diaspora. Charity has always had a systemic character in almost all diaspora communities. Armenian schools, kindergartens, national clubs, parties, and so on, were established and maintained by charity funds, mostly run by the Church. Charity and charitable foundation are among the main instruments for shaping social identities and social statuses in these communities.[19] Since Armenia became independent, a significant part of these charity projects have shifted to Armenia, the "suffering homeland," which really has suffered in the aftermath of the war, economic collapse and the earthquake. It is a widespread practice to spend charity money on humanitarian aid or charity projects in Armenia and Karabagh, in order to help the "homeland." During my fieldtrip to Lebanon, I met families that were proud to have taken care of a group of the poorest families in Armenia or renovated a village hospital. Participation in as many charity projects as possible undoubtedly has a positive impact on the social status of a person or family in the community. Social projects funded by American or European businessmen of Armenian origin look like typical examples of the contemporary "social" mode of doing business—social investments in a developing country; however they have a deeper meaning: they are also perceived as a moral and spiritual tribute paid to a symbolic homeland. The construction of a church is also one of the most reputable social projects: religion and the Church have always been central to the maintenance of national identity for Armenians of the diaspora. The diaspora's established foundations

---

[19] This conclusion draws on my field study of the charity sector in the Armenian communities of Syria and Lebanon and personal talks with diaspora representatives (now still unpublished).

(for example, the Jinishian Foundation) pay a lot of attention to projects of religious revival and "spiritual uplift,"[20] so building churches and "recovering" religion in Armenia after years of the Soviet atheistic ideology seems to be an important component of the "patriotic" (*hayrenasirakan*) activities of affluent members in the diaspora communities.

Besides the individual sponsorship of the church construction, there are collective initiatives, such as the "Land and Culture" organization, that bring diaspora youth to Armenia to renovate the "cultural and historical heritage," mostly churches. Young people spend their vacation visiting notable sites in Armenia and voluntarily renovating churches. The main purpose of such activities is "bonding with the land and locals."[21] The organization provides the financial means for these works of renovation, raised from private diaspora donors, while the young diaspora Armenians input their physical and spiritual efforts.

There are many cases of anonymous donations for a church construction or renovation. Donors obviously do not try to get social benefits and prefer to remain outside of the social games around the building process, but they do have serious reasons for making donations that would be "accepted" by God. Usually, an individual has a very personal reason for communicating with God in a non-public way and does not want others to know about this reason. People appreciate such behavior and interpret it in a moral way: "There are those who donate an insignificant thing and order a plaque with their name on it to be hung on a wall. And there are people making significant donations that do not demand to be memorialized" (from the interview with Father Avetis). Anonymous donations are valuable because they seem to be reward-free; they do not seek social benefits and do not get involved in the existing system of social relationships and hierarchies of the community. In the case of the renovation of the church in the village of Martiros, people only found out later that the donor had in fact attended the opening of the church, and lamented: "We didn't know he was the donor. Otherwise we would have welcomed him in a decent way. Instead, we sold him *matsun* (sour milk) for money! What a shame!" (from conversations with Hripsime Pikichyan).

---

[20] See this activity component at the official website of the Jinishian Foundation: www.jinishian.org/index.php?option=com_fjrelated&view=fjrelated&layout=blog&id=117&Itemid=99&lang=en, accessed on June 22, 2014.

[21] See the website of Land and Culture at: www.lcousa.org/, accessed August 28, 2013.

Church as a Miracle

There is another concept that puts a newly constructed church at the center of the web of social life in a community. This is the concept of miracle. Revelations, foretelling, dreams or other manifestations of the miraculous are frequently incorporated into the "dossier" of newly constructed churches; however, they are not necessarily at the center of related discourses and not always affecting the future history of a church.

In this section I will be discussing cases that are based on a miracle, where the miracle has been the motivation and justification for a church-building project. Typologically, such cases may recall the "churches built with tears," described by Tobias Köllner and discussed earlier in this chapter—but with several fundamental differences. First, they are not communal projects, but personal ones, and the personality of the builder, his or her life story, is exceptionally important in public perceptions and discourses related to the church. Second, the whole project is considered to be a miraculous intervention of the sacred regardless of people's will or personal intentions, unlike the Russian cases, where people deliberately choose to participate in church construction for religious reasons, motivated by the hardships of the work or asking God for penance.[22]

Here I will describe the cases of Sonya Papyan, a widow in her early sixties living in one of the remote districts of Yerevan, who built a church by spending the scarce money of her needy family and years of her life, and of Levon Arakelyan, an inhabitant of the village of Arinj, who sacrificed more than 20 years of his life in building a subterranean "church," carving it out of a cliff under his own house using nothing more than a hammer and chisel. Both of them were stirred by the perpetual miraculous intervention of the sacred in their reality through visions and dreams. As we have seen, the elements of a miracle, in the form of dreams and visions, are important for the "legitimation" of a church in the eyes of the devout. Sonya and Levon appeared as mediators between the sacred and people. Both of them constructed their "churches" not because they were stirred by communal or personal purposes, but because, as they claimed, they could not resist the divine powers forcing them to do what they did.

The history of the construction of Sonya Papyan's church is tightly intertwined with her life story. After the death of her younger son, she had ceaseless visions in which a saint ordered her to build a church. She mobilized all the humble resources of her family, sent her other two sons to Russia as labor migrants,

---

[22] Tobias Köllner, *Practicing without Belonging? Entrepreneurship, Morality and Religion in Contemporary Russia* (Zürich and Berlin, 2012), p. 135.

and started to erect a church. So far, the lion's share of their family income has been spent on this church. Sonya also tries to raise funds from different sources, through personal requests and a charity box placed on the premises of the church under construction.

What is Sonya's relationship with her community? Before addressing this important issue, it is necessary give some introductory explanations of the situation. With her church Sonya has triggered several crucial changes in the community landscape, both sacred and social. The relatively small space between apartment buildings where the church is located is contested by the religion-related constructions of the neighborhood. Across the road there is a Culture House for Children belonging to the Armenian Apostolic Church, where children receive religious and professional (handicrafts) education. Next to it, on the same side of the road, there is a *matur* (a "martyrium," a small shrine) of Surb Karapet (St. John the Baptist), constructed by Sonya herself. As Sonya said, she wanted to reconstruct the original shrine of Surb Karapet, which had previously been located somewhere in the area but was destroyed in Soviet times when multi-story buildings were built. However, a man living in the vicinity recalled that the original *matur* was located right at the hill where the church is now perched. According to him, Sonya displaced the shrine and provided it with a khachkar. The shrine does not look abandoned; numerous gifts to the saint in the form of "sacred" images or lighted candles can be found there. However, it seems like Sonya did "privatize" a saint who had been a common "property" because she is convinced that Surb Karapet was the saint who appeared in her dreams and ordered her to build a church after her son died.

Although Sonya's church was officially blessed by a priest of the Armenian Apostolic Church at the beginning of the construction, later some clashes between her and the official Church occurred. A conflict flared up because of some territorial disputes with the Culture House, leading to a significant deterioration in her relationships with Armenian Apostolic Church officials. Moreover, Sonya has created her own idiosyncratic belief system: for example, she believes that God is the Sun and the Sun is God. Her special type of devotion includes a strong mission-orientation and mysticism. All this makes her a kind of heretic in the eyes of the Church and alienates her from the local community of which she is a member, because she lives in one of its buildings. But, as she herself confesses, very few of her neighbors attend church, despite her efforts to involve community members in at least some devotional activity: "I celebrate all holidays here, at the church, by making *matagh* (sacrifice), offering food. Previously [allegedly before the conflict with the AAC] I gathered crowds, but people are not religious today, very few of them come." Sonya is moralistic about people's attitudes toward her: "There is much evil and envy in people. They look at me and think: Who is this woman, why does she build this church, who gives this space to her?"

But who in this case attends Sonya's church? There are several big hospitals and clinics right on the next street and the patients or their relatives are frequent visitors to Sonya's church, which is the closest place of worship. Most of the people lighting candles and praying there are the relatives of hospital patients. Their tiny but frequent donations sometimes make a significant contribution to the daily construction expenses (covering workers' daily salaries or food). Sonya hired an architect and a team of laborers for the construction. Since Sonya was not able to pay much and was periodically late in paying salaries, she found a team as much committed to this job as she was. All of them are deeply religious people and regard this job as a kind of religious duty. The architect and the laborers share Sonya's missionary aims and aspirations. Sonya tells about the mystical revelations and visions whereby she contacts the saint who then helps her to resolve the constantly emerging technical problems. The laborers believe her and say: "Sonya is resolving all our problems through dreams. If we face a problem, we say, well, let's wait until Sonya is given its solution through a dream." One of the workers belongs to one of the Protestant communities, but he still thinks that working on the construction of this church is his duty as a Christian.

The fact that most church attendees come from outside and are mostly hospital patients and their relatives makes the church a sort of asylum for the ill, the desperate, or those who are in trouble. I spoke to a local man who said that he comes and sits in the church quite often to seek tranquility and peace. He was a seasonal migrant and split his life between two countries, experiencing risks and difficulties, and leaving his family on their own for a long time. He grew up in the district and saw Sonya's church as a kind of continuity with the Surb Karapet *matur* of his childhood.

Yet even without the full acknowledgment of the community, Sonya's church has changed the community's life by transforming its social and religious landscape and creating a space that has become a functional center of the district together with a couple of mini-shops, a parking lot for minibuses, and a small square between the church, the shrine and the Culture House. This story problematizes the concept of "a church without a priest." At the time of writing Sonya's church was not yet completed, but it seems that it will not have a priest or a normal liturgical life because of the conflict between Sonya and the Church. It would hardly become a fully functioning ritual place with a regular liturgical practice and legitimate status, approved "from above," that is, by the Church hierarchy. But it would remain a sacred place whose legitimacy is really obtained "from above"—from the saints, and from God. Her religiosity belongs to the "grassroots" type of religiosity in post-Soviet Armenia that I identified in an earlier paper,[23] a type that is characterized by the perception of Christianity as a holistic system of religious and magical beliefs associated with the cults of God, Christ, Mariam (Mary) the Mother of God and various local and national saints. According to these beliefs, the "sacred" may be in contact with particular people, and God's or a saint's will is to be "mediated" through visions and dreams, while churches are perceived as sacred places similar in function to shrines. The role of institutionalized church practices and the clergy is neglected or considered unimportant for such types of religiosity, even despite the current processes of post-Soviet de-secularization and the restitution of the Armenian Apostolic Church infrastructure, accompanied by the ideological and physical attack on grassroots practices.[24] Many times in my fieldwork, I heard people confessing: "I accept churches and saints, but I don't accept priests."

The miraculous cave of Levon Arakelyan (who died in 2008) in the village of Arinj is embedded in the same format. To be fair, it is not a "church" in the regular sense of the word and might not seem to fit into the discussion here, but I argue that Levon's cave fits well into the web of meanings and values described in the cases mentioned above.[25] One of the seven halls of the cave is set out as a mini-church with an altar and *khorans* (niches). There is a "wish hole" just before the "altar." People who want their wishes to come true put their feet directly into the hollow, pray, and make a wish. Levon himself confessed that he built the kind of temple from which people come away completely purified. He started to construct his "temple" in the mid-1980s under the Soviet regime, and his version of a "church" was the only one possible at that time, because nobody would have allowed him to build an ordinary church.

The story of the construction started with the miracle. Since the early 1970s Levon had been going to Siberia for seasonal work.[26] In 1985, in Irkutsk, on the shore of Lake Baikal, he had a vision of God and heard voices announcing

---

[23] Yu. Antonyan, "Religiosity and Religious Identity in Armenia: Some Current Models and Developments," *Acta Ethnographica Hungarica* 56, no. 2 (2011), p. 322.

[24] Antonyan, "Religiosity and Religious Identity in Armenia," pp. 327–9.

[25] Levon Abrahamian regards the small hand-made sanctuaries erected everywhere throughout Armenia in Soviet times as almost identical to churches in terms of meanings, functions, and perceptions. See Abrahamian, *Armenian Identity*, pp. 128–9. I can add that at least at the vernacular level, non-acting canonical churches and "shrines" were not differentiated and both fell into the general category of "sacred places" ("surb," "khach").

[26] Labor migration to Siberia or the Far East was not a rare phenomenon in the Soviet republics.

that he would live a long life and would make a miracle.[27] After he came back, he began to dig up the floor of his kitchen. For more than 20 years Levon dug into the rock, smashing the basalt stone with just a hammer and a chisel down to a depth of as much as 21 meters. At the same time he decorated the walls of the cave with carved columns, ornaments, crosses, and other details like clay vessels or mosaic urns resembling those of late antiquity and the early Christian era. After his death, his life was characterized by his relatives as a heroic labor: he slept no more than three or four hours a day, communicating with "saints" through his dreams and getting further "instructions," ate very little and only once a day, communicated little with others and did not sustain his family financially. His wife had to work hard raising four children and enduring the enormous difficulties of the post-Soviet period. Neighbors felt sorry for her: they thought Levon was mad. The family seemed to agree with them, but his wife did not leave him.[28] His visions and ongoing communication with the sacred, minor miracles like breaking through the tough stone after carving a cross on it, or similar things convinced the family and neighborhood over time of the sacredness of his mission. When asked why he did it, Levon always answered that everything would be well and the saints would eventually reveal the true meaning of his doings to people. According to Levon, his cave will save people from a cataclysm such as a deluge. He might have imagined himself as a kind of Noah of our days.

The cave strikes the imagination with its size, construction forms, accuracy of calculations, intricate labyrinth and ventilation holes. It is hard to believe that one person made it practically with his bare hands. People believe in the "miraculous" emergence of the cave, which has already become one of the most frequented tourist attractions and a place of pilgrimage for the locals. Levon's family derives a significant income from this place (an entrance fee is charged). The widow has turned the second floor of the house into Levon's museum. She also keeps a detailed register of visits to the place in special notebooks. One of them, the so-called Wish Book, contains dozens of notes from those who have made a wish in the "wish hall" that came true. Most of the notes concern miraculous recoveries from diseases and the cave is labeled as "sacred place," a "sanctuary," or a "shrine." The cave and the museum really do look like shrines,

---

[27] Levon's case is well known in Armenia: there have been numerous articles in the media, and a film has even been made about the cave. I interviewed his widow and grandson after his death.

[28] In a typical Armenian family of the Soviet and early post-Soviet period, divorce was not a socially acceptable thing. Enduring an unsuccessful marriage has always been socially more "normal" than ending it.

with numerous attributes of devotion. Pilgrims bring presents to Levon's "shrine" (images of saints, icons, sculptures, ceramics, etc.) and make financial donations to the family as a sign of gratitude to Levon's sacred cave.[29] Yet, officially, Levon's cave is identified as a museum, as the plaque at the entrance says. It is the only "decent" definition, because it would have been recognized as a church neither by the Soviet authorities, at the time when construction on the cave began, nor would it now be recognized as such by the AAC.

Conclusion

As we have seen, every church is embedded in the social and cultural landscape of the space it is built in. Moreover, its construction appears to be a semiotic and functional transformation of existing landscapes. It also encapsulates social information about the person who initiated the construction and the community for which the church was built. The person who sponsored or carried out the construction becomes one of the key players in the social life of his or her community, and the new church becomes an instrument of his or her empowerment. One usually raises one's social status and improves one's position, directly or indirectly (for example, through an improvement in one's moral image, added on to one's wealth and influence).

Even in those cases where motivations are claimed to be purely religious, without additional personal incentives (like health or career purposes), the idea of one's own significance, of "being chosen," may be pivotal for the individual who undertakes the construction of a church. Hence the boundary between the secular (social) and the religious nature of motivations is always blurred. Be it through economic and political power, or through a capacity to communicate with the sacred, in most cases participating in such "faith-based initiatives," to borrow Arthur Farnsley's term,[30] seem to achieve the same goal: an exceptional position in the society, the position of one who has been "chosen" for power, for respect, for worship, for penitence, and therefore for salvation. In other words,

---

[29] Levon happened to live in the same village that one of the aforementioned church-constructing oligarchs, Gagik Tsarukyan, comes from. Therefore, Gagik's church and Levon's cave compete within a framework of oppositions: up–down, money-made and hand-made, canonical church–"metaphorical" church, canonical ritual services–miraculous healings, oligarch–poor mason and driver, etc. However, each construction lives its own life and impacts village life in its own way.

[30] Arthur E. Farnsley II, "Faith-Based Initiatives," in James A. Beckford and N.J. Demerath III (eds), *The SAGE Handbook of the Sociology of Religion* (London, 2007), p. 345.

motivations may be personal but the achievements are always social, even in cases of anonymous donors, because one can never be totally anonymous and he or she always keeps society in mind, and, presumably, wants eventually to be known for one's piety and social merits. This is true in Levon's and Sonya's cases. As a result, both of them have become local celebrities, whether this was their intention or not.

Religion and the Church have become more significant in the social and political life of Armenia due to post-Soviet de-secularization processes. Church buildings, along with their sacred significance, acquired new weight as symbols of power. Therefore, more individuals choose the construction of churches as an instrument for self-empowerment and social advantages, thus converting their money into social and cultural capital.

Church construction may also be seen as a kind of (religious) practice because of several important aspects. One aspect is instrumental, which allows people to regard a church as a tool for the religious legitimation of political and social power. One of the expected results of using this tool is then the cementing of an alliance between the oligarchy and the Armenian Apostolic Church as well as the ideological support of the latter. The other is a public demonstration of a reciprocal exchange of "goods" between God and the donor. I have not referred to Marcel Mauss's theory of the gift earlier in this chapter because the mere concept of a gift explains little about the reasons for church construction practices in post-Soviet society. However, the concept of the gift as revisited by Maurice Godelier[31] may provide a good theoretical background for understanding the nature of sacred objects in the construction of social relationships based on power. In terms of Godelier's theory, a church can be considered as a sacred object that cannot be sold or involved in any further exchange, and therefore is best for being "gifted" to God. In some sense, if we rephrase Mauss,[32] investing one's own money, presumably awarded to one by God in the first place, in a church converts the money back into godly property. And this, as Godelier writes, allows "the imaginary structure which enabled caste and class relations to crystallize, to take shape and to acquire meaning," because "the human donors are from the outset inferior to the godly receivers."[33]

The other aspect is linked to the conversion of individual religious feelings, fears and attitudes into socially meaningful and morally valued practices that have been made possible as a consequence of social and cultural changes in

---

[31] Maurice Godelier, *The Enigma of the Gift* (Chicago, 1999).
[32] Marcel Mauss, *The Gift* (London, 1966), p. 14.
[33] Godelier, *The Enigma of the Gift*, p. 30.

the post-Soviet period. These changes (the transition from a socialist politico-economic system to a liberal, market-oriented one) are mirrored, as Jarrett Zigon notes, in religious and moral conceptions valuing charity and individualism.[34]

As we have seen, some church construction initiatives integrate or re-integrate "church-builders" into a community, while others marginalize them; but both processes may be interpreted in terms of the re-negotiation and consequent reconfiguration of a social order either by opposing or by merging together morality and power, sacrifice and profit, religious and secular worldviews. Thus, the emergence of a new church may be compared to a kind of "systemic reloading" of society on either the local or national level, leading to the transformation and reconfiguration of social hierarchies, values, landscapes, meanings and practices.

References

Abrahamian, Levon, *Armenian Identity in a Changing World* (Costa Mesa: Mazda, 2006).
Abrahamian, Levon, "Zohi marmnits achogh erknayin tachary" [A heavenly temple raised of the body of a victim], in *Hayots srbery ev srbavairery* [Armenian saints and sanctuaries] (Yerevan: Hayastan, 2001), 361–7.
Antonyan, Yu, "Religiosity and Religious Identity in Armenia: Some Current Models and Developments," *Acta Ethnographica Hungarica* 56, no. 2 (2011): 315–32.
Brown, Peter, *The Cult of the Saints* (Chicago: University of Chicago Press, 1981).
Darieva, Tsypyima, "Bringing the Soil back to the Homeland: Reconfigurations of Representation of Loss in Armenia," *Comparativ* 16 (2006), Heft 3: 87–101.
Farnsley, Arthur E. II "Faith-Based Initiatives," in James A. Beckford and N.J. Demerath III (eds), *The SAGE Handbook of the Sociology of Religion* (London: Sage, 2007), 345–56.
Godelier, Maurice, *The Enigma of the Gift* (Chicago: Polity Press, 1999).
Hoffman, Douglas R., *Seeking the Sacred in Contemporary Religious Architecture* (Kent, OH: The Kent State University Press, 2010).

---

[34] Jarrett Zigon, *Morality: An Anthropological Perspective* (Oxford and New York, 2008), p. 62.

Kilde, Jeanne Halgren, *Sacred Power, Sacred Space: An Introduction to Christian Architecture and Worship* (New York: Oxford University Press, 2008).

Köllner, Tobias, "Built with God or Tears? Moral Discourses on Church Construction and the Role of the Entrepreneurial Donations," in Jarrett Zigon (ed.), *Multiple Moralities and Religions and Post-Soviet Russia* (New York: Berghahn Books, 2011), 191–213.

Köllner, Tobias, "Businessmen, Priests and Parishes: Religious Individualization and Privatization in Russia," *Archives des sciences sociales de religions* 162 (April–June 2013): 37–53.

Köllner, Tobias, *Practicing without Belonging? Entrepreneurship, Morality and Religion in Contemporary Russia* (Zürich and Berlin: LIT Verlag, 2012).

Mauss, Marcel, *The Gift* (London: Cohen and West Ltd, 1966).

Minasyan A., A. Poghosyan, T. Hakobyan and B. Hancilova, *Labor Migration from Armenia in 2005–2007: A Survey* (Yerevan: "Asoghik," 2007).

Petrosyan, Hamlet, "The Temple," in Levon Abrahamian and Nancy Sweezy (eds), *Armenian Folk Arts, Culture, and Identity* (Bloomington: Indiana University Press, 2001), 40–51.

Shahnazaryan, N., "Transgranichnye migratsii iz Armenii i Nagornogo Karabakha skvoz' prizmu konflikta i gendernykh otnoshenii" [Transborder migrations from Armenia and Nagorno-Karabagh through the lens of conflict and gender], *Diaspory* 1 (2013): 6–33.

Smith, Jonathan Z., *To Take Place: Toward Theory in Ritual* (Chicago: University of Chicago Press, 1987).

Tocheva, D., "Ot vosstanovleniia khrama k sozdaniiu obshchiny: samoogranichenie i material'nye trudnosti kak istochniki prikhodskoi identichnosti" [Rebuilding a church, creating a community: Self-restraint and material scarcity as markers of parish identity], in Alexander Agadjanian and Kathy Rousselet (eds), *Prikhod i obshchina v sovremennom pravoslavii: kornevaia sistema rossiiskoi religioznosti* [Parish and community in contemporary Orthodoxy: The grassroots system of Russian religiosity] (Moscow: Ves' mir, 2011), 277–97.

Zigon, Jarrett, *Morality: An Anthropological Perspective* (Oxford and New York: Berg, 2008).

Chapter 3

Where Did We Come From? Creationism versus Evolution in Armenian Public Schools

Satenik Mkrtchyan

During a history lesson my son had to defend the scientific hypothesis of human evolution, all alone against the teacher and entire classroom. The teacher kept on affirming that humanity evolved from Adam and Eve. (From the public status of a colleague on her Facebook wall)

Religion and the Public Education System in Armenia

The Educational Reform Act of 1984 in the USSR mentioned the necessity to "form atheistic views among students" as one of the tools for forming a Marxist-Leninist worldview. It was proposed to achieve this through various subjects taught in schools in both the natural and social sciences (*obshchestvovedenie* in Russian). The subject of biology was considered one of the key tools to impose an "atheist education." This can be illustrated with an example from *Sovetakan Dprots*, the Armenian weekly newspaper that served as the official publication of the Ministry of Education of Soviet Armenia, in which authors recommended improvements to atheistic education in schools and provided practical instruction for this. For example, one of the editions from March 1984 speaks about biology and atheistic education, saying that one of the modern requirements of biology programs and textbooks is the formation of the student's worldview, including atheistic views. In the proceeding passages, the author, who was at the time the director of the biology cabinet at the Institute for Training Teachers, advises teachers to highlight the idea of the impossibility of God's existence, and that it is mystic and supernatural. He also urges teachers to show students that animals and plants have emerged historically through evolution.[1]

---

[1] "Biology and Atheistic Education," *Sovetakan Dprots* [Soviet School], March 22, 1984, p. 4 [Սովետական դպրոց. "Կենսաբանությունը և աթեիստական կրթությունը"].

Atheistic education was supposed to be fulfilled even earlier in the elementary grades, before students study the subject of biology.[2] General education with the implementation of an atheistic upbringing would not leave any space in official curriculum and published textbooks for any form of creationist ideas.

The situation changed dramatically with the dissolution of the USSR and formation of new independent states. Even earlier than this, the end of the 1980s and the beginning of the 1990s were characterized as years of revival for many religious elements in different parts of Armenian society.[3] During the late Soviet period, it was widely discussed whether religion should be introduced into schools.[4] Since independence and during the transition period of the early 1990s, one could observe diverse practices of teaching religion and different forms of instruction at schools, though in a chaotic way and without any central regulation, including mini-lectures about Christianity, reciting prayers (particularly the Lord's Prayer), group baptisms for children at schools, and Christmas celebrations.[5] The 1,700th anniversary of the adoption of Christianity as a state religion, celebrated in 2001, brought to a certain extent of enlivenment of religious discourse for society in general and the education sphere in particular. Not only the celebration itself, but also the preparation and necessary mobilization of all sectors of society created an atmosphere where talks were triggered around Christianity, the Armenian Church, and Armenia being the first nation to adopt Christianity as a state religion. The education system was not an exception, although officially the program of the Government Committee created for the 1,700th anniversary celebration did not include any activities directly related to schools.[6] One article suggests that iconographic

---

[2] Satenik Mkrtchyan, "State and Church in Armenian State Schools: From Atheistic Soviet Education to the Contemporary 'History of the Armenian Church' Course," in Ansgar Jodicke (ed.), *Religious Education Politics, the State, and Society* (Ergon-Verlag, 2013), pp. 149–64.

[3] Felix Corley, "The Armenian Church under the Soviet and Independent Regimes, Part 3: The Leadership of Vazgen," *Religion, State and Society* 26, no. 3/4 (1998), pp. 295–355; Levon Abrahamian, *Armenian Identity in a Changung World* (Costa Mesa, 2006).

[4] Corley, "The Armenian Church," p. 308.

[5] "One More Generation has Become Literate," *Dprutyun* [Literacy], January 1, 1991, p. 3 [Դպրություն. "Եվս մեկ սերունդ տառաճանաչ դարձավ"]; "The Mother Tongue is Proudly Flying," *Dprutyun* [Literacy], May 21, 1992, p. 2 [Դպրություն. "Եվ հպարտ թևածում է մայրենի լեզուն"].

[6] Decree of the Government of the Republic of Armenia on "The Action Plan for the Celebration of the 1700th Anniversary of the Adoption of Christianity as a State Religion," June 13, 1997, N180, Yerevan, www.arlis.am/DocumentView.aspx?docid=6134, accessed January 27, 2012.

and ritual dimensions of the religious revival were fostered by this celebration in the schools in Armenia.[7] However, a wide range of religious themes entering into school life through rituals and celebrations was observed, the visual representations of which remained long after the year of the celebration in the form of wall-posters and decorations in Armenian schools. Not only the events and festive celebrations themselves were relevant, but also long periods of preparation and training for teachers themselves to develop scenarios, poems and texts for the celebrations, during which the teachers themselves were learning about the history of the Church, about Christianity and other religions, and about religious rituals and ceremonies.

In August 2002, not long after the 1,700th anniversary, the government of Armenia and the Armenian Apostolic Church signed an agreement requiring that the history of the Armenian Apostolic Church be gradually introduced into the general education system—meaning in secondary and high schools—over the period from 2002 to September 2004. This was to be implemented through joint efforts between the Church and state. The Christian Education Center would participate particularly in the areas of funding, developing textbook content, and training teachers. The subject's official title is "The History of the Armenian Church" and it is taught from the fifth grade to the eleventh grade. It is included in the social science group and considered a history subject, being taught mostly by history teachers and, in lesser cases, by geography and language teachers.

The head of the Christian Education Center of the Armenian Apostolic Church explained the purpose of introducing this subject during a TV program dedicated to the 10th anniversary of the subject's introduction:

> This wise decision came to fill a spiritual gap. During the transition from Soviet rule to independence, when diverse sects emerged and increased in number, the first and most important factor was not social hardships, but a serious lack of religious knowledge and information; people did not know anything about their own church and faith. That is why in their search for religion people took whatever they were offered at that period of time and followed it. I am sure that this subject will fill this gap and that the youth will know their identity and roots, and afterwards they will, of course, be free to follow it or not.[8]

---

[7] Mkrtchyan, "State and Church."

[8] *History of the Armenian Church: 10 Years in Schools* (part 1, 2), 01:38–01:51, Mother See of Holy Edchmiadzin, Shoghakat TV Company, www.youtube.com/watch?v=bcLi4ea8qrI, accessed January 8, 2014, 08:51–09:32, www.youtube.com/watch?v=_t-yu11n0gs, accessed January 8, 2014.

A brief review of the course indicates that the sphere of knowledge provided is wider than just an account of the history of the Church. Thus, in the first two years, the course presents the Bible, Church doctrine, the organizational structure of the Armenian Church, and its holidays. Part of the textbook for the third year of the subject teaching includes chapters about the ancient beliefs of Armenians and neighboring countries, the adoption of Christianity as a state religion, and historical events of the Armenian Apostolic Church. The next two years of the subject explore the whole period after Christianity became a state religion, including contemporary history of the Armenian Apostolic Church.

The introduction of this subject and its further implementation lead to a certain level of public discourse, mostly in the form of newspaper and analytic articles, as well as a few publicly held debates. One of the main "accusations" observed in public debates about the subject regards whether the introduction of such a course into the school curriculum is a violation of the principles of a secular state. The next argument for those debating the introduction of the subject concerns the fact that this policy provides the Armenian Church with an exclusive role, granting it predominance in the content of the subject, while other religions are underrepresented. It is also emphasized that minor attention in the textbooks is paid to the pre-Christian period, its beliefs, and cultural heritage.[9] Another argument relates to the worldview that is expected to form among schoolchildren as a result of completing the subject. It is said to be filled with intolerance and bias. During a public debate organized by the Eurasia Partnership Foundation in 2013, a participant spoke out against the subject regarding its form and the content actually taught, stating:

> In fact [students] only learn about the Armenian Apostolic Church and its beliefs, foregoing information and knowledge about other denominations, such as Catholicism, Evangelism, and other religions such as Islam and Buddhism. This lack of information also hinders the student's ability to understand and accept the existence of other possible religions, which in turn can lead to intolerance and psychological discomfort for them when they come across people of a different religious identity and behavior.[10]

---

[9] Vardan Jaloyan, "A History of the Armenian Church" [Վարդան Ջալոյան, "Հայոց եկեղեցու պատմությոն" դասագիրքը], www.religions.am/arm/articles/?p=18, accessed December 30, 2013.

[10] The debate was organized as a part of "Promoting Religious tolerance," a project by the Eurasia Partnership Foundation.

The response to these arguments refers to the fact that the exclusive role of the Armenian Church in education is related to the historically exclusive role of the Armenian Church in preserving Armenian identity and culture, which is even fixed in the Constitution. According to the Minister of Education and Sciences:

> The Armenian Apostolic Church is the 'national church' according to the Constitution, and the state recognizes the exclusive mission of the Armenian Apostolic Church in preserving Armenian identity and in spiritual and cultural development. It is impossible even to imagine how such an identity would be preserved if not by the Armenian Apostolic Church. Thus, this very important point of the Constitution serves as a foundation for us to continue the process of introducing the subject on the history of the Armenian Church in schools.[11]

Another objection is that the course is actually not purely about history. The contention is that, in the first two years of the course, the textbook teaches and explains more about the Bible and theology than about history.[12] Another argument raised in Armenian public debates is not so much about the subject itself, but more about diverse practices that reveal themselves as being more about teaching religion or diverse forms of instruction rather than teaching about religion, as NGOs have alarmingly mentioned in diverse reports and press conferences.[13]

---

[11] See Armen Ashotyan, an interview, at www.lragir.am/armsrc/print.country34232, accessed December 30, 2013.

[12] Aram Avetyan, "What Does the Textbook 'History of the Armenian Church' Teach?" [Արամ Ավետյան, Ինչ է ուսուցանում "Հայոց եկեղեցու պատմություն" դասագիրքը], www.religions.am/arm/articles/?p=18, accessed December 30, 2013.

[13] Stepan Danielyan, Hovhannes Hovhannisyan, Artur Avtandilyan and Ara Ghazaryan, "Religious Problems in Schools in the Republic of Armenia" [Կրոնական խնդիրները Հայաստանի Հանրապետության հանրակրթական դպրոցներում], www.religions.am/files/1706/pastathter/ps1.pdf, accessed December 30, 2013; H. Hovhannisyan, A Davtyan and S. Mkrtchyan, "School Textbooks of the History of the Armenian Church and their Influence on the Young Generation" [Հայոց եկեղեցու պատմություն դպրոցական դասագրքերի բովանդակային վերլուծությունն ու դրանց ազդեցությունը երիտասարդող սերնդի վրա], www.religions.am/files/3290/library/legal/L011.pdf, accessed December 30, 2013.

The Case about Creationism and the Latent "Culture War" within the Curriculum

Having provided the general context of introducing the subject in Armenian schools and its pursuant debates, we will further discuss one particular aspect, namely the ways that questions surrounding the origins of the universe, earth, and species—including humans—are being introduced to schoolchildren.

Among the subjects envisaged by the national curriculum for general education in Armenia operating for the academic year of 2011–12, we have chosen several subjects that might deal with related questions and themes and that could provide us with either answers or supporting ideas about the origins of the universe, the earth, and species, as they are meant for schoolchildren. The subjects reviewed lie within the fields of social and natural sciences, including world history, biology, and the history of the Armenian Church, which was mentioned above. These three subjects are taught at higher levels, rather than at the elementary grades. Ideas and topics taught at the basic level (grades 5–9) later on become broader and are presented with more details in high school (grades 10–12). The depth and volume of the topics depend on the field, whether it is humanities, social sciences, natural sciences, etc. Chronologically, the first subject within the curriculum where students come across ideas about the origin of creation is the History of the Armenian Church (one hour per week).

A subject on the history of the Armenian Church begins in the fifth grade, which is the first year of basic school in Armenia. In the program document for this subject, we find the Old Testament among one of the first themes for discussion. This theme consists of several sub-themes, such as the creation of the world and humans, including Adam and Eve. It is mentioned that, upon completing these lessons, "the student should know about the history of the Creation and the first people" and "the student should be able to describe the life of people in paradise." In a two-page passage accompanied by illustrations, the textbook describes the creation of the universe and of the world's first people, meaning Adam and Eve. The topic starts with a short introductory part that says, "We live on Earth, which is an interesting and wonderful planet full of plants, animals, and people. Who created it or how did it emerge? The Creation is described in the Bible."[14]

The subject of world history is taught starting from the sixth grade (one academic hour per week). The curriculum document developed for this subject

---

[14] Ghandilyan, Vardan, V. Parsamyan, A. Ghukasyan and A. Gyulbudaghyan, *History of the Armenian Church*, National Institute of Education (Yerevan: CED, 2003), p. 9.

says that one of the fields of the subject is historical development. One of the processes of historical development is mentioned to be anthropological, namely the origin and further development of human beings. The program starts with pre-history. One piece of knowledge included in the obligatory list that students should know upon completing one of the lessons is "the origin of the ancient (հնագույն) human and the period of formation of *homo sapiens*."[15] The textbook for world history starts from presenting pre-history as the first stage of world history. According to the textbook, "Humanity has a history of more than three million years."[16] Further, "The human being is different from other species of fauna, with its ability to act with purpose and to work, thanks to which labor activity was formed and developed over the course of thousands of years."[17]

One of the topics for the subject of biology in schools according to the national curriculum is "biodiversity and evolution." The curriculum says that, upon completion of this subject, students should be able to describe the mechanism of evolution and bring arguments for its role in the origin of biodiversity. Corresponding lessons are allocated to presenting the evolutionary theory of Darwin, the mechanisms of evolution, natural selection and the struggle for life, and the main topics of evolution, as well as the origins of life on earth and modern ideas about it. These lessons are included in the program for the ninth grade of the basic level of general education.

Thus, as we saw above from curriculum statements and textbook passages, there is a certain level of diversity with regard to ideas on the origin of the earth, life and humans. The subject of biology in the ninth grade speaks about the theory of evolution and explains the mechanisms of biodiversity, natural selection and the struggle for life. The subject of world history in the sixth grade speaks about the origins of the human race with a more vague concept of humans being different from other species with their ability to act purposefully, in an organized way, and with the principle of labor. However, ideas about where we are from are first given in the subject on the history of the Armenian Church, which is studied earlier than the two other subjects and offered as objective knowledge, rather than as a matter of subjective belief. These ideas concern the creation, the first humans and paradise.

---

[15] *World History (6–9 grades), a Program*. Yerevan, Ministry of Education and Science of the Republic of Armenia, 2014, http://lib.armedu.am/resource/122, accessed January 7, 2014.

[16] A. Stepanyan, H. Avetisyan and A. Qosyan, *World History: Ancient World 6* (Yerevan, Zangak 2013), p. 5 [Համաշխարհային պատմություն. հին աշխարհ 6].

[17] Stepanyan et al., *World History*, p. 10.

In other words, teachers and students are met with a certain level of the "culture war" between creationism and evolution as a part of official school curriculum. Teachers find themselves with a decision to either choose between the two concepts or to strike a balance between them and have the students understand these two forms of knowledge, meaning the scientific and the religious. Official approaches can be tracked within the national curriculum and in textbooks printed by the Ministry of Education and Sciences.

The next level of analysis concerns the daily implementation of teachers during classes and interpretations of the ideas, to what extent and in what ways are these two sides reflected, and are they contradicted, cooperated or reconciled? Below are two episodes of teacher practices in schools trying to negotiate and reconcile these two ideas. In what follows, instead of claiming to cover the whole range of possible practices and teachers' strategies, I will just provide a couple of illustrative narratives:

> (1) Children discuss and debate the concepts actively. They argue against the theory of evolution, saying that they know that God created humans. I do not want them to go into more detail and debate, I just try to bring them into the dimension of physiology and explain that, with regard to the body, it is a matter of evolution, while God regulates our soul. It is not a coincidence that we pray when we feel bad, I tell them. But when it comes to the body, it is a matter of evolution. (Biology teacher, Yerevan, 2013)

> (2) Adam and Eve are presented in the Bible as representations of many other people with their families. The Bible shows it on this one example. I give this as an answer to children who wonder how it had become possible for the population to increase this much if initially there was only one family. Then I add that no one can say for sure how human beings emerged; that there are only religious theories based on the Bible, natural theories based on the assumption that the earth emerged as a result of a great explosion, and scientific theories based on the theories of Darwin. I think that every person should think and decide for oneself which theory to believe. I cannot impose any of them upon the students. (History teacher, Yerevan, 2013)

This clash of ideas about the Beginning is not new in the modern world and has been a matter of controversy in the education systems of other countries. One of the earliest clashes was the famous John Scopes trial in the United States in 1925. This trial received the public's attention and fostered public debates between the two sides. One side believed the Bible to be literally true and was against the teaching of evolution. The other side tried to teach evolution in schools despite a law that prohibited doing so. In an article discussing this clash, Harding argues that the side pushing for creationism to be taught in school eventually "lost" in the eyes of the public, even though they officially won their case again John Scopes.[18]

Post-Soviet states have also witnessed publicized and juridical clashes between creationists and evolutionists. The "accused" side is evolutionism, and the demand is that the two ideas should be equally mentioned as theories about the origins of the earth and humans within a framework of general education. In St. Petersburg, a school student together with her father demanded that "outdated and mistaken" Darwinism be excluded from the school program and that creationism be included.[19] A more recent public debate in Russia was connected to a proposal for schools to use a biology textbook by S. Vartianov for grades 10–11.[20]

As a reaction to the activation of creationist ideas and their introduction to school systems, in 2007 the Committee on Culture, Science, and Education of the Parliamentary Assembly of the Council of Europe published a report entitled "The Dangers of Creationism in Education." This was thought as response to the spread of modern forms of creationist ideas all over Europe, especially that which was known as "intelligent design," which is said to have previously been a case for the United States. The report mentions some alarming evidence of creationist ideas taking the arena in education systems. One striking example is of Harun Yahya, a Turkish preacher, and his work "The Atlas of Creation," which was sent to many schools in France, Belgium, Spain and Switzerland. The report also warns about different cases of recent creationist initiatives in other countries such as Poland, Russia, Italy, Greece, Germany, Sweden, the Netherlands, Serbia and the United Kingdom. The Assembly called on education authorities in member states to "promote scientific knowledge and the teaching of evolution and to oppose firmly any attempts to teach creationism as a scientific discipline."[21]

---

[18]   Susan Harding, "Representing Fundamentalism: Representing the Cultural Other," *Social Research* 58, no. 2 (Summer 1991), pp. 373–93, p. 377.

[19]   "The Dangers of Creationism in Education," Report, Committee on Culture, Science and Education, Parliamentary Assembly Council of Europe, Doc. 11375, September 17, 2007.

[20]   Ksenia Koniukhova, "Uchebnik po biologii bez Darvina? Nu, s Bogom!" [A Biology textbook without Darwin? God bless!], *Komsomol'skaia Pravda*, March 21, 2013, www.kp.ru/daily/26049.4/2961617/, accessed January 30, 2013.

[21]   "The Dangers of Creationism in Education." In the United Kingdom, on June 2014 creationism was effectively prohibited from teaching as a scientific theory (or "evidence based theory") in all state-run ("free") schools and academies (including schools run by the Church

Further Discussion

In this concluding discussion, I wish to expand on the idea that the introduction of a religious course actually created or provoked this latent conflict within a scientific school curriculum inherited from the Soviet Union. The Soviet curriculum had an ideological framework in the form of Marxist materialism with Darwinism as one of its main pillars. The general education system of Armenia inherited much from its Soviet precedent, but not an ideological framework. As a post-Soviet society, Armenia needed a new and updated ideological framework for its education system. The old framework was removed and a Western-type secular pattern prevailed, with Darwinism remaining in an uncontested stronghold. Simultaneously, the general education system was being nationalized and linked to Armenian ethno-national and religious identity, which held the Armenian Apostolic Church as a key pillar of national identity. The introduction of a school subject on the history of the Armenian Church took place within this wider trend. But this much-needed new framework could not be purely religious, as such a framework was of course *nation*-oriented; religion was legitimized through a projection of national identity, national legacy and national heritage. As a part of the programs for the above-mentioned subject and textbooks, the idea of the world being created by God is taught in schools in the sixth grade. Thus, creationism was introduced within the official school curriculum and as an element of a national spiritual tradition, namely the Armenian Church. In fact, creationism is a certain substitution to the evolutionism officially taught in biology and, to a lesser extent, history classes.

In the early 1990s and up until 2003–4 when the history of the Armenian Church was introduced to the official curriculum, school life in its everyday practices and festivities had witnessed a certain level of religious revival as a reflection of similar trends in society.[22] If we put aside the issue of nationalization (nation-building), which is a major process, and stick to a religious aspect, we can see that post-Soviet Armenia is witnessing a wave of desecularization connected with a "world-wide resurgence of religion"[23] and such counter-secularization tendencies as a revitalization of religious content within a multiplicity of

---

of England and Catholic Church): see http://www.politics.co.uk/news/2014/06/18/secular-triumph-as-government-bans-creationism-from-free-sch, accessed on June 22, 2014.

[22] Mkrtchyan, "State and Church," pp. 150–52.

[23] Peter L. Berger (ed.), *The Desecularization of the World: Resurgent Religion and World Politics* (Washington, DC: Ethics and Public Policy Center/Grand Rapids: Eerdmans, 1999), p. 12.

sub-systems of culture.²⁴ One specific feature of counter-secularization put forth by Karpov suggests that the inclusion of creationist ideas in biology classes at schools has "weakened the monopoly of science as a radically secular cultural instrument of world-building."²⁵ In his 2011 lecture "Faith and Knowledge," Jürgen Habermas called to seriously respect the notion of the Creation, because such knowledge is a long-standing and deep tradition of Western culture, and perhaps contains some deep intuitions for all in a pluralist democratic society. It is interesting that Habermas mentioned the concept of creationism as legitimate in a diverse pluralist society. Among these two legitimate mentalities, meaning the religious and secular, or faith and knowledge, a mutual learning process should be established that would enable them to "live together in a self-reflective manner," if a balance of shared citizenship and cultural difference is desired.²⁶ This new type of interaction between secular and religious worldviews was conceptualized as a part of a "post-secular" perspective in the social sciences.

Thus, with creationist ideas being part of the History of the Armenian Church as a school subject and evolutionist ideas as part of the subjects of biology and history, a new situation for witnessing a contrast has been formed in Armenia. Such a "latent culture war" in the school curriculum has become possible and people—both students and teachers—need to somehow come to terms with this new contradictive complexity. In a way, this "war" leads to establishing clear borders between "the secular and the religious." It may also be that a certain level of eclecticism and a mixture of diverse attitudes and practices leads to the issue being something taken for granted, paying no attention to any contradiction, and simply assuming that evolution and creationism are various possibilities existing simultaneously and subject to individual choice. What is the situation in the field of the classroom and how are teachers dealing with the issue? Without pretending to "diagnose" the prevailing practice of how teachers deal with the issue, I would like to mention that creationist ideas have a stable position in school discourse for at least two reasons. First, creationism is connected to the Christian identity, which is regarded as a pillar of national identity and therefore receives legitimacy and weight. Second, creationist ideas are taught in earlier grades than biology is. Therefore, the evolutionist idea must "struggle" with already fixed knowledge, creating a challenge for biology

---

²⁴ Viacheslav Karpov, "Kontseptual'nye osnovy teorii desekuliarizatsii" [Conceptual bases of desecularization theory], *Gosudarstvo, religia, tserkov' v Rossii i za rubezhom* [State, Religion, and Church in Russia and Worldwide], vol. 30, no. 2 (2012), pp. 114–64.

²⁵ Karpov, "Kontseptual'nye osnovy teorii desekuliarizatsii," pp. 124, 136.

²⁶ Jürgen Habermas, "Faith and Knowledge," Speech accepting the Peace Prize of the German Publishers and Booksellers Association, Paulskirche, Frankfurt, October 14, 2001.

teachers who now have to negotiate and reconcile evolutionist ideas with those of biblical creationism.

References

Abrahamian, Levon, *Armenian Identity in a Changing World* (Costa Mesa: Mazda Publishers, 2006).
Ashotyan, Armen, Interview, www.lragir.am/armsrc/print.country34232, accessed December 30, 2013.
Avetyan, Aram, "What Does the Textbook 'History of the Armenian Church' Teach?" [Արամ Ավետյան, Ինչ է ուսուցանում "Հայոց եկեղեցու պատմություն" դասագիրքը], www.religions.am/arm/articles/?p=18, accessed December 30, 2013.
Berger, Peter L. (ed.), *The Desecularization of the World: Resurgent Religion and World Politics* (Washington, DC: Ethics and Public Policy Center/Grand Rapids: Eerdmans, 1999).
"Biology and Atheistic Education," *Sovetakan Dprots* [Soviet School], March 22, 1984, p. 4 [Սովետական դպրոց. "Կենսաբանությունը և րեեիստական կրթությունը"].
Corley, Felix, "The Armenian Church under the Soviet and Independent Regimes, Part 3: The Leadership of Vazgen," *Religion, State and Society* 26, no. 3/4 (1998): 295–355.
"The Dangers of Creationism in Education," Report, Committee on Culture, Science, and Education, Parliamentary Assembly Council of Europe, Doc. 11375, September 17, 2007.
Danielyan, Stepan, H. Hovhannisyan, A. Avtandilyan and A. Ghazaryan, "Religious Problems in Schools in the Republic of Armenia" [Կրոնական խնդիրները Հայաստանի Հանրապետության հանրակրթական դպրոցներում], www.religions.am/files/1706/pastathter/ps1.pdf, accessed December 30, 2013.
Decree of the Government of Republic of Armenia on "The Action Plan for the Celebration of the 1700th Anniversary of Adoption of Christianity as a State Religion," June 13, 1997, N180, Yerevan, www.arlis.am/DocumentView.aspx?docid=6134 (accessed January 27, 2012).
Ghandilyan, Vardan, V. Parsamyan, A. Ghukasyan and A. Gyulbudaghyan, *History of the Armenian Church*, National Institute of Education (Yerevan: CED, 2003).

Habermas, Jürgen, "Faith and Knowledge," Speech accepting the Peace Prize of the German Publishers and Booksellers Association Paulskirche, Frankfurt, October 14, 2001, www.habermasforum.dk/index.php?type=onlinetexts&text_id=253, accessed January 7, 2014.

Harding, Susan, "Representing Fundamentalism: Representing the Cultural Other," *Social Research* 58, no. 2 (summer 1991): 373–93.

History of the Armenian Church: 10 Years in Schools (part 1, 2). Shoghakat TV Company, Mother See of Holy Etchmiadzin, www.youtube.com/watch?v=bcLi4ea8qrI, accessed January 8, 2014; www.youtube.com/watch?v=_t-yu11n0gs, accessed January 8, 2014.

Hovhannisyan, Hovhannes, A. Davtyan and S. Mkrtchyan, "School Textbooks of the History of the Armenian Church and their Influence on the Young Generation" [Հայոց եկեղեցու պատմության դպրոցական դասագրքերի բովանդակային վերլուծությունն ու դրանց ազդեցությունը երիտասարդ սերնդի վրա], www.religions.am/files/3290/library/legal/L011.pdf, accessed December 30, 2013.

Jaloyan, Vardan, "A History of the Armenian Church" [Վարդան Ջալոյան, "Հայոց եկեղեցու պատմություն" դասագիրքը], www.religions.am/arm/articles/?p=18, accessed December 30, 2013.

Karpov, Viacheslav, "Kontseptual'nye osnovy teorii desekuliarizatsii" [Conceptual bases of desecularization theory], *Gosudarstvo, religia, tserkov' v Rossii i za rubezhom* [State, Religion, and Church in Russia and Worldwide], vol. 30, no. 2 (2012): 114–64.

Koniukhova, Ksenia, "Uchebnik po biologii bez Darvina? Nu, s Bogom!" [A Biology textbook without Darwin? God bless!], *Komsomol'skaia Pravda*, March 21, 2013, www.kp.ru/daily/26049.4/2961617/, accessed January 30, 2013.

Mkrtchyan, Satenik, "State and Church in Armenian State Schools: From Atheistic Soviet Education to the Contemporary 'History of the Armenian Church' Course," in Ansgar Jodicke (ed.), *Religious Education Politics, the State, and Society* (Würzburg: Ergon-Verlag, 2013), 149–64.

"The Mother Tongue is Proudly Flying." *Dprutyun* [Literacy], May 21, 1992, p. 2 [Դպրություն. "Եվ հպարտ թևածում է մայրենի լեզուն"].

"One More Generation has Become Literate," *Dprutyun* [Literacy], January 1, 1991, p. 3 [Դպրություն. "Եվս մեկ սերունդ տառաճանաչ դարձավ"].

Stepanyan, Albert, Hayk Avetisyan, Aram Qosyan and Armine Sargsyan, *World History: Ancient World 6* [Համաշխարհային պատմություն. հին աշխարհ 6] (Yerevan: Zangak, 2013).

World History (6–9 grades), a Program (Yerevan: Ministry of Education and Science of the Republic of Armenia, 2014), http://lib.armedu.am/resource/122, accessed January 7, 2014.

Chapter 4

The Religious Modernity of the Brotherhood: A New Face of Armenian Grassroots Christianity

Alexander Agadjanian

In this chapter[1] the analysis of Armenian religiosity will be made within the more general context of post-Soviet trends. I will make a tentative breakdown of various forms of current religious life in Armenia. I will then analyze one of these forms in more detail and show, using the example of a religious movement, an attempt to create a pattern of "religious modernity" within an old and conservative tradition that retains, by default, an almost total national monopoly on the sacred. By "religious modernity" I refer to the conceptual frame developed by Danièle Hervieu-Léger who analyzed major patterns of adaptive transformations within old religious traditions, including changes in the sources of authority, motives of belonging, and forms of solidarity.[2] I will finally assess the overall impact of this new type of religious agency on the post-Soviet Armenian society.

This research is based on fieldwork that included a number of interviews with priests, lay people and experts.[3]

---

[1] This work was partly supported by the Knights of Vartan scholarship granted by the National Association for Armenian Studies and Research (NAASR).

[2] Danièle Hervieu-Léger, *Religion as a Chain of Memory* (New Brunswick, 2000); Danièle Hervieu-Léger, *Le pèlerin et le converti* (Paris: Flammarion, 1999).

[3] The fieldwork was conducted with interruptions in 2009–10 and then in 2012–13 in collaboration with Konrad Siekierski, although all interpretations and conclusions in this chapter are mine. The data was collected in the forms of interviews. I will refer to these interviews according to my own system including the letter R (for respondent), the respondent's number and category (p–Priest, l–Lay, e–Expert), followed by the date of the interview. With some exceptions, the names of the respondents are not given to preserve their anonymity.

The Post-Soviet Religious Dynamic in Armenia

The post-Soviet religious revival had a few common features across various ethnic, national and denominational boundaries. The forced secularization during seven decades (in most regions except those annexed during World War II) led to breaks in the "chain of memory"[4] that is at the core of religion as a worldview and communicative system: some basic forms of verbal knowledge and practical *habitus* were simply lost along the way.

Yet religion did not disappear, but rather was deeply transformed. First of all, the very notion of "religion" changed: "religion" was conceptualized as a particular, specific "worldview" and "subculture," a closed and systemic set of ideas and practices, an object-in-itself—a transformation that goes back to the fundamental rationalistic episteme of the Enlightenment. Second, this "object" became linked to the "past," which socialist "modernity" was bound to replace forever, as a result of a radical, exclusivist version of the same Enlightenment episteme. Third, this "object" was seen as relating exclusively to private life, or even to the private consciousness; even more accurately, to a subconscious that would inevitably die out (a very radical form of the "privatization of religion," which was a general Western secularist trend). Fourth, when I say that religion became an *object*, I mean that it could be the *subject* of management and manipulation: one could eliminate it, struggle against it, or use it, construct it, interpret it, and sometimes even reify it—and, in fact, one could even invent a new "object" from its dispersed cultural fragments.

"Religion" in the Soviet Union—including the Armenian Apostolic Church (AAC)—was brutally repressed, mostly in the pre-World War II period, and then, with a new softer post-war policy, used and manipulated for certain purposes. However, while the initial objectives of the Soviet authorities did not go beyond creating a false image of religious freedoms, in the popular imagination and in intellectual interpretations religion gradually started to be associated with the national culture and heritage and, eventually, with nationalism. This association was implicitly accepted and even promoted in the Russian center of the Soviet empire. In colonial provinces like Armenia, religion of this new, objectified kind, became a legitimate pillar of local nationalism (or whatever "socialist" euphemism the Soviet official language might employ, such as "patriotism" or "cultural heritage"). Armenian "religion"—for policy-makers and for most ordinary people—was seen, in a deeply recast, reified way, as a symbol of national identity: substantially—a profane symbol, cut off from real

---

[4] Danièle Hervieu-Léger, *Religion as a Chain of Memory* (New Brunswick, 2000).

sacred or spiritual meanings; but semiotically—bearing reference to the semi-forgotten, semi-hidden spiritual tradition.[5]

The post-Soviet processes of the "exit from socialism" revealed a need for national consolidation as a symbolic basis for nation-building. Although the major factors in this consolidation were the drive for independence and the acquisition of Karabagh, religion played an important role in promoting cohesive nationalism—if not on the level of mass behavior or everyday social cohesion, but at least as a source of collective national symbolism. The AAC naturally claimed to perform this role of a major "community cult," in the Durkheimian sense.

In the development of the religious field as a whole, however, there was another process that went simultaneously: the growth of uncontrolled diversity and pluralism, as religious expressions were emancipated from the control and imposed uniformity of the Soviet era. After this late- and post-Soviet liberalization, the AAC's move to recover its traditional hegemony was challenged by other denominations, which aimed to re-establish their rights, like the Armenian Catholics, or found their way into the country, like many Protestant communities. Other groups also appeared from within the local cultural fabric in opposition to the dominant narrative of Christian hegemony, such as the local neo-pagans, *Arordiner*.[6]

Most importantly, this emancipated diversity even sprang up within the dominant Apostolic Orthodox Christian tradition itself. This tradition turned out to be less monolithic than it was imagined after its reification during the communist period, and it took various shapes. In fact, the policy of the Church leadership in Etchmiadzin was, predictably, to oppose diversity and potential splits, and to strengthen the imagined uniformity of the tradition; at some point, this image was further promoted by the government for the purposes of legitimation. However, the contrary trend of pluralization could hardly be stopped. First of all, the major split between the two centers of ecclesiastic authority—the Etchmiadzin and Cilician Catholicosates (Patriarchates)—

---

[5] Interestingly, this trend actually pre-dates socialism: it is well known that under the Ottoman *millet* system, the Armenian Church played the role of a political institution, representing and preserving the national tradition as a whole; in the nineteenth century, when the nationalist movement began, the Church partly remodeled itself, as one of the nationalist parties—what Bishop Sahak, former rector of the Etchmiadzin spiritual academy, called "the second tradition of the Armenian Church" (Interview: R-78P, November 8, 2009).

[6] Yulia Antonyan and Konrad Siekierski, "A Neopagan Movement in Armenia: The Children of Ara," in Kaarina Aitamurto and Scott Simpson (eds), *Modern Pagan and Native Faith Movements in Central and Eastern Europe* (Durham, 2013), pp. 267–8.

became apparent, in spite of a considerable rapprochement in the 1990s, and revealed clear differences in religious style, clergy orientations and political sensibilities. These differences roughly corresponded to the split between post-Soviet Armenia and the older Armenian diaspora worldwide.[7] The fact of growing interconnections between these two sub-traditions within Armenian Orthodoxy made their differences more clearly manifest, although, at the same time, the interaction led to mutual influences.

In this chapter, putting aside the issue of this split of ecclesiastic authority and its consequences in the narrow, institutional sense, I will keep in mind the very fact of growing interaction between the post-Soviet society of the Armenian "Third Republic" (since 1991) and the diasporas, which created truly transnational flows and networks. As we will see, the case study that follows is, in a very deep sense, a result of these newly opened flows.

Before turning to my case study, and in order to locate it more precisely within the religious field, I would like to propose the following breakdown of forms which emerged around and within the Armenian Apostolic tradition in the post-Independence society:

1. Church clergy, based upon the monastic order at Etchmiadzin, using the discourse of national identity and spiritual hegemony, supported, in various degrees, by the political regimes since independence in 1991.[8]
2. Continued and revived amalgam of folk religiosity, mostly festive and/or devotional, embedded in rural or semi-rural settings and partly controlled, partly rejected by the clergy (the degree of such control may vary).[9]

---

[7] See the chapter by Hovhannes Hovhannisyan in this volume (Chapter 6), as well as his previous article in Armenian: "Mayr At'or' s. Echmiadzin ev Metsi Tann Kilikio kat'oghikosneri verchin shrjani haraberut'yunneri verlutsut'yun" [The Mother See of Etchmiadzin and the Great House of Cilicia: An analysis of their relationships in recent times], *Kron ev hasarakut'yun* [Religion and Society] 8 (2009), pp. 42–67.

[8] In this list of religious forms I will not include "monastic life" as a separate item: the Holy See of Etchmiadzin itself is set as a "monastic order" which can be seen at the same time as the collective leadership of the Church. However, the monastic life *outside* the Holy See has not been restored with the current revival. No monasteries have reappeared, as was, for example, the case in the Orthodox churches of Russia or neighboring Georgia.

[9] This form is basically what Yulia Antonyan has called "vernacular religion" in her insightful paper on models of Armenian Apostolic religiosity: Yulia Antonyan, "Religiosity and Religious Identity in Armenia: Some Current Models and Developments," *Acta Ethnographica Hungarica* 56, no. 2 (2011), pp. 315–32.

3. Urban and rural church life within a re-established parish structure, mostly of the "consumerist" type, providing "spiritual goods" for mass symbolic needs (rites of passage and other sacramental "supplies") or, in some cases, seeking a deeper mystical and communal sociality.
4. Alternative religious life outside, or beyond, the established parish structure, creating new forms of community and moving, deliberately or unintentionally, beyond traditional Church culture toward a more spontaneous, congregational type of religiosity.
5. Individual, dispersed, volatile religiosity of various degrees of intensity, where people do not belong to either the Church or any alternative kind of associational life, and mostly related to symbolic consumption of nationally-colored religious meanings.

In this chapter my goal is to concentrate on item 4 in this list: the new form of associational religiosity, remaining within the tradition but partly moving beyond traditional forms and structures. By far the most prominent and vivid example of this trend was the emergence of the "Brotherhood," an organization that played an important role in the post-Soviet religious revival.

A Brief History of the Brotherhood: Analyzing Origins

The Armenian name for the Brotherhood is *Yekhpairakts'ut'yun*.[10] It considers itself to be a lay movement within the Armenian Apostolic Church. In my brief historical account I will follow the narrative as told by its spiritual head, Brother (as adepts call themselves) Hamlet Zakharian,[11] with comments or different assessments and observations made by other sources, other informants, and myself.

Mythologically, the foundation of the Brotherhood is sometimes claimed to go back to Mesrop Mashtots of the fifth century CE.[12] Historically, the Brotherhood was initially the product of a revival in the Ottoman Empire

---

[10] The full name is *Hay Arakelakan Ekeghetsu Ekeghasirats Ekhpairakts'ut'yun* (Brotherhood of Those Who Love the Church, of the Armenian Apostolic Church) or sometimes *Ekeghetsi Sirokhneri Miut'yun* (Union of Loving the Church).

[11] Interview with Hamlet Zakharian: R-39L, October 6, 2009.

[12] The myth containing this claim of antiquity was recorded in the mid-1990s by David C. Lewis, who devoted a chapter to the Brotherhood and was, perhaps, the first to give an account of this movement. See David C. Lewis, *After Atheism: Religion and Ethnicity in Russia and Central Asia* (New York, 2000), p. 243.

in the late nineteenth and early twentieth centuries. That time witnessed the intensification of public life across the empire and, quite obviously, in the Armenian communities. The Brotherhood was founded in Cilicia, a southern imperial province, in the early 1880s in the midst of a revivalist wave sparked by the Protestant missions. I would suggest that the Brotherhood was *both* an imitation of Protestant forms of piety and mission *and*, at the same time, a protective reaction against Protestants from within the Armenian Apostolic tradition—a pattern of resisting-through-imitation, common in religious history. It was a "spiritual Revival, a Revival in the bosom of the Armenian Church."[13] Its main religious agenda was, indeed, revivalist—active evangelization and mission, something that was almost entirely unknown in the institutional practices of the Armenian Church.

The Brotherhood's narrative includes the hagiography of a woman, Sister Elisabeth Labashlyan, or Haji Elisabeth, born in 1863 in Earpuz, Cilicia; she was a lower class, semi-educated woman who experienced a series of visions and dreams that led her to initiate in 1880, with the help of a few followers, including ordained clerics, a small prayer group who called themselves the Union of Love (*Siro Enkherut'yun*). This form of small prayer group then spread widely among Armenian communities.

The enmity against Armenians that culminated in the 1915 genocide strongly stimulated the expansion of the Brotherhood's prayer groups wherever the refugees settled—mostly in the Middle East, but also in more distant diasporas. The genocide also stimulated new spiritual needs among all the dispersed and traumatized communities, which the Brotherhood sought to fulfill. In 1931, in Lebanon, the association's charter was approved as belonging to the Cilician Catholicosate of the AAC.[14]

It was obviously unknown in Soviet Armenia until the post-war policy of repatriation declared by Stalin's government: at this point the "seeds" of the Brotherhood were planted in Armenian soil with the new immigrants. Beginning in 1948, very small communities (sometimes only three or four people) were settled in the semi-underground in a few cities, such as Yerevan, Leninakan (now Gyumri), Kirovokan (now Vanadzor) and Ararat. Over time, they were said to have been semi-legalized and continued to grow: in the early 1960s there were about a dozen communities bringing together up to 50–60 people for common prayer.

---

[13] See a history account at the Brotherhood's website: http://bclaac.org/am/, accessed on March 14, 2014
[14] Ibid.

Interestingly, most of the members of these communities were Turkish-speaking, and this situation continued until at least the 1970s, a fact that made them relatively harmless in the eyes of the Soviet authorities. In the 1970s, at a time of spiritual and nationalist revival accompanied by a new wave of urbanization (especially the growth of Yerevan), the prayer meetings started to be increasingly attended by Armenian speakers; this marked a new stage in the Brotherhood's acculturation.[15] The first peak of that revival occurred in the late 1970s, when a few members of the intelligentsia joined the meetings. At that point the authorities and the secret services started to monitor the movement. This period of gradual growth was also one of extensive contacts with similar revivalist movements in other parts of the Soviet Union, especially in Moscow.[16]

Like other similar underground religious movements in the Soviet Union, the Brotherhood and its religious life was, in a way, not fully incorporated into the official Church, which had no option but to be loyal to the anti-religious regime, and was thus seen as containing no charisma of "true spirituality." As in Ottoman Turkey a century before, the Brotherhood's stance vis-à-vis the Church was ambiguous. It claimed to be attached to it, but it was de facto autonomous and viewed with suspicion by the Church hierarchy. The Brotherhood's main agenda was free spiritual devotion, mission and association—functions that the contemporary Church was said to be unable to perform. "Spirituality," or "true spirituality," is the main emphasis in the movement as presented by its leader (R-39L, October 6, 2009). The Church is criticized for its lack of this "true spirituality." As another respondent said, the present Catholicos and his brother[17] are just "builders": they are concerned with "external things," while the Brotherhood is "concerned about the inner" (R-43L, October 15, 2009).

---

[15] Most prayer meetings were gradually Armenianized; prayer books and books of spiritual songs were published first in Western Armenian and later in Eastern Armenian as well. At some point the Brotherhood created its own hymnal in Armenian, now recognized as standard for all branches and groups.

[16] The leader, Hamlet Zakharian, went for prolonged stays in Moscow where he contacted (and received a blessing from) the well-known Russian Orthodox priest Alexander Men'. One of my Moscow informants, a woman from Alexander Men's circle and now a parishioner in one of the Moscow churches, told how profoundly the Brotherhood inspired her and her friends back in the 1980s with the spirit of devotion and solidarity. She and others went to Armenia several times to participate in the Brotherhood's gatherings (R-69L, May 6, 2009). Hamlet Zakharian also told me about the influence he and other brethren experienced from another Moscow reformist priest, Father Georgii Kochetkov, who created a strong community within the Russian Orthodox Church (R-39L, October 6, 2009).

[17] Ezras, the Catholicos' younger brother, the bishop of the AAC's Russian diocese (officially called Novo-Nakhichevan' and Russian diocese).

At the same time, the Brotherhood's distance from the official Church structures could not become too great: as an institution closely bound up with the national identity, the Church still provided a strong symbolic capital for many people who had joined the Brotherhood out of patriotic feelings. The main pattern in the religious life of the Brotherhood's members was getting together in a rented space for a community meeting, chanting, prayers and sermons; however, the members were also attached to a few existing parishes for taking Holy Communion. In such ways they combined allegiance to the "Mother Church" and experimentation with totally new forms, very close indeed to typical Protestant patterns.

The eventful period between 1988 and 1994 (the earthquake and the Armenian pogroms in Azerbaijan in 1988, independence in 1991, and the Karabagh movement and war in 1992–4) gave rise to an astonishing national revival—and the religious revival was a part of it. The Brotherhood grew dramatically in numbers, gathering together thousands of people. It offered forms quite appropriate to the new style of open public expression developed in these years; it also offered a means of coping with social upheavals for which the Church hierarchy was hardly prepared.

At this point, according to the master narrative presented by the current head of the Brotherhood, the organization was recognized by Vazgen, the Catholicos of the AAC (in 1991), and its mobilizing role was appreciated by the new regimes of the Third Republic. The Brotherhood claimed up to 150,000 members at the peak of its popularity in the early 1990s. It started many Sunday schools for children, widely distributed bibles, and initiated the first non-government charities, such as *Gtutiun* (Compassion).[18]

Beginning in 1992, the Brotherhood went through a series of organizational crises (its various interpretations will be discussed later); and then fell into a continuous decline. By the end of the 2000s, membership was assessed by Hamlet Zakharian at about 3,000 people, including all groups in Armenia (several centers in the capital, Yerevan, and a few elsewhere[19]) and abroad. According to its 1991 charter, the Brotherhood is managed through the elected Spiritual Council (*Hogevor Khorurd*), with 12–14 members, and the Council of Representatives, headed by an Elder (*Avag*); it is not a recognized legal entity, for it is regarded as an internal structure within the AAC. In Yerevan members

---

[18] See the detailed account of the activities of *Gtutiun* and its founder, Khachik Stamboltsian, in Lewis, *After Atheism*, pp. 244–53.

[19] Hamlet mentioned the towns of Ararat, Vanadzor, Stepanavan and Goris; he said that some of the centers were de facto autonomous, while the Karabagh branch was completely independent.

meet in small neighborhood groups, and also twice a week all together in a large hall at a building belonging to the Church's TV channel *Shoghakat*. In some smaller towns, such as Stepanavan and Ijevan, the meetings are held in the local churches. In my most recent interview, I was told that in Argel, a small village in central Armenia, the meetings of tiny groups were held in a church that had held no liturgies for many years; in other places in the same region, the small meetings were reported to be held in other buildings that functioned like "clubs" (*akumb*) (R-80-L, November 24, 2013).

The Type of Religious Agency Produced by the Brotherhood and its Place within the Church

My research has found that the Brotherhood was indeed an exceptional phenomenon in the religious landscape of Armenia during these dramatic years. Most of our informants—many of them with a clearly negative attitude toward the current activities of the Brotherhood—agreed that in the late 1980s and early 1990s it played an enormous role in introducing the Christian message and disseminating knowledge about it, providing moral and social empowerment in those hectic, disastrous times. As its numbers (even if somewhat exaggerated) and the scale of its activities suggest, the Brotherhood was a major religious focal point for the powerful energy of national revival.

We can say that the Brotherhood became a "school" for hundreds of religious neophytes, many of whom combined spiritual needs with public/civic activism. This sense of agency, generated by the Brotherhood at the height of its popularity, affected a large number of people who went on to become leaders in either the religious or the socio-political realm; many future priests or Protestant pastors, as well as many politicians and other activists, passed through the Brotherhood or were close to it. Some activities, such as quickly multiplying Sunday schools, burgeoning Bible and youth groups, and sermons and lectures by invited Christian missionaries (mostly Protestant) served the need for a renewed Christian identity and were engaged in by a wide spectrum of semi-urban, mostly educated strata, with the urban intelligentsia playing a strong role, especially in the eventful years of the national revival.

A local example in Mardakert, Nagorno-Karabagh, studied by Matsuzato and Danielyan, illustrates the Brotherhood's special role. Emerging in 1989, the local branch led a Christian revival, which was then replicated in a few other towns of Karabagh right before and during the war. Hence it provided a foothold for the future presence of the Church in the newly created Artsakh diocese of the AAC. Somewhat later, the Brotherhood's Christian "club" in Mardakert was transformed into a parish council.[20] We can speak of the Brotherhood's role of evangelizing the new territory and placing it under the Church's aegis, which accompanied Armenia's military acquisition of the Karabagh territory.

Speaking in terms of religiosity as such, this new Christian identity, addressed to the laity, put a strong emphasis on spiritual, rather than traditional institutional, ritual or folk (vernacular) piety of various kinds—that is, the ones that belong to forms 1, 2 and 3 in the classification that I gave above. It is clear that this kind of identity is ideally suited to these urban milieus, distanced from both institutional religion and folk culture. At the same time, the agency accumulated within the Brotherhood provided a sense of community, of a common cause, which was certainly necessary in a time of mass mobilization, when the privatized, individualized religiosity of form 5 in my classification could not be in much demand. Besides all this, the Brotherhood, by roots, represented a link to *Spyurkh*, the diaspora communities, and thus to transnational "Armenianness" (*Hayut'yun*), a fact that resonated to further strengthen the euphoria of national revival.

One of my respondents, a former Brotherhood member and at that time a prominent public official, said that already in Soviet times the Brotherhood provided something in its underground meetings that was, of course, unbelievable in the Armenian Church: Bible study, sermons by lay preachers, spontaneous contacts and sincere religious emotions; it was, after all, a "real parish life without the priest." It was the Brotherhood that began to explain to religiously uninformed people what Christianity was and what the Church was (R-53E, October 28, 2009). The mission of the Brotherhood, as understood by its leader, was to bring lay people to the Church (R-40L, December 14, 2009). Another respondent, a woman in her fifties, who was a member of an active Church parish in the Yerevan area, remembers how many people "came to faith through the Brotherhood, it was like a revelation! Half of our parish went through it!" She was baptized by a Cilician priest because the Brotherhood was perceived as belonging to the Cilician patriarchate (R-56L, October 25, 2009). Some members said that they felt closer to the Cilician Church because in it there was no that sharp cleavage between the priesthood and the laity (R-40L, December 14, 2009).[21] Another former member and one of the preachers in

---

[20] Kimitara Matsuzato and Stepan Danielyan, "Faith or Tradition: The Armenian Apostolic Church and Community-Building in Armenia and Nagorny Karabakh," *Religion, State & Society* 41, no. 1 (2013), pp. 18–34.

[21] In fact, Hamlet Zakharian never emphasized his belonging to the Church of Cilicia (Antelias), though as I already mentioned, this link is significant for the origins of the

the Brotherhood, a man in his fifties, said that "the Brotherhood was a salvation at that time; they preached the Word to people who badly needed it" (R-59L, October 12, 2009). Yet another former member, now an active Church layman, admitted that the Brotherhood "has the advantage: they know how to approach one's soul, something that we miss in the Church" (R-70L, June 4, 2010). A Church official in Etchmiadzin added his high assessment of the Brotherhood, calling them "our evangelicals"—and then he added, emphatically: "they are *ours, ours!*" (R-74P, November 3, 2009).

There was obviously ambivalence, however, in how the Brotherhood was positioned vis-à-vis the AAC. The Brotherhood was part of the Church, and willing to be such, but it accumulated and provided something that was definitely lacking in the AAC, or even foreign to its nature. The Church, as most respondents admitted, was inapt at satisfying the symbolic needs at this crucial time of national revival. Its structures were not dynamic enough and not responsive to the dramatic changes and troubles of the period; its liturgical and parish life was routinized and bleak, while its missionary work and social involvement were almost non-existent. It had no way "to approach one's soul": first, preaching (sermons) was practically not used; second, the individual confession was non-existent.[22]

In contrast, the Brotherhood's main business was relentless preaching at all levels, with the team of "preachers" (or elder brethren) being the core, the elite of the organization. In addition to common confessions led by "preachers" during their meetings, the Brotherhood also introduced individual confessions made *in public* (before the elder brethren), which was an unthinkable novelty. The sense of free, unfettered devotion was obvious through the common and individual prayer during the meetings. As worded by one respondent, a key person in spiritual chanting, prayer comes without preparation, spontaneously, "from the heart," for "God needs ours hearts and not chanting as such" (R-41L, October 22, 2009).

The ambivalence in the relationship between the Brotherhood and the Church mainstream and leadership came from these novelties, and also from

---

movement. However, Hamlet himself repeated the idea that the distinction between priests and laity was much less felt in the Cilician jurisdiction, and when he was invited there to preach he felt himself more easy and comfortable (R-40L, December 14, 2009).

[22] There is an opinion that the practice of individual confession was absent in the Armenian tradition until rather recent influences from the Eastern Orthodox churches. At the beginning of the twenty-first century the practice is being reintroduced in some parishes, although mainstream practice is still the collective confession during the liturgy right before the Eucharist.

the very contradiction of belonging: for the Brotherhood's members, belonging to *their* community was a priority. Also, though many of them attended regular church services and received Holy Communion there, this sacramental modus of their religion was definitely becoming less important. Finally, within the canonical constitution of the Armenian Church, there was simply no pattern set out for a lay association. These contradictions became obvious when the Brotherhood grew exponentially and became, in fact, ostentatiously *beyond* the Church, autonomous from it, and structurally, if not consciously, competitive with it.

Hence the ambivalent attitude toward the Brotherhood on the part of the Church leadership in Echmiadzin. Are they always considered as "ours," as the Church official quoted above insisted? Hardly so. Catholicos Vazgen (pontificate 1955–94) who seemed to have been informally supportive during Soviet times,[23] blessed the Brotherhood in 1991, at the very peak of its popularity, at his residence in Etchmiadzin, in a very emotional meeting with thousands of attendees. The next Catholicos, Garegin I (1995–9), wrote a letter of blessing (*orhnagir*). Yet the current Catholicos, Garegin II (1999–present), had mixed feelings back in 1980s and 1990s when he served as the bishop of the key Ararat diocese, and developed a rather negative attitude in the 2000s, although, according to the Brotherhood's leader, there were still a few bishops who supported the association's cause.

The Brotherhood's Identity Crisis and the Causes of Decline

The decline of the Brotherhood after the peak of the early 1990s can be seen within this frame of "competition" and the association's ambiguous positioning. Since the mid-1990s the Etchmiadzin-led AAC started to assert itself as having a sacred monopoly in representing the "national idea," which largely resonated among the population. At some point the Church started to push the Brotherhood into the margins as a community that was not truly traditional, truly national, and experimented too much with Protestant patterns of religiosity. The Church certainly feared the competition from a spontaneous, autonomous authority accumulated within the religious field outside its direct control. As Hamlet Zakharian went on to say in his interview, Etchmiadzin was

---

[23] Hamlet Zakharian remembers that Vazgen helped the Brotherhood to get a number of pocket editions of the New Testament and gave it a book with spiritual songs, printed in Lebanon, which became the basis of the current standard hymnal used by all members of the association (R-40L, October 12, 2009).

threatened by the explosive growth of this de facto autonomous structure and promptly strove to curtail its work, provoking the split within the organization.[24]

Yet there was also a deep *internal* crisis within the Brotherhood, which can be explained at two causal levels—the level of human relations and the level of structural controversy. At the personal level, former and current members referred to conflicts within the leadership and between factions; to "powers of temptation" and the "authoritarian biases" of the leaders; and to strong financial "temptations" (because of the active involvement of foreign missions and churches).

The personal issues, I would suppose, reflected deeper, more substantial controversies. The very acute fact of the Brotherhood's growing cooperation with Protestant organizations or individual missionaries, who had invaded Armenia in the critical time after the 1988 earthquake, was quite significant. Moreover, the type of religious practices described above had an undeniably Protestant flavor. At its very origin, as I have pointed out, the Brotherhood was an internal, Armenian response to the Protestant impact in the nineteenth and early twentieth centuries—not a conservative, "protective" response, but rather an instinctive impulse of imitation: an attempt to modernize Armenian Christianity by creating within it similar, competitive forms. This stance was further strengthened during Soviet times when the Brotherhood continued to exist outside the politically controlled Church and developed a kind of Christianity without priests. This stance became obvious after the national explosion at the end of the 1980s.

During the splits of the mid-1990s, many active Brotherhood people actually left the AAC and became Protestant ministers or ordinary members of Protestant groups. For example, in Mardakert, Karabagh, eight Sunday school teachers who belonged to the Brotherhood were among those who left the Armenian Church, and the leader of one of the Brotherhood communities became the leader of the local Armenian Evangelical Church.[25]

Many critical respondents, including former brethren, refer to the Brotherhood's "Protestantism" in negative terms. The individual and common confessions outside the Church were said to contradict the Armenian ecclesiastical tradition. The brethren have also been sharply criticized for regularly practicing *andastan*, a traditional prayer of blessing the four quarters of the world with the cross, a ritual traditionally performed by the priests only on special occasions or

---

[24] This claim may have some plausibility, though there is no evidence to support it.
[25] See Matsuzato and Danileyan, "Faith or Tradition," p. 27.

in a national emergency.²⁶ The brethren, assuming that the critical time for the nation had now come, have continued this ritual, thus, in fact, claiming unusual spiritual and sacramental rights for the laity. Importantly, women and men alike participated in the ritual, a practice that was doubly unthinkable in gender-sensitive Armenian Christianity.²⁷ Overall, gender equality came as a part of the general lay orientation, and the movement leader referred to the role of women in its history, starting with the fact that one of the Brotherhood's founders in the late nineteenth century was a woman, whose first task was said to be to "find a prayer place for women."²⁸

All these things were easily attributed to Protestant influence by the critics. A bishop of one of the Republican dioceses (whose mother attended the Brotherhood's meetings in Soviet times) believed that the brethren were trying to be "corporally" within the "Mother Church" but that their thinking [*myshlenie* in Russian] was purely Protestant (R-76P, June 5, 2009). Another person, a member of the university's department of theology, more bluntly called the Brotherhood a product of "sects," while the brethren were, as he said, the *kes-kes*—"half and half": half Armenian Orthodox, half "sectarians." This term—sectarians—was used a few times by the respondents.²⁹ In a more nuanced explanation, the same bishop said the Brotherhood lacked "true spiritual leaders" and therefore created "their own Christianity" (R-76P, June 5, 2009). Another former preacher said that the brethren proclaimed themselves to be "simply Christians," but that they were cut off from the tradition of the Church Fathers and did not do "true spiritual work." This respondent did, however, refer to one of the former leaders of the Brotherhood, commonly called "elder Asatur,"³⁰ who, in his opinion, "was truly spiritual and never permitted Protestant influence" (R-60L, June 3, 2009). At some point, the same respondent continues, "the Brotherhood ran out of gas," for "they should have come of age and worked as [spiritual] adults," whereas they continued "to be nourished with children's food."³¹

---

[26] The ritual is performed at regular meetings of the Brotherhood's small groups, when people move around the table with crossed hymnals in hands and with a special prayer.

[27] A female respondent remembers how they all, women especially, were inspired by participating in *andastan* prayer, forgetting, in the euphoria of the early 1990s, that, canonically, women were not supposed to bear the cross during the ritual blessing (R-81L).

[28] As at the Brotherhood's official website: http://bclaac.org/am/.

[29] "Sectarians" in Armenian sounds *aghandavor*, a term very emotionally pejorative in the Armenian public context, which is dominated by official Church rhetoric.

[30] Asatur Darbinian, 1895–1985, who repatriated to Soviet Armenia in 1948.

[31] Let us note in passing, how interesting the interpretation of the notion "spirituality" alters in this last statement: instead of being understood as an emphasis on "inner feeling" as usually associated with the Protestantism, or the discourse of "true spirituality" which is

These analyses are quite symptomatic. Becoming "too Protestant," or being "half-and-half," or creating "their own Christianity," or proclaiming themselves to be "simply Christians"—in every case what this rhetoric records is an identity shift arising from the Brotherhood's ambivalent relationship with Armenian churchliness. As I mentioned earlier, many Brotherhood preachers became Protestant pastors, while a few others became priests in the AAC, the Brotherhood's sharpest critics and promoters of a more *in-church* type of spirituality. Many ordinary members followed these priests in a turn toward a more traditional type of piety and practice and a closer symbolic affiliation with the "Mother Church." As one informant, with a deacon's rank, said, the question posed to the brethren was: "Are you Armenians with a Protestant bent, or are you Protestants pretending to be Armenians?" (R-66P, October 15, 2009). Thus, at first glance, the internal split in the critical time of the early 1990s was, roughly speaking, between Protestant modernity and Armenian Orthodox ecclesiastical traditionalism.

Over time, the Brotherhood's rhetoric itself had to become more traditional, particularly in response to being stigmatized as "Protestant" and therefore a-national in the Church's dominant discourse. One respondent, looking back to the early 1990s, emphasized the strong "anti-clericalism" in the Brotherhood's leadership, even though it sought Etchmiadzin's support and blessings from the Catholicos (R-53E, October 28, 2009). In contrast, by the late 2000s the leaders always emphasized the Brotherhood's being an integral part of the Church. The standard booklet listed among the main vows (*ukht*) the "belief in the Armenian Apostolic Church, Her rules and canons, Her bishops' traditions"; and in its brief history of the group, stressed that the Brotherhood was indeed rooted "in the bosom" of the Armenian Church.

This does not mean that the Brotherhood was not aware of its particular identity: to be, so to speak, the Church's missionary and reformist avant-garde. The same booklet, describing the Brotherhood's mission, said that its members "meet in small and large groups to read and discuss the Gospel, to pray together and to glorify God by singing. In those places where there are no churches, the bright faith of our fathers ... will be extinguished without such meetings." Meetings *outside* the church, in places where the church does not exist, thus *replacing* it—is, indeed, the credo of the association. As one of the active members said, the brethren intuitively understood that "we need to keep our

---

the main marker of the Brotherhood's central narrative, "spirituality" in the words of critics is linked to the millennial Church tradition, which is inseparable from Orthopraxy and the ecclesiastic authority.

distance from the priests; let them do what they do, while we are preaching the gospel to ordinary people" (R-43L, October 15, 2009).

The general opinion within the Church mainstream still placed the Brotherhood at the margins of the Tradition. The brethren were always challenged by the need to cope with this marginality. One of the respondents, an active preacher in the early 1990s and then a prominent member, remembered how in his youth, before joining the Brotherhood, he used to be aggressive in fighting against other religions and denominations. But at the very time he joined the Brotherhood, he heard God's voice saying: "Do you love Me more than the Church?"—and this question was the answer to his doubts: loving God leads you beyond denominational borders (R-42L, November 20, 2009).

The identity crisis and splits over the meaning of Church tradition thus marked the onset of the decline in the Brotherhood's membership and influence from the mid-1990s. Even independently of the major "Protestant-traditionalist" split, the mass participation and its decline both had their own logic. The huge numbers who once joined the Brotherhood on the wave of nationalist emotions turned away and dropped out for two main reasons: either they were just "free riders" with shallow and temporary religious motivations who simply dropped out along with the waning of revolutionary enthusiasm; or they returned to the Apostolic Church as the national religious institution that had firmly established itself in the course of the nation-building. Whatever weaknesses, inaptitude, and irrelevance the Armenian Church may have shown in comparison to the dynamic, active Brotherhood, it still possessed one critical advantage—the powerful authority of a millennial national memory that associated the Church with the state and the nation.[32]

Overall, the active, reformist agency once produced by the Brotherhood was no more in demand when the enthusiasm roused by independence and the Karabagh war victories was replaced by the routine and exhausting economic troubles of the 1990s. Interestingly, as one of the Brotherhood's preachers observed, men definitely outnumbered women at the peak of its glory, while later the gender composition became more equal and women eventually came to

---

[32] On the relation of the dominant religion to national identity, see Chapter 1 by Konrad Siekierski in this volume, as well as his other publications: "Nation and Faith, Past and Present: the Contemporary Discourse of the Armenian Apostolic Church in Armenia," *Journal of the Society for Armenian Studies* 18, no. 2 (2009), pp. 99–109 and "Religious and National Identities in Post-Soviet Armenia," in I. Borowik and M. Zawila (eds), *Religions and Identities in Transition* (Krakow, 2010), pp. 149–62.

predominate (R-42L, November 20, 2009), a fact that is quite significant in the Armenian cultural context with its distinctive patriarchal bias.[33]

Conclusion: The Overall Impact and Significance of the Brotherhood

Does the decline of the Brotherhood mean that this form of religious modernity was lost and inconsequential? Definitely not. It is true that any profound reform, much less a Reformation (an image that was always lurking in the background of this phenomenon), would have been unlikely; and in the early twenty-first century the Armenian Church seems to have been established itself along traditional lines: a strong symbolic weight with no real involvement in politics, an expanding physical presence in the countryside but a minor grassroots impact, mass symbolic belonging through life cycle rituals but a very low liturgical attendance. No real attempts have been made to officially reorganize the institution or to grasp theologically the current spiritual and sociocultural zeitgeist (only lip service is paid to any kind of "social doctrine"). The Brotherhood might then seem to have been an alien episode that could easily be forgotten within the Church and society at large.

Yet there are a few ways to speak about the significance of the movement. First of all, in a wider societal framework, the Brotherhood was one of the vehicles of emancipating people's agency in post-Soviet times: it emerged at the intersection of the national and religious revivals and served as one of the channels for national and individual self-empowerment. The Brotherhood produced a specific new agency at the juncture of religious and civic "social capital." In the Armenian context *civic* activism had very strong *nationalist* connotations, and therefore nationalist motives were very strong in all forms of civic activity. The "national idea" was indeed the common ground for *both* religious and civic activities; and many former "brethren" and "sisters" converted their religious agency into a civic one after they left the Brotherhood.

The Brotherhood was one of the strongest, if not *the* strongest, vehicle for acquiring Christian identity for many people. As I said in the introduction, by the end of the twentieth century "Christian identity" became something

---

[33] The absolute domination of women in small provincial groups in the 2010s was reported by an informant (R-80L, November 24, 2009). In my own observations in Yerevan, the percentage of men in the Brotherhood is still higher than in an average Church parish, but now obviously closer to it than it reportedly used to be. A youth group leader complained that recently boys have become rare and the group consists almost entirely of girls, while even in the late 1990s 80 percent were boys (R-44L, October 19, 2009).

that people "return to" and "re-appropriate." The spectrum of meanings encompassed by this identity might be wide. For many their Christian identity was mostly mixed with their national one and then merged into it. However, for a minority this was a deeper process, and precisely in the *religious* sense, as opposed to a national, civic or political one. For this minority, it was an attempt to "spiritualize" Armenian Christianity, to create a distinct "religious identity" within a modern differentiated culture.

At the same time, for many people the Brotherhood was, in a way, a laboratory of Armenianness. It emphasized the importance of the Christian dimension of Armenianness. It contributed to a stronger link between the Republic and the diaspora. The Brotherhood was thus an agent for broadening the scope of Armenianness. By working at the margin of what was conventionally accepted as "the national religious tradition," it contributed to the internal pluralization of this tradition, its negotiation with the plurality of other Christian traditions (mostly Protestant). By the very fact of doing such work, the Brotherhood questioned the conventional, narrower definitions of Armenianness.

Speaking in a different perspective, in terms of the Brotherhood's experimentation with religious modernity, we can say that it developed some new elements that certainly affected the Armenian Church at large—sometimes directly, and sometimes as a "foil" in revealing problems within the Church mainstream. Here we can cite not only the institutional projects initiated by the Brotherhood (such as Sunday schools or youth organizations) and not just some practices that it promoted among the faithful (sermons, the reading and discussion of the Bible), but also some subtler skills and patterns of religious life. It promoted patterns of stronger communal solidarity, greater interest in scripture, the practice of shared confession, and stronger missionary activism. These skills and patterns "infiltrated" the Church through former members who turned priests or became active laity. A really crucial fact, pointed out by one of the respondents, was that those Brotherhood activists who left to become ordained as priests managed to create a really active, committed parish life (R-60L, June 3, 2010). These priests broke with the Brotherhood and consciously rejected its "Protestantism," because it allegedly "lacked spiritual depth"; but even while doing so, they took with them some of the skills they had acquired when they were fired in the cauldron of the Brotherhood's missionary zeal.

In assessing the significance of the Brotherhood overall, we might call their attempt to produce "religious modernity" a failure, but this would be only part of the truth. The Brotherhood did show a certain path and created grassroots forms of religiosity relevant to a changing society. In the crucial 1990s it played an important role in producing social capital based on Christian rhetoric and experience. And, as we have just seen, it became a reference point for a new religious discourse inevitably developing in the official Church itself: a discourse about Armenian Christian identity, about the balance between new and old forms of religiosity, and about the wider societal relevance of Armenian Christianity.

References

Antonyan, Yulia, "Religiosity and Religious Identity in Armenia: Some Current Models and Developments," *Acta Ethnographica Hungarica* 56, no. 2 (2011): 315–32.

Antonyan, Yulia and Konrad Siekierski, "A Neopagan Movement in Armenia: The Children of Ara," in Kaarina Aitamurto and Scott Simpson (eds), *Modern Pagan and Native Faith Movements in Central and Eastern Europe* (Durham: Acumen, 2013), 266–82.

Hervieu-Léger, Danièle, *Le pèlerin et le converti* (Paris: Flammarion, 1999).

Hervieu-Léger, Danièle, *Religion as a Chain of Memory* (New Brunswick: Rutgers University Press, 2000).

Hovhanissyan H., "Mayr At'or' s. Etchmiadzin ev Metsi Tann Kilikio kat'oghikosneri verchin shrjani haraberut'yunneri verlutsut'yun" [The Mother See of Etchmiadzin and High House of Cilicia: An analysis of their relationships in recent period], *Kron ev hasarakut'yun* [Religion and Society] 8 (2009): 42–67.

Lewis, David C., *After Atheism: Religion and Ethnicity in Russia and Central Asia* (New York: St. Martin's Press, 2000).

Matsuzato, Kimitaka and Stepan Danielyan, "Faith or Tradition: The Armenian Apostolic Church and Community-Building in Armenia and Nagorny Karabakh," *Religion, State & Society* 41, no. 1 (2013): 18–34.

Siekierski, Konrad, "Nation and Faith, Past and Present: The Contemporary Discourse of the Armenian Apostolic Church in Armenia," *Journal of the Society for Armenian Studies* 18, no. 2 (2009): 99–109.

Siekierski, Konrad, "Religious and National Identities in Post-Soviet Armenia," in I. Borowik and M. Zawila (eds), *Religions and Identities in Transition* (Krakow: Nomos, 2010), 149–62.

Chapter 5

Evangelical and Pentecostal Communities in Armenia: Negotiating Identity and Accommodation

Anna Ohanjanyan

Introduction

The purpose of the present chapter is to explore the notion of identity in Evangelical, Evangelical Baptist and Pentecostal/Charismatic churches and movements in modern Armenia. The research is mostly based on fieldwork consisting of interviews with representatives and leaders of these churches in Yerevan city and the Shirak and Lori regions of Armenia. The most conservative churches, where interview and written material was unavailable, have been researched by observation. The relevant literature, mostly articles and interviews in journals, has been analyzed. The topic is broad, since it is related to various aspects of a large Evangelical family of churches, but our focus will be on the churches' identity and accommodation in Armenian society.

A number of scholarly works have been published on the Armenian Evangelical and Evangelical Baptist churches, especially when it comes to the more traditional forms of these churches. Nevertheless, before introducing them, it is worthwhile to give a short survey of the writings by nineteenth-century American and English Protestant missionaries that serve as primary sources for understanding the first steps towards the establishment of the Armenian Evangelical Church in the Ottoman Empire and the eastern part of Armenia, then under the rule of Persia. Among the most notable are those of Reverend Henry Martyn, perhaps the first British Protestant (Anglican) who traveled across Armenia, from west to east. His personal journals (those for the years 1811–12 are especially relevant) and his letters to his fiancée have survived and were published after his death.¹ Another significant source is the *Memoirs* of Reverend William Goodell,² a missionary of the American Board of Commissioners for Foreign Missions, who prepared the way for other missionaries coming to the Ottoman Empire. Perhaps the most complete and informative memoirs belong to the missionaries who arrived in the Ottoman Empire after Goodell—Eli Smith and Henry O. Dwight, who did tremendous work among the Armenians and established the Armenian Evangelical church in Constantinople.³ Many articles on missionary activities among the Armenians have been preserved in *The Missionary Herald*, the annual journal of the American Board.⁴ Apart from these sources, a lot of information on the divisions, both doctrinal and structural, of Armenian Evangelical and Evangelical Baptist churches can be found in the letters published periodically in the journal called *Byurakn* in the late nineteenth and early twentieth centuries and containing comments and discussions on various doctrinal issues.⁵

As for scholarly researches, the first attempt at writing a more or less complete history of the Armenian Protestants was made by Leon Arpee. In his book *The Armenian Awakening* he demonstrates an eagerness to connect the origin of the Armenian Evangelical Church to medieval religious movements such as the Paulicians and the Tondrakians.⁶ This idea was based on the famous hypothesis of the nineteenth-century scholar F.C. Conybeare in his book *The Key of Truth: A Manual of the Paulician Church of Armenia*.⁷ Almost six decades later, two

---

¹ See *Journals and Letters of the Rev. Henry Martyn, B. D.* (London, 1837), 1811, 1812, http://anglicanhistory.org/india/martyn/journal.html.

² See William Goodell, *Forty Years in the Turkish Empire, or Memoirs of Rev. William Goodell, D. D., Late Missionary of the A.B.C.F.M. at Constantinople* (New York, 1878), http://babel.hathitrust.org/cgi/pt?id=uva.x000531168;view=1up;seq=9.

³ See E. Smith and H.G.O. Dwight, *Researches of the Rev. E. Smith and Rev. H.G.O. Dwight in Armenia: Including a Journey through Asia Minor, and into Georgia and Persia with a visit to the Nestorian and Chaldean Christians of Oormiah and Salmas* (Boston and New York, 1833), http://books.google.gr/books?id=M0tVcWnUDWMC&printsec=frontcover&hl=el&source=gbs ge summary r&cad=0#v=onepage&q&f=false.

⁴ "Letter from Mr. Peabody," *The Missionary Herald, Containing the Proceedings of the American Board of Commissioners for Foreign Missions*, vol. XLVIII (December 1852). Also, "Letter from Mr. Coan, Armenians," *The Missionary Herald, Containing the Proceedings of the American Board of Commissioners for Foreign Missions*, vol. XLVIII (December 1852).

⁵ See, *Byurakn*, No. 74, 28/16 July, No. 75, 1/13 August, No. 76, 16/28 August, No. 81, 13/1 November (Constantinople, 1885, in Armenian).

⁶ Leon Arpee, *The Armenian Awakening: A History of the Armenian Church, 1820–1860* (Chicago, 1909).

⁷ F.C. Conybeare, *The Key of Truth: A Manual of the Paulician Church in Armenia* (Oxford, 1898). For an historiography analysis of this work see: Ohanjanyan, A., The

other historiographers of the Armenian Evangelical Church, H. Boghosian and A. Keorkezian,[8] developed in their books the same idea concerning the origin of the Armenian Evangelical Church. Around the same time a new book by Buzand Yeghiaian appeared, in which the author tried to contest the widespread hypothesis on the origin of the Armenian Evangelicals and provided important historical data on the establishment and structure of the Armenian Evangelical Church as a "Protestant millet."[9] In 1982 a new book on the history of the Armenian Evangelicals was published by Vahan Tootikian.[10] The book begins with the events relating to the preaching of British and American missionaries and develops the history of the Armenian Evangelicals up until the 1970s, classifying the Evangelical churches and showing their development and organizational divisions in Armenia and the diaspora. Another book by Reverends H. Aharonyan and E. Kasuni, *The Armenian Evangelical Church at the Crossroads*, is of great importance in terms of the identity issues of Armenian Evangelicals all over the world. It focuses on the post-genocide generation of Evangelicals, indicating the paths of their migration to Syria and Lebanon.[11] All of these books were published outside of Soviet Armenia by Armenian Evangelical scholars living in the diaspora (except Buzand Yeghiaian, who was not an Evangelical author). Most of them are therefore slightly biased, since they represent the subject only from the point of view of the Armenian Evangelical churches.

Tootikian's book was translated into Armenian in 2001, on the occasion of the 1,700th anniversary of the adoption of Christianity by Armenians. In 1999 another valuable book, titled *The Evangelical Church of Armenia*, was co-authored by R. Levonyan (the former leader of the Armenian Evangelical Church) and A. Ghazaryan. This might be regarded as the most recent complete book on the Armenian Evangelicals, which introduces the history of the Armenian Evangelical and Evangelical Baptist churches from the early nineteenth century to the 1990s. Nowadays authors attempting to sketch the history of the

---

Manuscript The Key of Truth and its Historiographical Significance, PhD Thesis (Yerevan, 2011) (in Armenian).

[8] A. Keorkezian, *The Paulician-Tondrakian Movement within the Armenian Apostolic Church from the Seventh to the Twelfth Centuries* (Beirut, 1970, in Armenian).

[9] B. Yeghiaian, *The Separation of the Armenian Catholic and Evangelical Denominations in the Nineteenth Century* (Antelias: Press of the Catholicosate of Great House of Cilicia, 1971, in Armenian).

[10] V. Tootikian, *The Armenian Evangelical Church* (Detroit: Armenian Heritage Committee, 1982).

[11] H. Aharonyan and Y. Kasuni, *The Armenian Evangelical Church at the Crossroads* (Middle East Council of Churches, 1988).

Armenian Evangelicals rely mainly on these two books. Tigran Gharanalyan's recent article on Evangelical churches is a nice summary of relevant data collected from the above-mentioned books and other encyclopedias and articles.[12] Tigran Ghanalanyan, along with Vahan Hovyan, continues to publish sketches of the Armenian Protestant communities in various countries—Georgia, Iran, Egypt, South America, and so forth.

As for the history of the foundation and development of Pentecostal/Charismatic communities, both traditional and modern, the sources are quite scarce. Possibly the very first data on Pentecostal or Charismatic practices in Armenia can be found in the articles of Alexander Yeritsian, in which he describes small communities of believers, who were not properly identified at that time, but displayed glossolalia.[13] In 2010 research was conducted on the Evangelical and Pentecostal communities in Armenia,[14] where the communities of Charismatic Christians are described. Another source on Pentecostal communities in Armenia is the doctoral dissertation of Armen Lusyan, the spokesperson of the Church "Word of Life," who gives a brief description of Evangelical, Baptist, Pentecostal and Adventist Churches in Armenia.[15] The most up-to-date information, however, is contained in *Challenges for Awakening*, a book by Samvel Navoyan, the head of the Full Gospel Church. In his book Navoyan outlines all the existing Pentecostal/Charismatic communities and unions in today's Armenia.[16] Nevertheless, there is a need for more and better historiographical work on the subject, since most of the rare existing materials are mainly biased.

Brief Historical Background

The history of the Armenian Evangelical churches goes back almost 200 years. The first Armenian Evangelical church was established in Constantinople

---

[12] T. Ghanalanyan, "Armenian Protestants," *21st Century* 2 (2010), www.academia.edu/4132351/Armenian_ Protestants, accessed on June 22, 2014.

[13] A. Yeritsian, "Tondrakian Armenians of Our Days," *Pordz* 10 (Tbilisi, 1880, in Armenian), pp. 91–132; A. Yeritsev, "On the Sect of Armenian Tondrakians," in *The Works of the 5th Archeological Conference in Tbilisi in 1881* (Moscow, 1887, in Russian), pp. 187–92. See also A. Ohanjanyan, "The Key of Truth and the Problem of the 'Neo-T'ondrakites' at the End of the 19th Century," *JSAS* 20 (2011), pp. 130–36.

[14] *Freedom of Religion in Armenia: Research* (Yerevan, 2010, in Armenian), p. 101.

[15] A. Lusyan, *State-Church Relations in Modern Armenia: Current Situation and Potential Developments*, PhD Thesis (2012, in Russian), pp. 97–101.

[16] S. Navoyan, *Challenges for Awakening* (Yerevan, 2012, in Armenian), pp. 85–6.

through the efforts of the American Board of Commissioners for Foreign Missions (A.B.C.F.M.), which was founded in Boston, Massachusetts in 1810 and incorporated in 1812. The American Board sent its first missionary, William Goodell, to the Ottoman Empire in early 1831. The missionaries Eli Smith and Henry O. Dwight arrived in Constantinople soon after Goodell to "evangelize the heathens in foreign lands," particularly in the Middle East.[17] At first the Board missionaries aimed at evangelizing among Jews and Muslims, but facing severe resistance from these groups, they turned to the so-called historical Christian nations. As a result, the Armenian Evangelical Church was established in the Bera section of Constantinople in 1846, with a membership of 37 men and three women. Four years later, in 1850, it was granted the status of a "Protestant millet (literally, nation)" by the Ottoman Sultan Abdul Mejid, which means that it was granted formal recognition as a separate religious community. Multicultural Ottoman society was organized into communities known as *millets* (nations) according to their religious affiliation, each of which established and maintained institutions to exercise the functions not carried out by the state—education, religion, justice and social security. Under Ottoman rule the Armenian Apostolic Church (AAC) had been organized into a separate *millet* since 1461, and the patriarch acquired authority over the Armenian Apostolic *millet*. In 1830 an Armenian Catholic *millet* was established. As for the Protestant *millet*, it was established for the Armenian Evangelical community only. In fact, the status of *millet* granted to the Armenian Evangelical Church was indeed significant, since Armenian Protestants, according to the very meaning of the term *"millet,"* were thus determined to be a separate "nation."

The "evangelization" of Armenians, however, had already started and continued in the eastern parts of Armenia and on the whole territory of the Caucasus of the time. In the 1820s a wave of European Baptist missionaries from the Basel Theological School of Switzerland began moving to Eastern Armenia, which was then under the rule of Persia. The missionaries first settled in Karabagh, in the city of Shushi, as well as in Shamakhi, and launched several schools and printing houses. Karabagh and Shamakhi became the centers for the Armenian Evangelical Baptists from the 1820s until the 1890s. After 1828 Armenia had undergone the rule of Russian Empire, which refused to formally recognize the Eastern Armenian Evangelicals as a separate community until 1914.[18] By the middle of the nineteenth century there were Evangelical Baptist

---

[17] Smith and Dwight, *Researches of the Rev. E. Smith and Rev. H.G.O. Dwight in Armenia*, pp. 44–5.
[18] Ghanalanyan, "Armenian Protestants," p. 74.

communities in Yerevan, Vagharshapat, Alexandropol, Kars, Tiflis, Baku, Batumi and Sukhumi. In 1914 the Armenian Evangelical Union of Ararat was formally registered, which included the Armenian Evangelical communities of Yerevan, Vagharshapat, Alexandropol, Kars and Nor Bayazet.[19] In 1946 the Evangelical Baptist churches of Yerevan and Gyumri (formerly Alexandropol) were officially recognized by the government of Soviet Armenia.[20]

After the downfall of the Soviet Union, in 1994, the Armenian Evangelical and Evangelical Baptist churches obtained the right to work officially in Armenia. In May 1995 the Union of Evangelical Churches was established in Yerevan. Later in August of the same year the Armenian Evangelical Union of Armenia, Georgia, Eastern Europe and Central Asia was established, with Rene Levonyan as chairman.[21]

As for the Holiness Movement and the Pentecostal churches, it is difficult to determine the exact date when they were established in Armenia. The first evidence of Pentecostal manifestations in the Armenian population occurred in the late nineteenth century. This was largely due to contacts with missionaries coming from Russia. According to Demos Shakaryan, the former head of the International Association of Full Gospel Pentecostal Churches, the very first Charismatic community was organized in 1891 in the village of Kara-Kala.[22] The revival of Pentecostal/Charismatic movements in Soviet Armenia is linked to the name of pastor Sergey Kevorkyan, who moved from Krasnodar to Yerevan in 1960. In Yerevan he was affiliated with the Evangelical Baptist church, and a few months later he established the Charismatic church. Its first pastor was Akop Mkrtchyan (1960–77), who was followed by Samvel Navoyan (1977–80) and David Manukyan (1980–92).[23] There is not much published material on the state of traditional Pentecostal/Charismatic churches in Armenia after independence in 1991, whereas the new revival of Pentecostal movements, according to our respondents, may have occurred in the period from the late 1980s to 1991.[24]

---

[19] Ghanalanyan, "Armenian Protestants."
[20] Ghanalanyan, "Armenian Protestants," p. 75.
[21] Ghanalanyan, "Armenian Protestants," p. 76.
[22] See *Freedom of Religion in Armenia*, p. 101.
[23] See S. Navoyan, "The Full Gospel Movement in the Context of the Mission of Christ's Church," *Religion and Society* 5 (Yerevan, 2009), p. 97.
[24] This assumption is based on data collected from interviews.

Mapping Armenian Protestantism

Nowadays the Protestant churches of Armenia can be divided into three large groups: Evangelical churches, Evangelical Baptist churches and Pentecostal/Charismatic churches. A list of the churches studied here in the Yerevan, Shirak and Lori marzes can be found in the Appendix.

1. *Evangelical churches*: Evangelical churches in Armenia in comparison to the other Protestant denominations might be called "classical" churches, as they have the reputation of being one of the oldest and largest churches. In the modern mosaic of Protestant churches the Evangelical churches can still be regarded as the most "traditional," in the sense of being closest to the early Protestant models, or even as "historical," since they claim to be the churches that did a great deal for preserving the nation (language, culture, customs), mostly in the diaspora. Armenian Evangelical churches have relatively good relationships with the AAC, are deeply rooted in the diaspora, and are closely connected to other Protestant denominations.
2. *Evangelical Baptist churches*: According to my observations, Armenian Evangelical Baptist churches may be divided into two types—the more conservative, which keep to the old traditions of Baptist churches in doctrine and ritual, but are rather marginalized, and the more modern, which are trying to adhere to tradition, but in the meantime are open to change and active socialization. The Evangelical Baptist churches of Armenia generally have good connections with other Baptist churches in Russia and the Caucasus.
3. *Pentecostal churches*: Pentecostal churches are the most diverse in Armenia. Like the Evangelical Baptist churches they are divided into traditional and neo-Pentecostal or Charismatic branches. In this sense the typological scale of Pentecostal/Charismatic churches runs from hyper-modern to hyper-marginalized. Probably the oldest traditional Pentecostal Church is the Full Gospel Church of Armenia (*Amboghjaavetaranakan ekexeci*), with Samvel Navoyan in charge. The largest neo-Pentecostal church is the Church "Word of Life" (*Kianki khosk*) which is supposed to be the most socially active and liberal church. Together with the United Church of Christians of Evangelical Faith (*Avetarani havatqi kristonyaneri miavorvats ekeghetsi*) (a Presbyterian church with maximalist doctrines), the "Unity" Church of Christians of Evangelical Faith (*Avetarani havatki qristonyanieri "Miabanutyun" ekeghetsi*) and The Union of Churches of

Evangelical Faith (*Avetaranakan havatqi ekeghetsineri miutyun*), they formed the Alliance of Full Gospel Churches.²⁵ The smaller Pentecostal/Charismatic communities are not as active in social life as the ones I have mentioned. All Pentecostal/Charismatic churches have connections with other Pentecostal/Charismatic churches in Russia as well as good relationships with Pentecostal churches abroad.

The majority of Evangelical, Evangelical Baptist and Pentecostal/Charismatic churches have mutual relationships and dialogues on different levels and platforms. The largest open platform, on which all the churches from these groups are allowed to participate in dialogue on significant issues, such as the law on freedom of conscience and religious organizations, is the so-called Family of Evangelical Churches.²⁶ In the Shirak and Lori regions the pastors from these three groups meet once or twice a month and discuss the existing issues and share experiences, consult with each other, and pray jointly. However, not all the pastors of all the churches in the region express their willingness to attend such meetings. For instance, in Gyumri the pastor of the Church of the Nazarene, Seyran Vardanyan, doesn't have any relations with the Pentecostal/Charismatic churches and claims that he has amicable relations only with the Armenian Church of Evangelical Baptists.

There is a smaller dialogue platform within the three groups on which the pastors of churches from the same families—Evangelical, Baptist and Pentecostal—meet and consult about dogmatic and disciplinary concerns. At times online social networks, like Facebook, appear to be the only platforms for mutual understanding and support.²⁷ Comparatively small Pentecostal/Charismatic churches, such as "The Nation of God," "The Army of God," "The House of God," and "Grand Grace," which belong to the same Charismatic family, organize amicable seminars and joint devotions.

Despite the efforts toward unity and mutual understanding, there is a huge competition among Evangelical, Evangelical Baptist and Pentecostal churches. The most conservative churches, such as the United Church of Christians of Evangelical Faith, tend to persuade their adherents not to attend more liberal churches. Controversially, the most liberal ones, like the Church "Word of Life," encourage people, especially women, to be engaged in their practices in much

---

[25] Navoyan, *Challenges for Awakening*, pp. 85–6.
[26] Interview with rev. Ruben Pahlevanyan, the head of the Armenian Church of Evangelical Baptists of Shirak, August 8, 2013.
[27] Interview with rev. Mamikon Hambaryan, the former pastor of "Veratsnund" ("Renaissance") Church of Evangelical Baptists, August 9, 2013.

more liberal terms. The latter also proselytize among other religious groups, such as Jehovah's Witnesses.²⁸

Evangelical Baptist and Pentecostal/Charismatic churches have tried to start a dialogue with the AAC, but the relationship between them still remains cold. As previously mentioned, only the Armenian Evangelical Church and the Evangelical Church of Yerevan have to some extent a mutual understanding and relationship with the AAC. The leader of the Church "Word of Life," Artur Simonyan, has called for the organization of a round table for all Christian churches, where the AAC will have precedence, since it is the root of Armenian churches and a sister church; according to him, this would be a good start for launching a dialogue at an appropriate level.²⁹ The dominant Church, however, has not responded to such proposals.

Armenian Protestants: Myths of Origins and Construction of Identity

There is a popular tendency among Armenian churches in the Evangelical family to deal with their foundational history and construction of identity by way of what I call "mythos-weaving." It is closely connected to the stories of the "ancient" origin of the respective churches: for the most part, Armenian Evangelical and Evangelical Baptist churches.

Armenian Evangelical and Evangelical Baptist churches show a penchant for moving their foundation dates to earlier times and connecting the emergence of the Armenian Evangelicals with an outstanding event in the history of Armenia. The most important instance of this is a belief that all Armenian Evangelical churches have their historical and ideological roots in the medieval Paulician and Tondrakian movements, which troubled the Byzantine Empire from the eighth century onwards. This hypothesis has been popular since the 1960s, when a group of Western scholars, following the ideas of F.C. Conybeare, tended to search for the roots of Protestantism in the doctrines of the Paulician and Tondrakian heresies.³⁰ According to the primary sources, the Paulician

---

²⁸ According to Artur Simonyan, head of the Church "Word of Life," over 60 Jehovah's Witnesses have recently joined his church. Interview with rev. Artur Simonyan, November 27, 2012.

²⁹ Interview with rev. Artur Simonyan, head of the Church "Word of Life," November 27, 2012.

³⁰ See Conybeare, *The Key of Truth*. Also see N. Garsoïan, *The Paulician Heresy: A Study of the Origin and Development of Paulicianism in Armenia and Eastern Provinces of the Byzantine Empire* (The Hague and Paris, 1967).

movement emerged in Armenia and expanded throughout Byzantium, while the Tondrakian heresy retained only a local Armenian character.

The link between the medieval movements and modern Protestantism hinges on an eighteenth-century manuscript titled *The Key of Truth*. This manuscript was confiscated in 1835 from a group of migrant believers in the village of Arkjveli in the Shirak region, who moved from the Ottoman Empire to Eastern Armenia during the Russo-Turkish war (1828–9). Since 1835, the Holy Synod of Etchmiadzin condemned these people, labeling them "neo-Tondrakians" because of some general doctrinal similarities with the medieval Tondrakians (for example, rejection of a mediator between God and man, rejection of the clergy and most of the sacraments).

Conybeare was the first person to pay heed to the case of these sectarians and the confiscated manuscript in the 1890s. His investigations resulted in the assumption that the manuscript, whose content is extremely close to some basic Protestant ideas, was a Paulician–Tondrakian text, preserved up until his own time.[31]

A number of historians of the Armenian Evangelical churches (L. Arpee, A. Keorkezian, V. Tootikyan, R. Levonyan) borrowed this hypothesis in trying to prove that the Armenian Evangelical church is the one that had its roots in Paulician–Tondrakian doctrines. By localizing this hypothesis, they wove an "antiquity" mythos describing the origin of Armenian Evangelicalism. It is obvious that the key point for the adoption of this theory by Armenian Evangelicals was the fact that both the Paulician and, in particular, the Tondrakian movements originated in Armenia.

However, both the Western scholarly hypothesis on "neo-Tondrakians" and the new "Paulician–Tondrakian mythos" of origin created by Armenian Evangelicals are entirely groundless. Since the publication of Conybeare's research, the manuscript of *The Key of Truth* has been thoroughly examined, and it has been proved that it has no ties with medieval heretical doctrines. Moreover, the content of the book is not purely Protestant, but rather an individual symbiotic interpretation of the doctrines of different denominational churches (Protestant Baptist and Anabaptist as well as Armenian Apostolic, among others).[32]

For reasons of identity construction some Armenian Evangelical authors have attempted to link the "believers" in the doctrine of *The Key of Truth* with

---

[31] Conybeare identifies Paulician and Tondrakian movements. For details see Ohanjanyan, "The Key of Truth and the Problem of the 'Neo-T'ondrakites,'" pp. 130–36.

[32] Ohanjanyan, "The Key of Truth and the Problem of the 'Neo-T'ondrakites.'"

a small ethnic group in the eastern part of Armenia. Leon Arpee, an early historiographer of the Armenian Evangelical Church, compares the people of *The Key of Truth*, who allegedly had the name "*pahk utoghk*" (meat eaters during Lent) and lived in Chevirmeh village in Western Armenia, with a small ethnic group in Oudik county of Eastern Armenia bearing the name "*udi*" or "*udetsi*."[33] The latter were mentioned in the memoirs of American missionaries, who came across them while traveling to Gyanja in the 1830s. Since the two expressions sound very similar, Leon Arpee concluded that "*pahk utoghk*" and "*udi*" might have been the remnants of those same "protestant" believers, who were scattered over both Western and Eastern Armenia. But in the end, Arpee felt that the theory was groundless and dropped it.[34] Nevertheless, the very phenomenon is important: an old mythos develops for the sake of identity construction, and religious affiliation, ethnicity and "antiquity" are combined in the image of Armenian Protestants.

Nowadays "mythos-weaving" is still an ongoing process among the churches of the Evangelical family. It is interesting to follow the recent transformation of the "Paulician–Tondrakian mythos" among Evangelical Baptists. In spite of the fact that until the mid-2000s all the historians of the Evangelical Church claimed that the Paulicians and Tondrakians were the brilliant predecessors of Armenian Evangelicals, today we witness new developments on this topic. In his interview with the e-journal *Religions in Armenia* Ruben Pahlevanyan, the leader of the Armenian Church of Evangelical Baptists in the Shirak region, "reconstructs the Paulician-Tondrakian mythos," remarking that "at first the Evangelical movement was perceived as a revival of the Paulician movement, but in reality it has nothing in common with the fifth-century heretical Paulicians. This incorrect assumption led to a mistrust of Evangelical communities, for it was created by the dark powers of the time and the secret services of Tsarist Russia."[35] Hence, a "mythos-transformation" occurs: instead of rejecting the old mythos as historically inaccurate, some modern Protestants renovate it by dressing it up with a new notion according to which the state (laymen or the Tsarist Russian special services in the nineteenth century!) and the dominant Church ("dark powers") are enrolled as enemies.

---

[33] Leon Arpee, "Armenian Paulicianism and The Key of Truth," *The American Journal of Theology* 10, no. 2 (April 1906), p. 274.

[34] See A. Ohanjanyan, "The Attempts of Identification of the Names 'Pahk utoghk' and 'Udi' by Some Armenian Evangelical Historiographers," *Hay Astvatsaban* [Armenian Theologian] 2 (2008), 179–85.

[35] Interview with Ruben Pahlevanyan, the leader of Armenian Church of Evangelical Baptists of Shirak, www.religions.am/arm/religions/, accessed on June 22, 2014.

On the local level the same tendency of "mythos-weaving" occurs when it comes to the foundational history of each concrete local Evangelical church: adherents try to emphasize the "antiquity" of their church by connecting its foundation to the names of the first Protestant missionaries in Armenia. For instance, according to Ruben Pahlevanyan, "the first Baptist community was founded by the missionaries from Basel since 1820 (!), who on their arrival in Alexandropol (nowadays Gyumri) discovered a group of believers reading the Bible."[36] Nevertheless, other Protestant sources[37] prove that the Evangelical Baptist Church in Alexandropol was established by the joint efforts of the Armenian missionary M. Kotikyan and missionaries from Tiflis at the beginning of the twentieth century. So there is a 100-year gap between the two foundation stories. It may turn out that separate small groups of Protestants did exist in Alexandropol before the arrival of the missionaries, although their origin is completely unknown: the first written evidence of Protestants in Alexandropol dates to the 1850s.

The second level of modern "mythos-weaving" is the creation of an "old-new mythos," which is connected with the narratives about personal conversions common to all Christian churches. All the hierarchical churches anchor their foundation upon a mythos or legend about a "great vision" that led to the conversion of a person, group, or even a nation and the consequent establishment of a new Christian church, by analogy with the great vision of Gregory the Illuminator.[38]

"Old-new mythos" creation is a significant axis in the conversion stories of the leaders of the churches under study. The majority of those interviewed confirm that they had been converted to Christianity after having a "mystic vision/talk with God," which they regarded as a "call" to start a new church. Some leaders emphasize that their talk with God is an ongoing process. This is how they get their answers to problems about the future steps and disciplinary organization of the community.

Most respondents confirmed that they had a "vision or dream" at the turning point of history, in 1985–91, the period of the dissolution of the Soviet Union. This transformation of real historical period into a mythological narrative of

---

[36] Interview with rev. Ruben Pahlevanyan, the head of the Armenian Church of Evangelical Baptists of Shirak, August 8, 2013.

[37] A. Ghazaryan, R. Levonyan, *The Armenian Evangelical Church (Armenia – Caucasus)* (Yerevan, Armenia Encyclopedia Press, 1999), pp. 139–41.

[38] L. Abrahamian, *Armenian Identity in a Changing World* (Costa Mesa, 2006), p. 117.

the modern churches matches with the analysis by Mircea Eliade[39] as well as with my own "mythos-weaving" concept. Even the year 1985, the initial year of Gorbachev's Perestroika, might have been perceived as "a new call" for revival.

To be sure, the pastors of traditional Evangelical or Charismatic churches, such as Mamikon Ghazaryan, the leader of the United Church of Christians of Evangelical Faith, were actually converted in an earlier period of Soviet history. Mamikon says: "My conversion was in 1974, after my father's and mother's conversions ... In 1974 I received a spiritual baptism, and then in 1975 I was baptized with water."[40] However, most younger churches, such as "New Generation" Church, "Rhema" Evangelical Church of the Republic of Armenia, and "Renaissance" Evangelical Baptist Church, were established in the late 1990s or even in the 2000s. Most of them split from other churches: only in rare cases were they founded from scratch. The splits themselves were also predominantly attributed to the same old-new mythos of "vision." My respondents stressed that "visions" were the stimulus to act, that is, to separate and organize new churches.

Diversity and the Search for Family Resemblances

Protestant churches can easily split and organize new communities. Such is the case with the pastors of "Grand Grace" Evangelical Church of Armenia. Brothers rev. Vahagn and rev. Vahan Poghosyan were ordained in the Armenian Church of Evangelical Baptists of Shirak. But on account of misunderstandings, they separated from the Baptist Church and built a church in the Pentecostal family. Another case is the leader of the "Nazarene" Church, who converted in the Pentecostal Church. Then, after several years, he joined the Church "Word of Life" and finally created his own small church, which now has no more than 60 adherents. Thirty members of the church are baptized.[41]

In rare cases churches may re-unite as well. For instance, *"Veratsnund"* ("Renaissance") Church of Evangelical Baptists separated six years ago from the Armenian Church of Evangelical Baptists of Shirak, in order to get a separate

---

[39] Mircea Eliade, *The Myth of the Eternal Return, or Cosmos and History* (Princeton, 1971), pp. 75–6.
[40] See the interview with Mamikon Ghazaryan, www.youtube.com/watch?v=Zot0GLhghRU, accessed on June 22, 2014
[41] Interview with rev. Seyran Vardanyan, the head of "Nazarene" Church in the Shirak region, August 10, 2013.

registration; but today, according to the former pastor of *"Veratsnund"* Mamikon Hambaryan, it has reunited with the same church.[42]

Sometimes the dialogue between Evangelical Baptist and Pentecostal churches stops or moves in a new direction depending on the transformation of one of the churches from a more liberal to a more conservative or socially marginalized type or vice versa. We observed such an example after the departure of Rene Levonyan, the leader of the Armenian Evangelical Church: with the appointment of new leader Mkrtich Melkonyan in 2012, the Armenian Evangelical Church has changed its stance on interchurch dialogue and civic activism, which affects its relationships with other churches in the Evangelical family. Now it hews to a more pro-Apostolic strategy with a focus on traditionalism. As Mkrtich Melkonyan states, the Armenian Evangelical Church differs from the Armenian Apostolic Church only in its rituals.[43]

There are horizontal links among all Protestant communities, so that people's affiliations may be mixed before they can find the church that best fits their spiritual requirements. In more liberal churches adherents are not forbidden to attend even the Armenian Apostolic or Armenian Catholic churches, while in conservative churches, like the Church of Evangelical Christians, members are discouraged from leaving even for another Evangelical church. Another factor that influences people in their choice of a church is geographical: attendance at certain types of churches in the various regions of Armenia depends on the particular neighborhood and the distance of the church from their homes.

Religious Identity versus National Identity

During his meeting with the Armenian diaspora in the United States in 2008 the Armenian president Serzh Sargsyan defined Armenian identity as follows:

> The identity of an Armenian should not be complicated and mysterious ... It should reject linguistic, religious, cultural, political, ideological disunions. An Armenian who speaks English, Turkish, Russian, or Armenian, who is

---

[42] Interview with rev. Mamikon Hambaryan, the former pastor of *"Veratsnund"* ("Renaissance") Church of Evangelical Baptists, August 9, 2013.

[43] Press conference with Mkrtich Melkonyan, the leader of the Armenian Evangelical Church, http://haynews.am/hy/1343912848, accessed on June 22, 2014.

Apostolic, Catholic, Protestant, or Muslim, a socialist or a democrat, a liberal or a fundamentalist still remains simply Armenian. Diversity is the key to continuity.[44]

This statement has provoked excitement among the liberal layers in Armenian society, whereas people of a more traditional mentality were dismayed.

The identity issue is essential for the churches under study, and the major issue is a correlation between two factors: religion/denomination and nationality/ethnicity. Both of them are dimensions that offer collective identity.[45] In this particular case, the first dimension alternates between the notion of being a Christian and an affiliation with a given church/group. The second dimension is a bit harder to determine because of the divergence between the notions of "nationality" and "ethnicity."[46] Collective identity includes cultural markers like ethnicity, language, customs and history on the one hand, and, on the other hand, civic markers like the state, patriotism and national symbols.

The words "Armenia" or "Armenian" in the names of registered Evangelical, Baptist and Pentecostal churches prove that national identity is emphasized. Some of the respondents mentioned that the word "Armenian" shows that national identity is a constant and does not vary with belief. As Ruben Pahlevanyan has said: "By using the word 'Armenian' in the title of the Armenian Church of Evangelical Baptists we accentuate the fact that our not belonging to the Armenian Apostolic Church doesn't mean that we are not Armenians."[47]

In fact, all the churches under study here attempt to separate the notion of "national belonging" from that of "religious affiliation." The widespread opinion in Evangelical circles is that the most dangerous and destructive thing is the fusion of national and religious identities.[48] In the opinion of Ruben Pahlevanyan, the statement "being Armenian means being Christian" is a historical illusion:

---

[44] Quoted from the speech of Serzh Sargsyan, president of the RA, made in the USA, http://www.president.am/hy/statements-and-messages/item/2008/09/24/news-18/, accessed on June 22, 2014.

[45] B. Donahoe et al., "The Formation and Mobilization of Collective Identities in Situations of Conflict and Integration," Max Planck Institute for Social Anthropology, Working Paper 116 (Halle/Saale, 2009), p. 13.

[46] Brackette F. Williams, "A Class Act: Anthropology and the Race to Nation across Ethnic Terrain," *Annual Review of Anthropology* 18 (1989), p. 429; see also Steve Fenton, *Ethnicity* (Cambridge, 2003).

[47] Interview with rev. Ruben Pahlevanyan, the head of Armenian Church of Evangelical Baptists of Shirak, August 8, 2013.

[48] Rafael Grigoryan, head of Christians of Evangelical Faith, "The most dangerous thing is the identification of ethnic and religious identities," www.religions.am/arm/interviews/, accessed on June 22, 2014.

an Armenian may even not speak Armenian and not follow Armenian traditions, but he or she can still uphold Armenian dignity.⁴⁹ According to Gor Karapetyan, the youth projects coordinator of the Charismatic Pentecostal church "New Generation," "religious discrimination is unavoidable in a country having Christian roots, where Christianity and national self-consciousness are indivisible." As for the inter-confessional dialogue, he adds: "There is no dialogue, and if there were one, it would sound like this: if you are an Armenian, you are a Christian. It is just an absurdity, because an opposite question may arise: if you are a Christian, are you an Armenian? Certainly, no! ... Apart from being a religion in a broader sense, Christianity is also a lifestyle, a mentality, and after all, Christianity is just life."⁵⁰

This contradicts the official opinion of the AAC, according to which being Armenian does mean being Christian. This claim means that Christianity was indeed a path to ethnic survival and the preservation of Armenian identity.⁵¹ In fact, Christianity is a "must" for evangelicals as well: that is why, despite their willingness to separate ethnic and religious identities, none of them dares to insist that an Armenian might also be a Muslim.

It is true that for some mainstream Armenian Evangelical and Evangelical Baptist churches, which belong to a more traditional branch of Protestantism, nationality might even be regarded as a priority. Some of them emphasize the importance of ethnic culture and traditions, from ways of running households to traditional Armenian cuisine and hospitality.⁵²

However, in those churches that we have defined as less "historical" or "traditional," religious affiliation is stressed as the primary factor of identity, and national-ethnic belonging is subordinate to it. Here the ethnic culture is sometimes downplayed to avoid the subconscious linkage, or even total equation, of ethnicity and religious denomination, which is the traditional image of the AAC. The soterological orientation, which is central to Christian identity, plays a significant role here. As Seyran Vardanyan has said, "First of all

---

⁴⁹ Interview with rev. Ruben Pahlevanyan, the head of Armenian Church of Evangelical Baptists of Shirak, August 8, 2013.

⁵⁰ Gor Karapetyan, youth projects coordinator of the Pentecostal church "New Generation," "Being Evangelical Armenian one can face serious legal issues nowadays," www.religions.am/arm/interviews/.

⁵¹ Abrahamian, *Armenian Identity*, p. 125.

⁵² E. Melkonyan, "Ethnic Culture and Tradition," *Patma-banasirakan handes* [Journal of History and Linguistics] 4 (1980, in Armenian), p. 73.

we are Christians and then we are Armenians, because salvation doesn't depend on nationality."[53]

However, religious and national factors are flexibly interchangeable when it comes to interrelations with other ethnic groups and nations. In this regard, a new psychological model for "us–them" discourse has been created within Evangelical churches on the basis of nationality/ethnicity. During joint worship sessions with sister church members from other countries, the only distinguishing factor is nationality/ethnicity. On the whole, although nationality and religion often coincide, Christianity and nationalism do not totally fuse together: we should speak rather of a religious-national mythos that has been adapted and transformed so that the Christian religion is called upon to preserve the Armenian heritage.[54]

One national dimension of Armenian Evangelical identity is the concept of "chosenness." Levon Abrahamian calls this the "pioneer complex" of Armenians;[55] we can rephrase it as a "chosen nation complex." Some churches of the "traditional" type share this notion of Armenians as a "chosen nation": "We are chosen, since Noah's ark came to rest on the peak of Mount Ararat. Everybody knows this, this is a Biblical narrative."[56]

Moreover, we can sometimes find a notion of being "doubly chosen": most Evangelical/Pentecostal leaders tend to believe they have been "elected" to preach among a chosen nation. This idea is presented with the help of biblical and state symbolism on the emblems or logos of Armenian Protestants, the core element of which is Mount Ararat. Usually, the latter is combined with the Bible or the dove of Noah with a blooming branch in its beak. One respondent declared, "We all believe in the symbolism of Ararat, since it has roots in the Bible. Being Armenian obliges me to serve the Armenian people."[57] And another said, "I am

---

[53] Interview with rev. Seyran Vardanyan, the head of "Nazarene" Church in the Shirak region, August 10, 2013.

[54] V. Guroian, "Religion and Armenian National Identity: Nationalism Old and New," paper presented at the Annual Meeting of the American Academy of Religion, Washington, DC, November 1993, www.georgefox.edu/academics/undergrad/departments/soc-swk/ree/Guroian_Religion_articles_previous.pdf.

[55] Abrahamian, *Armenian Identity*, p. 113.

[56] Interview with Ruben Pahlevanyan, the head of the Armenian Church of Evangelical Baptists of Shirak, August 8, 2013.

[57] Interview with Ruben Pahlevanyan, the head of the Armenian Church of Evangelical Baptists of Shirak, August 8, 2013.

not a nationalist, neither am I a cosmopolitan, but it is painful to look at Mount Ararat from this side. My heart is full of pain."[58]

In the opinion of Samvel Navoyan, the leader of the Full Gospel Church of Armenia, the modern Western legalistic way of thinking identifies nationality with citizenship, which undermines the real meaning of nationality. Being Armenian and preaching among Armenians is to preserve the national heritage, to create new values and transmit them.[59]

Another aspect of national identity, which is still very peculiar to Armenian Evangelical churches, is, in the words of H. Marutyan, "dominating traumatic memory."[60] Memory, and historical memory in particular, is one of the fundamental features defining the boundaries of an "ethnic community," a "nation" and a "national identity."[61] In the case of Armenians, including all Evangelical churches, it is related to "crucial dates in real or mythological history, which were turning points for identity preservation."[62] One such crucial date for Armenians, independently of religious affiliation, was the genocide in the Ottoman Empire. The genocide is perceived as a symbol of identity among all Evangelical churches. The official commemoration for the victims of the genocide on the day of April 24 is a remarkable event. The head of the "Nazarene" Church in Yerevan mentioned that every April 24 he attends the *Tsitsernakaberd* memorial along with his family and encourages the adepts of the church to follow his example.[63]

Patriotism is also regarded as a pillar of national identity. The head of the Church "Word of Life" Artur Simonyan has noted that people shouldn't leave

---

[58] Interview with rev. Seyran Vardanyan, the head of "Nazarene" Church in the Shirak region, August 10, 2013.

[59] Interview with rev. Samvel Navoyan, the head of Full Gospel Church of Armenia, "A number of facts witness the spiritual fall of society," www.religions.am/arm/interviews/, accessed on June 22, 2014

[60] H. Marutyan, *Iconography of Armenian Identity: The Memory of Genocide and Karabagh Movement*, vol. 1 (Yerevan, Gitutyun, 2009).

[61] A. Smith, *National Identity* (Reno, 1991), pp. 14, 21.

[62] Abrahamian, *Armenian Identity*, pp. 121–2.

[63] On the emblem of Armenian Evangelical church, as pictured on the floral wreaths to the monument of genocide in 1995, the two peaks of Mount Ararat stand out. Just next to it stands the wreath by the Armenian Catholic church. This makes it obvious that the past is not only "commonly shared but also jointly remembered, that is, co-memorialized." Thus, "pastism" as a type of collective memory is common to all Armenians when it refers to such a "crucial date for identity preservation" as the date of the genocide. See Marutyan, *Iconography of Armenian Identity*, p. 22.

their homeland. He declares: "This is my country, this is my mission. If you leave, you become a traitor."[64]

Rubik Tumanyan, the leader of the "Unity" Church of Christians of Evangelical Faith, persuades his "parish" to stay in Armenia in spite of hard times, to stay in the motherland and to rely on God and pray for the achievements of the Republic of Armenia in day-to-day life.[65]

In this regard it is worth mentioning that the notion of "homeland" seems to be a sort of "brand," a "hallmark," or, what is more acceptable, another modern mythos predominantly for those Armenian Evangelical churches whose founders and leaders are originally from the diaspora. The modern "homeland mythos" is mainly endorsed among the "traditional" or "historical" Evangelical churches. The idea of the motherland becomes the essential core in the worldview of such Evangelical leaders, since it is regarded as a real home, a "lost and regained paradise," *Ergir* (Country)—they consider the Republic of Armenia to be the replacement for the lost homeland (in Greater Armenia, now Turkish Anatolia). H. Marutyan justly remarks that "visions of Armenia, Armenia Minor, free, independent and United Armenia, and the lost homeland (i.e., Greater Armenia) in general have always moved the hearts of Armenians for many centuries."[66] The Evangelical Church of Yerevan and the Armenian Evangelical Church may be taken as examples of this orientation.

Service in the Armenian military is also considered to be a witness of patriotism. The churches of the Evangelical family encourage their young male adherents to complete their military service with great distinction. All the church leaders among my respondents stated that Evangelical churches try to build a trusting relationship with the state and not to interfere in state affairs. Armenian flags and emblems are common attributes in all Evangelical, Evangelical Baptist, and Pentecostal/Charismatic churches. A few younger Charismatic churches—especially the Church "Word of Life"—are extremely active in social and civil movements. According to most Evangelical Baptist churches, they try their best to educate a patriotic and socially active new generation, which is not bound by the limits of the church and takes responsibility for social changes. As one respondent advises: "The preacher

---

[64] Interview with Artur Simonyan, head of the Church "Word of Life" in Armenia, November 27, 2012.
[65] Rubik Tumanyan, Sermon, www.youtube.com/watch?v=T-NGz6UW3nA, accessed on June 22, 2014
[66] Marutyan, *Iconography of Armenian Identity*, p. 17.

should keep a newspaper in one hand and in the other—the Bible. We should live fully in the present day, putting aside all illusions."[67]

As for the smaller churches in the Evangelical family, they prefer not to engage in political activities, since they believe that it diverts them from the main goal of the church; they purposely isolate themselves. Others, such as the "Rhema" Evangelical Church, feel that they are being marginalized.[68]

Relating to the Armenian Christian Tradition: Rituals, Language and the Bible

Rene Levonyan, the leader of the Eurasia Union of Evangelical Churches and the former leader of the Armenian Evangelical Church, has remarked that the Armenian Apostolic Church gave birth to Armenian Evangelicals and that Evangelicals do not focus on mass conversions, being satisfied with just thousands of adherents.[69] The image of the "mother-Church," the AAC, is accepted by almost all the Evangelical and Pentecostal churches, even the most liberal and socially active. Why is this so? Creating such a "mythos of the mother" might be either an attempt at compromise or a good defense against those who label them as "sectarians."

When discussing the identity issues for Pentecostal/Charismatic and Evangelical churches, the impact of the Armenian Apostolic "culture and tradition" is of particular significance. Currently, there is a strong tendency among Evangelical churches to adopt a number of traditional elements of Armenian Apostolic Christianity in order to emphasize their Armenian identity. The adoption of such elements as the spiritual hymns (*sharakans*) of the composer Komitas (1869–1935) and the poems of the medieval mystic Grigor Narekatsi (951–1003) gives rise to a very contradictory picture, because Evangelical and Evangelical Baptist churches are supposed to follow the Protestant legacy, which normally distances itself from earlier traditions. We could say that some of the more traditional or historical churches in the Evangelical family are being "nationalized" through the adoption of these old elements of Apostolic Christianity.

---

[67] Interview with rev. Mamikon Hambaryan, the former pastor of "*Veratsnund*" ("Renaissance") Church of Evangelical Baptists, August 9, 2013.

[68] Interview with rev. Karen Khachatryan, the head of the Pentecostal "Rhema" church, http://rhemachurch.net/, accessed on June 22, 2014.

[69] Interview with Rene Levonyan, http://arminfo.info/index.cfm?objectid=693301 E0-1D17-11E2-85BFF6327207157C, accessed on June 22, 2014.

According to respondents, such fathers and teachers of the Armenian Apostolic Church as Grigor Narekatsi, Nerses Shnorhali (1102–73) or Grigor Tatevatsi (1346–1409/10) do not belong only to the AAC. They are pan-Armenian, even pan-Christian authors, and there is an attempt to make them universal. One respondent explained: "We always quote Armenian authors during our exhortations. If we had a good music band we would also sing spirituals (*sharakans*). We sing the songs of Sayat-Nova, and though he is considered to be an Armenian minstrel, he is a Christian author and our young people should know him."[70]

In the United Church of Christians of Evangelical Faith, which is a traditional Charismatic church, the usage of Armenian Church *sharakans* is a common thing. They run a nice choir with a director and frequently sing the *sharakans* "*Ter voghormea*" (Lord, have mercy) and "*Surb, surb*" (Holy, Holy) during their devotions.[71] Despite its Pentecostal orientation, this church feels very close to the musical traditions of the Armenian Apostolic Church, as well as to Armenian folk music. The choir is accompanied by such unique musical instruments as the *tar* (lute) and the *k'anon* (a string instrument). On the whole, the church openly associates itself with the history of the AAC.[72]

Younger Pentecostal churches, like the Church "Word of Life," have a different strategy: the strategy of "change." They do not aim to adopt the old ecclesiastical traditions but rather to create a new Armenian Christian culture, to make a change in Armenian minds towards the idea of Christian culture. As the head of the church has said: "We are not authorized to use the Armenian Apostolic Church spirituals. We should show a new thing to the world, whatever it is. The culture should develop."[73]

Moreover, the confidence to shape new cultural patterns finds its basis in personal prophetic visions or "talks" with God. For instance, during his sermons, Artur Simonyan, the head of the Church "Word of Life," mentions that he has been commanded to launch new cultural projects: "I spoke to Him [God] and

---

[70] Interview with rev. Ruben Pahlevanyan, the head of Armenian Church of Evangelical Baptists of Shirak, August 8, 2013.

[71] "Holy, Holy" spiritual song (music by Komitas *vardapet*): the devotion of the United Church of Christians of Evangelical Faith, http://youtube.com/watch?v=zCMib(WN 0fI, accessed on June 22, 2014.

[72] Folk music and musical instrument usage during the devotions of the United Church of Christians of Evangelical Faith, www.youtube.com/watch?v=0aAQ4PeubSw, accessed on June 22, 2014.

[73] Interview with rev. Artur Simonyan, head of the Church "Word of Life" in Armenia, November 27, 2012.

after that we realized several cultural projects. Then after 2000 I spoke to Him and He commanded me to turn to TV (to start broadcasting on TV)."[74]

I assume that a number of Evangelical Baptist as well as traditional Charismatic churches widely use the elements of Armenian Apostolic Church literature and spiritual music, whereas the new liberal Pentecostal churches strictly reject them, partly in order not to be accused by the Apostolic Church of "assimilation." However, some Evangelical churches that reject the adoption of Armenian Apostolic Church cultural elements are still respectful of its ritual traditions. For instance, some Evangelical churches accept the role of godfather during the baptism, which goes against Protestant doctrine.

Christian and state holidays are also unique markers of religious and national identity. All churches in the Evangelic Family of Armenia accept Christmas and Easter. Evangelical and Baptist churches celebrate them according to the same calendar as the Armenian Apostolic Church, which differs from other major branches of Christianity.[75] There are several Baptist churches, however, which celebrate "Western" Christmas on December 25. Evangelical Baptist churches also have a separate harvest holiday, which is celebrated on the last Sunday of September.

While the liturgical language of the Armenian Apostolic Church is classical Armenian (*grabar*), the ritual language of Armenian Evangelical and Pentecostal churches tends to be Western Armenian. This conclusion is based not only on the words of respondents, but also on the fact that Evangelical, Evangelical Baptist and Pentecostal churches basically use the Western Armenian translation of the Bible, done by the first Protestant missionaries in the Ottoman Empire. This tradition is kept up among Evangelicals and even Pentecostals, because the original translation text looks more sacred—it creates a sacred space between the listeners and the readers. In other words, paradoxically, but not without logic, Western Armenian has become the sacred language of the Holy Scripture to the ears of Eastern Armenian evangelicals, making the same impact as ancient languages like Latin or Old Slavonic in the liturgies of traditional churches.

---

[74] Artur Simonyan, Fall Summit of the Alliance, www.youtube.com/watch?v=pj-AM1zJpk0, accessed on June 22, 2014.

[75] The Armenian Apostolic Church follows the oldest Jerusalem version of Canons of Calendar, based on the Julian Calendar, and therefore celebrates Christmas and Theophany on the same day, January 6; while Greek Orthodox and Catholic churches accept the Byzantine Canons of Calendar adopted at the Ecumenical Council of Chalcedon in 451, according to which Christmas and Theophany are celebrated separately on December 25 and January 6.

Pentecostal and Evangelical churches widely use the so-called Ararat translation, published by the Armenian Bible Society in 1896. Still, the pastors are not limited to it. Those pastors who speak English also compare passages in Armenian with the King James Bible as well as with the New Living Translation. In several communities they have also started to use the Eastern Armenian translation of the Bible, as in the young "Rhema" and "New Generation" Pentecostal churches. Evangelical and Evangelical Baptist churches, in turn, also use the so-called Shushi translation and Grigor Zohrabyan's translation, last published in 1997 in Etchmiadzin. All these translations, of the Bible, except the latter, are based on the Protestant (Hebrew) canon, which does not include the Deuterocanonical books. Nevertheless, there is some flexibility in exceptional situations, crucial to the Armenian nation: "During the [Karabagh] war, we were continuously reading the books of the Maccabees from the Armenian Bible canon, especially the first book, to raise the morale of our soldiers."[76]

Globalization and Its Effects: Focus on Gender Roles

The majority of Evangelical and Pentecostal churches are to some extent anti-globalists, mostly in issues concerning the preservation of the traditional family. The main point of disagreement with the liberal human rights agenda appears to be LGBT marriages and child adoption by such families. Recently, the pastors within the Alliance of Evangelical Churches of Armenia have shown their concern about the concept and the new law on social gender.[77] In this regard, globalization is perceived to lead to the demolition of Christianity since it is believed that social gender and LGBT communities have their roots in paganism. Hence conclusions like the one drawn by one prominent Charismatic leader: "Better the Armenian Apostolic Church than the Council of Europe."[78]

In the more moderate opinion of R. Pahlevanyan, globalization doesn't unconditionally mean the disappearance of the boundaries of what is called "national-ethnic-traditional." The adoption of Western values is to be strictly selective: there are indeed values that will stimulate development in Armenia, but in the meantime we should be very attentive not to become accustomed

---

[76] Interview with rev. Ruben Pahlevanyan, the head of the Armenian Church of Evangelical Baptists of Shirak, August 8, 2013.
[77] See, http://www.aravot.am/2013/07/24/269393/, accessed on June 22, 2014.
[78] Interview with Artur Simonyan, head of the Church "Word of Life" in Armenia, November 27, 2013.

to the destructive forces of Western civilization.[79] One of the advantages of globalization is the Internet, which is widely used by all the churches, who sometimes even design and disseminate online lessons.[80]

Moving back to the central issue of gender, let us concentrate on the role of women in the churches of the Evangelical family. In almost all these churches women are in the majority: on average 60–70 percent of church attendees are women.[81] This can be attributed to various causes. One purely social factor is the higher migration rate of men: today, in some regions of Armenia the rate of out-migration is enormous. By migrating—more or less temporarily, and mainly to Russia—the men lose their connection with the church because they are too busy and their workload is quite heavy. On the other hand, several Baptist Armenians started attending Pentecostal rather than Baptist churches, because in Russia Baptist churches are isolated closed communities, and not very welcoming toward outsiders. Another reason for the greater number of women is connected to a behavioral stereotype: men are usually more restrained when they pray in public;[82] moreover, in villages men are ashamed to go to church even if they want to.[83]

The approaches toward gender roles are quite diverse—from very conservative to very liberal. The United Church of Christians of Evangelical Faith (leader: rev. Mamikon Ghazaryan), the most maximalist and rigorist church among Armenian Evangelicals, forbids women to put on makeup, restricts what clothing they can wear, and restricts their participation in social services, whereas most new Charismatic churches have a much more liberal approach. In Charismatic churches like "Word of Life" and the Charismatic Church of the Erebuni quarter in Yerevan, women have more freedom: they are allowed to serve not only in the social but also in the pastoral ministry. Moreover, the founder and senior pastor of the "Erebuni" Charismatic Church is a woman—Ninel Movsisyan.

In most churches women deal with social and educational services. In Evangelical Baptist churches they also conduct Bible lessons and are members

---

[79] Interview with rev. Ruben Pahlevanyan, the head of the Armenian Church of Evangelical Baptists of Shirak, August 8, 2013.

[80] In some small communities, however, the adepts frequently do not have Internet access ("Grand Grace" Evangelical Church, the former "Renaissance" Church, "Atoned of God" Church). Interview with rev. Mamikon Hambaryan, the former pastor of "*Veratsnund*" ("Renaissance") Church of Evangelical Baptists, August 9, 2013.

[81] This assumption is based on the data gathered from all our interviews.

[82] Interview with Artur Simonyan, head of the Church "Word of Life" in Armenia, November 27, 2012.

[83] Interview with rev. Seyran Vardanyan, the head of "Nazarene" Church in the Shirak region, August 10, 2013.

of boards of trustees, but do not perform any pastoral service. In some churches, women are allowed to become preaching pastors, for instance, in the "Nazarene" Church.[84]

Concluding Discussion: A Precarious Identity for Armenian Protestants

Summing up our research, we have seen that the Armenian Protestant churches are quite diverse in terms of orientation, social engagement, and, most importantly, the correlation between national and religious identity. To overcome this diversity of views, several platforms for dialogue between them have been formed. The largest is the Family of Evangelical Churches; there are also regional platforms on the level of pastoral meetings and smaller platforms designed for pastoral meetings within the same Protestant branch (Evangelical, Baptist or Pentecostal/Charismatic). This diversity of views is also reflected in the official social doctrines adopted by some churches.

Identity construction in Armenian Protestant churches is based on what I have called self-legitimizing "mythos-weaving." It conveys the idea of the "ancient" origin of Armenian Protestantism, allegedly rooted in medieval "Armenian heresies" (Paulician and Tondrakian) and historically connected with the activities of the first Protestant missionaries in Armenia during Ottoman times. Another manifestation of this is the "old-new mythos" linked with the narratives of personal repentance and conversion, which often coincided with the historical turning point of the collapse of the Soviet Union and the gaining of independence by the Republic of Armenia.

The same "visionary" tradition provides the Armenian Protestant churches with a legitimate tool to split easily, thus organizing new communities, or to re-unite, or even to turn from the conservative into the modern type and vice versa, allowing the adepts to move from church to church as much as they want.

For Armenian Protestants, the issue of national versus religious identity remains open. Most of them strive to separate "national belonging" from "religious affiliation," stating that the most dangerous thing is the fusion of national and religious identities. Nevertheless, there is a variety of combinations. Historical or traditional Protestant churches put a stress on the ethnic and national element, whereas less traditional or liberal churches subordinate it to the religious/denominational element and downplay ethnic culture.

---

[84] Interview with rev. Seyran Vardanyan, the head of "Nazarene" Church in the Shirak region, August 10, 2013.

As we have seen, the "national ethos" for Protestant Armenians is often projected through the notion of a "chosen nation," and even the idea of being "doubly chosen," which means that "evangelizing" among a chosen nation is a sign of being elected. The idea of being "chosen" is manifested in the frequent use of Mount Ararat as a symbol, recalling the narrative of Noah's Ark. Also important for all Evangelical churches is the collective traumatic memory relating to the 1915 genocide and its commemoration. To some extent this evokes the memory of the lost homeland, especially for those church leaders and members who are originally from the Armenian diaspora. The image of the "homeland" works as a hallmark of the "regained" land that had been lost by previous generations.

When drawing up a typology of Armenian Protestants it is useful to apply Bert Waux's suggestion of three general types of identity: *solipsic* (what an individual feels himself/herself to be), *endothetic* (what a community feels itself to be) and *exothetic* (what outsiders consider an individual or community to be).[85] On the level of individual self-consciousness, that is, the solipsic type, most Armenian Protestants feel themselves to be Armenian "true Christians," which means, in practice, being a non-Apostolic Armenian believer. At the level of endothetic identity, we may say that, according to our data, Evangelical and Pentecostal communities feel like a complete "body," "a crew," where individual adherents feel protected by the group they belong to.

On the other hand, Armenian Protestant churches are struggling to avoid marginalization through the popular label "sect," used by a wider public to create an image of Protestants as alien, which relates to what Waux called "exothetic type of identity." To cope with this pressure, Armenian Protestants use several strategies. Most of all, they try to project the negative meaning of the terms "sectarian" and "other" onto other groups, such as Jehovah's Witnesses or the Neo-Pagans. Sometimes, though, certain churches, like the Seventh Day Adventists, *make* themselves "others" by self-isolation and the creation of a closed community; they are quite passive in public life and eventually become marginalized.[86]

The modern globalist impact, which the Protestant churches in Armenia are trying to withstand, is largely associated with "paganism." The majority of Evangelical and Pentecostal churches in Armenia are anti-globalists in

---

[85] See Bert Waux, "Language and Religion in the Construction of Modern Armenian Identity," December 4, 2004, www.academia.edu/183324/Language_and_religion_in_the_construction_of_Modern_Armenian_identity, accessed on June 22, 2014.

[86] Vigen Khachatryan, pastor of the Adventist Church of the Seventh Day, "Every Believer has to make an investment in his/her own country," www.religions.am/arm/interviews, accessed on June 22, 2014.

terms of wanting to preserve traditional family patterns and opposing liberal interpretations of gender issues and LGBT rights. Accordingly, globalization should not blur the boundaries of the "national-ethnic-traditional," and the adoption of Western values is to be strictly selective. Nowadays there is a strong tendency among Evangelical churches to adopt some traditional elements of the Armenian Apostolic Church (hymnals, music and theological texts) to display and accentuate their Armenian identity. This is most true for the older, historical Protestant churches (Evangelical and Baptist), whereas the new Pentecostal churches, in their efforts to avoid "assimilation," aim rather at creating a new Armenian Christian culture. Yet the rejection of Armenian Apostolic traditional elements does not preclude some of them, including the most publicly active, from acknowledging, for pragmatic and/or ideological reasons, the Armenian Apostolic Church as the Mother Church for all of them.

Appendix: A List of Evangelical, Evangelical Baptist, and Pentecostal/ Charismatic Churches in Armenia (as of mid-2013)

Evangelical churches: Armenian Evangelical Church (rev. Mkrtich Melkonyan) in Yerevan, Evangelical Church of Yerevan (rev. Levon Partakchyan).

Evangelical Baptist churches: Armenian Church of Evangelical Baptists (rev. Garegin Khachatryan) in Yerevan, Armenian Church of Evangelical Baptists of Shirak (rev. Ruben Pahlevanyan) in Gyumri, The Church of Nazarene (pastor rev. Seyran Vardanyan) in Akhuryan village,[87] former Armenian "*Veratsnund*" ("Renaissance") Church of Evangelical Baptists (the former pastor rev. Mamikon Hambaryan) in Gyumri.[88]

Pentecostal/Charismatic churches: Full Gospel Church of Armenia (pastor rev. Samvel Navoyan) in Yerevan, "Unity" Church of Christians of Evangelical Faith or "Emmanuel" Church (rev. Rubik Tumanyan) in Yerevan, Church "Word of Life" of Armenia (rev. Artur Simonyan) in Yerevan, "Rhema" Evangelical

---

[87] The church also has a small community in Yerevan about which rev. Seyran Vardanyan provided some information.

[88] Besides the city of Gyumri, the Armenian Church of Evangelical Baptists of Shirak has communities in villages of the Shirak region such as Harich, Artik, Amasya, Shirak, Kaghnut, Marmashen, Tsoghamarg and Kamo. In some villages there are no formal communities, just several families which belong to the Armenian Church of Evangelical Baptists of the Shirak region.

Church of the Republic of Armenia in Yerevan, Church "New Generation" (rev. Tigran Tadevosyan) in Yerevan, "Christian Church of Evangelical Faith" (the branch of rev. Mamikon) in Yerevan, "Grand Grace" Evangelical Church (rev. Vahagn Poghosyan and rev. Vahan Poghosyan) in Gyumri and Yerevan, Pentecostal Church of Erebuni District of Yerevan (Ninel Movsisyan), "Family of God" Evangelical Church (rev. R. Sahverdyan) in Yerevan, Church "Atoned of God" in Yerevan and Gyumri, Church "The Nation of God," Christians of Evangelical Faith (rev. Rafayel Grigoryan) in Vanadzor, Church "Army of God" (rev. Misak Grigoryan, founder Hovhannes Jalafyan in Los Angeles, The House of God (rev. Grigor Simonyan) in Moscow, Church of Adventists of the Seventh Day (rev. Vigen Khachatryan, who is currently in Georgia).

References

Abrahamian, Levon, *Armenian Identity in a Changing World* (Costa Mesa: Mazda Publishers, 2006).

Aharonyan, H. and Y. Kasuni, *The Armenian Evangelical Church at the Crossroads* (Middle East Council of Churches, 1988).

Arpee, Leon, *The Armenian Awakening: A History of the Armenian Church, 1820–1860* (Chicago: University of Chicago Press, 1909).

Arpee, Leon, "Armenian Paulicianism and the Key of Truth," *The American Journal of Theology* 10, no. 2 (April 1906): 267–85.

Byurakn, No. 74, 28/16 July, No. 75, 1/13 August, No. 76, 16/28 August, No. 81, 13/1 November (Constantinople, 1885, in Armenian).

Conybeare, Fred C., *The Key of Truth: A Manual of the Paulician Church of Armenia* (Oxford: Clarendon Press, 1898).

Donahoe, B., J. Eidson, D. Feyissa, V. Fuest, M.V. Hoehne, B. Nieswand, G. Schlee and O. Zenker, "The Formation and Mobilization of Collective Identities in Situations of Conflict and Integration," Max Planck Institute for Social Anthropology, Working Paper No. 116 (Halle/Saale, 2009).

Eliade, Mircea, *The Myth of the Eternal Return* (Princeton: Princeton University Press, 1971).

Fenton, Steve, *Ethnicity* (Cambridge: Polity Press, 2003).

Freedom of Religion in Armenia: Research (Yerevan, 2010, in Armenian).

Goodell, William, *Forty Years in the Turkish Empire, or Memoirs of Rev. William Goodell, Late Missionary of the A.B.C.F.M.* (New York, 1878), http://babel.hathitrust.org/cgi/pt?id=uva.x000531168;view=1up;seq=9, accessed on June 22, 2014.

Garsoïan, Nina G., *The Paulician Heresy: A Study of the Origin and Development of Paulicianism in Armenia and the Eastern Provinces of the Byzantine Empire* (The Hague and Paris: Mouton, 1967).

Ghanalanyan, Tigran, "Armenian Protestants," *21st Century* 2, no. 8 (2010), www.academia.edu/4132351/ARMENIAN_PROTESTANTS, accessed on June 22, 2014.

Ghazaryan, A. and Levonyan, R., *The Armenian Evangelical Church (Armenia-Caucasus)* (Yerevan, Armenian Encyclopedia Press, 1999, in Armenian).

Guroian, Vigen, "Religion and Armenian National Identity: Nationalism Old and New," paper presented at the Annual Meeting of the American Academy of Religion, Washington, DC, November, 1993, www.georgefox.edu/academics/undergrad/departments/soc-swk/ree/Guroian_Religion_articles_previous.pdf, accessed on June 22, 2014.

Journals and Letters of the Rev. Henry Martyn, B. D. (London: Seeley and Burnside, 1837), http://anglicanhistory.org/india/martyn/journal.html, accessed on June 22, 2014.

Keorkezian, A., *The Paulician-Tondrakian Movement within the Armenian Apostolic Church from the Seventh to the Twelfth Centuries* (Beirut: Tonikian Publishing House, 1970, in Armenian).

"Letter from Mr. Coan, Armenians," *The Missionary Herald, Containing the Proceedings of American Board*, vol. XLVIII (December 1852).

"Letter from Mr. Peabody," *The Missionary Herald, Containing the Proceedings of American Board*, vol. XLVIII (December 1852).

Lusyan, A., *State-Church Relations in Modern Armenia: The Current Situation and Potential Developments*, PhD Thesis (2012, in Russian).

Marutyan, H., *Iconography of Armenian Identity: The Memory of Genocide and the Karabagh Movement*, vol. 1 (Yerevan: Gitutyun, 2009, in Armenian).

Melkonyan, E., "Ethnic Culture and Tradition," *Patma-banasirakan handes* [Journal of History and Linguistics] 4 (1980): 72–83 (in Armenian).

Navoyan, S., *Challenges for Awakening* (Yerevan, 2012, in Armenian).

Navoyan, S., "The Full Gospel Movement in the Context of the Mission of Christ's Church," *Religion and Society* 5 (Yerevan, 2009), 105–78.

Ohanjanyan, A., "The Attempts of Identification of the Names 'Pahk utoghk' and 'Udi' by Some Armenian Evangelical Historiographers," *Hay astvatsaban* [Armenian Theologian] 2 (2008), 179–85.

Ohanjanyan, A., "The Key of Truth and the Problem of the 'Neo-T'ondrakites' at the End of the 19th Century," *JSAS* 20 (2011): 130–36.

Ohanjanyan, A., *The Manuscript* The Key of Truth *and its Historiographical Significance*, PhD Thesis (Yerevan, 2011, in Armenian).

Sargsyan, Serj, President of the Republic of Armenia, speech delivered in the USA, www.president.am/hy/statements-and-messages/item/2008/09/24/news-18/, accessed on June 22, 2014.

Smith, A., *National Identity* (Reno, Las Vegas and London: University of Nevada Press, 1991).

Smith, E. and H.G.O. Dwight, *Researches of the Rev. E. Smith and Rev. H.G.O. Dwight in Armenia: Including a Journey through Asia Minor, and into Georgia and Persia with a visit to the Nestorian and Chaldean Christians of Oormiah and Salmas* (Boston and New York: Crocker and Brewster, 1833).

Tootikian, V., *The Armenian Evangelical Church* (Detroit: Armenian Heritage Committee, 1982).

Waux, B., "Language and Religion in the Construction of Modern Armenian Identity," December 4, 2004, www.academia.edu/183324/Language_and_religion_in_the_construction_of_Modern_Armenian_identity, accessed on June 22, 2014.

Williams, Brackette F. "A Class Act: Anthropology and the Race to Nation across Ethnic Terrain," *Annual Review of Anthropology* 18 (1989): 401–44.

Yeghiaian, B., *The Separation of Armenian Catholic and Evangelical Denominations in the Nineteenth Century* (Antelias: Press of the Catholicosate of Great House of Cilicia, 1971, in Armenian).

Yeritsev, A., "On the Sect of Armenian Tondrakians," in *The Works of the 5th Archeological Conference in Tbilisi in 1881* (Moscow, 1887, in Russian), 187–92.

Yeritsian, A., "Tondrakian Armenians of Our Days," *Pordz* 10 (Tbilisi, 1880): 91–132 (in Armenian).

Interviews, etc.

Ghazaryan, Mamikon, interview, www.youtube.com/watch?v=Zot0GlhghRU, accessed on June 22, 2014.

Grigoryan, Rafael, head of Christians of Evangelical Faith, "The most dangerous thing is the identification of ethnic and religious identities," www.religions.am/arm/interviews/, accessed on June 22, 2014.

Hambaryan, Mamikon, former pastor of "*Veratsnund*" ("Renaissance") Church of Evangelical Baptists, interview, August 9, 2013.

Karapetyan, Gor, youth coordinator in Pentecostal church "New Generation," "Being Evangelical Armenian one can face serious legal issues nowadays," www.religions.am/arm/interviews/, accessed on June 22, 2014.

Khachatryan, Karen, the head of "Rhema" Evangelical church, interview, http://rhemachurch.net/, accessed on June 22, 2014.

Khachatryan, Vigen, pastor of the Adventist Church of Seventh Day, "Every Believer Have to Do Investments in his Country," www.religions.am/arm/interviews/, accessed on June 22, 2014.

Levonyan, Rene, the former leader of Armenian Evangelical Church, interview, http://arminfo.info/index.cfm?objectid=693301E0-1D17-11E2-85BF F6327207157C, accessed on June 22, 2014.

Melkonyan, Mkrtich, the leader of Armenian Evangelical Church, Press Conference, http://haynews.am/hy/1343912848, accessed on June 22, 2014.

Navoyan, Samvel, the head of Full Gospel Church of Armenia, "A number of facts witness the spiritual fall of the society," www.religions.am/arm/interviews/, accessed on June 22, 2014.

Pahlevanyan, Ruben, the head of Armenian Church of Evangelical Baptists of Shirak, interview, August 8, 2013.

Simonyan, Artur, head of Church "Word of Life" in Armenia, interview, November 27, 2012.

Simonyan, Artur, Sermon on Fall Summit of the Alliance, October 26, 2012, www.youtube.com/watch?v=pj-AM1zJpk0, accessed on June 22, 2014.

Tumanyan, Rubik, Sermon, www.youtube.com/watch?v=T-NGz6UW3nA.

Vardanyan, Seyran, the head of "Nazarene" church in Shirak region, interview, August 10, 2013.

YouTube Music Links

Folk music and musical instruments usage during the devotion of United Church of Christians of Evangelical Faith: www.youtube.com/watch?v=0 aAQ4PeubSw, accessed on June 22, 2014.

"Holy, Holy, Holy" spiritual song (music by Komitas *vardapet*): the devotion of United Church of Christians of Evangelical Faith, Sharakan: http://youtube.com/watch?v=zCMib9WN0fI, accessed on June 22, 2014.

PART II
Armenian Diasporas: Puzzles of Identity

Chapter 6

Identity, Borders and Religious Belonging: Armenians between Two Spiritual Centers, Etchmiadzin and Cilicia

Hovhannes Hovhannisyan

The historical and current situation between the two spiritual centers of Armenians—the Mother See of Holy Etchmiadzin and the Great House of Cilicia, as they are officially titled—is a complex issue that has not been sufficiently studied from different perspectives. In public discourse the relationship between the two Holy Centers is conceived as one of the basic factors affecting the maintenance of Armenian identity abroad, while also having an impact on the relationships and contacts among the different Armenian groups in foreign countries.

This chapter will analyze the relationship between the two Armenian spiritual centers in recent years in an attempt to understand how this affects Armenian identity, especially in the diaspora. The historical development of this relationship will also be analyzed for a better understanding of the current situation and current problems.

The chapter will draw on documents from the archives of both spiritual centers, as well as on materials published in their official journals (although the official newspaper of Etchmiadzin is quoted more frequently for reasons of accessibility). Articles in other newspapers and magazines, as well as the interviews and speeches of the spiritual leaders, and letters exchanged between the two centers have also been used. During a stay in Boston, Massachusetts, in July and August 2006, the author was able to observe the relationship of the two ecclesiastical jurisdictions in the United States and their perception in public discourse. Several interviews with the clergy of the Etchmiadzin and Cilician churches, as well as with some believers, were also conducted, in order to discover the strength of religious identity and religious belonging and to find out how this identity influences the relationship between believers and the adepts of both Sees. The city of Boston is very important for the relationship between the Sees, since the positions of the traditional Armenian political parties are very strong here and directly influence both Sees. Boston is also home to a diversity of groups—Armenians from Syria, Iran, Iraq, Lebanon, Russia and the Republic of Armenia—whose relationship is also quite important for understanding the relationship between Cilicia and Etchmiadzin.

The Two Centers of the Armenian Church in the Twentieth Century

The Armenian Apostolic Church has four basic spiritual centers—the Etchmiadzin and Cilician Catholicosates and the Constantinople and Jerusalem Patriarchates. The first two centers are the main Sees and play an important role among Armenians in both the diaspora and Armenia. The Etchmiadzin Catholicosate is situated in the territory of the present-day Republic of Armenia and to a certain extent is under the influence of the Armenian government. Since 1930 the Cilician Catholicosate has been located in Antelias, Lebanon, and is under the influence of the powerful Armenian political party abroad—the Armenian Revolutionary Federation (*Dashnaktsutyun* in Armenian).[1] The relationship between the two Catholicosates has been complicated at times for a number of reasons, including the contest for ecclesiastical power and the competition for influence over Armenians at home and abroad; and such controversies have had a direct impact on the unity of the Armenian Church and hence on the whole issue of Armenian identity.[2]

After its re-establishment at Antelias, Lebanon, the House of Cilicia had quite amicable relation with Etchmiadzin. This statement is proved by the letter (No. 897) of the Etchmiadzin Catholicos Khoren I to the Cilician Catholicos Sahak II on December 30, 1932. Catholicos Khoren wrote: "My heart is full of joy and happiness when I remember the bonds of mutual love among the Cilician Catholicosate, the Jerusalem and Constantinople Patriarchates, and the Mother See of Holy Etchmiadzin."[3] During this period regular contacts between

---

[1] The Cilician religious center was first established at Sis, in the Armenian Kingdom of Cilicia, in 1293. Shortly after the fall of the Cilician kingdom (1375), the Holy See was reestablished in Etchmiadzin (1441), and since then the two spiritual centers, Etchmiadzin and Cilicia, have existed simultaneously. After the Armenian genocide in 1915, the Cilician Catholicosate moved from Turkey to Antelias, Lebanon.

[2] Interview with a priest of the Etchmiadzin church in Boston, July 2006.

[3] Eghyan Byuzand, *The Peaceful Solution of the National-Ecclesiastical Problem* (Antelias, 1960), p. 3 (in Armenian).

Cilicia and Etchmiadzin were established and both Sees tried to deal with the common challenges facing the Armenian Nation and showed their unity as one Armenian Church. In 1935 the Cilician Catholicos Babken prepared the Holy Muron (*surb miuron*, the anointed oil used during church rituals)[4] by mixing together Muron from both Sees, thus symbolizing in the most meaningful way their unity and common mission.[5] One of the memorable events attesting to the good relations between the two centers at this time was the participation of the Cilician Catholicos Garegin I Hovsepyan in the election and anointment of the Etchmiadzin Catholicos Gevorg VI Chorekchyan. Both centers also cooperated in organizing the "Sasuntsi Davit" tank division, facilitation immigration to Armenia, and celebrating the 1,500th anniversary of S. Vardan.[6]

In the post-war period, the history of the relationship between the two centers can be divided into four basic phases:

1. from the 1950s to the Great Earthquake of 1988;
2. from 1988 (the Spitak earthquake and the start of Karabagh movement) to the death of Catholicos Vazgen I in 1994;
3. the Pontificate of the Catholicos Garegin I, 1995–9;
4. the Pontificate of the Catholicos Garegin II, 1999–present.[7]

The relationship worsened in the 1950s when Khad archbishop Ajapahyan became the *locum tenens* of the Cilician Catholicosate, and especially after the election of Catholicos Zareh in 1956. This situation lasted until the end of the 1980s. The Etchmiadzin Catholicos Vazgen I (1955–94) wrote in one of his letters: "From the very beginning of my enthronement I unfortunate in inheriting a situation where the Church in the Diaspora was split into two opposing sides. The Church turned into a battlefield for the struggle between the parties, which was conditioned by the position of the Party [i.e., the ARF

---

[4] *Muron* (μυρων) is a Greek word meaning "fragrant oil." The word is derived from the root meaning "to rub," "to anoint." The Muron is prepared once every seven years with a special ritual and ceremony. It is used in baptism and is considered very important for the practices of the Church. For more about the origin and preparation of Holy Muron see: www.armenianchurch.org/index.jsp?sid=1&id=11938&pid=11937.

[5] Byuzand, *Peaceful Solution*, p. 45.

[6] Byuzand, *The Contemporary History of the Armenian Catholicosate in Cilicia 1914–1972* (Antelias, 1976), pp. 669–70 (in Armenian).

[7] Hovhannes Hovhannisyan, "An Attempt to Analyze the Relationship between the Mother See of Holy Etchmiadzin and the Great House of Cilicia in the Second Half of the Twentieth Century," Faculty of Theology, Yearbook C (Yerevan, 2008), p. 318, www.religions.am (in Armenian).

Dashnaktsutyun] towards Soviet rule and ideology. This tension increased."[8] In another letter Catholicos Vazgen I mentioned that "every effort has been made to portray Etchmiadzin as a Soviet propaganda center," citing the political factor as the major reason for the division of the Armenian nation.[9] The relationship between the two spiritual centers turned from non-amicable to hostile when the Cilican Catholicosate opened new dioceses in North America, on the east coast in 1957 and on the west coast in 1972. At the same time the Antelias Catholicosate "owned" the dioceses of Tehran, Isfahan, Atrpatakan (in Northern Iran), as well as part of the diocese in Greece.

The party Dashnaktsutyun had long regarded Etchmiadzin as a Soviet agent and used every means to prevent people from having a favorable view of it. In 1933 Ghevond Duryan, the Church Primate in North and South America, was killed by Dashnaktsutyun members because of his loyalty to the Soviet Union.[10] (The other two traditional parties—Ramkavar and Hnchak—were more loyal to Etchmiadzin.)

From the 1960s through the 1980s some meetings, negotiations and discussions were held to try to resolve the problems between the two Sees, but no progress was made. After these failures, the relationship between the two centers was virtually interrupted.[11] In public discourse the opinion prevails that the unresolved conflict was not the result of the inner disposition of the two Catholicosates but was imposed on them by two historically opposed political parties—the Communist party ruling Soviet Armenia and the party Dashnaktsutyun which had a great influence in the diaspora.[12]

Even after the Cold War was becoming less virulent in the 1970s and 1980s, the Dashnaktsutyun continued the policy of "motherland without land," addressed to the 1915 genocide generations and asserting the independence of the Cilician center was regarded as an integral part of this policy. This proves that political interests prevailed in the Etchmiadzin–Cilicia relationship, and that only through a reconsideration of this factor would it be possible to achieve any kind of cooperation between them. Support for this statement also comes

---

[8] *Etchmiadzin* magazine, December, L, 1992, p. 10 (In Armenian).

[9] Archive of Contemporary History, f. 823, l. 3, h. 150, No. 19.

[10] E. Melkonyan, "Armianskaia Apostol'skaia tserkov' vo vzaimootnosheniakh Armenii i diaspory" [The Armenian Apostolic Church in the relationships between Armenia and the Diaspora], in A. Iskandaryan (ed.), *Religia i politika na Kavkaze* [Religion and politics in the Caucasus] (Yerevan, 2004), p. 34.

[11] *Etchmiadzin* magazine, December, L, 1992, p. 10 (in Armenian).

[12] A. Kalashayan, "The Current Phase of the Canonical Unification Processes of Etchmiadzin-Cilicia (1988–2008)," *Armenian Theologian*, C (Yerevan, 2009), p. 143 (in Armenian).

from the fact that during his visit to New York in 1968 Catholicos Vazgen I invited the head of the Cilician diocese to take part in the celebrations and in discussions on ways to restore the unity of the two jurisdictions. This offer was rejected by the Cilician diocese and no further steps were taken to resolve the issue.[13]

After the breakdown and demise of the Soviet Union, the political factor continued to play a major role. Dashnaktsutyun, which was exiled from Armenia for 70 years, was mainly active abroad and regarded the diaspora as its main source of power and authority. For this reason the party ascribed special importance to the Cilician center and endeavored to use its network, resources and scientific and financial capabilities for its own political goals. At the same time, the party Dashnaktsutyun did not want the Cilician center to become too independent and powerful, because a powerful spiritual center could oppose the party's policies and political programs. From this point on, any move toward a closer relationship between Etchmiadzin and Cilicia was mainly regarded as an attempt to weaken the political position of Dashnaktsutyun in the worldwide Armenian diaspora.

In public discourse the relationship between Etchmiadzin and Cilicia has often been regarded as an ecclesiological problem, while the political, economic and other aspects of this issue have largely been ignored. Both centers used the term "Catholicos" as the title of their highest prelate, which presumably meant that they were equal; the Holy See of Etchmiadzin, however, had always firmly asserted its claim to primacy. Etchmiadzin has always considered itself to be the only and undivided spiritual center for all Armenians, the highest in the hierarchical structure, and it could not accept the equal use of term Catholicos by the Cilician spiritual center. Opposing such an approach, Cilician writers emphasized that the Great House of Cilicia had never been part of the hierarchical structure of the Mother See of Holy Etchmiadzin, although it accepted the primacy of Etchmiadzin in the chronological and spiritual senses.[14] The basic argument of the Cilician See is founded on the priority of its own role as the spiritual center integrating the all the Armenians who were saved from the genocide of 1915 in the Ottoman Empire. The Cilician representatives have always maintained that "Mother See" is only a title ascribed to Etchmiadzin and

---

[13] Melkonyan, "Armianskaia Apostol'skaia tserkov'," p. 37.

[14] One of the vivid expressions of such trends is the article of St. Alajajyan. See "Open Letter to the Armenian Catholicos," in *Grakan Tert* [Literary Paper] November 25, 2005 (newspaper, in Armenian). The "primacy of honor" of the Catholicosate in Etchmiadzin, Armenia was recognized by the Catholicosate in Sis, Cilicia. see: www.armenianorthodoxchurch.org/en/history, accessed on June 22, 2014.

does not imply any subordination or hierarchical relationship between the two centers.[15] During the Soviet period the Cilician clergy always claimed that they served the Armenians who had lost their motherland, whereas Etchmiadzin served the atheist state and a people without faith.[16]

There is another aspect, a psychological one, which has great importance for defining these issues. With regard to the identity and security of the diaspora, great importance is given to the understanding of the term "motherland" and its misuse by diaspora Armenians.[17] In its historical memory the Armenian diaspora, formed after the genocide, has continued to consider its motherland to be only the so-called Western Armenia,[18] but not the territory of the Republic of Armenia, which is a serious challenge from the viewpoint of connecting diaspora Armenians to the present-day Republic of Armenia.[19] This challenge was supported by the Dashnaktsutyun party, which was actively trying to connect the diaspora Armenians mainly with the Cilician center. However, during the visits of Catholicos Vazgen I to the diaspora, which began in 1956, the majority of Armenians referred to the Mother See of Holy Etchmiadzin as the spiritual center of all Armenians.[20]

At the end of the 1980s, the Etchmiadzin Catholicosate began work on a new Church constitution, a move that was strongly criticized by the Dashnaktsutyun party. In particular, one of the political organs of the Dashnaktsutyun party criticized the unresolved conflict between the two centers, pointing to the "unhealthy situation that has existed for over thirty years."[21] To resolve this "unhealthy situation" and its concomitant problems, the following basic steps were suggested:

1. To proclaim the unity and oneness of the Armenian Apostolic Church in Armenia and the diaspora without any political stipulations. The Church should keep itself free from any party influence.

---

[15] *Grakan Tert*, November 25, 2005 (newspaper, in Armenian).
[16] *Grakan Tert*, November 25, 2005 (newspaper, in Armenian).
[17] Interview with *Hayk*, in Los Angeles, March 6, 2006.
[18] In the sixteenth century Armenia was divided between Turkey and Persia, that is, into Western (Turkish) Armenia and Eastern (Persian) Armenia. The territory of Western Armenia covers the region of Turkey called Eastern Anatolia.
[19] Interview with *Hayk* in Los Angeles, March 6, 2006.
[20] For more details see *Etchmiadzin* magazine, Press reaction in international journals of the visits of Catholicos Vazgen), January–March, A-B-C, pp. 253–63. The first visit of Vazgen I was in 1956, just after his election as Catholicos. Later on he continued his visits to many diaspora centers in South and North America, Europe, Asia, etc.
[21] *Hayrenik*, November 22, 1986 (newspaper, in Armenian).

2. To proclaim the canonic unity of the Church, especially the spiritual cooperation and unity between the Mother See of Holy Etchmiadzin and the Great House of Cilicia with clearly defined spheres of competence.
3. To create harmonious cooperation among the clergy and laity, providing equal rights in ecclesiastical, administrative and financial issues.
4. To establish a democratic administration in Church communities and dioceses.
5. The clergy shall discuss the issues concerning the reformation of all spheres of Church life, including its dogmatic, ecclesiastical, canonic, disciplinary, and ritual aspects.[22]

The reaction from Etchmiadzin, which appeared in the pages of its official journal, was very negative. The editorial called upon the Cilician See to reject the political provocations of the Dashnaktsutyun, although it also remarked that it was understandable that "the piper calls the tune."[23]

In an interview with the Russian newspaper *Novoe Vremia* [New Times], Catholicos Vazgen I acknowledged the chilly relations between Etchmiadzin and Cilicia. He also affirmed that the center of the Armenian Church was the Mother See of Holy Etchmiadzin and remarked that the relationship between the two Armenian Holy Centers depended on changes in the world political situation.[24] At the same time he pointed out that the ideological and religious division of the diaspora was having a negative impact on Armenian identity and national unity abroad.[25]

During this period, the efforts toward the development of an Armenian Church constitution were rejected by Dashnaktsutyun and the Cilician See, which wanted to limit the participation of the laity in the governance of the Armenian Church. The Dashnaktsutyun party, which has traditionally had a great influence on the Cilician See and on the diaspora in general, was against a constitution that might limit the party's influence on Church affairs. During his visit to the United States in 1988 Catholicos Vazgen I rejected all these arguments on the limitation of secular participation in Church affairs. He clearly explained that lay people should be involved in Church affairs and that the new constitution would not limit their participation in the governance

---

[22] *Hayrenik*, November 22, 1986 (newspaper, in Armenian).
[23] *Etchmiadzin* magazine, November–December 1987 (in Armenian).
[24] The interview of the Catholicos was published in *Etchmiadzin*, November–December 1987 (in Armenian).
[25] As of December 1, 1987 approximately 20 percent of Church dioceses were not under the competence of Etchmiadzin.

of the Armenian Church.[26] Eventually, however, the Cilician See preferred to avoid active participation in the elaboration of such constitution, because such a document would be supposed to clearly define the subordination between the two Sees. At the same time the draft constitution was intended to restore the unity of the Armenian Church under the auspices and authority of Etchmiadzin, which was also unacceptable to the Cilician Catholicosate. Any clause in any draft document that imposed a hierarchical structure in the Church would automatically be opposed by the Cilician See, since it accepted the priority of Etchmiadzin only in a chronological (but not in the ecclesiastical or any other) sense. Although the two spiritual centers were negotiating and cooperating during this period, they could not resolve their conflict over the elaboration of the Church constitution. Any sign of cooperation between the centers, however, went against the political agenda of the Dashnaktsutyun party, which criticized their collaboration in the *Hayrenik* (Fatherland) newspaper.[27]

Many political actors and intellectuals emphasized that, in order to remedy the chaotic situation in the diaspora, the Armenian Church in Armenia and in the diaspora should be unified and one, apart from any politics and parties. There should also be clear cooperation among the dioceses of the Armenian Church, clergy and laity, for discussing the challenges and solving the problems of the various layers of the Armenian nation. For this reason, democratic order and relations should prevail in ecclesiastical relationships and in the Church system.[28]

One of the basic factors in the controversies between Etchmiadzin and Cilicia was the intolerant attitude of clergymen toward each other and the absence of any will to compromise. The competition for financial resources diverted the clergy from their basic responsibilities. In this respect, both centers were quite uncompromising and based their activities on the interests of their own Sees. Consequently, any attempt to reach unity or move toward closer cooperation would fail, since the problem of national unity was subordinated to the interests of each Catholicosate.

---

[26] Interviews in the newspapers *Payqar* and *Armenian Mirror Spectator*, 1988.
[27] *Hayrenik*, November 22, 1986 (newspaper, in Armenian).
[28] Kalashayan, "The Current Phase," pp. 160–167.

The Earthquake of 1988 and Independence in 1991: Icebreaking and a New Stage

The Spitak earthquake of 1988 created a situation that changed the relationship, stagnant for 30 years, between the two Catholicosates. Both spiritual centers worked together to remedy the consequences of the disaster and to help the suffering people in the earthquake zone. The head of the Cilician center hurried to Armenia to express his condolences to the Armenian nation. In 1989 Catholicos Garegin II of the Great House of Cilicia officially visited Etchmiadzin for the first time in history, and took part in the events commemorating the genocide of 1915. It should be mentioned that at the end of his visit the two Catholicoses signed a joint announcement called "one Church, one Nation, one Motherland," in which the memory of the Armenian genocide of 1915 and the earthquake of 1988 were seen as the fundamental bases for cooperation between the two centers. The Cilician Catholicos declared that "the Diaspora is the gate to death without the Motherland" and therefore the need of cooperation between Armenia and the diaspora strongly depends on good contacts between the two spiritual centers. After a friendly meeting, the two Catholicoses issued their common statement to the Armenian nation, in which the spirit of cooperation based on the slogan "one nation, one Church" was highlighted.[29] Evidence of the close cooperation between the two centers is provided by the pilgrimage then organized by Cilician Catholicos Garegin II to Der-Zor, Syria, where in May 1991, along with the delegates of Vazgen I, he consecrated the Armenian Genocide Martyrs Memorial Church and conducted a liturgy in memory of the genocide victims in Turkey.

One of the main achievements of this announcement was a new interpretation of the term motherland, which provided a firm basis for recognizing the Republic of Armenia as the physical and spiritual motherland of all Armenians. This was quite important in the sense that, after the genocide, the generations of Armenians now spread all over the world had not perceive the Republic of Armenia as their motherland, while the name of "Cilicia" exerted a magical influence, reminding them of the medieval independent Armenian state in the southeastern part of today's Turkey, which was seen as their lost motherland. The concurrent movement for independence and signs of the future war in Karabagh ignited the spirit of cooperation between the two Catholicosates and

---

[29] For more details see *Etchmiadzin* magazine, "The Preaching of Garegin B Catholicos in the Mother Temple of the Mother See of Holy Etchmiadzin," November–December, N-O, 1988, p. 33 (in Armenian).

played an essential role in the growing perception of Eastern (and not Western) Armenia as the motherland of all Armenians.[30]

The positive nature of these events raised the hope in Armenian society at large that the damaged relationship between Armenia and the diaspora would continue to improve. In a 1989 interview with radio "Ayb" in Paris, Catholicos Vazgen I asserted that "the two Sees had come to a final agreement."[31] In his interview with the Belgian newspaper *La Libre Belgic* on May 14, 1990, Vazgen I, in talking about the Armenian Sees and dioceses, used the expression *primus inter pares* (first among equals) meaning that the four main Armenian Church centers (Etchmiadzin, Cilicia, Jerusalem, Constantinople) have equal rights and cooperate closely with one another, but that the primacy belongs to the Mother See of Holy Etchmiadzin.[32] This primacy is conceived in both its chronological and legal sense.

Significant events took place in the relationship of Etchmiadzin and Cilicia in the first years of Armenia's independence, which coincided with the last years of the pontificate of Catholicos Vazgen I. The high point of this relationship was the *kondak* (order) of the Catholicos of All Armenians on the unity of the churches from December, 1992. Although the order concerned the Universal Church and dealt with universal principles, its publication was an essential fact and might become a serious basis for cooperation among the Armenian ecclesiastical centers in the diaspora. Even though the *kondak* referred to the ecumenical church and reflected general principles, the core message was addressed to the three Armenian Sees historically located outside the motherland. Thus, the mutual relationship entered into an amicable phase and if there were no influence from the political parties then cooperation and unity at all social levels would not have seemed impossible.

After the independence of the Republic of Armenia was proclaimed in 1990 and recognized in 1991, the relations between Etchmiadzin and Antelias developed to a new level. During the Soviet period the diaspora dioceses avoided any interaction with Etchmiadzin because of the communist government, but after independence this situation radically changed. The Republic of Armenia

---

[30] *Etchmiadzin* magazine, "The Preaching of Garegin B Catholicos in the Mother Temple of the Mother See of Holy Etchmiadzin," November–December, N-O, 1988, p. 33 (in Armenian).

[31] *Etchmiadzin* magazine, September–October, I-J, 1989.

[32] It was the first time in Armenian history that the two Catholicoses had anointed a church together: in this case, the Mary Magdalene Church in Brussels. By this action the Catholicoses of the Mother See of Holy Etchmiadzin and the Great House of Cilicia began a new era of joint activities.

re-emerged as the national anchor, while Armenians abroad were faced with the growing threat of assimilation. This new interpretation somewhat weakened the role of the Dashnaktsutyun party and, accordingly, the Cilician religious center.

The earthquake, the Karabagh (Artsakh) movement, independence, and the opening of relations with the diaspora—all these events taken together spurred the two spiritual centers to deeply reconsider their relationship. The last years of Catholicos Vazgen I's pontificate were marked by the regular mutual visits between the Etchmiadzin and Cilician clergy; in particular, many believers had the chance to hear the preaching of Cilician Catholicos Garegin II in Etchmiadzin from 1988 to 1994.

In 1995 Garegin II of Cilicia was elected as the Catholicos of the Mother See of Holy Etchmiadzin with the name of Garegin I, and his pontificate lasted until his death in 1999. The cooperation that had been established between two spiritual centers continued. After the election of Garegin I there were some new achievements in motherland–diaspora relations. As we have mentioned, after the genocide Armenians worldwide identified the motherland with Western Armenia. In his speeches, however, the newly elected Catholicos referred to Eastern Armenia as the motherland, reinforced now by the newly independent state and the "return" of people from the diaspora to Armenia.[33] It is interesting that, as the previous head of the Cilician center, Garegin I, even subconsciously, identified the Etchmiadzin–Cilicia relationship with the motherland–diaspora relationship. This identification emphasizes the spheres of influence of the two centers, which continued to be the main source of controversy between them. The first visit of the newly elected Catholicos, in January 1996, was to Canada. In a speech in Montreal the Catholicos declared that "our nation needs a spiritual 'restoration' ... We all represent unleavened bread, and if a piece of the bread is divided, the whole bread will desiccate."[34]

In their 1995 election speeches, all the speakers emphasized that this was a historical moment, since it was the first time in Armenian history that a Cilician Catholicos had become the Catholicos of the Mother See of Holy Etchmiadzin. It was also the first time that the Cilician Catholicos—Aram I, also newly elected in 1995—was ordained by the Catholicos of All Armenians. During these days when two new prelates were elected, the idea of one nation, one motherland, and one Church was emphasized, underpinning the indivisible unity of the Armenian Apostolic Church. The election of a former Cilician Catholicos as the

---

[33] See *Etchmiadzin* magazine, "Preaching on the Catholicos Anointment," April, D, 1995, p. 75 (in Armenian).

[34] *Etchmiadzin* magazine, B-C, February–March 1996, p. 85 (in Armenian).

Catholicos of All Armenians was made possible also by the support of the first president of Armenia, Levon Ter-Petrosyan.[35] He declared that the separation of the two Sees was a "national shame" and suggested that the best step towards reconciliation would be the election of the Cilican Catholicos as the Catholicos of All Armenians in Etchmiadzin, in order to symbolize the restored unity.[36] According to E. Melkonyan, Levon Ter-Petrosyan's idea was to try to unite the Church under the hierarchy of the Mother See of Holy Etchmiadzin, but after a short time it became clear that the process of unifying the dioceses in the diaspora and any further unification would fail.[37]

After his election, Catholicos Garegin I continued the positive relationship with the House of Cilicia, his own former office, and deepened the established cooperation. He actually took part in the election process of the new Catholicos of Cilicia, Aram I, and in his speech he made a clear distinction between the roles of the two centers, emphasizing that "after Holy Etchmiadzin the Cilician Catholicosate is the most important center of our Church and this fact cannot be disputed."[38] During the election of the Cilician Catholicos every speech mentioned that this was the first time in Armenian history that the head of Cilicia had become the Catholicos in Etchmiadzin and that the anointment of the Catholicos of the Great House of Cilicia had been performed by the hand of the Catholicos of All Armenians.[39] The declarations about the unity of motherland and Church were perceived as a basis for the unity of the entire nation.

An essential step toward solving the problem may have been the formation of a commission by mutual agreement of Catholicoses Garegin I and Aram I. The commission would consist of four members from each See; it would discuss all the issues under dispute and their origins, and try to find solutions and prevent such issues from arising again in the future. This dialogue continued in September 1995 and October 1996 during the visits of the Cilician Catholicos to Etchmiadzin to participate in the meeting of the "Hayastan" All-Armenian Fund in Armenia. On August 1997 four delegates from Cilicia arrived in Etchmiadzin and, with their four colleagues from Etchmiadzin, established the

---

[35] *Hayk* magazine, March 8, 1995 (in Armenian).
[36] See *Republic of Armenia* newspaper, 47 (1167), March 8, 1995; *Etchmiadzin* magazine, D, April 1995, pp. 52–4.
[37] Melkonyan, "Armianskaia Apostol'skaia tserkov'," pp. 44–7.
[38] *Etchmiadzin* magazine, H-L, August–September 1995, p. 20 (in Armenian).
[39] It is interesting that, in the not too distant past, in 1945, the newly elected Catholicos of Cilicia Garegin Hovsepyants had visited Etchmiadzin and presided over the election process of the Catholicos of All Armenians Gevorg V Chorekchyan and anointed him.

commission for the discussion of the issues under dispute. The agenda of the first meeting was "The Enforcement of the Unity of the Armenian Church" and the basic points to be discussed were: (1) the diocese issue; (2) contacts and cooperation among dioceses; and (3) the reformation of the Armenian Church. The discussions were held in a friendly atmosphere and a decision was made to establish a commission to analyze the suggestions for Church reformation and to adopt a working program to pursue reformation in rituals, the development of ethical approaches, the theological interpretation of many phenomena, and so on.[40]

It is interesting to note that all parties agreed upon Church reform as part of the agenda. Reform ideas had emerged at the beginning of the twentieth century and were revisited after the independence of Armenia, especially when they were enriched through the dialogue between the two Armenian Catholicosates and the elimination of sources of conflict that had prevailed since the 1950s in the "cold war" between the two Catholicosates. Even during the negotiations in 1956 in Antelias and in the agreement signed by both parties on June 23, 1956, both Catholicosates had accepted the need for reforms in various spheres of social life. However, no real reforms in the canonical system were performed. The representatives of both Sees involved in the mentioned commission accepted the need to reform the rituals of the Armenian Church and have a unified ritualistic system. There were plenty of different canonical issues to reform or to consider its reformation but the members of commission decided not to touch different issues but to start from ritualistic and less problematic ones.

One of the proofs of the high level of the relationship between Etchmiadzin and Cilicia was the visit of Cilician Catholicos Aram I to Etchmiadzin on the personal airplane of the prime minister of Lebanon on August 26, 1998. He arrived in Armenia to visit the Catholicos of All Armenians who had just returned to Etchmiadzin after a long stay abroad for medical treatment. At the end of the meeting Garegin I stated: "We are not two churches and this idea should be widely spread. We are one Church and the evidence of this oneness is the visit of Your Excellency today."[41] Both Catholicoses asserted that the Church would show its oneness not just in words and speeches but in deeds.

The pontificate of Catholicos Garegin I was in a way a revolutionary period in the history of the Armenian Church. His legacy has been analyzed in detail by Hermann Goltz, the head of the Faculty of Theology at Halle-Wittenberg, who emphasized that Garegin I maintained Armenian identity in the diaspora and

---

[40] Kalashayan, "The Current Phase," p. 153.
[41] *Etchmiadzin* magazine, J-I, August–September 1998, p. 105 (in Armenian).

promoted the unification of Armenians all over the world, overcoming the gap created by the Cold War between Eastern and Western Armenians. According to Goltz, the election of Garegin I and his activities while in office constituted a milestone in the Armenian history.[42]

The New Pontificate and New Challenges after 1999

After the death of Garegin I, the new Catholicos was elected in 1999 under the name Garegin II. The new Catholicos was Armenian-born and deeply rooted in the Etchmiadzin clerical hierarchy. The relationship between the two centers entered into a new phase. During the first part of his pontificate, 1999–2004, positive relations prevailed, but after the opening of the diocese in Canada (2004) by the See of Cilicia, the relationship between the two Armenian Holy Centers totally changed again—they started to freeze and worsen.[43]

In his annual report at the end of 1999 the new Catholicos expressed his hope that any dispute between Etchmiadzin and Cilicia would be resolved, on a mutually shared ground, for the "restoration of canonical unity." Yet the terms of such a "restoration" were conceived differently by the two Sees. For Etchmiadzin it meant the subordination of the Cilician See, while the latter interpreted it as equal, friendly, and mutually beneficial relations between the two centers.

The 1,700th anniversary of the adoption of Christianity as the state religion in Armenia, celebrated in 2001, was intended to mark a crucial point in the relationship between the Catholicosates. In addressing the challenges of spiritual and church life Catholicos Garegin II declared: "We shall overcome the challenges of our history. After the resolution of the disputes between the Mother See of Holy Etchmiadzin and the Great House of Cilicia we shall initiate the reformation of the Armenian Church and promote brotherhood among nations, religions, and churches with our two-thousand-year-old Christian heritage. We shall move forward as one Church, one State and nation."[44]

The speech of Catholicos Aram I was motivated by the same vision, which he expressed on September 22, 2001 in Etchmiadzin during the blessing of the Holy Muron. Mixing the Muron of Cilicia with the Etchmiadzin Muron, Catholicos Aram I said: "The Armenian Church is one with its Muron, mission,

---

[42] *Etchmiadzin* magazine, G, July 1999 (in Armenian).
[43] *Azg*, March 19, April 3, 2004 (daily newspaper, in Armenian).
[44] *Azg*, January 2001, p. 19.

service, and nation."[45] This was the high point of harmony between the two Sees in modern Armenian history.

The relationship between the two centers became tenser, however, during 2002–3. This was quite evident, because during the second conference on "Armenia–Diaspora" in May, 2002, the relations were severed between the representatives of two centers. The official protocol, used during the visits of the Cilician Catholicos to Armenia, was cancelled. The official magazine of Etchmiadzin and other information organs stopped regularly illustrating the events in the See of Cilicia after the election of Catholicos Garegin II in 1999. In our view, it was not only the projected opening of a new diocese in Canada by the Antelias center but also the renewal of the work of the commission on the elaboration of the Armenian Church constitution in 2003 that played a negative role in the relationship between the two Holy Centers. The commission included only representatives of Etchmiadzin, Constantinople and Jerusalem, without the participation of Antelias, whose position might be expected to be negative. Cilicia's negative attitude to the elaboration of such a constitution was well-known, because the main point in previous concepts of the constitution was to emphasize the hierarchical priority of the Mother See of Holy Etchmiadzin.

The relations between the Holy Centers worsened even more during the second half of 2004. The main obvious reason was obviously Cilicia's creation of the new diocese in Canada. In 2004, when the diocese was officially opened, Garegin II indirectly criticized the decision of Cilicia as anti-canonical. Garegin II regarded such a step on the part of Cilicia as an issue of State security because, in his opinion, the integrity and unity of the Armenian nation in the diaspora and the motherland would face new challenges and threats.[46]

Since that time, a sort of "cold war" broke out between the two Catholicosates and has continued up to the present day. To be sure, Catholicos Aram I visited Armenia in 2006 and 2011 to participate in the third conference on "Armenia–Diaspora" and in the meeting of the "Hayastan" All-Armenian Fund. During his visit to Etchmiadzin he made some general pronouncements on national

---

[45] *Azg*, January 2001.

[46] Since September 3, 1983, Etchmiadzin had had its own diocese in Canada, and it had always opposed the attempts of the Cilician Catholicosate to open a diocese there. On October 6, 1984, the Diocesan Assembly convening at the St. Gregory the Illuminator Church of St. Catharines elected Bishop Vazken Keshishian as the first primate of Canada. Before the establishment of the Canadian prelacy, Canada had been included in the Eastern Prelacy of the Cilician Catholicosate. Despite the opposition from Etchmiadzin and many attempts to stop the process, the Cilician See managed to declare the opening of Canadian prelacy in 2002 and officially opened the diocese in 2004.

and ecclesiastical issues, the importance of national unity, and the preservation of the national identity, but he did not go into details and did not touch on the deeper and more problematic issues. Otherwise, there have been no regular relations between the two centers.

The Catholicosates were especially divided by their different approaches to the foreign policy implemented by the Republic of Armenia and, in particular, to the controversial protocols signed by Armenia and Turkey in Zurich in October, 2009.[47] Armenians living in the diaspora, for whom the memory of the genocide was an integral part of their national identity, were especially affected, and considered the protocols to be a national betrayal. This led to demonstrations and rallies in various countries during the visits of the president of Armenia, Serzh Sargsyan. The protocols were also opposed by the Dashnaktsutyun party and the Great House of Cilicia, and personally by Catholicos Aram I. The Mother See of Holy Etchmiadzin, however, convened a session of the Spiritual Council and accepted a formula accroding to which a general statement would be made in support of the policy of the Armenian government.

The difference between the approaches of the two Catholicosates to the signed protocols was used by the Dashnaktsutyun party and various sections of the Armenian diaspora to deepen the gap between the Republic of Armenia and the diaspora, as well as between diaspora Armenians and the Mother See of Holy Etchmiadzin. The clamor over the signed protocols damaged the chances for a deepening rapprochement between the diaspora and Armenia and gave new life to the ideology of a "motherland without land." The newly created situation was quite profitable for the Dashnaktsutyun party and the Cilician center, reinforcing their influence among the nationalistically inclined circles of the diaspora. This growing divide has become a challenge to the maintenance of national identity across the world: the alienation of the diaspora Armenians could become a serious threat to the security and unity of the nation as whole.

Recent developments indicate, however, that relations between the two Catholicosates may be improving as the commemoration of the 100th anniversary of the genocide approaches. On September 24, 2013 the joint Bishops' Council (62 delegates) was opened with the participation of both Catholicoses, Garegin II and Aram I. The two main issues under discussion at the council were the possible canonization of the genocide victims and the uniformity of the ritual of Baptism. Both Catholicoses in their opening speeches emphasized the need

---

[47] The protocols were aimed at resuming diplomatic relations and opening the borders between the two countries. The protocols were never ratified by both sides, and the normalization process was frozen.

for reforms and improvements in the Armenian Apostolic Church. Aram I declared: "The Armenian Apostolic Church will turn into a museum if there are no reforms."[48] A deification commission was established which would elaborate the principles of deification, the canons, and the system of rituals. The council also decided to adopt a uniform ritual for baptism and confirmation. The council was deemed "historical," since such a joint council had never before taken place in the Armenian Apostolic Church. The bishops decided to continue their work in the future, and the next council is scheduled for the fall of 2014. The common mourning, the common memory of the genocide induced the clergy of both Sees to put aside their differences and sit around the table to discuss possible Church reforms together.

Conclusion

Judging from the history of the last few decades, we can conclude that relations between the two Catholicosates have been quite delicate and sometimes explosive, and that careless approaches may lead to clashes and alienation among the Armenian centers in the diaspora and their representatives. The rapprochement of the two Catholicosates was precluded by the political factor, the agenda of the Armenian Revolutionary Party (Dashnaktsutyun), which drove a serious wedge between Soviet Armenia and the diaspora. This situation continued in part even after Armenia gained her independence. The result was that diaspora Armenians had no way of fully assessing the restoration of independent Armenia and remained spiritually isolated from the new Republic. And, as we mentioned the Dashnaktsutyun party continued the policy it adopted during the Cold War, impeding the improvement of Etchmiadzin–Cilicia relations.

Although the relationship between the two centers was friendly but remote during the first decades of Soviet rule, after the mid-1950s it quickly worsened. From 1956 to 1988 there were no relations between them at all, a situation which was also conditioned by the political factor. But after the Spitak earthquake in 1988 the ice broke, and thanks to the efforts of Catholicos Vazgen I and the Cilician Catholicos Garegin II relations were re-established, and became even better when the latter became Catholicos Garegin I of Etchmiadzin in 1995. Peace, friendship and unity during the period from 1988 to 2001 were the result of objective and subjective reasons. The objective reasons were the earthquake and the assistance provided by the Cilician See, as well as the collapse of Soviet

---

[48] Available at: www.azatutyun.am/content/article/25116085.html.

Union, which led to the facilitation of relations between the Sees. The subjective reason was political: the initiative taken by the first president of Armenia Levon Ter-Petrosyan to assist in the election of Garegin I. However, after the election of Garegin II Nersisyan in Etchmiadzin in 1999, the relationship became more complex and ambiguous. It was mostly conditioned by power conflicts (over the Canadian diocese of Cilicia, for example) and by the issue of hierarchy, as Etchmiadzin periodically emphasized its primacy. The political factor was also vitally important, since the Dashnaktsutyun party always impeded the close cooperation between Etchmiadzin and Cilicia, trying to retain its power and authority in the Cilician See and in the diaspora as a whole.

The diaspora dimension is, in the final analysis, truly crucial. Most of the financial resources for both Catholicosates come from the diaspora. The division of the diaspora supports the differentiation of the components of Armenian identity because the terms "Armenians of Armenia" and "Armenians of the diaspora" and the meanings imputed to them often contradict each other. The ecclesiastical centers also have a role in fomenting this contradiction. The "Armenians of Armenia" are mostly regarded as belonging to the Etchmiadzin hierarchy and the "Armenians of the diaspora" to the House of Cilicia; and the followers of the two Catholicosates often do not have regular contact with each other. Such issues are especially evident in the Armenian diaspora in America, where the various divisions of Armenian identity are deeper and uniquely different.

This division in the Armenian diaspora does not exist in former Soviet countries, especially in the biggest Armenian diaspora—in Russia. The Armenian community there was formed during Soviet times and afterwards, and consists entirely of immigrants from the territory of Soviet and independent Armenia as well as from the other Caucasian republics. Traditionally the Russian Armenians fall under the jurisdiction of the Holy See of Etchmiadzin, and the Cilician See is not represented there. Hence the conflicts between the two Catholicosates that cause such problems in other countries do not affect the Russian-Armenian diaspora.

The second largest Armenian diaspora, in the United States, is more complex and therefore more divided. It emerged after the genocide of 1915 in the Ottoman Empire, and later after the mass immigration of Armenians from the Middle East. Another migration—from both Armenia and Azerbaijan—took place after the collapse of the Soviet Union and the Karabagh war: this wave continues. Thus, succeeding waves of immigrants formed diaspora groups that differ essentially in language, identity perception, political orientation, perception of the "motherland," and religion. The first wave, immigrants from the Middle East, mostly belongs to the Cilician See; the more recent immigrants from Armenia and Azerbaijan belong to the jurisdiction of Etchmiadzin (if they belong to the Church at all). The differences in identity among these groups sometimes have an influence on Church relationships. The controversies between the two Holy Centers have been transferred into the public sphere, a situation that is widening the gap among the various Armenian groups.

References

Byuzand, Eghyan, *The Peaceful Solution of the National-Ecclesiastical Problem* (Antelias: Antelias Publishing House, 1960) (in Armenian).

Byuzand, Eghyan, *The Contemporary History of the Armenian Catholicosate in Cilicia 1914–1972* (Antelias: Antelias Publishing House, 1976).

Hovhannisyan, H., "An Attempt to Analyze the Relationship between the Mother See of Holy Etchmiadzin and the Great House of Cilicia in the Second Half of the Twentieth Century," Faculty of Theology, Yearbook III (Yerevan: Yerevan State University press, 2008), 316–38; www.religions.am, accessed on September 23, 2013 (in Armenian).

Kalashayan, A., "The Current Phase of the Canonical Unification Processes of Etchmiadzin-Cilicia (1988–2008)," in *Armenian Theologian* III (Yerevan: Yerevan State University Press, 2009), 141–67.

Melkonyan, E., "Armianskaia Apostol'skaia tserkov' vo vzaimootnosheniakh Armenii i diaspory" [The Armenian Apostolic Church in relationships between Armenia and Diaspora], in A. Iskandaryan (ed.), *Religia i politika na Kavkaze* [Religion and politics in the Caucasus] (Yerevan: Caucasus Institut, 2004), 31–52.

Chapter 7

Venerating the Saints, Remembering the City: Armenian Memorial Practices and Community Formation in Contemporary Istanbul[1]

Christopher Sheklian

As we entered the Şişli Armenian Cemetery in Istanbul, I admit I was a little perplexed. I, no stranger to the city, was accompanying a friend on his first visit from California as he toured "Armenian Istanbul" led by Deacon Vagharshag[2] from the Armenian Patriarchate of Istanbul. Thirty-five active Armenian Apostolic churches in the city, not to mention the plentiful schools, newspapers, and even the monuments built by the Balyan family, the Ottoman palace architects—why go to the cemetery? Allan was visibly excited to see the grave of the mid-twentieth century Patriarch of Istanbul Shnork Kaloustian,[3] who had served in America for some time and whom Allan had known. Having never

---

[1] The research for this chapter has been made possible through a series of grants and fellowships. The earliest phases of the research were supported by the University of Chicago, including summer research grants through the Social Sciences Division. Subsequent research was made possible through a research grant from the American Research Institute in Turkey, with funding from the US Department of State, Bureau of Educational and Cultural Affairs. Currently, my research and this publication is made possible by support from the Social Science Research Council's International Dissertation Research Fellowship, with funds provided by the Andrew W. Mellon Foundation. I would like to thank several friends and colleagues who have read portions of this chapter at various stages. I am very grateful for the help provided by Elizabeth Hewitt, Shefali Jha and Ryan Tellalian. Any errors and omissions are, of course, mine.

[2] Other than recognized public figures such as Hrant Dink and Archbishop Ateşyan, or where others have explicitly given permission for their names to be used in print, I use pseudonyms throughout.

[3] September 27, 1913–March 7, 1990. The 82nd Armenian Patriarch of Constantinople, elected in 1963 and served until his death.

met him, I allowed the two men to pay their respects while I wandered around, still feeling strange at the excitement over the dead.

As I shuffled away from Shnork Patriarch's grave and turned a corner, I looked up at the magnificent marble statue affixed atop a grave, and froze. Transfixed, I may have crossed myself. Malachia Ormanian. Head of the Seminary of Armash, which arguably not only revived but outright saved Armenian theological knowledge. Author of the *Azkabadum*, the definitive history of the Armenian nation and Church. Known for being so difficult and detailed that no one has undertaken the task of translating it into English.[4] Despite the controversies over his Catholic background and the extent to which Catholic theology influenced his interpretation of the Armenian Apostolic Tradition, he is probably the greatest theologian of the Armenian Apostolic Church since the fourteenth-century Gregory of Datev (incidentally, also highly influenced by Catholic theology). And there he was, right in front of me. A slight chill came over me. Turning to Deacon Vagharshag, I asked if he would take a picture of me with the tombstone. He chuckled at me, noting the reversal of my apprehension and discomfort from only a moment before.

I left the cemetery excited after I saw Daniel Varujan, the great nineteenth-century romantic poet, and other famous Armenians. Yet I was no less perplexed than when I entered. In fact, now I had to explain my own excitement, and the chill that came over me in the presence of the grave of the great Patriarch.

Memory and Community in Istanbul: Mapping the Case in Theoretical Perspective

As part of a larger anthropological study on the relationship of Turkish secular law to the Armenian population of Turkey, this encounter in the Şişli Armenian Cemetery and the attention paid to Shnork Patriarch in particular provides the opportunity to reflect on the ways in which certain figures and practices are central to the ability to conceive of an entity like the Armenian community. Community, writes Zygmunt Bauman in a work of the same name, "feels good because of the meanings the word 'community' conveys– all of them promising pleasures, and more often than not the kinds of pleasures we would like to experience but seem to miss."[5] While I do not share Bauman's suggestion that

---

[4] Ormanian lived February 11, 1841–November 19, 1918. Malachia Ormanian, *Azkabadum* (3 vols, Jerusalem, 1913–27).

[5] Zygmunt Bauman, *Community: Seeking Safety in an Insecure World* (Cambridge, 2001), p. 1.

"community" necessarily conveys a certain kind of nostalgia for an impossible condition, I point to his comments to note that while the object of this inquiry is in part "the Armenian community of Turkey (Istanbul)," as a theoretical notion, community is both "fuzzy" and "feel good." This chapter explores the conditions under which we recognize a group of people as a community.

Arguably, collective memory becomes a crucial way in which a group can be recognized as more than a mass of people, as something we would be willing to call a community. This chapter, through my encounter in the Şişli Armenian Cemetery, tackles a subset of my doctoral dissertation research to explore in detail one way we can recognize the Armenians of Istanbul collectively: ideas about exemplary figures within that collective, how they are remembered and suffuse group memory, the practices by which they are remembered, and the role of the Apostolic Church in such practices of memory formation.[6]

Specifically, I argue that liturgical practices of saint veneration in the Armenian Apostolic Church are ways of remembering exemplary figures who provide a basis for collective identification. In other words, it is exactly by placing people and events into the collective memory that the collective, i.e. "community," is itself constituted. By looking at three very different theoretical approaches toward connections between memory, community and ethics, my goal is to describe specific memories of events and figures, as well as the practices through which they are remembered, as a heuristic device for the contours of community. If we accept that community is always "fuzzy," that its boundaries are always unclear, then we can move beyond policing those boundaries to look at how different people relate to different practices of/and memory in order to explore how they relate to an already amorphous community.

I then go on to explore the relationship between "canonical" saints remembered liturgically and more recent figures like Shnork Patriarch. Are the liturgical practices similar? Do the liturgical practices influence or support other practices of remembrance? Finally, I ask about the relationship between these practices and broader memorial practices within the city to see how a specifically Armenian Apostolic Church practice of remembrance is taken up by those (Armenians and not) outside of the Church. In other words, I trace the memorial practices of the Armenian Apostolic Church through three different contexts in order to demonstrate the similar yet distinct ways these practices are

---

[6] My broader dissertation research interrogates the way in which Turkish law and governance, explicitly secular in nature, sets the parameters by which Armenians collectively constitute themselves. I have conducted research in Istanbul in the period from 2009 to September 2012.

taken up and used by various members and parts of the Armenian community as a way of thinking about the way that community is identified and bounded.

Mary Carruthers, in a rich and influential book on medieval memory and mnemonic techniques, emphasizes how in Western Late Antiquity through the Middle Ages, memory was more than an intellectual tool or even part of liturgical mastery, but was a consummately moral virtue. As she notes, "the choice to train one's memory or not, for the ancients and the medieval, was not a choice dictated by convenience: it was a matter of ethics. A person without memory, if such a thing could be, would be a person without moral character and, in a basic sense, without humanity."[7]

In other words, memory becomes crucial to the formation of a moral person. Yet she goes beyond the individual to stress how memory is central also to communal formation. In discussing the idea of a medieval self, she says that "every person had domesticated and familiarized these *communes loci*, these pieces of public memory."[8] As we will see, public memory in this sense both reaffirms and constitutes the public[9]—the community—itself.

Michael Daniel Findikyan, in the Armenian Apostolic context, has stressed the same point in a series of published and unpublished discussions of the centrality of *anamnesis* to the Armenian Apostolic liturgy.[10] Glossing it as the "sacred, corporate recalling of the mighty acts of God," he traces the concept of *anamnesis* from Deuteronomy through the Old Testament. In particular, he dwells on the Psalms as Jewish liturgical texts, demonstrating how important this collective remembering is for a Jewish and subsequently Christian liturgical tradition. He states that "anamnesis was central to Jewish worship because it guarded against the human inclination to forget God,

---

[7] Mary Carruthers, *The Book of Memory: A Study in Medieval Culture* (second edition, Cambridge, 1990 and 2008), p. 14.

[8] Carruthers, *The Book of Memory*, p. 224.

[9] Carruthers unproblematically introduces a concept with its own set of theoretical baggage, the public. Since Habermas' *The Structural Transformation of the Public Sphere* the concept of public has received an incredible amount of scholarly attention. Here, I try not to rely too heavily on it, although I often use the term here to mean "a person who, by work or position, is known by a large number of people," as in "a public person."

[10] See, in particular Michael Daniel Findikyan, "Liturgical Usages and Controversy in History: How Much Diversity Can Unity Tolerate?" in *St. Nersess Theological Review* 1, no. 2 (1996), pp. 191–212; "The 'Unfailing Word' in Eastern Sacramental Prayers," in Maxwell Johnson and L. Edward Phillips (eds), *Studia Liturgica Diversa: Essays in Honor of Paul F. Bradshaw* (Portland, 2004) pp. 179–89; and "An Introduction to Liturgy and Worship in the Armenian Church" (n.d.), unpublished manuscript used with permission of the author.

that is, to credit other agents—be they pagan deities or people themselves—for what God himself had accomplished."[11]

Findikyan then traces this Jewish concept of worship into the Christian and ultimately Armenian Christian experience of liturgy. Importantly, the word *anamnesis* is used by Jesus himself during the "words of Institution" during the Last Supper: "Do this in remembrance of me." From this foundational moment of Christian worship, he demonstrates the use of *anamnesis* in the central, Eucharistic prayer of the Divine Liturgy, *Badarak*, of the Armenian Church. He concludes: "liturgy is based on anamnesis, a sacred, corporate remembering, by which a community recalls and recounts those historical events it perceives as constituting its common identity and outlook. Anamnesis allows Christians to remember the Lord and all he has done for us."[12]

He continues with an insightful discussion of liturgy, memory, and temporality; however, for our purposes, there are three aspects of Findikyan's discussion that are of supreme importance. First, as noted above, *anamnesis*, this particular form of remembering, is liturgical. Second, we should note that the form of remembering Findikyan describes, which is central to Armenian worship, is also ethical. It keeps Christians from forgetting what God has done for them, and thereby misattributing the works of God to other deities, or simply to man. This is different from the way in which Carruthers describes memory as an ethical imperative, but we can nonetheless see how they are both ethical injunctions. Here, memory quite directly keeps us from the sin of idolatry, and moreover spurs us to good ethical action through the example of previous events. In liturgical prayer, these are usually biblical events. Carruthers, on the other hand, is describing a broadly Aristotelian concept of ethics, wherein memory necessarily contributes to the habituated formation of a holistic ethical self who can recognize through *phronesis*, a certain wisdom, the proper way to act at a given time. From either perspective, remembrance is consummately ethical. We will return to the importance of the ethical aspect of memory when we see the contours of the Armenian community in Turkey emerge from these memorial practices.

Finally, we should note that such remembrance is crucially communal. Findikyan describes it, in the quote above, as "corporate remembering." Similarly, Carruthers has emphasized that medieval practices of reading and authorship depended upon a shared set of texts which all would have in the memory. In other words, "corporate remembering" concretizes the community

---

[11] Findikyan, *Introduction to Liturgy*, p. 9.
[12] Findikyan, *Introduction to Liturgy*, p. 14.

exactly through that shared remembering. Not only does it make individuals and individual experience intelligible, it also works in the other direction: while we will explore various institutional aspects to community recognition, one could give a definition of community as exactly coterminous with those who can draw on these shared memories. In the liturgical setting, this mutually imbricating dynamic means that the individual draws upon the corporate memories of God's previous actions to worship meaningfully and to place herself within the liturgical community, while at the same time, the corporate nature of this remembrance is exactly what constitutes the liturgical community.

Theoretically, it is this mutual interaction of community and memory that organizes the ethnographic exploration which follows. After a brief overview of the Armenian presence in Turkey and Istanbul, I delve into the question of how certain memorial practices help organize amorphous demographic data into something we could call an Armenian community. First, I discuss the explicitly liturgical practices of memory used to venerate the saints of the Armenian Apostolic Church. This discussion is expanded to recent important clergymen, still remembered through ecclesial means, and finally to a broader look at memorialized people. Through this expansion, I hope to be able to ask about how memorial practices of the Armenian Apostolic Church, which helps constitute a particular church-going subset of the Armenians of Turkey, may also interact with broader memorial practices taking place outside the church walls. In this way, this chapter offers not only an insight into one aspect of contemporary religiosity, but also how specific practices we deem "religious" may have broader importance.

Istanbul and Anatolian Armenians

Exact numbers of Armenian in Istanbul vary by source; there are probably around 60,000 or 70,000.[13] In addition to that, recent years have seen an influx in the number of Armenians from the Republic of Armenia living and working in Istanbul. Many of these are undocumented workers, and thus there is no way

---

[13] Dr Tessa Hoffman, in *Armenians in Turkey Today: A Critical Assessment of the Situation of the Armenian Minority in the Turkish Republic* (Brussels, 2002), p. 6, states that "Some 70 000 Armenians still live in Turkey, most of them in Istanbul." Ruben Melkonyan, in *Aknark Stambouli Hay Hamaynki Patmoutyan* [Review of the history of the Armenian community in Istanbul (1920–till present day)] (Yerevan, 2010), p. 97, says that "According to official statistics now there are around 60 thousand Apostolic Christian Armenians which live mainly in Istanbul."

to figure them into the number of Armenians in the city, though it may increase the number to just over 100,000 in a city of almost 14 million.

Most of the active Armenian population of Turkey is to be found in Istanbul. Outside of the city, demographics begin to take a more contested shape. While until only a couple of decades ago there were still a number of Armenians who were recognized as such in cities such as Malatya and Diyarbakır, today those numbers have dwindled. The region of Hatay hosts the only two active Armenian churches outside of Istanbul, one of them in the last remaining Armenian village in Turkey, Vakıflıköy. The only permanently stationed Armenian Apostolic priest in Anatolia serves the families in the village and in the city of Iskenderum. St. Giragos Church in Diyarbakır, recently renovated, stands with the St. Gregory the Illuminator Church in Kayseri among churches which are active in the sense that they are repaired, open, and occasionally house services but do not have a full-time priest. So in terms of "Armenians who are recognized as such," most today are to be found in Istanbul.

By saying "Armenians who are recognized as such," I mean to avoid in part both the demographic question and a larger debate over Armenian identity. Identity discourse itself can be incredibly problematic, and surveys of the concept in the social sciences show how it emerged as a central concept in the 1980s and peaked sometime thereafter. As the *Stanford Encyclopedia of Philosophy* puts it, "although 'identity politics' can draw on intellectual precursors from Mary Wollstonecraft to Frantz Fanon, writing that actually uses this specific phrase, with all its contemporary baggage, is limited almost exclusively to the last twenty years."[14] Anecdotally, it is interesting to note that in the oral history project with Diyarbakır Armenians mentioned below, older interviewees often referred to "Armenian-ness (*Ermenilik*)" while it was mostly younger people who explicitly used the language of identity (*kimlik* in Turkish).[15] Yet both phrases indicate self-ascriptive recognition of a relation to Armenian heritage and community. Thus, when I speak of "Armenians who are recognized as such," I want to include not only those who have "Christian" written on their identity cards, are baptized in the Armenian Apostolic Church and speak clear Western Armenian, but who

---

[14] Cressida Heyes, "Identity Politics," *The Stanford Encyclopedia of Philosophy* (spring 2012 edition), ed. Edward N. Zalta, http://plato.stanford.edu/archives/spr2012/entries/identity-politics/.

[15] Ferda Balancar, *The Sounds of Silence II: Diyarbakır's Armenians Speak* (Istanbul, 2013).

both self-ascribe and participate in some way in the Armenian community, even if that is minimal.¹⁶

Beyond this debatable but still fairly clear set of "Armenians who are recognized as such," the question of an Armenian presence in Turkey becomes more complicated. First, there are the Hemşin Armenians, living in the Black Sea region. Converted to Islam a few centuries ago but still speaking a form of Armenian, their status as Armenians has been the subject of recent debate.¹⁷ Diyarbakir, a city where many Armenians lived at least partially in the open as Armenians until only a couple of decades ago, has seen a revival of the Armenian population in the wake of the re-dedication of the St. Giragos Church on October 22, 2011 with a second dedication of the bells on October 20, 2012. Indeed, a number of Armenian converts to Islam have been re-baptized in the Armenian Church.¹⁸ Finally, there is the issue of the "hidden" (*gizli* in Turkish) Armenians. We can define these as people who have some Armenian ancestry, with or without knowledge of it, but in the wake of 1915 have lived as Muslim

---

¹⁶ Melkonyan, *Aknark*, p. 98, divides Armenians in Istanbul into three groups based on "their attitude towards the community life and existing problems": indifferent, conforming and active. As my discussion of community above demonstrates, I find the ontological certainty of the "Armenian community" to be problematic. Nonetheless, these categories help us think about the ways in which Armenian self-ascription occurs. As should be clear, my category "Armenians who are recognized as such" would include all three of Melkonyan's "conditional groups," while some of the entirely indifferent, who are not active at all, could fall outside this category.

¹⁷ Although the debate over the identity of the Hemşin Armenians is not entirely a new one, with early work done by Levon Haçikiyan in Armenian in the 1970s (the major work translated into Turkish in 1996 as *Hemşin Gizemi*), there has been a renewed interest in them. In addition to a recent, widely circulated piece written in Beirut about them (see the commentary in *AGOS*, p. 2 of the Armenian pages of May 17, 2013, entitled, "The Hamshin and the Armenians"), a documentary by Lusine Sakaryan titled "Hamshen at the Crossroads of Past and Present" was recently screened at the 10th annual Golden Apricot Film Festival in Yerevan (www.gaiff.am/en/1372678208).

¹⁸ See, for instance, the October 23, 2011 article in *Hurriyet Daily News*, "Armenians Claim Roots in Diyarbakır," www.hurriyetdailynews.com/default.aspx?pageid =438&n=armenians-claim-roots-in-diyarbakir-2011-10-23. In conjunction with this, the Hrant Dink Foundation has published two important books on Diyarbakır Armenians. The first is the proceedings from a conference organized by the Foundation in Diyarbakir in November of 2011 about the Diyarbakır Armenians published as *Diyarbakır Tebliğleri*. The other is the second book in their series of oral history projects. While the first was a collection of oral histories about Turkish Armenians generally, entitled *The Sounds of Silence: Turkey's Armenians Speak* (published in both Turkish and English), the second is specific to Diyarbakir Armenians: *Sessizliğin Sesi II: Diyarbakırlı Ermeniler Konuşuyor*. The English translation was just published as Balancar, *The Sounds of Silence II*.

Turks or Kurds. In an April 26, 2013 interview on Bügün TV, Deputy Patriarch Archbishop Aram Ateşyan claimed that there were as many as 100,000 of these hidden Armenians.[19]

Thus, in contemporary Turkey, Istanbul is the clear center of Armenian life. The texture of Armenian Istanbul is variegated, and since the eighteenth century, has included a strong Armenian Catholic presence, and later, in the nineteenth century, an Armenian Protestant presence. In the Ottoman period, Armenian was largely coterminus with the Armenian Apostolic Church until a significant number of Catholic Armenians received recognition from the Sultan as a *millet*. The Armenian *millet*, essentially a confessional group organized around ecclesial structures for tax purposes, was headed by the Armenian Patriarch of Istanbul. However, in 1831, the first legally recognized cleavage of the Armenians in Istanbul occurred between the Apostolic Church and the Armenian Catholic Church with the latter's official recognition. Later, in 1850, an Armenian Protestant *millet* was recognized.[20] Both the Armenian Catholic Church and the Armenian Protestant Church have a continued presence in the city today: there are 12 Catholic Churches, and two Protestant Churches, and both denominations run schools.

Today's Istanbul Armenians are not defined solely by religious affiliation, however, as there are several other important Armenian institutions throughout the city. A long-standing press includes the dailies *Jamanak* and *Marmara* as well as the Turkish/Armenian bilingual weekly *AGOS*. A new monthly magazine, *Luys*, put out its first issue in late April 2013 and the monthly *Paros* has been printing important cultural articles for the past three years. Additionally, the publishing house of Aras, printing books in Armenian, Turkish, and English on Armenian issues, is also a lively center. The schools, while often physically situated near or on Church property, enjoy a large degree of autonomy. Their alumni associations are also important cultural centers—for instance, the Pangaltı Armenian High School Alumni association recently performed a ballet version of the classic Armenian opera *Anush* in late May of 2013. Thus, I would stress that there are many non-ecclesial aspects to Armenian life in Istanbul, despite this chapter's focus on liturgical and thus ecclesial aspects.

In fact, there is push by some of the newspapers and other intellectuals for what is called in Turkish *sivileşme*, "civilianization," the reduced importance of ecclesial institutions in the collective life of the Armenian community of

---

[19] See *AGOS*, "Ateşyan: '100 bin gizli Ermeni var,'" May 2, 2013, p. 7.

[20] Vartan Artinian, *The Armenian Constitutional System in the Ottoman Empire 1839–1863: A Study of its Historical Development* (Istanbul, 1988).

Istanbul.²¹ As opposed to the state-dictated *laiklik* or secularism/laicism which forms the official legal situation, "civilianization" hopes to work through civil society institutions to propose a different conception of the link between Armenian citizen of Turkey and Armenian community. Hrant Dink, the founder and assassinated editor of the newspaper *AGOS*, was an early and vocal proponent of "civilianization," addressing the issue in a series of articles.²²

These debates over Armenian identity and Armenian community also condition my own use of these terms throughout this chapter. Yet whichever conception of Armenian community one operates with, there are shared entanglements which exceed the institutional.

More than nostalgia for a glorious past or pride in their eternal city, the new Rome, memory among the Armenians in Istanbul takes on an ethical bent of a character much different than the one alluded to either by Findikyan or Carruthers. As the remaining Armenian community in Turkey, which includes the Western portion of the areas where Armenians historically lived (see discussion above about Armenian presence in Turkey generally), there is a special burden upon those who stayed. Tellingly, diaspora is a difficult concept to apply to the Armenians of Istanbul. While Istanbul was never geographically in an entity we can recognize as Historical Western Armenia, it was nonetheless the capital of Western Armenian life in the Ottoman Empire. Given that there are many Istanbul families who are either direct descendants of genocide survivors, or now, who have migrated from Diyarbakir, Malatya, etc. during the Republican era, we could perhaps call them an "internal diaspora." Yet this would still do disservice to those genuine *Istanbullus* (residents of Istanbul). As one interviewee in *The Sounds of Silence II* mentions after their family moved from Diyarabakır to Istanbul, while most of her friends at school had recently arrived from Sivas or Kayseri, "none of them were Istanbul Armenians in the true sense. Although there might have been some, because there were Armenians in Istanbul even a thousand years ago."²³ These alone would be the true *Istanbullus*, but there is still a sense in which Istanbul Armenian existence is a direct descendent of Western Armenian life, albeit not the "traditional village life" which might characterize

---

²¹ See the August 29, 2011 article in *Hurriyet Daily News*, "Minority Communities Ready for Civilianization," www.hurriyetdailynews.com/minority-communities-ready-for-civilianization.aspx?pageID=438&n=minority-communities-ready-for-civilianization-2011-08-29.

²² Some of these have been collected with many other of his articles in Hrant Dink, *Bu Köşedeki Adam* [The Man on This Column] (Second Printing, Istanbul, 2009), pp. 151–61.

²³ Balancar, *The Sounds of Silence*, p. 43.

a stereotypical Western Armenian existence, such as that described in *Armenian Village Life Before 1914*.²⁴

Carrying this burden of being the remnant of Armenian life in former Ottoman lands, memory does in fact take on a moral weight. As Melissa Bilal has described beautifully through detailed ethnographic work on Armenian lullabies, "in such a context where cultures are detached from lived experiences and memory, it becomes impossible to share the stories of violence and pain in the public sphere."²⁵ She goes on later to argue that:

> For decades, Armenians in Turkey could not easily transmit their lullabies, stories, songs, or any other artifact referring to their presence in Anatolia, since national identity in Turkey, Turkish national culture, and official Turkish History were constructed through repression, denial or assimilation of ethnic identities and cultures in Anatolia.²⁶

From this perspective, memorializing the deeds of those actors who, since 1915, have worked to preserve not only Armenian ethnic identity and culture, but also the memory of life before the excision of Armenians from Anatolia, is an act of defiance of this official line which surely comes from a moral compulsion to remember. Memory here takes an ethical bent, not only in the construction of self or group, but its preservation in the face of loss—both past loss and the potential of further assimilation.

Venerating the Saints

In what follows, I trace out the Armenian Apostolic Church's various ways of commemorating and venerating the saints. I consider the liturgical remembrance of saints to be one particular practice of memory which is current not only in Istanbul, but in the Armenian Apostolic Church generally. Thus, I take it to be one way among many that the memorial burden described above is expressed.

Not only the Armenian Apostolic Church venerates the saints. In the introduction to a book on the Jews of Morocco, Issachar Ben-Ami goes so far to

---

²⁴ Susie Hoogasian Villa and Mary Kilbourne Matossian, *Armenian Village Life Before 1914* (Detroit, 1982).
²⁵ Melissa Bilal, "The Lost Lullaby and Other Stories About Being Armenian in Turkey," *New Perspectives on Turkey* 34 (2008), pp. 67–92, p. 67.
²⁶ Bilal, "The Lost Lullaby," p. 73.

assert that "Veneration of the saints is a universal phenomenon."[27] Arguably, the invocation of the Patriarchs ("Abraham, Isaac, and Jacob") throughout the Old Testament already forms a nascent veneration which influences early Christian practices. These begin to take more concrete shape with early patristic writings. St. Athanasius' *The Life of St. Anthony* stands as one of the earliest hagiographies and sets both form and content for later writings about the lives of the saints. In both the Christian Church at large and the Armenian Apostolic Church in particular, remembrance of and edification by holy men and women is found in the earliest writings.

Yet the Armenian Church has its own particular set of practices for venerating great men and women of the Church.[28] For instance, a collection of homilies supposedly delivered by the founder of Armenian Christianity, St. Gregory the Illuminator, includes homily 16, "On Edification from Teaching About the Martyrs."[29] Mostly, however, in the Apostolic Tradition, saints are memorialized liturgically. There are three types of liturgical days in the Armenian Apostolic Church. In an ordinary week, Sunday is designated a "dominical" day, literally, "the day of the Lord." Other major feast days, as well as the entirety of the 50-day period following Easter fall into this category. Wednesday and Friday are normally designated fasting days. This leaves Monday, Tuesday, Thursday and Saturday as "Saints Days." Each day is given to the memory of a particular saint or set of saints. These vary from biblical figures to saints recognized in all the ancient churches to particularly Armenian saints. If Divine Liturgy, *Badarak*, is offered that day, there is a special litany during what I call the "Remembrance Litanies"[30] which inserts their name(s). During the Night and Morning Services, the two services outside of *Badarak* which are most commonly performed, prayers vary by type of day. So at the end of the Morning Service, there is both a litany by the deacon and a prayer said by the priest which inserts the names of the saint(s) of the day.

---

[27] Issachar Ben-Ami, *Saint Veneration Among the Jews of Morocco* (Detroit, 1998), p. 1.

[28] Much of this information comes from courses taken on liturgy taught by Fr. Michael Daniel Findikyan at the St. Nersess Armenian Seminary. Any errors are, of course, my own.

[29] This is known in Armenian as the *Hajakghabadum Jark'*. An English translation is being prepared by Dr Roberta Ervine and Dr Abraham Terian of the St. Nersess Armenian Seminary.

[30] The technical term is the "Diptychs," but I use "Remembrance Litanies" throughout to emphasize what they do. During the *Badarak*, they occur shortly before the singing of the Lord's Prayer. See Michael Daniel Findikyan (ed.), *Divine Liturgy of the Armenian Church with Modern Armenian and English Translations, Transliteration, Musical Notation, Introduction and Notes* (New York, 1999).

It is precisely this liturgical invocation which marks one as a saint in the Armenian Church. Unlike the Catholic tradition, there is no rigorous canonization process, requiring a minimum of two miracles and so on. Rather, in the liturgically-oriented Armenian Church, if one is considered worthy to be included in the litanies read during the service, then the Church considers that person a saint. We can note that this same concept of being liturgically "canonical" also applies in part to the Scripture: an astute observer of the daily readings in the Armenian Church will notice that the book of Revelation is never read in an official status in the Church. While it is included in the Armenian Bible, the fact that it is not read during the liturgy marks the ambivalence with which it was held by many early Armenian theologians. So from this perspective of liturgical canonicity, the fourteenth-century Gregory of Datev is actually the last official saint of the Armenian Church, since he is the "youngest" saint whose name is mentioned during the *Badarak*.

There are two main textual resources for thinking about the saints in the Armenian Apostolic Church. The first is the *Donats'oyts'*, the comprehensive caldendar of the liturgical year. This book, which contains all possible yearly variations, is calculated for any given year as the Ōrats'oyts'. For practical purposes it is the Ōrats'oyts' which is used in the Church, rather than the more encyclopedic Donats'oyts'. The other major book dealing with the saints is the *Haysamavurk*, a book of readings about the lives of the saints. Each ecclesiastical center renders its own version of the Ōrats'oyts', so that while the one calculated out of Etchmiadzin every year is the more pervasive, the Istanbul Patriarchate also produces its own Ōrats'oyts'.[31] This liturgical book includes all of the variable hymns and litanies for a given day, and when that day is a saint's day as described above, it lists the saints remembered.

Using the Istanbul Ōrats'oyts' and limiting ourselves to the summer of 2013, we can see the vast range of saints who are memorialized liturgically, and thus, canonically. On June 11, Emperor Constantine and his mother Helen are commemorated. On Monday, June 17, a number of "Holy Witnesses," including St. Anthony, the same described by St. Athanasius, are remembered. And June 20 celebrates the uniquely Armenian saints the "Holy Translators" Sahag and Mesrob. Thursday, July 11 commemorates "St. Isiah the Prophet," and the following Saturday "Our St. Thaddeus the Apostle and the Virgin Santoukht."[32] So within the span of a few days an Old Testament Prophet and one of the 12 disciples are remembered. The July memorial to St. Thaddeus emphasizes his

---

[31] Istanbul Armenian Patriarchate, *Yegeghets'agan* Ōrats'oyts' (Istanbul, 2013).
[32] Istanbul Armenian Patriarchate, *Yegeghets'agan* Ōrats'oyts', pp. 66–8, 76.

role in the conversion of Armenia, and pairs him with a particularly Armenian saint who was influential in that history. In other words, we see in the calendrical cycle that everyone from Old Testament Prophets, New Testament figures, early monks and important figures in universal church history, as well as saints important to the Armenian conversion and history are all "canonized" through their remembrance during liturgical services.

This wide gamut of saints is further enlarged in the *Haysamavurk*, a book about the lives of the saints. Additional figures who are not recognized in the *Badarak* are also included in this book, and stories about their lives are told which expands on the idea of saints as exemplary figures to be emulated. Despite its rare use in the Armenian liturgy today—I know of its regular use only in Jerusalem—the *Haysamavurk* points to the importance given in the Armenian Apostolic Church to the role of holy men and women.

Additionally, this daily march through the canon of accepted saints pushes out from liturgical to daily practice. The same day a saint is venerated is also seen as the "name day" for anyone who shares a name with that saint. For instance, St. Christopher (Krisdapor), a fourth-century figure who is supposed to have carried a manifestation of Jesus across a river is remembered usually sometime in October (the details of the Armenian liturgical calendar are well beyond the scope of this chapter). This would be my name day, and while practices vary as to what exactly that entails, at the very least, after *Badarak* everyone would wish me "*Anunovut dzeranas,*" that is, "May you grow old with your name," or simply, "*Anunovut abris,*" "May you do well with your name!"

Istanbul, the Liturgical City

Throughout Istanbul, these weekday celebrations of the saints and various practices related to saint commemoration are ubiquitous. Due in part to the presence of the Armenian Patriarchate, an institution supposedly established in 1461 by the Ottoman Sultan Mehmed II (the Conqueror) shortly after the conquest of Constantinople,[33] Istanbul Armenian life remains heavily ecclesial, and moreover, liturgical. In fact, in Istanbul, *Badarak* is celebrated nearly every

---

[33] See Benjamin Braude's discussion of the "foundation myths" of the *millet* system: Benjamin Braude, "Foundation Myths of the *Millet* System," in Benjamin Braude and Bernard Lewis (eds), *Christians and Jews in the Ottoman Empire* (New York and London, 1982), pp. 69–88. The Patriarchate of Istanbul, like that of Jerusalem, recognizes the Catholicos of the See of Etchmiadzin as the head of the Armenian Apostolic Church, the "Catholicos of All Armenians." While both Patriarchates have a large degree of autonomy, Istanbul

day. As mentioned, there are 35 open Armenian Apostolic churches (the number rises to a total of 49 Armenian churches when we include the 12 Catholic and two Protestant churches).[34] However, due to both a dwindling and centralizing Armenian population, not all of them can be considered active. For instance, in Beykoz, a neighborhood far north on the Asian side of Istanbul, there is a church which is open, maintaining an active Church Foundation. Without a parish, however, it would be difficult to describe it as an active church. However, *Badarak* is sometimes celebrated on special occasions at these "open but not active" churches, often in conjunction with the saint's day of the name of the church.

Churches which are more central, but which do not necessarily have many local Armenian families in the neighborhood, figure into a weekly cycle of liturgical services. This is what makes Istanbul the liturgical city: Monday–Friday *Badarak* is performed in at least one church somewhere in city, if not more than one. A handful of dedicated choir members, deacons and even parishioners move around the city, dealing with the constant construction on public transportation to get to various corners of Istanbul where there are Armenian churches. Priests who are assigned to more active parishes on Sundays perform the rite at these weekday churches. Choir members have their favorite churches, based on everything from proximity to home to the fact that a church is located on the same grounds as their *alma mater*. Different choir masters, experts in the singing of Armenian liturgical *sharagans* or hymns, lead the choirs at each of the churches. Choir members follow their chosen teachers during the week, who instruct and encourage others in the learning of the modal system on which Armenian *sharagans* are based.

Istanbul, then, is the Armenian liturgical city *par excellence*. There are very few places in the world where *Badarak* is celebrated as frequently as in Istanbul. In the cathedral of Etchmiadzin, daily services include the Night, Morning and Evening Services, but not the Divine Liturgy. In Jerusalem, *Badarak* is celebrated in the closed Church of the Holy Sepulchre in the middle of the night

---

bishops are elevated to the episcopate by the Catholicos of Etchmiadzin at the request of the Patriarch of Istanbul.

[34] This data is taken from a chart on page 187 of the 2012 Declaration of Armenian foundation properties in Istanbul, published by the Hrant Dink Foundation: Mehmet Polatel, Nora Mıldanoğlu, Özgür Leman Eren and Mehmet Atılgan, *2012 Beyannamesi: İstanbul Ermeni Vakıflarının El Konan Mülkleri* [2012 Declaration: The Seized Properties of Armenian Foundations in Istanbul] (Istanbul, 2012). An invaluable resource which has an online component, the Declaration is a nearly comprehensive record of the *vakıf* (religious foundation) property of the Armenians in Istanbul, prepared in conjunction with the announced return of properties in August 2011.

and Morning and Evening Services are offered daily in the St. James Monastery Church in the Armenian Quarter. Thus, the only places in the contemporary Armenian world which rival the amount of Istanbul's liturgical celebration are the monastic centers such as Etchmiadzin, Jerusalem and Antelias.

More importantly, there is a precision and comprehensiveness which characterizes the performance of liturgy in Istanbul. Assuredly, the American liturgical experience is decidedly different than many of the other parts of the Armenian world, where the Armenian Apostolic Church competes not only with Sunday morning football but in a marketplace of churches where "church-shopping," the casual search for the "right" church, is common.[35] This had led to a general shortening of the liturgy, and in many parishes to a total neglect of the daily offices. While such worldwide comparison is beyond the scope of this chapter, I note not only this shortening in America, but also the fact that most parish churches in Armenia do not regularly celebrate the Morning Service on Sunday in order to demonstrate how thorough liturgical performance is in Istanbul.

So we find in Istanbul a sheer quantitative liturgical primacy both in terms of the number of services celebrated per week and also in the comprehensive nature of the service. More than this quantitative aspect, however, is the way in which liturgy is celebrated. Earlier, I alluded to the choir masters who teach their devoted students the modal system of Armenian hymns and the hundreds of variable daily hymns. While perhaps only a couple of choir masters are worthy of the term *hoca*, "teacher," there are close to a dozen choir masters who are fluent in the modal system and have mastery of a significant number of the *sharagans*.

Finally, there is a stress upon memorization which is unlike many other dioceses. After a month or so of serving, using a *Badarak* book small enough to be carried while doing *purvar*, the elaborate ritualistic censing during the liturgy, one of the older deacons approached me to let me know that it was about time I stopped using the book as a crutch. While there are certainly other monastic centers and older individuals throughout the world serving for many years who have learned the *Badarak* and other services by heart, I was surprised by the value given to memorization.

---

[35] Amy Sullivan, "Church-shopping: Why Americans Change Faiths," *TIME Magazine* (April 28, 2009), http://content.time.com/time/nation/article/0,8599,1894361,00.html.

Modern-Day Saints in Contemporary Istanbul

In Istanbul, there is not only commemoration of these "canonical" saints, but the ubiquity of liturgical commemoration also often recalls more recent figures, clergymen in particular. I want to ask about these more recent churchmen and laypeople and how remembering them relates to the more official saint veneration. Later in the same day we visited the cemetery, Deacon Allan presented the younger Deacon Vagharshag with a recently released history of the Western Diocese of the Armenian Church in America.[36] At the same time, Deacon Vagharshag was compiling a book which would record all of the clergy in Istanbul since the foundation of the Republic. The two archivists spent over an hour talking, turning the pages in the Western Diocese book slowly, discussing figures they both knew, since many of the priests who served in America, especially in the early twentieth century, had been born, educated, ordained, or had served previously in Istanbul.

There is clearly a connection between the veneration of the saints and the more contemporary remembrance of great Istanbul clergy. Given that canonicity is a product of liturgical innovation which has largely been closed since the sixteenth century, many people simply go on as if the saintly men and women of the previous five centuries really are officially saints. They may not have a designated day in the Church calendar,[37] but their individual piety or brave leadership has not stopped a popular veneration of them.[38] Perhaps

---

[36] *A History of the Western Diocese*, published in conjunction with the 80th anniversary of the diocese in 2008. See the History section of the Diocesan website, www.armenianchurchwd.com/diocese/history-of-the-western-diocese/, where a pdf of the book is available.

[37] See discussion above. As mentioned, due to the Patriarchal status of Istanbul and Jerusalem they both produce an Ōrats'oyts', the daily calendar calculated for a given year, which is separate from Etchmiadzin. In this way, there is the possibility of adding particular local saints to the calendar. While Istanbul has not really used this prerogative, there has been some innovation in the Jerusalem calendar. For instance, in Jerusalem, the seventeenth-century Patriarch Krikor, "The Chain Bearer," renowned for wearing chains until he collected enough money to pay off the Patriarchate's debts, is included among those who have their own saint's day.

[38] There was no official decision to stop designating saints through their inclusion in the Ōrats'oyts' or *Badarak* in the sixteenth century, but several factors may have played a role. The Armenian monasteries generally suffered a decline during this period, thus producing fewer "saints." This decline itself is understudied and deserves treatment. Another factor may have been the introduction of the printing press, which leads to both a standardization and calcification of texts. Whatever the reason, there have been almost no new officially designated saints (see previous footnote for exceptions). Interestingly, while writing this chapter, at the

most prominent among them is Mktrich Khrimian, the Patriarch of Istanbul in the late nineteenth century who later went on to become the Catholicos in Etchmiadzin, known affectionately as Khrimian *Hayrig* (a diminutive for Father). During the tumultuous years of the late nineteenth and early twentieth century, he championed the rights of Armenians and even led a delegation to the Treaty of Berlin in 1878 for that same purpose.[39]

While Deacon Vagharshag's forthcoming book is full of more mundane examples than this great Patriarch, it is in part the prominence of characters like Khrimian *Hayrig* and Malachia Ormanian which drives the remembrance of later saintly clergy. On the same day as our trip to the Şişli Cemetery, we walked by a house where the great composer Gomidas had lived, and on a visit to the Gentronagan School which he had attended, I lovingly stroked a piano he used to play. While Gomidas, like the two patriarchs, has not been liturgically canonized, his work and reputation secures him a place in the pantheon of saintly men in the Armenian imagination. That Gomidas, a figure more easily recognized than Ormanian, also has a connection to Istanbul, underlines the prominence of Istanbul which is also at play in the drive to remember all of those who have contributed to its greatness.

The ways in which these clergy, prominent or merely devoted, are remembered throughout the city varies from the personal to the monumental. At the very minimum, clergy are always included in the *Hokehankisd*, memorial services which often accompany *Badarak*. Yet on such a day when a priest's name is read in the context of the memorial service, they inevitably become the subject of conversation. Many times, such conversations are sparked spontaneously, but the *Hokehankisd* explicitly recalls certain people. For instance, at one of the churches I attend, the list of names of people for whom *Hokehankisd* would be offered was printed in one of the papers. In the morning, before *Badarak*, I sat with the priest and an older deacon in the priest's office. As he looked at the paper, he discussed his own time training with that priest. On this particular morning, thinking about this spawned a wide-ranging and nostalgic conversation between the two men with a common refrain I have heard in America as well: when so-and-so was alive, the churches were full of people, and he always did the

---

high-profile Synod of Bishops convened on September 24, 2013 in Etchmiadzin, the topic of the collective canonization of the victims of the Armenian genocide was discussed. See Asbarez, "Bishops' Synod Considers Canonization of Genocide Victims" (September 30, 2013), http://asbarez.com/114512/bishops-synod-considers-canonization-of-genocide-victims/.

[39] Mkrtich I Khrimian lived April 4, 1820–October 27, 1907. He served as Patriarch of Istanbul from 1869 to 1873 and as Catholicos of All Armenians from 1892 until his death.

complete service. "Before, people had all the verses of *Aravod Lusoh* ['Morning Light,' an acrostic hymn of the Night Service] memorized, now, they only know a few from memory," Der Hayr opined.

Similar conversations often occur after liturgy, when there is a meal which follows the service. Depending on the church the meal ranges from sandwiches for the altar servers to elaborate homecooked meals in the church courtyard (during summer months) for the whole congregation. Conversations will meander but any time there is a *Hokehankisd*, some of the discussion will center on the life of the person for whom prayers were offered. And while *Hokehankisd* for a prominent layman might elicit stories of someone as devoted father, good football player or excellent craftsman, there is a greater chance that everyone present will remember and have some memory of the clergy. Thus, like the exemplary lives of saints, reflection on the clergy invites an engaged encounter with present practice. This is one way in which commemoration of more recent clergy is reminiscent of the role of saint veneration.

The Importance of Remembrance

Venerating the saints and remembering recent spiritual leaders becomes, then, a multifaceted way of remembering Istanbul as a city with a vibrant Armenian presence, and extends to include the city itself as metonym for the former vibrant Armenian life in Anatolia, even if Istanbul has its own Armenian history disparate from that of Anatolia. It takes on the moral weight of preservation in the face of loss, while retaining many of the other important features of memory described earlier. While the Istanbul Armenians are not reducible to the Church, public figures in the twentieth century have often been ecclesial. As Bilal notes, and her emphasis on the consummately private practice of lullabies underscores, not only violence and pain, but mere existence is difficult to assert in public. Any figure who is by necessity in the public eye gains prominence in an otherwise quite sequestered Armenian community. This was underscored for me when I tried to get two older men at a small church I frequent on the Asian side of Istanbul to discuss prominent members of the Armenian community. "Since the Republic?" one asked. "Well, the main person since the Republic is Atatürk." "But from *our* community, the Armenian community," I pressed. After some discussion, it was in fact the names of the twentieth-century patriarchs that they supplied: Shnork Patriarch and the current Patriarch Mesrob Mutafyan. Thus, the clergy are most easily incorporated into the collective memory which not only provides exemplary moral individuals, but also, as detailed above, construct that very collective.

In a sense it is unremarkable that *Hokehankisd* service is offered for clergymen and forms a basis for remembrance. It is as common as are *Hokehankisd* services for regular Armenian men and women who have passed away. As one of my friends, Deacon Yeprem, states, "the type of every person's [work] is different: a builder—the work a builder does is different, the work Bishop Mutafyan [the current Patriarch of Istanbul] has completed is different, our responsibilities are different, for instance. Everyone does their own work. I can't construct a way of measuring great or small." Jokingly, he suggested, "maybe someone will say Yeprem" is great. Yet, when I asked about Shnork Patriarch, who had played such a central role in my own introduction to this topic, Deacon Yeprem was happy to agree that "certainly, he was a good Patriarch." At the very least, he fulfilled his role, one which allowed both of us to talk about him in the same way as we could talk about the current patriarch, and which, modesty aside, made talking about himself in the same way difficult. The exemplarity which forms the rationale for hagiographies since St. Athanasius wrote about St. Anthony is operative in the special place given to these priests. We can view Dn. Vagharshag's book as a contemporary *Haysamavurk*, and understand the *Hokehankisd* as a way to liturgically remember them. I would suggest, then, that the public nature and exemplarity is what sustains a unique commemoration for clergyman versus the average parishioner.

In a very public remembrance of the same Shnork Patriarch, we see clearly all of these factors of memory at work. On Monday, April 1, 2013, at the Balıklı Armenian Cemetery, a statue of Shnork Patriarch was unveiled. Melkon Karaköse, who was the former head of the Samatya Church Foundation and who was influential in the creation of the statue, mentioned in a short speech during the dedication that although Shnork Patriarch was buried in the Şişli Cemetery, he had been instrumental in the building of the beautiful, small chapel on the Balıklı Cemetery grounds, and so they decided to erect the statue there.[40] As Archbishop Aram Ateşyan, Patriarchal Vicar, asserted, this was really a momentous occasion. It was the first statue of its kind—free-standing and not attached to a headstone—to be erected. Although the large statues adorning the graves of Ormanian, and indeed, Shnork Patriarch himself at the Şişli cemetery, were not much smaller than this statue, it was a free-standing statue. In other words, the purpose was sheer remembrance of a great and beloved man. The

---

[40] Vartan Estukyan, "Şınorhk Patrik'in Büstü Balıklı'da açıldı," *AGOS*, April 5, 2013, p. 11.

archbishop underlined that the Turkish authorities had let this happen, which was rare. Thus, a very public assertion (even if still in the cloistered space of an Armenian cemetery) of the Armenian presence was allowed to be built. It is not incidental that this public presence recognized a clergyman, the most public Armenian figures of the twentieth century.

Archbishop Ateşyan's short sermon at the dedication utilized and emphasized all of the memorial tropes and functions we have discussed above. To the murmuring approval of the crowd, he noted how beloved the Patriarch was. That is to say, Shnork Patriarch serves as a figure which everyone can collectively remember, and in that memorial we were all tied into the Armenian community of Istanbul. Although I have no memories of him, I too was drawn in and included in this communal reassertion, as I drew on the stories the two deacons had told me and my memory of the earlier visit to the Şişli Cemetery. Asserting the beloved nature of the Patriarch and remembering his deeds, he is made into an exemplary figure, one who fulfills all three of the ethical models discussed above: he is the Aristotlean mean for individual ethical life, he is the saintly exemplar, and he was a public Armenian figure who insisted on the Armenian presence in Turkey.

Perhaps most interestingly, Archbishop Ateşyan's sermon drew on the wellspring of collective Armenian memory to locate both Shnork Patriarch and all of those present into the long line of exemplary Armenian figures. Tellingly, Archbishop Ateşyan described Shnork Patriarch as one of many great figures who were both *yegheghets'agan* (ecclesial, as opposed to say *gronagan*, "religious") and *azkagan* (national). He thus claimed the Patriarch's importance as a figure for the whole Armenian community, not just that of the Apostolic Church. Moreover, he placed him in a long line of both canonical and other later saints, beginning with St. Vartan Mamikonian and explicitly mentioning the Battle of Avarayr in 451. This battle, seen as the iconic defense of the Armenian nation and the fledgling Armenian Church, is one of the most widespread events in collective Armenian memory. By invoking it in his description of Shnork Patriarch, he not only places the Patriarch in illustrious company, but also recreates the collective exactly through that invocation. There are perhaps only a few other events more widely known than *Vartanatz*, and invoking it helps the audience to understand the importance of Shnork Patriarch while simultaneously reasserting the collective memory which binds the Armenians of Istanbul together.

Archbishop Ateşyan then continued: "In the nineteenth century we had Khrimian Hayrig, Patriarch Tourian, Patriarch Malachia Ormanian, and in the twentieth century we had Shnork Patriarch." All of these figures are clergy, but they are not canonized like Vartan Mamikonian is. Nontheless, according to

Archbishop Ateşyan, they share the characteristic of being both ecclesial and national heroes, exemplary figures in the history of both Church and nation. Shnork Patriarch falls in this illustrious line of heros, and those gathered in the cemetery on April 1 are swept up into the community which remembers these figures together.

Final Discussion: Hrant Dink and the Contours of Community beyond Religious/Secular Divide

In order to see how the practices of saint veneration also influence how people outside of the Church hierarchy are commemorated, I turn to the funeral of Hrant Dink, the founder of the weekly Turkish/Armenian newspaper *AGOS*, assassinated in 2007. Through the funeral, we will see how the memorial services of the Armenian Apostolic Church we have traced throughout were taken up and used in a different context. We will see how the use of the service for somebody who was a non-clergyman exceeded the physical boundaries of the Church and served to delimit a community.

I do not want simply to suggest that ways of honoring important, influential Armenians in Istanbul are somehow a "secularized" version of saint veneration. Even if we found the evidence to suggest something this straightforward (I, certainly, have not found such evidence), Talal Asad suggests that "we should focus on the differential results rather than on the corresponding forms in the process referred to as 'secularization.'"[41] Using Hrant Dink's funeral as a case in point, we see here not only "corresponding forms," but actually the same practice of the memorial service of the Armenian Apostolic Church. Yet this same practice, as we will see, clearly has differential results—that is, it does different things and is put to different work—while at the same time, it remains a Christian funeral and memorial service for the dead.

The reaction to Hrant Dink's assassination was remarkable in itself. Marching from the office in Osmanbey several miles to the St. Mary Cathedral across from the Armenian Patriarchate in Kumkapı, those present, the large majority of whom were not Armenian, chanted "We are all Hrant, We are all Armenian!" The funeral, which liturgically uses many of the same prayers and hymns as the *Hokehankisd*, was then performed at the church. While this is a use of the practice of *Hokehankisd* entirely in line with the Armenian Apostolic

---

[41] Tala Asad, *Formations of the Secular: Islam, Christianity, Modernity* (Stanford, 2003), pp. 189–90.

tradition, the impromptu demonstration around the funeral exceeded that context. To simply insist that it is the same practice which has been secularized by its placement in an explicitly "political" setting is to focus merely on its form. Rather, we should see the complex ways in which there was an affective response of empathy on the part of the large number of non-Armenians who made their way to the funeral, or that a figure who was not always the most enthusiastic supporter of the Patriarchate was laid to rest according to a practice which locates him inside one of the most important Armenian institutions in Istanbul, or even the way in which some Armenians who rarely go to the church were emotionally affected by the funeral service.

Dink himself had a complex relationship to the Armenian Apostolic Church. After an initial education at an Armenian Protestant orphanage and camp, he studied at the Surp Haç Tıbrevank School in Üsküdar. Dink, like others, was greatly influenced by Shnork Patriarch, who served and taught at Tıbrevank while Dink was a student there. In both *Bu Köşedeki Adam* and an article rerun in *AGOS* after the dedication of Shnork Patriarch's statue, there is a picture of young Dink serving at Surp Haç with the late Patriarch. In the article, originally printed on March 7, 2003, Dink calls Shnork Patriarch "My Father," and discusses his respect for the man who was influential during his youth.[42] Despite frequent criticism of the Patriarchate as an institution and its sway over Armenian life in Istanbul, as in the "civilization" articles discussed above, Dink continued to recognize the importance of the Apostolic Church in his own life.

Dink's relationship to Shnork Patriarch emphasizes that even those Armenians who do not attend liturgy on a weekly (or near-daily) basis, also have some connection to the practices of memory which are central to the Armenian community. By looking at his relationship to these important figures and the ways in which they are memorialized, we can discern Dink's own relationship to the Armenian community, and indeed what his ideas about such a community were. The section heading in *Bu Köşedeki Adam* where the three articles about "civilization" are reprinted is telling in this case: "Cemaat mı, Toplum mu?" That is, are Armenians in Istanbul are a *cemaat*, the Turkish word derived from the Arabic for a group of believers, or the more contemporary Turkish *toplum*, which can also be translated as community?

Many Armenians related to the liturgical form of commemoration operative during Dink's funeral, including many who were not usual participants in such a liturgy. Whether they did so solely for "political" and therefore "secular" reasons

---

[42]   *AGOS*, "Hrant Dink: Sayın ki o benim babam," reprinted in *AGOS* 885, p. 11.

seems to me beside the point. The "differential results" Asad alludes to allows for the possibility that not all the Armenians present at the funeral knew the words to every hymn and prayer, but it would be disingenuous to suggest that the funeral thereby became a "political rally." Moreover, the assertion of thousands of non-Armenians, "We are all Hrant, we are all Armenian," can be seen in a similar light. Clearly not Armenian in any recognizable way, they fleetingly claimed solidarity or participation in the Armenian community—and they did so through participation in an Armenian Christian practice of memorialization.

For me, it is more important to see the heuristic value in the ways different people have related to a "religious" practice, rather than suggesting that Dink's funeral was a "secular" event or a "secular" use of a "religious" practice. Rather, we can discern people's relationship to a community which has been largely defined through its ecclesial hierarchy at a time when many self-ascribing Armenians are not practicing Armenian Apostolic Christians. Are all Armenians involved in memorials of exemplary saints and clergymen? Of course not. Just as the figure of Shnork Patriarch would be known but not upheld in the same way by an Armenian Catholic, many of the Armenians present at Dink's funeral would have seen a funeral service but not been able to sing along with some of the hymns. Once we recognize that the boundaries of community will always be "fuzzy," then practices such as saint veneration become a heuristic device to explore the contours of that amorphous community. The necessary work, then, is identifying and exploring the shifting boundaries of community rather than policing strict borders. Other than the explicitly legal forms of recognition like the Turkish identity card, collective memories and the practices associated with them are the clearest ways to see the limits of a community.

References

AGOS, "Ateşyan: '100 bin gizli Ermeni var,'" May 2, 2013.
AGOS, "Hrant Dink: Sayın ki o benim babam," March 7, 2003, reprinted April 5, 2013.
Artinian, Vartan, *The Armenian Constitutional System in the Ottoman Empire 1839–1863: A Study of its Historical Development* (Istanbul, 1988).
Asad, Talal, *Formations of the Secular: Islam, Christianity, Modernity* (Stanford: Stanford University Press, 2003).
Asbarez, "Bishops' Synod Considers Canonization of Genocide Victims," (September 30, 2013), http://asbarez.com/114512/bishops-synod-considers-canonization-of-genocide-victims/, accessed October 25, 2013.

Balancar, Ferda, *The Sounds of Silence II: Diyarbakır's Armenians Speak* (Istanbul: Hrant Dink Foundation Press, 2013).
Bauman, Zygmunt, *Community: Seeking Safety in an Insecure World* (Cambridge: Polity Press, 2001).
Ben-Ami, Issachar, *Saint Veneration Among the Jews of Morocco* (Detroit: Wayne State University Press, 1998).
Bilal, Melissa, "The Lost Lullaby and Other Stories About Being Armenian in Turkey," *New Perspectives on Turkey* 34 (2008): 67–92.
Braude, Benjamin, "Foundation Myths of the *Millet* System," in Benjamin Braude and Bernard Lewis (eds), *Christians and Jews in the Ottoman Empire* (New York and London: Holmes and Meier Publishers, Inc., 1982), 69–88.
Carruthers, Mary, *The Book of Memory: A Study in Medieval Culture*, 2nd edn (Cambridge: Cambridge University Press, 1990 and 2008).
Dink, Hrant, *Bu Köşedeki Adam* [The Man on This Column] (Second Printing, Istanbul: Hrant Dink Foundation Press, 2009).
Estukyan, Vartan, "Şınorhk Patrik'in Büstü Balıklı'da açıldı," *AGOS* (April 5, 2013), 885.
Findikyan, Michael Daniel (ed.), *Divine Liturgy of the Armenian Church with Modern Armenian and English Translations, Transliteration, Musical Notation, Introduction and Notes* (New York: St. Vartan Press, 1999).
Findikyan, Michael Daniel, "An Introduction to Liturgy and Worship in the Armenian Church" (n.d.).
Findikyan, Michael Daniel, "Liturgical Usages and Controversy in History: How Much Diversity Can Unity Tolerate?" *St. Nersess Theological Review* 1, no. 2 (1996): 191–212.
Findikyan, Michael Daniel, "The 'Unfailing Word' in Eastern Sacramental Prayers," in Maxwell Johnson and L. Edward Phillips (eds), *Studia Liturgica Diversa: Essays in Honor of Paul F. Bradshaw* (Portland: The Pastoral Press, 2004), 179–89.
Heyes, Cressida, "Identity Politics," *The Stanford Encyclopedia of Philosophy*, ed. Edward N. Zalta (spring 2012 edition), http://plato.stanford.edu/archives/spr2012/entries/identity-politics/, accessed September 15, 2013.
Hoffman, Tessa, *Armenians in Turkey Today: A Critical Assessment of the Situation of the Armenian Minority in the Turkish Republic* (Brussels: The EU Office of Armenian Associations of Europe, 2002).
Hoogasian Villa, Susie and Mary Kilbourne Matossian, *Armenian Village Life Before 1914* (Detroit: Wayne State University Press, 1982).
Hurriyet Daily News, "Minority Communities Ready for Civilianization," August 29, 2011, www.hurriyetdailynews.com/minority-communities-ready

-for-civilianization.aspx?pageID=438&n=minority-communities-ready-for-civilianization-2011-08-29, accessed October 25, 2013.

Istanbul Armenian Patriarchate, *Yegeghets'agan Ōrats'oyts'* (Istanbul: Armenian Patriarchate of Istanbul, 2013).

Melkonyan, Ruben, *Aknark Stambouli Hay Hamaynki Patmoutyan* [Review of History of the Armenian Community in Istanbul (1920–till present day)] (Yerevan: VMV Press, 2010).

Ormanian, Malachia, *Azkabadum*, 3 vols (Jerusalem: Armenian Patriarchate of Jerusalem, 1913–27).

Polatel, Mehmet, Nora Mıldanoğlu, Özgür Leman Eren and Mehmet Atılgan, *2012 Beyannamesi: İstanbul Ermeni Vakıflarının El Konan Mülkleri* [2012 Declaration: The Seized Properties of Armenian Foundations in Istanbul] (Istanbul: Hrant Dink Foundation Press, 2012).

Sullivan, Amy, "Church-shopping: Why Americans Change Faiths," *TIME Magazine*, April 28, 2009, http://content.time.com/time/nation/article/0,8599,1894361,00.html, accessed October 25, 2013.

Western Diocese of the Armenian Church of America, *A History of the Western Diocese* (Glendale, 2008), www.armenianchurchwd.com/diocese/history-of-the-western-diocese/, accessed June 20, 2014.

Chapter 8
The Three Religions of Armenians in Lebanon

Irina Papkova

This chapter examines the religious situation of that part of the Armenian diaspora that presently resides in Lebanon. The Levant, traditionally a refuge for persecuted religious groups, has proved a safe haven for all three Armenian denominations—the Apostolic, the Catholic and the Evangelical. At its height, Lebanon's Armenian community exhibited a religious diversity unmatched anywhere else among Armenians, with the percentage of non-Apostolic faithful reaching as high as 20 percent in some regions of the country in the mid-1970s.[1] Today, Lebanon remains home to the second Apostolic See (of Cilicia), and the center of the global Armenian Catholic Church. The Union of Armenian Evangelical Churches of the Near East, one of the five Unions of the Armenian Evangelical Church, is also based in Beirut, contributing to the importance of Lebanon as a center of Armenian religion in the diaspora.

"Religion" has many definitions, with the distinction between religion understood as faith per se or as organized institution being the most obvious.[2] This chapter privileges the institutional aspect of the question. Among other things, there have been no previous studies focused specifically on the religion of Lebanese Armenians. As a result, the subject remains a virtual *terra incognita*, requiring the most basic mapping of the empirical situation. Accordingly, I trace the historical development of the "Armenian religions'" presence in Lebanon, in the process identifying the percentages of Lebanese citizens who belong to each of the three denominations, and describing the spatial location of their churches and affiliated institutions.

---

[1] Nikola Schahgaldian, *The Political Integration of an Immigrant Community into a Composite Society: The Armenians in Lebanon, 1920–1974*, PhD Diss. (New York, Columbia University, 1979), pp. 74–5.

[2] Clifford Geertz, *The Interpretation of Cultures: Selected Essays* (Waukegan, 1993), pp. 87–125; Paul Tillich, *Theology of Culture* (Oxford, 1959), p. 8.

The research conducted for this chapter was qualitative in nature, involving a close reading of the available scattered secondary historical sources and analysis by other scholars in English, French and Russian.[3] Several scholarly volumes are available on the general topic of "Armenians in Lebanon," most notably Nicola Migliorino's *(Re)constructing Armenia in Lebanon and Syria*; and *Armenians of Lebanon*, a collection of edited conference papers published by Haigazian University in Beirut.[4] Both volumes reference as self-evident the role of religion, particularly of the Armenian Apostolic Church, in the continuing survival of the community, but focus primarily on political and cultural (in the non-religious sense) aspects of Armenian Lebanese life. Relevant journal articles also treat religion as a present, stable and secondary factor, if they mention it at all.[5]

Two other literatures consulted for this chapter proved more fruitful. The first is a number of historical monographs and anthologies published under the auspices of the three Armenian denominations themselves.[6] These were particularly useful in providing data regarding the history and locations of churches and associated institutions. The second literature is a series of unpublished graduate dissertations on topics relating to Armenians in Lebanon. In discrete chapters supportive of their overall arguments, they provide substantial demographic and historical data unavailable elsewhere.

Besides a close reading of written sources, this chapter is based on a series of semi-structured interviews conducted in Beirut and its environs over the course of the spring and summer of 2013. I interviewed representatives of both clergy and laity across all three denominations, for a total of 28 conversations in English, French and Russian.

---

[3] Due to the author's linguistic limitations, this chapter ignores any available written material in Armenian, Arabic and Farsi.

[4] Nicola Migliorino, *(Re)constructing Armenia in Lebanon and Syria: Ethno-Cultural Diversity and the State in the Aftermath of a Refugee Crisis* (New York, 2007); Aida Boudjikanian (ed.), *Armenians of Lebanon: From Past Princesses and Refugees to Present-Day Community* (Beirut, 2009).

[5] For example, S.S. Kazarian and M.D. Boyadjian, "Validation of the Multigroup Ethnic Identity Measure Among Ethnic Armenian Adolescents in Lebanon," *Identity: An International Journal of Theory and Research* 8, no. 4 (2008), pp. 335–47; Ohannes Geukjian, "The Policy of Positive Neutrality of the Armenian Political Parties in Lebanon during the Civil War 1975-1990: A Critical Analysis," *Middle Eastern Studies* 43, no. 1 (2007), pp. 65–73.

[6] Several of these publications were not available anywhere outside Lebanon; some were obtained from representatives of the three denominations during the course of interviews in the spring and summer of 2013.

Background

The majority of Armenians are concentrated in central Lebanon, most significantly in the Matn District immediately to the north of Beirut. The municipality of Bourj Hammoud is the center of the community's economic and political activity. From Bourj Hammoud, the Armenian population spills over into the neighboring boroughs of Dora, Fanar, Raouda, Jdeide, Zalka, Jal El Dib, Antelias, Mzher, Naccash, Dbayeh and Awkar. Moving northeast into the Lebanese mountains, Armenians can be found throughout the region linking Antelias to Bikfaya. Considerable concentrations of Armenians are also located in Beirut itself, particularly in the neighborhoods of Greater Achrafiye and Hamra. In Northern Lebanon, there are Armenian populations dispersed between Jounieh, Jbeil and Tripoli. In the east, Armenians have a significant presence in the towns of Zahle and Anjar in the Beqaa Valley.[7]

The presence of a large Armenian population in Lebanon is a relatively recent development. Part of the Medieval Armenian Kingdom of Cilicia occupied portions of present-day Lebanese territory from the twelfth to fourteenth centuries.[8] However, after the collapse of the Cilicians, Armenian presence was minimal until the arrival of Catholic refugees from Constantinople in the eighteenth and early nineteenth centuries. By the 1850s, there were perhaps several thousand Armenians in Lebanon.[9] In the last quarter of the century, Armenians of all denominations from Central and Southern Anatolia began migrating toward the relative safety of Lebanon, fleeing increasing persecution from the Ottomans. The greatest wave of refugees arrived in the early 1920s, in the wake of the genocide.[10] After Lebanese independence in 1946, the Armenian community continued to grow, as economic opportunities combined with a political system that fostered the recovery of social capital lost during the genocide. At its height, just before the Lebanese civil war of 1975–90, the population of Armenians stood at approximately 250,000.[11]

---

[7] Armineh Johannes, "Attached to the Land: Anjar Recalls its Roots and Fights to Retain Them," *Armenian International Magazine* 13, no. 5 (2002), p. 22.
[8] Migliorino, *(Re)constructing*, p. 10.
[9] Schahgaldian, *Political Integration*, p. 51.
[10] Tsolin Nalbantian, *Fashioning Armenians in Lebanon, 1946–1958*, PhD Diss. (New York, Columbia University, 2011), p. 34.
[11] Schahgaldian approximates "well over 250,000." *Political Integration*, p. 55. Bedoyan provides a lower estimate, of 200,000. Hratch Bedoyan, *Armenian Political Parties in Lebanon*, MA Thesis (Beirut, American University of Beirut, 1973), p. 69.

The exact number of Armenians currently in Lebanon is a matter of dispute. Due to concerns about sectarian strife, there has been no census conducted in the country since 1932. During the civil war, the community's political leaders (of all three denominations) pursued a well-defined policy of neutrality, professing adherence to Lebanon's legitimate government and refusing to lend military support to any of the warring militias. The strategy aimed at protecting the Armenian enclaves, and was generally respected by all sides in the war. Still, the economic and physical destruction of the civil war resulted in a sizeable outmigration of Armenians, which has continued in the post-war period, if at a lesser rate. In the interviews I conducted for this chapter, I encountered estimates as low as 20,000 and as high as 150,000 Armenians still in Lebanon. Broadly speaking, the figure of "100,000 Lebanese Armenians" emerged as a sort of mantra repeated by most of my respondents.[12] Of this population, approximately 93 percent is Armenian Apostolic, 5 percent Armenian Catholic and 2 percent Armenian Evangelical.[13]

Previously, I described the Lebanese Armenians as "belonging" to three specific denominations, a turn of phrase conditioned by the unique Lebanese political context. There are certainly atheists among the Armenians of Lebanon,

---

[12] For example, Antranik Dakessian, director of Haigazian University's Armenian Diaspora Research Center, puts the figure at between 20,000 and 100,000, telling me that "it's not just that we don't want to know—we really don't know," given the scattered nature of the Armenian population across Lebanon. Zaven Messerlian, a historian and long-time principal of the Armenian Evangelical College in Kantari/Beirut, estimates "plus or minus" 100,000. The figure of "100,000" came up repeatedly in most of the interviews I conducted.

[13] Earlier in the twentieth century, the combined proportion of Catholic and Evangelical Armenians in Lebanon was significantly higher—much of the literature available for the pre-civil war period mentions a breakdown of 85 percent to 15 percent. In my interview with the Prelate of the Armenian Apostolic Church, Archbishop Kegham Khatcherian, he quoted the same distribution as reflecting the present situation. My conclusion, however, is that presently either the figure of actual Armenians in Lebanon is far lower than 100,000, or that the proportion of Catholics and Evangelicals has dropped precipitously since the civil war. I arrived at this conclusion after my interviewees consistently put the number of Catholic Armenians at 5,000 and Protestants at 2,000. If this is the case, and if we assume a stable figure of 100,000 for the overall population, then the proportion becomes 93 percent to 7 percent in favor of the Apostolic Armenians. Even then, ascertaining exact numbers is difficult; for example, in an interview with *Armenian International Magazine* in 2000, Reverend Mgrdych Karagoezian, President of the Union of Armenian Evangelical Churches of the Near East, placed the number of Evangelicals in Lebanon at "between 5,000–6,000." When I interviewed him, he cited a number closer to 3,000. "Coping With the Effects of the War: The Armenian Evangelical Union of the Near East," *Armenian International Magazine* 11, no. 1 (2000), p. 50.

or those who might adhere to other confessions (there are discrete numbers of Muslim or Greek Orthodox Armenians, for example). However, the Lebanese political system is set up in such a way that religion inevitably becomes an immutable individual characteristic.

The law of the Republic of Lebanon recognizes 18 "sectarian groups," and grants them legal prerogatives in regulating internal communal affairs. Religious authorities handle all matters of personal status, such as marriage, divorce and inheritance. Sectarian designation regulates many aspects of personal and public life, regardless of one's actual beliefs or lack thereof. In the case of the Armenians, the "internal affairs" of the community are channeled through three institutions—the Armenian Apostolic (Orthodox) and Catholic churches, and a generic Lebanese Protestant representation in the case of the Evangelicals.

In accordance with the Taef Agreement that ended the civil war in 1990, the Lebanese parliament consists of 128 seats, evenly distributed between Christians and Muslims. Within the quota set aside for Christians, the Armenian community has six fixed seats, five representing the Armenian Apostolics, and one representing the Catholics. In theory, an Armenian Evangelical can hold one or two additional seats, one broadly representing the Lebanese Protestants, and one reserved for the country's minority Christian denominations.[14]

This would suggest that in Lebanon, political differences between the Armenians should be channeled through their religious affiliations, and that the divisions between the three communities should be highly politicized in addition to any theological divergences. The more so that this is precisely the way in which politics are generally conducted among the other Lebanese sects. The final section of this chapter briefly discusses the extent to which reality meets with expectations in this case.

The Armenian Apostolic (Orthodox) Church in Lebanon[15]

The Lebanese municipality of Antelias houses the seat of the Catholicosate of the Great House of Cilicia, one of four—sometimes competing and sometimes complementary—Armenian Apostolic Sees. Headed since 1995 by Catholicos

---

[14] A. Alexandrian, "New Alliances Fresh Possibilities: The Dawn of a New Era for the Armenian Community of Lebanon," *Armenian International Magazine* 11, no. 10 (2000), p. 45.

[15] In local parlance, the Armenian Apostolic Church in Lebanon is referred to as the Armenian Orthodox Church. For this reason, this section and the rest of this chapter use the term "Orthodox" interchangeably with "Apostolic," even though it is technically incorrect.

Aram I (Keshishian), Antelias is widely seen as the most important spiritual center of the Armenian diaspora outside of Russia and the CIS, a factor that augments its symbolic importance to Lebanese Armenians. At the same time, a local diocese known as the Armenian Orthodox Prelacy (subordinated to the Catholicosate) administers the affairs of the community living in Lebanon proper. As both the Prelacy and the Catholicosate play visible roles in the lives of Armenian Orthodox, I devote attention to both institutions while providing an overall historical context to the contemporary situation.[16]

Prior to the collapse of the Ottomans, the Armenian Orthodox population actually residing permanently in Lebanon was negligible. According to a 1913 census, the Apostolic Armenians of Mount Lebanon numbered 67 individuals, with perhaps 100 families residing in Beirut itself.[17] Before the twentieth century, the literature does not refer to any significant construction of churches other than a monastery dedicated to the Holy Cross built in 1851.[18] In 1914, the monastery was confiscated and later destroyed by the Ottomans, together with other communal properties belonging to the minuscule community.[19]

As Armenian Orthodox began arriving en masse to Lebanon in the early 1920s, they found only two existing churches to minister to their spiritual needs, both located in Beirut. The first was the church of St. Nishan, originally built as a pilgrims' chapel in the mid-nineteenth century and administered by the Armenian patriarchate of Jerusalem. The other was the Church of the Holy Cross, under the jurisdiction of the Catholicosate.[20] Reflecting the chaos of the refugee situation, both the Jerusalem patriarchate and the Catholicosate claimed supreme authority in the internal affairs of the constantly swelling community of Armenian Orthodox.[21] Jerusalem ceded jurisdiction only in 1929, by which point Catholicos Sahag II had permanently relocated to Lebanon, establishing the See's headquarters at a complex in Antelias.

In 1931, the Catholicos sponsored a representative assembly of Armenians living in Lebanon, which endorsed the 1863 Armenian National Constitution [*Hay azkayin sahmanatroutioun*] (originally granted to the Armenian Apostolic

---

[16] For complicated relationships between the Catholicosates of Etchmiadzin and Antelias, see Chapter 6 in this volume. In what follows I will be focusing on the specifically Lebanese aspects of its jurisdiction.

[17] Zaven Messerlian, *Armenian Representation in the Lebanese Parliament*, MA Thesis (Beirut, American University of Beirut, 1963), p. 4.

[18] Bernadette Harboyan, *The Political Integration of the Armenian Community in Lebanon*, MA Thesis (Beirut, American University of Beirut, 1998), p. 5.

[19] Harboyan, *The Political Integration of the Armenian Community in Lebanon*.

[20] Nalbantian, *Fashioning*, p. 6.

[21] Messerlian, *Armenian Representation*, p. 11.

millet by the Ottomans) as the basis for Orthodox self-governance.[22] Since then, the constitution has regulated the life of Armenian Orthodox living in Lebanon, with periodic modifications to reflect evolving realities.[23] The emphasis of the constitution on regular elections and lay participation in the governance of the Armenian Apostolic Church has served to consolidate the stakes of the lay constituency in the institution's long-term survival as a symbol of Armenian nationality.[24]

The Catholicosate's complex in Antelias includes a cathedral dedicated to St. Gregory the Illuminator (built in 1939), the Catholicos' residence, a memorial chapel dedicated to the victims of the genocide, a library containing rare Armenian manuscripts, and a museum (inaugurated in 1998).[25] In addition to the compound at Antelias, the Catholicosate established a secondary headquarters in the mountain town of Bikfaya in 1952. The monastic property in Bikfaya houses a church dedicated to the Assumption of the Mother of God, as well as the Catholicos' summer residence and a theological seminary.[26]

The administrative offices of the Antelias Catholicosate primarily concern themselves with coordinating the various diaspora dioceses under the jurisdiction of the Great House of Cilicia, with providing priests for parishes worldwide through the Bikfaya seminary, and with activities on the ecumenical front.[27] At the same time, while leaving the internal governance of the Armenian Orthodox to the Lebanese Prelacy, the Catholicosate does play an important symbolic role in the life of the local community. First and foremost this includes commemorations related to the genocide, of which the most important is held at Antelias every year on April 24 and draws thousands of pilgrims from all over Lebanon.[28] The Catholicosate also oversees two major pilgrimages every year. The first is once more to Antelias, on the occasion of the feast of St. Gregory the

---

[22] Arpi Hamalian, *Lebanese-Armenians: A Study of Generational Differences in Assimilation*, MA Thesis (Beirut, American University of Beirut, 1973), p. 55.

[23] Hamalian, *Lebanese-Armenians*, p. 56.

[24] Interview with Archbishop Nareg Alemezian.

[25] Amine Jules Iskandar, *La Nouvelle Cilicie: Les Armeniens du Liban* (Antelias, Catholicosate of Cilicia, 1999), p. 115.

[26] Messerlian, *Armenian Representation*, p. 18; Iskandar, *La Nouvelle Cilicie*, p. 106.

[27] Felix Corley, "UN of Christianity at 50: The World Council of Churches is being Pulled in Different Directions; Aram I Struggles to Keep the Organization Together," *Armenian International Magazine* 9, no. 11 (1998), p. 46.

[28] Iskandar, *La Nouvelle Cilicie*, p. 109; interview with Archbishop Nareg Alemezian.

Illuminator as the Antelias cathedral houses the relic of the saint's right hand.[29] The second is to the monastery at Bikfaya, on the feast of the Assumption.[30]

The Catholicosate has also played a role within the Lebanese Armenian Orthodox community in more material ways. For example, since 1970, the Catholicosate has superintended an orphanage for Armenian children in Jbeil, known as the "The Bird's Nest."[31] Furthermore, in 1992 the Catholicosate launched a major construction project in an ultimately successful effort to reconstruct Armenian Orthodox churches that had been damaged in the course of the civil war.[32]

For all that, the administration of the specifically Lebanese Armenian Orthodox population is left entirely to the Prelacy.[33] The seat of the presiding prelate and the Prelacy's central offices are located at the church of St. Nishan. During the civil war, downtown Beirut was the center of major fighting, making the continuation of the Prelacy's activities impossible; as a result, the Prelacy temporarily relocated to new premises in Bourj Hammoud. Since the end of the war, the complex in Bourj Hammoud continues to house the Prelacy's secondary offices.[34]

Every four years, an electorate composed of Armenian Orthodox over the age of 18 who have paid their parish dues elects a 42-member national council for the Lebanese diocese.[35] Each parish elects a certain number of delegates, between one and nine, depending on the demographic weight of the parish in relation to the others. The council is composed of 36 laymen, and six clergymen. While the clergy presides at all meetings, the lay council members make the actual decisions. These representatives in turn elect the

---

[29] Interview with Archbishop Nareg Alemezian.

[30] Interview with Archbishop Nareg Alemezian.

[31] The "Birds' Nest" was founded by a Danish missionary in the 1920s, but was transferred to the Catholicosate's auspices in 1970. "Providing a Brighter Future: The Armenian Evangelical School in Anjar," *Armenian International Magazine* 11, no. 1 (2000), p. 48. Seta Khedeshian, "The Diakonia of the Armenian Church," in Seta Dadoyan (ed.), *The Contribution of the Armenian Church to the Christian Witness in the Middle East* (Antelias, the Armenian Catholicosate of Cilicia, 2001), p. 176.

[32] Iskandar, *La Nouvelle Cilicie*, p. 114.

[33] Messerlian, *Armenian Representation*, p. 19; Interview with Archbishop Nareg. Initially, the affairs of the Lebanese Armenian Orthodox community were managed by a vicar of the Catholicos. The Lebanese Prelacy was established in 1952. Interview with Archbishop Kegham Khatcharian.

[34] Interview with Archbishop Kegham Khatcharian.

[35] The elections are partial, with one-third of the delegates renewed every four years. Interview with Zaven Messerlian.

prelate, presently Archbishop Kegham (Khatcharian). The prelate is usually a bishop, but in principle can be a high-ranking priest.[36]

During the course of the year, the prelate and council meet twice, to elect smaller councils for the day-to-day administration of the Prelacy's affairs. These committees, divided between religious, educational, economic and civil responsibilities, have constant meetings throughout the year. The spiritual council is composed solely of priests, whereas the other councils consist entirely of parishioners.[37] The pattern is replicated on the parish level, where parishioners attached to each church in Lebanon elect a parish council every four years.[38]

While ultimately responsible in a spiritual sense to the Catholicosate, the Prelacy is also the official representative of the Orthodox Armenians in Lebanon to the government.[39] As such, the Prelacy is in charge of the channeling of affairs relating to personal status, through a lower level and appeals courts. These courts are staffed by some priests as well as by psychologists, nurses and other lay Armenian Orthodox.[40]

In addition to the St. Gregory the Illuminator cathedral in Antelias, St. Nishan and the church of the monastery in Bikfaya, there are presently 14 other functioning Armenian Orthodox churches in Lebanon, of which two are chapels (one in Fanar and one in Raouda). Most of the churches are located in and around Beirut, with a heavy concentration of parishes in Bourj Hammoud. There are also individual parishes in Jounieh, Zahle, Anjar and Tripoli.[41]

Prior to 1975, the Prelacy ran a network of 23 elementary and secondary schools throughout the country.[42] Currently, the Prelacy is responsible for 11 schools, as outmigration due to continuing political instability forced the closure of some schools and parishes.[43] Most parishes continue to run regular Sunday schools and catechism sessions.[44]

As with any aspect of the demographic situation of the Armenian community in Lebanon, the question of church attendance is somewhat elusive. On the one hand, my interviews revealed what seems to be the official view that

---

[36] Interview with Zaven Messerlian.
[37] Interview with Zaven Messerlian.
[38] Interview with Zaven Messerlian.
[39] Interview with Archbishop Kegham Khatcharian.
[40] Interview with Archbishop Kegham Khatcharian.
[41] Interview with Archbishop Kegham Khatcharian. See also Iskandar, *La Nouvelle Cilicie*, pp. 122–3 for high quality illustrations of Armenian Orthodox Churches in Lebanon.
[42] Messerlian, *Armenian Representation*, p. 18.
[43] Interview with Archbishop Kegham Khatcharian.
[44] Interview with the rector of St. Nishan (Father Mgrdych); interview with Zaven Messerlian.

churches—particularly in Bourj Hammoud—are full every Sunday, and that the attendance is spread fairly evenly among most age groups.[45] Other interviews and participant observation suggest that the demographic decline of the Armenian community in Lebanon has had a tangible negative effect on church attendance levels, and that there is a visible lack of youth presence in particular.[46] The overall impression is that attendance is relatively high in the parishes of Bourj Hammoud and Anjar, reflecting the high concentration of Armenians in those areas; other parishes in areas of Beirut where Armenian outmigration has been most significant are clearly on the decline. Another factor limiting attendance is language—the services are conducted entirely in Armenian, guaranteeing that in-conversion from other segments of Lebanese society is extremely rare.[47]

Still, the level of church attendance does not in itself serve as the most accurate indicator of the strength of the attachment of the Armenian Orthodox community to their Church in Lebanon. Parishes keep detailed lists of families attached to particular churches, and priests visit their parishioners at regular intervals throughout the year, most specifically to bless houses during the Christmas and Easter seasons.[48] Moreover, attendance tends to spike on days when memorial services are added on to the regular Sunday service.[49] Other Lebanon-wide celebrations also annually bring together thousands of Armenian Orthodox, for example a pilgrimage to a shrine in Anjar on the September feast of the Holy Cross, and a week of prayer and meditation dedicated to St. Ripsime at a Bourj Hammoud church that houses her relics.[50]

Chapter 6 in this volume explores the complicated relationship between the Apostolic Sees of Etchmiadzin and Cilicia. On the specifically Lebanese level, the interviews I conducted suggest that while Orthodox attitudes toward the Armenian Republic are positive and supportive, there is a certain degree of alienation based not on religious but cultural differences. These stem from the historical differentiation between Western and Eastern Armenians, bolstered

---

[45] Interview with Zaven Messerlian. Archbishop Kegham also told me that the average Armenian Orthodox church in Lebanon accommodates 150–200 people. Assuming that all the AOC churches in Lebanon are full every Sunday, this would suggest attendance levels of approximately 2,500 Armenians across the country, still a small portion of the overall population (which in turn suggests that either the majority does not go to church regularly or that the number of churches is inadequate to serve demand).

[46] Interview with Father Mgrdych, rector of St. Nishan, and participant observation of a service at St. Nishan in spring 2013; interview with Antranig Dakessian.

[47] Interview with Father Mgrdych.

[48] Group interview with St. Nishan parishioners; interview with Antranig Dakessian.

[49] Interview with Father Mgrdych; interview with Archbishop Nareg Alemezian.

[50] Interview with Archbishop Nareg Alemezian.

by differences in dialect. In other words, Armenian Orthodox in Lebanon might have more in common with Armenian Orthodox in Teheran than in Yerevan. Still, this does not affect exchanges between the two communities, with priests, seminarians and lay Lebanese Armenian Orthodox frequently visiting Etchmiadzin and vice versa.[51]

Finally, a few words should be said about local traditions of Armenian Orthodox piety that are influenced by specifically Lebanese conditions. Traditionally, the Armenian Orthodox Church (whether under the jurisdiction of Cilicia or Etchmiadzin) does not encourage frequent communion, reserving the sacrament for major feast days. Up until the 1970s, this appears to have been the custom in Lebanon as well. However, under the influence of Arab Christian tradition (most likely Maronite and Greek Orthodox), frequent communion has become common practice.[52] Furthermore, possibly for the same reason, the Armenian Orthodox Prelacy does not permit weddings to be held during the season of Lent, deviating from the practice of Etchmiadzin.[53]

The Armenian Catholic Church in Lebanon

The establishment of the Armenian Catholic community in Lebanon dates to the eighteenth century.[54] Toward the end of the seventeenth century, dozens of Armenian Catholics from Aleppo began to arrive in Mount Lebanon, fleeing persecution from the Ottoman authorities.[55] In 1721, several Armenian monks founded an Armenian Congregation of the Order of St. Anthony at Kreim, in the Kisrawan district of Mount Lebanon.[56] The foundation of the monastery coincided with the arrival in Lebanon of probably the most important figure in the history of the Catholic Armenian Church, Archbishop Abraham Ardzivian.[57] Formerly the Apostolic bishop of Aleppo, Ardzivian converted to Catholicism and was, as a result, imprisoned and then exiled from his homeland.[58] His presence on Mount Lebanon led to a steady in-migration of Armenian Catholics

---

[51] Interview with Archbishop Khegham Khatcharian.
[52] Interview with Father Mgrdych.
[53] Group interview with St. Nishan parishioners.
[54] Iskandar, *La Nouvelle Cilicie*, p. 69.
[55] Panos Jeranian, *Catholic Armenian and Maronite Relations in Mount Lebanon, 1720–1840*, MA Thesis (Beirut, American University of Beirut, 1971), p. 15; Iskandar, *La Nouvelle Cilicie*, p. 61.
[56] Jeranian, *Catholic Armenian*, pp. 37–40.
[57] Iskandar, *La Nouvelle Cilicie*, p. 61.
[58] Jeranian, *Catholic Armenian*, p. 43.

from Aleppo, Damascus and Istanbul.[59] By the middle of the eighteenth century, there were at least a dozen Armenian Catholic villages in the Kisrawan.[60]

In 1742, Ardzivian was confirmed by the Vatican as patriarch of the Armenian Catholic See of Cilicia, with the name Apraham-Bedros I.[61] In October 1749, the patriarchate purchased a large property in Bzoummar, building a new monastery and ecclesiastical headquarters.[62] In the meantime, the Antonine monks of Kreim built yet a third Armenian Catholic monastery in Mount Lebanon, at Beit-Khochbao.[63]

From the early to mid nineteenth century, the combination of the existence of the three monasteries and favorable economic conditions in the Levant attracted an increasing number of Armenian Catholics.[64] During this period, Bzoummar increased its landed possessions and wealth, while the social standing of the Catholic Armenians in the Levant rose steadily.[65] In 1861, the Ottoman Empire, facing pressure from the European powers, agreed upon a new status for Lebanon as a so-called Christian "Mutasarrifate," to be ruled by a Christian governor. Under this new arrangement, Armenian Catholics played an increasingly important role in the governance of the country. Of the eight Mutasarrifat governors, the first and last were Catholic Armenians.[66]

This long-established presence of the Armenian Catholics in Lebanon played a positive role in rescuing victims of the genocide, as the reputation of Bzoummar and the community overall proved crucial in overcoming objections by other groups in Lebanese society to the unexpected and massive influx of refugees in the 1920s.[67] In turn, the arrivals augmented the size of the Armenian Catholic population in Lebanon.[68] The wealth of the "native" community allowed the Armenian Catholics to recover quicker than their Orthodox counterparts,

---

[59] Jeranian, *Catholic Armenian*, p. 50.
[60] Harboyan, *Political Integration*, p. 3.
[61] Jeranian, *Catholic Armenian*, p. 48.
[62] Iskandar, *La Nouvelle Cilicie*, p. 71; Jeranian, *Catholic Armenian*, p. 53. The establishment of the patriarchate at Bzoummar was important on a symbolic level, since the property was in close proximity to the patriarchal seats of other Eastern Rite Catholic churches in Lebanon (the Melkites, Syriacs and Maronites).
[63] Iskandar, *La Nouvelle Cilicie*, p. 63.
[64] Harboyan, *Political Integration*, p. 3.
[65] Jeranian, *Catholic Armenian*, p. 89.
[66] Jeranian, *Catholic Armenian*.
[67] Jeranian, *Catholic Armenian*, p. 90.
[68] Interview with Father Vartan, of the Armenian Catholic patriarchate in Achrafiye, Beirut.

aided greatly by already existing philanthropic and religious institutions.[69] The connection of the Armenian Catholics to Rome led to significant funding from the Vatican, spent on refugee assistance and the building of new churches in Lebanon.[70]

In the late 1920s, Pope Pius XI financed the construction of a second residence for the patriarch in the Beirut Christian quarter of Achrafiye.[71] Since then, Bzoummar has remained the spiritual center for Armenian Catholics globally, playing a role similar to that of the Catholicosate of Cilicia for the diaspora Orthodox. The current patriarch, since 1999 Nerses Bedros XIX (Tarmouni), lives at the residence in Achrafiye; however, Bzoummar remains the patriarchal seat and the site of all synodal and ecumenical meetings.[72]

The Catholic Armenian patriarchate is concerned primarily with the direction of the jurisdiction's affairs on a global scale, while leaving the administration of the specifically Lebanese diocese to a separate bishop, in this case a vicar of the patriarch. On the surface, this appears similar to the division of labor between the Orthodox Catholicos of Cilicia and the Lebanese Orthodox prelate. Still, in the case of the Catholics, the relationship between the priests and the patriarch is more highly centralized than in the Orthodox, as it is the patriarch and not the vicar who assigns priests to particular parishes or missionary duties; the priests in turn are responsible directly to the patriarch.[73] The patriarchate runs the network of Sunday schools in the country.[74] In sharp contrast to the Orthodox community, the role of lay people is minimal, with all administrative affairs run by clergy who are free to appoint parishioners to assist in the direction of religious or educational needs of a particular parish.[75] Finally, the Catholic Armenian vicar for Lebanon does not, unlike the Orthodox Prelate, function as a representative of the Lebanese state in matters of personal status.[76]

---

[69] Schahgadlian, *Political Integration*, p. 59; Father Antranig Granian, *Bzoummar a Travers l'Histoire* (Bzoummar, 1979), p. 33.
[70] Interview with Antranik Dakessian.
[71] Iskandar, *La Nouvelle Cilicie*, p. 76.
[72] Interview with Father Antranig Granian.
[73] Messerlian, *Armenian Representation*, p. 22.
[74] Messerlian, *Armenian Representation*, p. 23.
[75] Messerlian, *Armenian Representation*, p. 22; interview with Zaven Messerlian.
[76] On this question my interviewees were not quite clear. According to Father Vartan of the Catholic Armenian patriarchate, the processing and registration of annulments, inheritances, marriage, etc. takes place on the parish level. M. Tchouhadarian, head of the Benevolent Association of Armenian Catholics, on the other hand, informed me that at least some of these functions (marriage and annulment) are channeled through a pan-Catholic tribunal chaired by a Maronite. Interviews with Father Vartan and M. Tchouhadarian.

Presently, the Armenian Catholic patriarchate in Lebanon counts eight functioning churches, headed by the Cathedral of St. George-St. Elias in downtown Beirut. The vicar for Lebanon serves at the church of the Annunciation in Achrafiyeh. There are individual churches in Bourj Hammoud, Zalka, Zahle and in Anjar. In addition, there is a chapel in Jounieh associated with the seminary at Bzoummar.[77] Finally, there is the church of the Bzoummar monastery, which remains at the heart of the Armenian Catholic community in Lebanon, through its seminary and affluent museum and library. The seminary trains priests who are then sent for mandatory study to Rome; upon their return to parishes in Lebanon they bring with them a degree of sophistication and an appreciation for the connection of the Armenian Church to the broader Catholic communion.[78]

The Armenian Catholic community in Lebanon is further augmented by three institutions not directly responsible to the patriarch, but rather under the direct control of the Vatican. These are the Venetian and Viennese branches of the Mekhitarist monastic order, and the Armenian Congregation of the Sisters of the Immaculate Conception. The Mekhtarists have three monasteries, in Raouda (with its own chapel), Bikfaya and Hazmieh. In Hazmieh, the Viennese Mekhitarists run a school and chapel; in Bikfaya, the Venitian Mekhitarists oversee a seminary.[79] The sisters of the Immaculate Conception administer three schools in Lebanon—one each in Fanar, Bourj Hammoud and Anjar.[80]

In addition to the schools run by the Mekhitaristes and the sisters of the Immaculate Conception, there are two other Armenian Catholic secondary schools in Lebanon—one associated with the Church of the Holy Savior in Bourj Hammoud, and one at the church of the Holy Cross in Zahle.[81] Altogether, the schools serve approximately 2,700 students.[82]

The Armenian Catholic Church in Lebanon also sponsors a number of benevolent associations. Four of them are Ladies' Benevolent Associations affiliated with the parishes of Bourj Hammoud, Achrafiye, Zalka and Anjar. While these are engaged mainly in the upkeep of the parishes themselves,

---

[77] Interview with M. Tchouhadarian; Iskandar, *La Nouvelle Cilicie*, pp. 82–3.

[78] Interview with M. Tchouhadarian; interview with Father Vartan; interview with Father Antranig.

[79] Hamalian, *Lebanese-Armenians*, pp. 57–8; interview with M. Tchouhadarian; website of the Armenian Catholic Church, www.armeniancatholic.org/inside.php?lang=en&page_id=311, accessed September 28, 2013.

[80] Interview with M. Tchouhadarian.

[81] Interview with M. Tchouhadarian.

[82] www.armeniancatholic.org.

the Benevolent Society of Armenian Catholics, with distribution centers in downtown Beirut and Bourj Hammoud, serves hundreds of needy individuals and families throughout Lebanon, regardless of confessional affiliation.[83]

There are number of youth organizations, beginning with the Young People's Diocesan Committee, consisting of 14 people including two representatives of each Armenian Catholic parish. Other youth organizations include the Association of Armenian Catholic University Students, the Armenian Catholic Youth Association (Anjar), and the Armenian Catholic Youth Association (Bourj Hammoud). The youngest age groups are served by the St. Mesrob Scouts (in Bourj Hammoud), the Armenian Catholic Juvenile Association in Zalka, Bourj Hammoud and Achrafiye.[84] By all accounts, the various youth organizations are rather vital, bringing together approximately 630 active young people in Lebanon.[85]

In terms of church attendance, the picture is as murky as it is in the case of the Armenian Orthodox. Some of my interviewees described the levels of attendance as relatively low, particularly among young people.[86] At the same time, the Catholic Armenians I interviewed unanimously characterized their community as "more practicing" than the Orthodox, even if the numbers are "fluctuating."[87] Unlike the Armenian Orthodox community, the Catholic parishes offer daily masses (following the Armenian-rite Catholic liturgy—largely similar to the Orthodox—established in the eighteenth century), providing the population with a variety of options as to when to worship; this may account for low numbers of Sunday attendance if such a trend exists.[88]

As far as the relationship of the Armenian Catholic Church in Lebanon with the Catholics in the Armenian Republic is concerned, the community in Armenia is subject directly to the patriarchate in Bzoummar (thus there is not, as in the Orthodox case, a competition between two legitimate Sees). The revival of the Catholic parishes in Armenia has been supported by the Bzoummar hierarchy, with the patriarch making periodic pastoral visits.[89] Since 1994, the Catholic parishes in Armenia have been served by a local seminary, lessening their dependence on Bzoummar for the formation of priests.

---

[83] Interview with M. Tchouhadarian.
[84] Interview with M. Tchouhadarian. Website of the Armenian Catholic Church, www.armeniancatholic.org.
[85] Ibid.
[86] Interview with Mimi and Taline Yozgatian; interview with Father Vartan.
[87] Interview with Father Antranig Granian.
[88] Interview with Father Vartan.
[89] Interview with M. Yozgatian.

Finally, a few words should be said about an issue affecting the Armenian Catholic community that is absent in the case of the Orthodox and Evangelicals. By the mid-nineteenth century, approximately 10,000 Armenian Catholics were politically and economically well integrated in Mount Lebanon and its environs, as a group closely tied to the larger and politically dominant Maronites. More than any factor, Catholicism served as the prime source of the Armenians' identification; intermarriage with Maronites was common. The Armenian Catholics did not build schools in Lebanon, but rather sent their children to either Maronite or French school, resulting in the decline of Armenian as the primary language at home.[90]

The long-term nature of the denomination's presence in Lebanon and its ties with the wider Catholic world served to dilute the strength of the community's Armenian identity. The arrival of the refugees in the 1920s brought with it an injection of Armenian nationalist ideology, an understandable phenomenon in the wake of a national disaster of such proportions. As the Catholicos at Antelias positioned the Orthodox Church as central to Armenian identity, the reaction among many Armenian Catholics was to rediscover their own "Armenianness," particularly since many Armenian Catholics from Anatolia also lost their lives and property in the genocide and could now claim to be equally "Armenian" in their suffering.[91]

Still, as the 100-year anniversary of the genocide approaches, not all Armenian Catholics in Lebanon have "rediscovered" their Armenian roots. As late as the 1970s, a large proportion of the population did not speak Armenian (preferring Turkish, French and Arabic), privileging the religious Catholic identity. In the 1970s, under the reign of Patriarch Bedros XVIII (Casperian), the balance began to swing the other way, as Casperian made a concerted effort to bring the Arabized portions of his flock back into the Armenian milieu. This, combined with the galvanizing outside threat of the Lebanese civil war (in which Armenians in Lebanon of all denominations temporarily retreated to the "ghetto" of Bourj Hammoud), contributed to arresting and even reversing the assimilationist trends among the Armenian Catholics despite continuing mixed marriages.[92] Today, the proportion of Armenian-speaking to Arabo-phone Catholics is perhaps two-thirds to one-third.[93] In the end, it is not obvious that the Armenian Catholic hierarchy in Lebanon sees the existence of an Arabized portion of the community as a problem, given the universalist character of the

---

[90] Harboyan, *Political Integration*, p. 3.
[91] Interview with Father Antranig Granian.
[92] Interview with Mimi Yozgatian.
[93] Interview with M. Tchouhadarian.

Catholic Church, even given the differences in liturgical practice between the Armenians and other Eastern Rite Catholic groups in Lebanon. Unlike the Orthodox or Evangelicals, the Catholic Armenian parishes do offer Arab-language mass (still conducted according to the Armenian Eastern Catholic rite) for those who no longer understand Armenian, and with rare exception the question of mixed marriages is not seen as problematic as long as the marriage is with a non-Armenian Catholic.[94]

The Armenian Evangelical Community in Lebanon

Of the three Armenian denominations in Lebanon, the Armenian Evangelical Church is by far the youngest. Records from the mid-nineteenth century mention a total of five Armenian Evangelicals worshiping at the Arabic Evangelical Church in Beirut. The period of World War I and the genocide saw the arrival of a steady stream of Armenian Evangelical refugees to Beirut and surrounding areas; initially, they gathered for worship in premises on loan from the local Presbyterian mission.[95] As the wave of survivors from Anatolia crested in the early to mid 1920s, approximately 2,000 Armenian Protestants settled in and around Beirut. In 1922, the community elected a church board, as a first step toward establishing a church proper. Between 1922 and 1926, the Evangelicals operated two rented church premises under the umbrella of the First Armenian Evangelical Church, one in East Beirut and one in the western part of the city. In 1926, the two parishes began to function independently of each other, with the eastern parish eventually moving to a permanent location in the Achrafiye neighborhood.[96] In the meantime, Evangelicals settling in Anjar established a parish in 1939.[97] In 1949, the First Armenian Evangelical parish bought a property on rue Mexique and built the first permanent Armenian Evangelical church in Beirut.[98]

At its height, from the late 1940s to 1975, the Armenian Evangelical Church constituted about 5 percent of the total Armenian population in Lebanon, and operated 12 churches and 12 schools across the country. As a consequence of the

---

[94] Interview with Father Vartan.
[95] http://en.wikipedia.org/wiki/First_Armenian_Evangelical_Church, accessed September 29, 2013.
[96] *The Armenian Evangelical Church* (Armenian Missionary Association of America, 2000), p. 57.
[97] "Providing a Brighter Future," p. 48.
[98] *The Armenian Evangelical Church*, p. 57.

outmigration associated with the Lebanese civil war, several of the Evangelical communities went entirely extinct, forcing the closure of churches and schools in Tyre, Zahle, Shtora and Tripoli. By the end of the war in 1990, the Evangelical Armenian Church was reduced to five churches and eight schools; of the latter, two were subsequently closed down in the post-war period. Presently, the Armenian Evangelicals operate five churches, of which four are in and around Beirut and one is in Anjar. Each church runs an affiliated school, with an additional elementary school outside parish walls, for a total number of 1,400 students.[99]

In terms of structure, the Armenian Evangelicals in Lebanon are administered by an elected council dominated by the laity. The parishes are virtually independent of each other, and choose their own pastors, who are expected to be highly educated. Each parish also has a board responsible for running the parish school, which may or may not be directed by the local pastor.[100]

Unlike the Orthodox and Catholic Armenian denominations, the Evangelical Armenian Church in Lebanon does not have the status of an independently recognized sect. Legally, it is part of the Lebanese Protestant community, through which matters of personal status and political representation are worked out.[101] The Lebanese Protestants have a joint Synod, of which the Armenians constitute one-fourth of the membership.[102]

Despite the relatively small size of the Armenian Evangelical community in Lebanon, it plays a highly visible role both in the diaspora and locally. Since 1924, Beirut has been the headquarters of the Union of Armenian Evangelical Churches in the Near East (UAECNE), one of the oldest among the five unions that comprise the Armenian Evangelical Church worldwide. The UAECNE comprises over two-dozen churches and congregations in seven countries in the Middle East. Although each member church is autonomous in its internal affairs, certain union-wide functions such as the education of ministers are centralized. Here, the Lebanese community plays a central role, as future pastors study at the

---

[99] Interview with Reverend Mgrdych Karagoezian.
[100] Interview with Zaven Messerlian.
[101] Messerlian, in his 1965 dissertation, writes that matters of personal status are handled through the Union of Armenian Evangelical Churches of the Near East. However, in my interview with Reverend Mgrdych Karagoezian, he did not mention this as a function of the Union; all of my interviewees rather referred to their legal status as part of the Lebanese Protestant sect, albeit without specifying its role as a tribunal for divorces, marriages, etc. "Coping," p. 50.
[102] Interview with Zaven Messerlian.

Near East School of Theology (run by the UAECNE in cooperation with Arab Evangelicals) and at Haigazian University, both in Beirut.[103]

Haigazian University stands out for its central role in the life of Lebanese Armenians of all three denominations. The university was established in 1955 in a partnership between the Armenian Missionary Association of America and UAECNE, and is the only specifically Armenian institution of higher education outside of the Republic of Armenia. Originally meant to train leaders for the Armenian Evangelical community, Haigazian now welcomes students without regard for religious affiliation, both within the Lebanese Armenian population and broader Lebanese society. But the governance of Haigazian remains Evangelical, with university presidents historically chosen among Armenian Evangelical theologians.[104]

In additions to the university and schools, the Armenian Evangelical Church in Lebanon curates a number of charitable institutions. These include a social services office, a hospital and old persons' home in Azounie, an old persons' home in Beirut, and a center for the blind and handicapped. The latter three institutions are all run in partnership with the Orthodox Catholicosate.[105]

Similarly to the Orthodox and Catholic Armenian communities, the Evangelicals in Lebanon have drastically declined in number since the Lebanese civil war. This has had a discernible effect on church attendance. For example, whereas prior to the war the First Evangelical Church on rue Mexique drew 800 worshipers on an average Sunday, current levels of attendance are of perhaps 50–60 people.[106] Furthermore, the exclusive use of Armenian in worship essentially eliminates the possibility of in-conversion from non-Armenian members of Lebanese society.[107] Perhaps 15 percent of the approximately 2,000–3,000 Armenian Protestants in Lebanon regularly attend Sunday services.[108]

One factor contributing to low turnout has to do with the cessation of civil strife—just as in the Orthodox and Catholic cases, the signing of the Taef peace accords in 1990 freed the Evangelicals of the necessity to live in exclusively Armenian areas of Lebanon, leading to dispersal away from their original parish

---

[103] "Coping," p. 50; interview with Reverend Mgrdych Karagoezian; Iskandar, *La Nouvelle Cilicie*, p. 87; interview with Dr. Yervant Kassouni.

[104] Interview with Reverend Paul Haidostian, rector of Haigazian University.

[105] "Coping," p. 50; interview with Reverend Mgrdych Karagoezian.

[106] Interview with Reverend Hrayr Chalokian, pastor of the First Armenian Evangelical Church in Beirut; Interview with Dr. Arda Ekmekji.

[107] Interview with Reverend Hrayr Chalokian.

[108] Interview with Rev. Mgrdych Karagoezian.

churches.¹⁰⁹ A second factor has to do with a singular characteristic of Armenian Evangelical theology, namely, the refusal of the Church to claim for itself the exclusivity of revealed truth. The Evangelicals regard the Apostolic Armenian Church as the "mother Church," and do not generally discourage conversions from Protestantism to Orthodoxy.¹¹⁰ As a result, it is not infrequent for Armenians who consider themselves Protestant to attend Orthodox services if the Orthodox parish happens to be geographically more convenient.¹¹¹ Finally, in contrast to the Orthodox, the Evangelicals offer opportunities for worship throughout the week in addition to the Sunday services, which may also perhaps explain lower levels of attendance on Sundays.¹¹²

The Evangelicals also do not purposefully proselytize amongst the Orthodox or Catholic Armenians, although conversions have been known to occur. The Evangelical schools—which serve predominantly non-Evangelical Armenian students—place a high emphasis on teaching the Bible, but with the express purpose of bringing "the Word" to students in a way that will strengthen their personal religious faith, rather than privileging a specifically Evangelical interpretation.¹¹³ At the end of the day, the Evangelical community is increasingly feeling the negative effects of mixed marriages, with Armenian members of such unions tending to attend Arab Christian churches.¹¹⁴ Of the three denominations, the general impression is of a more serious demographic decline among the Protestants than among the other two.

Lastly, in terms of relations with the Armenian Protestant community in Armenia proper, here as with the Orthodox and Catholics one can speak of a system of fairly regular exchanges, in this case largely of an academic nature, as theological students from Armenia come to study at the Near Eastern School of Theology.

---

[109] Interview with Rev. Mgrdych Karagoezian.
[110] Interview with Reverend Hrayr Chalokian.
[111] Interview with Reverend Mgrdych Karagoezian.
[112] Interview with Reverend Hrayr Chalokian. Curiously, Chalokian also told me that prayer meetings held during the week—whether by women's groups or youth groups—draw a high proportion of Orthodox Armenians.
[113] Interview with Reverend Hrayr Chalokian.
[114] Interview with Reverend Mgrdych Karagoezian.

Concluding Discussion: Key Issues of Armenian Religiosity in Lebanon

Finally, this chapter briefly considers two issues without which the picture of Armenian religion in Lebanon would not be complete. The first regards internal plurality in the Lebanese Armenian community, considered in terms of integration into Lebanese society, political agenda and class differences. Do these differences exist, and if so, are they correlated with denominational belonging? The final question is the blunt issue of the long-term prospects for the survival of Armenian religion in Lebanon, given the ongoing turmoil in the region.

I have already mentioned the high level of Arabization among Catholic Armenians, a process that is currently in fact being reversed as the Catholics increasingly rediscover their Armenian roots. Broadly speaking, the Protestant and Orthodox have been historically more intent on holding on to a specifically Armenian identity, which has not prevented the populations from learning Arabic and effectively functioning in the local habitus. While there does remain a high degree of at least rhetorical yearning for the restoration of Cilician Armenia, all the interviews I conducted led to the conclusion that Armenian youth across all three denominations are far more interested in surviving in the specific Lebanese context than in recovering lost territories.

Certainly researchers have noted the fragmented nature of the Lebanese Armenian community in terms of political orientation—historically, differences between the Armenian political parties in the country have been quite dramatic, occasionally spilling over into violence.[115] And yet, both the interviews I conducted and the written sources consulted all lead to the conclusion that, while political factionalism among Lebanese Armenians is alive and well, theological differences have historically played no role the community's internal disputes. The major factor here seems to be the genocide itself: if, prior to the genocide, the Apostolic Armenians posed the question of the national loyalty of the Catholics and Evangelicals, the common experience of persecution and near-annihilation seems to have imbued the Armenian community in Lebanon with a sense that religious differences matter far less than the core common ethnic identity.[116] This in turn, it should be emphasized, is imbued with a strong loyalty to Western Armenia. The trials of the civil war, in which Lebanese Armenians

---

[115] Ara Sandjan, "Podiem i upadok armianskoi obschiny Livana" [The rise and decline of the Armenian community in Lebanon], *Diaspory* 1 (2004), pp. 121–46; Nalbantian, *Fashioning*.

[116] Here, I do not cite specific interviews or written works consulted, only because every single interview/written work I reference for this chapter adds to this conclusion in some fashion.

remained entirely neutral, further cemented the bonds of common nationality among those who did not emigrate.[117]

In a pattern similar to that of Lebanon generally, there are obvious degrees of economic inequality, with a relatively small segment of Armenian families faring visibly better than the majority. The community has overall declined in economic wealth over the past 20 years for reasons having to do with Lebanon's chronic post-war instability, and not with any particular characteristic of the Armenians themselves.[118] In short here, too, social and economic differences do not appear to be related to the theological divisions.

Although theological disputes periodically crop up in the pages of the denominations' monthly publications, in practice the relations between the three communities are fluid and generally amicable, allowing for occasional rhetorical barbs.[119] The Evangelicals invite Orthodox priests to preach at their services; notable Orthodox clergy (including the current Catholicos of Antelias) have studied at the Near East School of Theology.[120] The board in charge of the Catholicosate's museum in Antelias includes Evangelical members; Catholics and Evangelicals work together in producing the most important Lebanese Armenian scholarly periodical, *The Armenological Review*.[121] Furthermore, at present the curricula of the schools run by the three denominations are largely the same, as are the textbooks.[122] In turn, the schools themselves do not discriminate on the basis of religion when it comes to student enrollment.

Moreover, the dominant lay presence within the administrative structures of both the Catholicosate and the Lebanese Prelacy has made it relatively easy for Armenian political parties to exercise considerable influence over these institutions. During the Cold War in particular, the Dashnak (ARF) party played a dominant role.[123] As a result, the Armenian Orthodox Church in Lebanon did not become a political actor in its own right in the manner of the Maronite Church, but rather has at times acted as a proxy for the Dashnaks. The Union of Armenian Evangelical Churches in the Near East and the Catholic patriarchate, have, for their part, remained traditionally entirely apolitical on the Lebanese

---

[117] Interview with Arda Ekmekji.
[118] Sandjan, "Podiem," p. 126.
[119] Sandjan, "Podiem."
[120] Interviews with Reverends Chalokian and Karagoezian.
[121] Interview with Arda Ekmekji.
[122] Interview with Antranik Dakessian.
[123] Seta Kalpakian, *The Dimensions of the 1958 Inter-Communal Conflict in the Armenian Community in Lebanon*, MA Thesis (Beirut, American University of Beirut, 1983), p. 25.

scene.¹²⁴ In other words, while religion has provided Armenians with political representation and legitimized the community's right to exist as a three-pronged part of the country's sectarian mosaic, the Armenian denominations do not have an independent political role beyond managing some internal communal affairs.¹²⁵ In this they are exceptional on the Lebanese scene.

Finally, there is the question of the long-term survival of the Armenian denominations in Lebanon. Here, the answer seems to be that the prospects for survival are high, although perhaps not at the current demographic levels. The three "Armenian religions" are well integrated in the country, and have deeply embedded educational and social institutions in addition to actual parishes themselves. Just as the Catholic Armenians identified their interests with those of the Christian Emirs of Mount Lebanon in the nineteenth century, so too do the Lebanese Armenians of all three faiths interpret the confessional arrangement of present-day Lebanon as optimal for survival of the Armenian ethnicity. Although outmigration is continuing (mainly for economic reasons), the pace of emigration appears to be slowing down, as previously attractive locations such as Los Angeles and Paris are themselves experiencing the protracted effects of the 2008 global crisis.¹²⁶

Furthermore, those Armenians who do leave Lebanon tend to replicate the pattern of Lebanese citizens in general, and return to the country at least periodically during their lifetimes. The dramatic situation in neighboring Syria may actually have had a positive demographic effect on Armenians in Lebanon, as my interviewees periodically mentioned the influx of their Catholic, Orthodox and Evangelical co-religionists from across the border. At the same time, the unpredictable dynamics of the regional turmoil periodically threaten to engulf Lebanon in a second civil war, in which case we can predict a further decline of all three Armenian denominations.

References

Alexandrian, A., "New Alliances Fresh Possibilities: The Dawn of a New Era for the Armenian Community of Lebanon," *Armenian International Magazine* 11, no. 10 (2000): 45.

---

[124] Interview with Father Vartan; interview with Arda Ekmekji.
[125] Interview with Antranik Dakessian.
[126] Interview with Archbishop Nareg Alemezian.

The Armenian Evangelical Church (Armenian Missionary Association of America, 2000).

Bedoyan, Hratch, *Armenian Political Parties in Lebanon*, MA Thesis (Beirut, American University of Beirut, 1973).

Boudjikanian, Aida (ed.), *Armenians of Lebanon: From Past Princesses and Refugees to Present-Day Community* (Beirut, 2009).

Boyadjian, M.D. and S.S. Kazarian, "Validation of the Multigroup Ethnic Identity Measure Among Ethnic Armenian Adolescents in Lebanon," *Identity: An International Journal of Theory and Research* 8, no. 4 (2008): 335–47.

"Coping With the Effects of the War: The Armenian Evangelical Union of the Near East," *Armenian International Magazine* 11, no. 1 (2000): 50.

Corley, Felix, "UN of Christianity at 50: The World Council of Churches is being Pulled in Different Directions; Aram I Struggles to Keep the Organization Together," *Armenian International Magazine* 9, no. 11 (1998).

Geertz, Clifford, *The Interpretation of Cultures: Selected Essays* (London, Hutchinson, 1975).

Geukjian, Ohannes, "The Policy of Positive Neutrality of the Armenian Political Parties in Lebanon during the Civil War 1975–1990: A Critical Analysis," *Middle Eastern Studies* 43, no. 1 (2007): 65–73.

Granian, Father Antranig, *Bzoummar a Travers l'Histoire* (Bzoummar: Metpa Group, 1979).

Hamalian, Arpi, *Lebanese-Armenians: A Study of Generational Differences in Assimilation*, MA Thesis (Beirut, American University of Beirut, 1973).

Harboyan, Bernadette, *The Political Integration of the Armenian Community in Lebanon*, MA Thesis (Beirut, American University of Beirut, 1998).

Iskandar, Amine Jules, *La Nouvelle Cilicie: Les Armeniens du Liban* (Antelias, Catholicosate of Cilicia, 1999).

Jeranian, Panos, *Catholic Armenian and Maronite Relations in Mount Lebanon, 1720–1840*, MA Thesis (Beirut, American University of Beirut, 1971).

Johannes, Armineh, "Attached to the Land: Anjar Recalls its Roots and Fights to Retain Them," *Armenian International Magazine* 13, no. 5 (2002): 22.

Kalpakian, Seta, *The Dimensions of the 1958 Inter-Communal Conflict in the Armenian Community in Lebanon*, MA Thesis (Beirut, American University of Beirut, 1983).

Messerlian, Zaven, *Armenian Representation in the Lebanese Parliament*, MA Thesis (Beirut, American University of Beirut, 1963).

Migliorino, Nicola, *(Re)constructing Armenia in Lebanon and Syria: Ethno-Cultural Diversity and the State in the Aftermath of a Refugee Crisis* (New York, Berghahn Books, 2007).

Nalbantian, Tsolin, *Fashioning Armenians in Lebanon, 1946–1958*, PhD Diss. (New York, Columbia University, 2011).

"Providing a Brighter Future: The Armenian Evangelical School in Anjar," *Armenian International Magazine* 11, no. 1 (2000): 48.

Sandjan, Ara, "Podiem i upadok armianskoi obschiny Livana," *Diaspory* 1 (2004): 121–46.

Schahgaldian, Nikola, *The Political Integration of an Immigrant Community into a Composite Society: The Armenians in Lebanon, 1920–1974*, PhD Diss. (New York, Columbia University, 1979).

Tillich, Paul, *Theology of Culture* (New York, Oxford University Press, 1959).

Chapter 9

The Chronotopes of the Armenian Diaspora in Romania: Religious Feasts and Shrines in the Making of Community

Konrad Siekierski

Introduction

This chapter examines two religious feasts celebrated at Armenian shrines in Romania. It focuses on the historical context in which these feasts are embedded, as well as the acts, moods and discourses that currently sustain them. Furthermore, it argues that being in a diaspora—along with an attachment to a faraway homeland and participating in transnational networks—can also mean drawing upon and engaging in its own local heritage.

This chapter is based on multi-sited ethnographic fieldwork conducted in Romania in March–August 2011 and June–September 2012,[1] particularly in Bucharest, Cluj-Napoca, Dumbrăveni, Iași, Gherla, Gheorgheni and Suceava. The fieldwork focused on the Feast of the Assumption of the Holy Mother of God, celebrated in mid-August in the monastery of Hagigadar in Suceava, and the Feast of St. Gregory the Illuminator, celebrated in June–July in the Armenian Catholic Holy Trinity Cathedral in Gherla.[2]

---

[1] The author's first research stay in Romania was made possible thanks to a fellowship from the New Europe College, the second thanks to a scholarship from the Romanian Cultural Institute.

[2] In course of the fieldwork, the author participated twice in both feasts, conducted around 50 loosely structured interviews with their Romanian Armenian, Hungarian Armenian, Romanian and Polish participants, and studied press materials on the Armenian diaspora in Romania, including two journals, *Ararat* and *Nor Ghiank*, published in Bucharest by the Union of Armenians in Romania.

As observed by Paul Christopher Johnson, a "diaspora is a series of interventions, not a permanent state of being."[3] At the moment of such "interventions" a diasporic identity is evoked; a sense of belonging to a distinct group, other than that of the host society in which everyday life is lived, is experienced and expressed. The main argument of this chapter is that the aforementioned religious feasts and shrines are central elements of Armenian diasporic life in Romania, and these are when and where the "interventions" that re-create diasporic bonds take place. This assertion brings us to Mikhail Bakhtin's concept of the "chronotope." In his words, chronotopes are:

> points in the geography of a community where time and space intersect and fuse. Time takes on flesh and becomes visible for human contemplation; likewise, space becomes charged and responsive to the movement of time and history and the enduring character of a people ... Chronotopes thus stand as monuments to the community itself, as symbols of it, as forces operating to shape its members' image of themselves.[4]

By invoking the notion of chronotope this chapter adds to the academic discussion on diasporic strategies of community making. While classic approaches to diaspora studies (as epitomized by William Safran's seminal definition[5]) focus on various forms of diaspora members' attachment to their homeland and transnational studies stress the importance of migrants' formal and informal networks that cross political and cultural borders, this chapter aims to shows that a fundamental trait of the modern Armenian diaspora in Romania is its enrootedness in and drawing on the history of their ancestors' settlement in the region. Such drawing on a local diasporic heritage is a "two-edged sword," since it provides, on the one hand, an effective mechanism for identity creation and collective mobilization, while on the other hand it brings about internal divisions among Armenian sub-groups, differentiated by the time of their migration as well as by the pace and direction of their assimilation.

---

[3] Paul Christopher Johnson, *Diaspora Conversions: Black Carib Religion and the Recovery of Africa* (Berkeley, 2007), p. 36.

[4] Mikhail Bakhtin, *The Dialogic Imagination: Four Essays,* ed. Michael Holquist (Austin, 1982), p. 7. A pioneering adaptation of this concept to anthropological research was offered in Keith H. Basso's study *Wisdom Sits in Places: Landscape and Language among the Western Apache* (Albuquerque, 1996).

[5] William Safran, "Diasporas in Modern Societies: Myths of Homeland and Return," *Diaspora: A Journal of Transnational Studies* 1, no. 1 (1991), pp. 83–4.

Armenians in Romania: History and the Present Day

The first wave of Armenian migrants, who reached Bucovina and Moldavia (the northeastern part of today's Romania) as early as the fourteenth century, considered themselves the heirs of the Armenian capital of Ani: a tradition that is still recalled by Armenians in Romania in the present day.[6] From the Middle Ages until the nineteenth century, Armenians were mostly merchants and craftsmen, often granted special juridical, economic and religious status. As Nicolae Iorga wrote: "The Principality of Moldavia was created through trade and the traders collaborated in the creation of the state in Moldavia. In this way, the Armenians were, so to speak, the founding fathers of Moldavia."[7] However, due to a deteriorating situation, a significant number of Armenians moved from Moldova westward to Transylvania in the second half of the seventeenth century.[8]

Religious autonomy was one of the most important factors in differentiating Armenians from their host society. It is usually accepted that the first bishopric of the Armenian Apostolic Church on the territory of modern Romania was created in Suceava as early as 1401. Later, religion also became the main force behind an important division among the Armenian population. At the end of the seventeenth century, the Transylvanian Armenians accepted a union with Rome and established the Armenian Catholic Church, an act which accelerated the process of their Magyarization. Meanwhile, the rest of the Armenian population (those living in Moldavia and Wallachia—the southern part of the country) remained faithful to the Armenian Apostolic Church, and they gradually

---

[6] See for example Suren Golanchean, *Rumanahayut'ean Anin' Suchavayi Hay Gaghut'e* (Yerevan, 2000) [Ani of the Romanian Armenians: The Armenian Colony of Suceava]; Datev Hakobian, *500, 1512–2012 Hagigadar, The Holy Hagigadar Monastery of Suceava: Miracle Maker* (Bucharest, n.d.); and Hakob Siruni, *Hay Yekeghets'in Rumen Hoghi Vra. Nicola Yorga* (Ējmiatsin, 1966) [The Armenian Church in Romanian Lands. Nicola Yorga]. These titles also offer good insights into the history of Armenian settlement in Romania. Other sources on this topic include: Dimitrie Dan, *Armenii ortodocși din Bucovina* (Bucharest, 1981); Sergiu Selian, *Schita istorica a comunitatii armene din România* (Bucharest, 1999); and Leon Stacescu, *Armenians in Romania*, www.personal.ceu.hu/students/02/Leon_Stacescu/rh/htm, accessed on June 15, 2014.

[7] Quoted in Judith Pál, *Armenians in Transylvania* (Cluj-Napoca, 2005), p. 88.

[8] On the history of the Transylvania Armenians see Pál, *Armenians in Transylvania*; Bálint Kovács and Emese Pál (eds), *Far Away from Mount Ararat: Armenian Culture in the Carpathian Basin* (Leipzig, 2013); Sándor Öze and Bálint Kovács (eds), *Örmény diaszpóra a Kárpát medencében* (Piliscsaba, 2006); and Sándor Öze and Bálint Kovács (eds), *Örmény diaszpóra a Kárpát-medencében II* (Pilicsaba, 2007).

assimilated into the Romanian milieu. This part of the Armenian diaspora took on an entirely new shape when the wave of Armenian migrants escaping the extermination of Armenians in Turkey in 1915–22 arrived in the country. As a result, according to different estimates, some 12,000–40,000 Armenians were living in the country in the 1930s.[9]

Later, the vibrant community life was strongly affected by the establishment of the communist regime in Romania in 1947. Gradually, all Armenian organizations, except for the Armenian Apostolic and Armenian Catholic churches,[10] were disbanded and to a large extent public diasporic life ceased to exist. In 1946–8 some 3,000 former refugees took part in a repatriation campaign to Soviet Armenia, and during the following decades most of the Romanian Armenians left the country and joined their compatriots in the United States and other Western countries.

After the fall of Ceausescu's regime in 1989, official statistics show a continual decrease in the number of people who declare Armenian nationality. According to the census of 1992, there were 2,023 Armenians in Romania; 10 years later this number had dropped to 1,708, and by 2011 to 1,361. However, according to the internal sources of the Union of Armenians in Romania, the numbers should be much higher, reaching as many as 7,000 people.[11]

Armenians are one of 19 ethno-national minorities officially recognized by the Romanian state and subjected to legal regulations, including state sponsorship and a seat in parliament. The main benefactor of state support is the Union of Armenians in Romania, a Bucharest-based cultural, social and political organization with branches in most parts of the country. A number of local Armenian organizations also exist in Transylvania.

Today, as in the past, the confessional organization of Armenians in Romania is divided into the Armenian Apostolic Church and the Armenian Catholic Church. The former has a separate bishopric (with its head residing in Bucharest) and 10 parishes in the southern and eastern parts of the country, served by four priests (in 2012). The Armenian Catholic Church is organized under the

---

[9] The first number is quoted from Ioan Scurtu and Ioan Dordea (eds), *Minoritățile Naționale din România 1925–1931* (Bucharest, 1996), p. 465; the latter from Leon Stacescu's article *Armenians in Romania*.

[10] However, the Armenian Catholic Churches lost its autonomy: in order to avoid the fate of the Romanian Greek Catholic Church, disbanded by the state, it was subordinated directly to the jurisdiction of the Roman Catholic bishop of Alba Iulia.

[11] Third Report Submitted by Romania Pursuant to Article 25, Paragraph 2 of the Framework Convention for the Protection of National Minorities, 2011, www.coe.int/t/dghl/monitoring/minorities/3_fcnmdocs/PDF_3rd_SR_Romania_en.pdf, p. 23 (accessed on June 15, 2014).

name of the "Ordinariate for the Faithful of the Eastern Rite in Romania" and subject to the Catholic bishop of Alba Iulia. Nowadays it has only one priest (of Hungarian origin) authorized to serve the liturgy in the Armenian-Catholic rite, who resides in Gherla and occasionally visits the Armenians in Cluj-Napoca, Dumbrăveni, Gheorgheni and Frumoasa.

The present, rather favorable, conditions regarding minority issues in Romania has given rise to the phenomenon sometimes referred to (by both Armenians themselves and in the literature) as "Neo-Armenism" or "Neo-Armenianism," which has attracted a number of people who have "rediscovered" their Armenian roots.[12] This phenomenon has also brought about a renewed interest in the Armenian heritage, a tangible part of which finds its most important representation in a number of old Armenian churches and monasteries,[13] while the intangible part includes important religious feasts that gather Armenians from around and from outside the country. Two such shrines and their respective feasts, earlier identified as chronotopes of the Armenian diaspora in Romania, will now be described in more detail.

Hagigadar and the Feast of the Assumption of the Holy Mother of God

Hagigadar (officially Surb Astvatsatsin—the Holy Mother of God) monastery[14] is a part of Suceava's unique Armenian architectural ensemble, which comprises today two monasteries (Hagigadar and Zamca or St. Oxentius), two churches (Holy Cross and St. Simeon), and the Holy Resurrection chapel. The first of them, Hagigadar, is located on a hill in the southern outskirts of the city, while the rest are along Strada Armenească and Strada Zamca stretching toward the northeast from the center of Suceava. The name Hagigadar, usually explained as "dream-fulfilling" or "petition-fulfilling,"[15] refers primarily to the widespread

---

[12] Pál, *Armenians in Transylvania*, p. 158.

[13] On Armenian religious art and architecture in Romania see Vlad Bedros, *Armenian Artistic Heritage in Romania: Between Exilic Nostalgia and Cultural Integration* (Bucharest, 2011); Kovács and Pál, *Far Away from Mount Ararat*.

[14] At the time when it was active, Hagigadar was a kind of semi-nunnery, where pious Armenian women lived, without following any specific monastic order. In administrative terms, Hagigadar was not referred to as a separate monastery but as a metochion. However, it is popularly called a monastery, a custom followed in this chapter.

[15] As stated by Bishop Datev Hakobian, a primate of the Romanian diocese of the Armenian Apostolic Church, there is a long tradition of miraculous monasteries in Armenian Christianity, some of which have received the name Hagigadar. In the region, the Armenian church in Lviv (Ukraine) was also referred to as "Hagigadar" (Hagobian, *500*,

belief in the miraculous power of the monastery. Also miraculous is the history of its construction. Various versions of Hagigadar's foundational myth exist today, one of the most popular saying that on their way to a cattle fair in Vienna two Armenian brothers—Astvatsatur and Trakan (Drăgan) Tonavag (Donavag, Tonavagian, Donavagian)—stopped for a rest on the hill where the monastery now stands. Both of them saw the Mother of God in a night vision and in the morning they made a vow that if they successfully sold their herd, they would build a shrine as a sign of their gratitude. In other versions only Trakan is mentioned,[16] the cattle fair is sometimes located in Pest (today's Budapest) or even in Leipzig,[17] and angels (rather than the Mother of God) appeared to the merchant(s).[18] What is generally agreed upon is the date of Hagigadar's foundation—1512.

Hagigadar gained its fame no later than the beginning of the seventeenth century and this name for the monastery is mentioned for the first time in a colophon of an Armenian manuscript written in Suceava and dated 1629.[19] Two hundred years later in a document issued by the town hall one could read: "thousands of pilgrims come to Suceava during the whole summer to visit the shrines of Zamca and Mitoc [Hagigadar] and they spread all over the city."[20] As an Armenian priest, Father Petros Manikonean, noted at the end of the nineteenth century, "The Holy Hagigadar became a Saint Karapet of Romanian Armenians,"[21] comparing Suceava's monastery to the most venerated pilgrimage site in Western Armenia.[22] The importance of Hagigadar as a pilgrimage site and miraculous shrine is also attested by votive gifts collected in the monastery,

---

pp. 68–70). The name Hagigadar (Hachkatar in Armenian) is a compound word. The word "hach" means "a wish" and "katarel" means "to do," "to fulfill." In the nineteenth-century sources the monastery is also referred to as Hajoyakatar (Siruni, Hay Yekeghets'in, p. 115). Yet another version of its name is Khendrakatar, where the word "khendrank" also means "a wish," "a request." In Romanian, Hagigadar is known as Biserica Dorințelor—the Church of Wishes. I am grateful to Anna Ohanjanyan and Vartan Martaian for providing me with this information.

[16] For example, an 1896 inscription on Hagigadar's wall mentions only his name. See also Siruni, Hay Yekeghets'in, p. 107.
[17] Varujan Vozganian, *Cartea șoaptelor* (Iași, 2009).
[18] Three versions of the legend are handed down in Hagobian, 500, p. 70.
[19] Hakobian, 500, p. 71.
[20] Hakobian, 500, p. 76.
[21] As quoted in Golanchean, *Rumanahayut'ean*, p. 262.
[22] Surb Karapet monastery (today in ruins) is located in the province of Moush (Muș) in Turkey.

by records in Hagigadar's pilgrim book,[23] and by a song that used to be sung by Armenians ascending to the sanctuary. The song starts with the following words:

> Holy Hagigadar, merciful mother
> Open for us the door of your mercy,
> Give health to the sick
> And support the pilgrims.[24]

It is worth mentioning that for a long time now Hagigadar has been a mixed shrine,[25] where not only Armenians, but also Orthodox Romanians and, to a lesser extent, local Catholic Poles gather.[26] Nowadays, since there are so few Armenians left in Suceava (and their overall number in Romania is low), Orthodox Romanians are the most numerous visitors to the shrine, both on a daily basis and during Hagigadar's feast. They come here individually, in families, or in groups to engage in traditional devotional practices—prayers, offerings and a prescribed set of bodily actions—which are believed to help one's wishes come true. These practices include crawling around the church on one's knees (usually three times), and sometimes also all the way up the hill, praying at each corner of the shrine, and leaving money and small sheets of paper with the names of those for whom one is praying in the cracks of the walls, the pillars of the belfry,

---

[23] For late nineteenth- and early twentieth-century excerpts from Hagigadar's pilgrim book see Golanchean, *Rumanahayut'ean*, pp. 319–21 and Siruni, Hay Yekeghets'in, pp. 114–18.

[24] Golanchean, Rumanahayut'ean, p. 327.

[25] Using the word "mixed" instead of more common "shared" when talking about shrines such as Hagigadar, I follow Glenn Bowman, who explains: "I programmatically abandoned the term 'shared' in the delineation of shrines, replacing it with 'mixed' ... — a term capable of embracing interaction ranging from antagonistic mobilization to amicable mutuality—allowed the nuances of each case to emerge" (Glenn Bowman, "Orthodox-Muslim Interactions at Mixed Shrines in Macedonia," in Chris Hann and Hermann Goltz (eds), *Eastern Christians in Anthropological Perspective* (Berkeley, 2010), p. 199). Although today there is little doubt that Hagigadar is peacefully shared by the groups mentioned above, historically relations between the Armenian Apostolic Church and the dominant Romanian Orthodox Church used to be more tense. A vivid example of this may be the traditional iconography of the Last Judgement, depicted in several sixteenth-century outer wall paintings in orthodox monasteries from Northern Moldavia and Bucovina; it features Christ at the top, heaven and saved souls on the right, and hell and condemned sinners on the left. Among the latter the figure of an Armenian monk is depicted (I am grateful to Vlad Bedros for providing me with this information).

[26] The village of Bulai, next to which Hagigadar is located, is predominantly populated by Poles, who settled here in the second half of the nineteenth century.

or on grave slabs around the church, or tying them to the clapper of the bell. Some light candles, and many drink from the spring located in the corner of the courtyard or from a special vessel filled with water blessed each Friday by the Armenian priests coming from Suceava. As one of the Romanian pilgrims explained:

> When you wish something, you have to go around three times and it will make your wish come true. People know about it and they come from the whole country. I am from Suceava, but I do not live here anymore, and now I come to Hagigadar every time I visit the city ... I think you will not see anything like this anywhere else in Romania. It is really a special place.

Once a year Hagigadar becomes an even more special place when it witnesses a flow of Armenians coming from around Romania and from abroad. The occasion for this gathering is the main feast of the monastery—the Assumption of the Holy Mother of God—celebrated according to the Armenian calendar on the nearest Sunday to August 15, and accompanied by the blessing of the grapes. The tradition of Armenian pilgrimage to Hagigadar was not interrupted, although its scale diminished, in the communist period. After the fall of Ceausescu's regime, the feast gradually became a central focus in redeveloping diaspora life. In its current shape, the celebration starts with a Saturday afternoon service in the Holy Cross Church in the center of Suceava, which serves as the parish church for the tiny local Armenian community. After the service, the preparation of the next day's festive meal takes place. This is the time when most Armenian pilgrims gather in the churchyard, where behind long tables women prepare small dumplings filled with meat, called *akanjner* (ears). According to popular tradition, whoever prepares 40 of them deserves to have a wish fulfilled after visiting Hagigadar the next day. The preparation process is also seen in terms of a unifying collective work and a good occasion for socialization with fellow countrymen. Along with *akanjner*, boiled meet is blessed and prepared for *madagh*.[27] On Sunday morning the pilgrims gather at the footsteps of the hill on which Hagigadar is located, from where a solemn procession led by the Armenian Apostolic clergy climbs up to the monastery. On the way the highest ranking clergyman blesses those who have gathered, including the Romanian pilgrims. It is customary that no one should enter the church before the Armenian procession reaches it. During the liturgy many people pass money to

---

[27] Madagh is an Armenian benevolent tradition, which usually takes the form of offering parts of the sacrificial animal to neighbors, guests and those in need.

the altar along with pieces of paper with the names of those for whom they are asking for prayers and venerate the miraculous icon of Virgin Mary placed in the church. After the liturgy, non-Armenian pilgrims are offered packages with *madagh* food. The Armenians (and some non-Armenians too) head toward the Holy Cross Church where a common meal is served, including *akanjapur*—a soup with dumplings, which among the Armenians in Romania has taken on the status of an obligatory festival food and a symbol of Armenian cuisine.[28] The dinner is sometimes accompanied by performances by Armenian dance and music ensembles. Most pilgrims, especially those from distant locations, leave after dinner. On Monday morning local Armenians and those who have stayed overnight participate in a Repose of Souls service held in the Zamca monastery.

Gathering in Hagigadar is described in the Romanian Armenian press as both a religious pilgrimage and an occasion for experiencing, enlivening and expressing one's Armenianness. As one can read in *Ararat* journal:

> Taking the road to Hagigadar, which is followed by Armenian and non-Armenian believers, is a special moment for the spirit. Our presence here proves our existence as an ethnic group. The Hagigadar is taking you really close to God and to your soul, this is felt in every step taken in this blessed place. And as long as at least one Armenian is present there, our existence is ensured. This is the place where hope is born ... When one reaches Hagigadar one realizes that one is an Armenian not only because of one's name.[29]

This statement corresponds with a more general approach toward religion and the Church shared by many Armenians in Romania and elsewhere, in which the Armenian Apostolic Church and its tangible and intangible heritage are perceived, above all, as a unifying force and a crucial part of national history and identity.[30] During the liturgy in Hagigadar, some of the Armenian pilgrims stay inside the Church, while others go in and out, or spend time in the yard of the monastery, busy with mundane conversations. Although the aforementioned

---

[28] The soup itself is made out of khourout—dried curdled milk with herbs: local Armenians call it "the first instant soup in the world."

[29] E.A., "Hagigadar 2000," *Ararat* 16, no. 205 (August 2000).

[30] This attitude was clearly expressed by one of author's interviewees, an Armenian from Bucharest: "I am not a religious man, but I think the Church plays an important role in bringing the community together. A large part of us come to the Church not for religious reasons, but to get together, to talk. Probably if the Church did not exist we would not gather so often, but now there is a reason to come every week." Next year this same man accepted the priests' invitation to serve as a sub-deacon during the Hagigadar feast.

kinetic devotional practices are well known to them and perceived as Hagigadar's endemic tradition, Armenians today usually do not engage in them bodily, but rather only discursively. Instead it is the Orthodox Romanians who, in a way that is perceived by them as standing apart from their own religious tradition, invest their physical suffering in search of the sanctuary's intercession. In Max Weber's terms, it can be said that for the latter Hagigadar is mostly about its charismatic authority (the authority of the "gift of grace"), while for the former this authority has been, at least partially, routinized and replaced by traditional authority (the authority of the "eternal yesterday").[31] Such traditional authority sustains modern diasporic nationalism and transforms the Hagigadar sanctuary into a powerful symbol of the endurance and accomplishments of the community.[32]

Gherla and the Feast of St. Gregory the Illuminator

Similarly to Suceava and the monastery of Hagigadar, the town of Gherla, where the feast of St. Gregory the Illuminator is celebrated in June–July, is a central symbol of the centuries-long existence of the Armenian community in this region. The town, located in Northern Transylvania and also known as Armenopolis (*Hayakaghak*), is not only dotted with Armenian churches, but actually was built from scratch by Armenians in the seventeenth century. On its central square stands the monumental Holy Trinity Armenian-Catholic Cathedral constructed in 1748–1808, the largest Armenian-Catholic church in Europe.[33] On one of the altars of the Holy Trinity Cathedral the miraculous painting of the Queen of the Rosary, surrounded by votive gifts, used to be

---

[31] Laura Desfor Edles and Scott Appelrouth (eds), *Sociological Theory in the Classic Era: Text and Readings* (Thousand Oaks, 2009), p. 201.

[32] In this context it is worth noting that in 1912 and 2012 the 400th and 500th anniversaries of Hagigadar's construction were officially celebrated (Hakobian, *500*, p. 81). The special status of Hagigadar for Romanian Armenians is also strengthened by the fact that this is where the future Catholicos (supreme patriarch) of the Armenian Apostolic Church—Vazgen I (1955–94) went in 1943 for his 40-day seclusion after being ordained to a celibate priesthood. Furthermore, in 1997 Hagigadar hosted the first of five pan-Armenian pilgrimages organized on the occasion of the 1,700th anniversary of the Christianization of Armenia, which had their culmination in 2001 in Etchmiadzin (the spiritual and administrative center of the Armenian Apostolic Church).

[33] It is rivaled in this title by the church of Saint Elizabeth of Hungary located in Dumbrăveni (Southern Transylvania). Aside from the cathedral, there is also an older Armenian Solomon's Church of the Annunciation of the Virgin Mary in Gherla.

venerated.[34] However, contrary to the tradition of celebrating the feast of St. Gregory, the "charismatic" character of the cathedral, endowed by the Queen of the Rosary, has been forgotten.

The feast, a part of the cult of St. Gregory the Illuminator that has been particularly strong among Transylvanian Armenians, has a long tradition.[35] In the nineteenth century it was marked by a procession during which a massive flag of St. Gregory was carried around Gherla's main square on each corner of which the altar was installed. After the religious part of the feast was over, Armenians continued the celebration in their homes, while a special dinner was offered to visiting clergymen. During socialist times the feast was celebrated on a very small scale, the liturgy was deprived of part of its Armenian flavor, and the flag was lost. Re-established after socialist times, today the feast is an occasion for the most important Armenian gathering in Transylvania,[36] and it is the most visible sign of "Neo-Armenism" ("Neo-Armenianism")—the recent ethnic awakening of heavily assimilated (mostly to Hungarian culture) Transylvanian Armenian-Catholics.

The feast in Gherla starts with a procession that goes from the parish house to the cathedral. It is led by the so-called "Red Robes"—the last Armenian-Catholic parish society preserved in Transylvania (and today limited to purely symbolic functions),[37] who on this occasion come to Gherla from Gheorgheni. Later, during the liturgy, the members of the society, equipped with long and thick candles, stand between the celebrant and the gathered people.

---

[34] Emese Pál, "The Sacral Art of Transylvanian-Armenians," in Kovács and Pál, *Far Away from Mount Ararat*, pp. 81–2.

[35] As Emese Pál shows, while representations of other saints of the Armenian Christian tradition are scarce in the region, there are 13 altarpieces, as well as numerous sculptures, flags and murals depicting this saint. It is worth noting that, according to her, in the second half of the nineteenth century "instead of [St. Gregory's] miracles, which had been emphasized in the eighteenth-century medallion pictures in Gheorgheni and Armenopolis, his historical role came to the foreground. Interestingly (parallel with the shifting image of King St. Stephen of the Hungarians), [Armenians] began to focus on St. Gregory's missionary achievements, without which the Armenian nation might well have become extinct" (Pál, "The Sacral Art," p. 80).

[36] Two other important feasts celebrated by Armenians in Transylvania are the feast of the Assumption, celebrated in Dumbrăveni, and the feast of the Nativity celebrated in Gheorgheni.

[37] In the eighteenth century as many as 20 Armenian parish societies were active in Dumbrăveni, Frumoasa, Gherla and Gheorgheni. They fulfilled various community tasks such as supporting the poor and the orphaned, the funding of new churches, commissioning the elements of their decoration, organizing religious feasts, etc. ("Catalogue: IV. Church and the Veneration of Saints," in Kovács and Pál, *Far Away from Mount Ararat*, p. 146).

During the procession, the Red Robes are followed by women from Gherla dressed in "traditional" costumes, as well as by clergymen from four historical Transylvanian Armenian centers—Dumbrăveni (Erzsébetváros), Frumoasa (Csikszépviz), Gherla (Szamosújvár) and Gheorgheni (Gyergyószentmiklós).[38] The solemn liturgy is served in Hungarian with Armenian church hymns sung in their original language by a choir, which at the end of the liturgy also performs the Hungarian and Armenian national anthems. After the religious ceremony, a festive meal is offered to all guests, who gather in the hall and cellar of the parish house. Here too, as in Suceava, *akanjapur* is served, although no customs related to its preparation are observed, and it is the local Armenian community that prepares all the food, including homemade cognac. Depending on the year, cultural events may take place following the dinner, including visits to the cathedral's catacombs and a chapel where a painting (allegedly by Rubens) is displayed, book presentations, music performances or exhibitions.

The feast in Gherla—aside from being a central event for local Armenians, requiring a significant mobilization of human and financial resources and elevating Armenian sentiments above the everyday immersion in Hungarian (or at times Romanian) social milieu[39]—also serves as a unique meeting place for Transylvanian Armenians, Romanized Armenians from Southern and Eastern Romania, and Armenians from Hungary. As the leader of the local Armenian community states:

> Every year we expect more and more people to come. We hope that Armenian customs that have been forgotten here will be brought again to us from Bucharest or Bacău or other places. And we hope that we also have something to share with them ... It is because of this feast that we have become such a big community. I have even heard Romanian Armenians saying that Gherla is like Mecca for the Armenians in Romania. Everybody is proud of this town.

---

[38] Except for priest from Gherla, other participating clergymen are regular Roman Catholic priests. Dumbrăveni Armenian Catholics are served by a priest from Mediaş. In Frumoasa there are no Armenians left, but the Armenian Catholic church still exists there, served by a local priest who is also in charge of village's Roman Catholic church. The descendants of Frumoasa Armenians still live nearby, in the city of Miercurea-Ciuc.

[39] Based on research conducted in Gheorgheni, Kinga Kali calls this phenomenon a "positional identity." As one of her respondents stated: "We are Hungarians during the week and Armenians on the weekends, in the church." Kinga Kali, "Vasárnapi örmények—valami a pozicionálisidentitásról," in Sándor Öze and Bálint Kovács (eds), *Örmény diaszpóra a Kárpát-medencében II* (Piliscsaba, 2007), p. 155 [Sunday-Armenians and something about the positional identity, in: The Armenian diaspora in Carpathian basin].

This meeting prompts a plethora of various strategies aimed both at establishing links and at reinforcing boundaries, and it reveals rifts and internal differences in what is often labelled by a collective term "the Armenian diaspora." While the religious differentiation between the Armenian Apostolic Church and the Armenian Catholic Church is downplayed today, and in 2012 the feast was celebrated for the first time in the presence of both the Armenian Apostolic Bishop of Romania and the Catholic Archbishop of Alba Julia, the complexities of historical and present-day Romanian–Hungarian relations also affect Armenians who have assimilated to these two host societies. Today's Armenian community in Gherla is in the midst of a number of socio-cultural and demographical processes on different scales, including a decline in the Hungarian population in Transylvania, and the growing activity of the Union of Armenians in Romania in the region. A few years ago a branch of the Union was established in the town, connecting local Armenians to their compatriots in Bucharest and bringing state funding for the operation of the community.[40] This rapprochement also brings a growing number of Romanian Armenians to the feast of St. Gregory the Illuminator.[41] On the other hand, this development has not been well received by a part of the Hungarian Transylvanian Armenians, including those who live today in Hungary. Certain tensions between the current leadership of the Gherla Armenians and the Transylvanian Armenian Roots Cultural Association from Budapest are reflected symbolically in the fact that the leaders of the latter organization are seated in the cellar of the house, and not in the "prestigious" parish hall, as are most other Armenian leaders.[42] Furthermore, since the internal situation in the modern Hungarian Armenian diaspora is also marked by multiple animosities and tensions, some of this enmity "travels" to the feast in Gherla together with the Hungarian guests.

With regard to this complex situation, it is noteworthy that in many respects Gherla's feast shares similarities with the Hungarian mass pilgrimage

---

[40] Today, the Union of Armenians in Romania has three branches in Transylvania: in Cluj-Napoca, Dumbrăveni and Gherla.

[41] In 2012 some 300 people were present during the feast, including around 80 Romanian Armenians from Bacău, Bucharest, Constanţa, Iaşi, and other towns, as well as Transylvanian Armenians from Cluj Napoca, Dumbrăveni, Gheorgheni, Miercurea Ciuc and Târgu Mureş. Furthermore, Armenians from Budapest as well as local guests were present.

[42] In turn, the recently developed Armenian feast in Gheorgheni may be seen as a kind of counter-balance to Gherla's feast. In Gheorgheni Hungarian sentiments are strong enough to block any official contacts with Romanian Armenians, associated with the Romanian state and society. Thus, compared to Gherla, this feast reflects and reinforces another set of strategies of identification, inclusion and exclusion.

to Șumuleu (Csiksomlyó) in Eastern Transylvania. In Anne-Marie Losonczy's words, this annual event has recently been transformed into the "ritual staging of Hungarian 'homeland' across borders and regardless of religious affiliations. [T]his pilgrimage provides a sophisticated ritual framework and the symbolic tools to negotiate the various groups' belonging to, and their hierarchic ordering in, the cultural construct of 'fatherland.'"[43] In Gherla too, Armenianness, in its various amalgamations with local cultures, is staged, the Armenian "homeland away from homeland" is re-created, and the right to the diasporic heritage is claimed and negotiated.

Conclusion

As discussed by the author elsewhere in this volume, the paradigm of ethno-religious inseparability plays a key role in modern Armenian identity discourse. As a result, religious traditions and ecclesiastic institutions hold a central place in many Armenian diaspora communities,[44] while at the same time being subjected to the ultimate goal of preserving Armenianness. The two feasts and shrines described in this chapter illustrate well this phenomenon. Hagigadar Monastery and Holy Trinity Cathedral share a status as crucial landmarks of Armenian historical and contemporary presence in Romania. They create the geography of the diaspora, marking the space of the host land with familiar and semantically saturated places. In turn, the ecclesiastic calendar determines to a large extent the rhythm of diaspora life. Religious feasts are the high points of the communal activities of Armenians in Romania, being the most important occasions for experiencing, practicing and publicly expressing not only one's religious convictions, but also—and often first of all—one's belonging to a distinct ethno-national group, and to a particular subgroup within this wider entity. Thus, on the one hand, they allow (in the spirit of Turnerian *communitas*) for the manifestation and affirmation of common Armenianness, often not expressed on a daily basis, while on the other hand (closer to Durkheimian thought)

---

[43] Anne-Marie Losonczy, "Pilgrims of the 'Fatherland': Emblems and Religious Rituals in the Construction of an Inter-Patriotic Space between Hungary and Transylvania," *History and Anthropology* 20, no. 3 (2009), p. 265.

[44] See for example Denise Aghanian, *The Armenian Diaspora: Cohesion and Fracture* (Lanham, 2007); Timothy Norman Fisher, *In Church with My Ancestors: The Changing Shape of Religious Memory in the Republic of Armenia and North American Diaspora*, Doctoral Diss. (University of Southern California, 2005); and Susan Paul Pattie, *Faith in History: Armenians Rebuilding Community* (Washington, DC, 1996).

they are an occasion for confirming existing relations of power, hierarchies, alliances and divisions within the shared cultural field.[45] Their important role in group cohesion and fractures turns the shrines and feasts examined here into chronotopes: the fundamental symbols of community.

References

Aghanian, Denise, *The Armenian Diaspora: Cohesion and Fracture* (Lanham: University Press of America, 2007).
Bakhtin, Mikhail, *The Dialogic Imagination: Four Essays*, ed. Michael Holquist (Austin: University of Texas Press, 1982).
Basso, Keith H., *Wisdom Sits in Places: Landscape and Language among Western Apache* (Albuquerque: University of New Mexico Press, 1996).
Bedros, Vlad, *Armenian Artistic Heritage in Romania: Between Exilic Nostalgia and Cultural Integration* (Bucharest: NOI Media Print, 2011).
Bowman, Glenn, "Orthodox-Muslim Interactions at Mixed Shrines in Macedonia," in Chris Hann and Hermann Goltz (eds), *Eastern Christians in Anthropological Perspective* (Berkeley: University of California Press, 2010), 195–219.
"Catalogue: IV. Church and the Veneration of Saints," in Bálint Kovács and Emese Pál (eds), *Far Away from Mount Ararat: Armenian Culture in the Carpathian Basin* (Leipzig: Leipziger Universitätsverlag, 2013), 137–53.
Dan, Dimitrie, *Armenii ortodocși din Bucovina* (Bucharest: Zamca, 2010).
E.A., "Hagigadar 2000," *Ararat* 16, no. 205 (August 16–31, 2000).
Eade, John and Michael J. Sallnow, "Introduction," in John Eade and Michael J. Sallnow (eds), *Contesting the Sacred: The Anthropology of Christian Pilgrimage* (Urbana: University of Illinois Press, 2000), 1–29.
Edles, Laura Desfor and Scott Appelrouth (eds), *Sociological Theory in the Classic Era: Text and Readings* (Thousand Oaks: Pine Forge Press, 2009).
Fisher, Timothy Norman, *In Church with My Ancestors: The Changing Shape of Religious Memory in the Republic of Armenia and the North American Diaspora*, Doctoral Diss. (University of Southern California, 2005).

---

[45] For more on Victor Turner's concept of communitas and its foundational role for the studies of pilgrimage and on Emile Durkheim's interpretation of feasts as reinforcing a social order, and pilgrimage sites as an arena of contesting discourses, see John Eade and Michael J. Sallnow, "Introduction," in John Eade and Michael J. Sallnow (eds), *Contesting the Sacred: The Anthropology of Christian Pilgrimage* (Urbana, 2000).

Golanchean, Suren, *Ṛumanahayutʻean Aninʼ Suchavayi Hay Gaghutʻe* (Yerevan: Hayastan, 2000). [Ani of the Romanian Armenians: The Armenian Colony of Suceava].

Hakobian, Datev, *500, 1512–2012 Hagigadar, The Holy Hagigadar Monastery of Suceava: Miracle Maker* (Bucharest: Zamca, n.d.).

Johnson, Paul Christopher, *Diaspora Conversion: Black Carib Religion and the Recovery of Africa* (Berkeley: University of California Press, 2007).

Kali, Kinga, "Vasárnapi örmények—valami a pozicionálisidentitásról," in Sándor Öze and Bálint Kovács (eds), *Örmény diaszpóra a Kárpát-medencében II* (Pilicsaba: Pázmány Péter Katolikus Egyetem, 2007), 145–55. [Sunday-Armenians and something about positional identity, in: Armenian diaspora in Carpathian basin].

Kovács, Bálint and Emese Pál (eds), *Far Away from Mount Ararat: Armenian Culture in the Carpathian Basin* (Leipzig: Leipziger Universitätsverlag, 2013).

Losonczy, Anne-Marie, "Pilgrims of the 'Fatherland': Emblems and Religious Rituals in the Construction of an Inter-Patriotic Space between Hungary and Transylvania," *History and Anthropology* 20, no. 3 (2009): 265–80.

Öze, Sándor and Bálint Kovács (eds), *Örmény diaszpóra a Kárpát medencében* (Piliscsaba: Pázmány Péter Katolikus Egyetem, 2006). [The Armenian diaspora in Carpathian basin].

Öze, Sándor and Bálint Kovács (eds), *Örmény diaszpóra a Kárpát-medencében II* (Pilicsaba: Pázmány Péter Katolikus Egyetem, 2007). [The Armenian diaspora in Carpathian basin II].

Pál, Emese, "The Sacral Art of Transylvanian Armenians," in Bálint Kovács and Emese Pál (eds), *Far Away from Mount Ararat: Armenian Culture in the Carpathian Basin* (Leipzig: Leipziger Universitätsverlag, 2013), 73–83.

Pál, Judith, *Armenians in Transylvania* (Cluj-Napoca: Romanian Cultural Institute, 2005).

Pattie, Susan Paul, *Faith in History: Armenians Rebuilding Community* (Washington, DC: Smithsonian Institution Press, 1996).

Safran, William, "Diasporas in Modern Societies: Myths of Homeland and Return," *Diaspora: A Journal of Transnational Studies* 1, no. 1 (1991): 83–99.

Scurtu, Ioan and Ioan Dordea (eds), *Minoritățile Naționale din România 1925–1931* (Bucharest: Arhivele Naționale ale României, 1996).

Selian, Sergiu, *Schita istorica a comunitatii armene din România* (Bucharest: Ararat, 1999).

Siruni, Hakob, *Hay Yekeghets'in Rumen Hoghi Vra. Nicola Yorga* (Ējmiatsin: Mayr At'oṛ Surb Ējmiatsin, 1966). [The Armenian Church in Romanian Lands. Nicola Yorga].

Stacescu, Leon, *Armenians in Romania*, www.personal.ceu.hu/students/02/Leon_Stacescu/rh/htm, accessed on June 15, 2014.

Third Report Submitted by Romania Pursuant to Article 25, Paragraph 1 of the Framework Convention for the Protection of National Minorities, 2011, www.coe.int/t/dghl/monitoring/minorities/3_fcnmdocs/PDF_3rd_SR_Romania_en.pdf, accessed on June 15, 2014.

Vozganian, Varujan, *Cartea șoaptelor* (Iași: Polirom, 2009).

Chapter 10

Armenians in St. Petersburg: Belonging to the Church as a Key Marker of Ethnic Identity

Anatolii Tokmantcev

In this chapter I analyze how Armenians in St. Petersburg, Russia, consider affiliation with the Armenian Apostolic Church (AAC, or the Armenian Church) and the Russian Orthodox Church (ROC, or the Russian Church) as a mechanism of self-identification and as a marker or measure of assimilation.

Fear of complete assimilation into a host society is a widespread phobia among national minorities and migrants. People who live in alien surroundings often consider preserving the uniqueness of their culture as their most important aim. The earliest scholars of migration studies tended to regard assimilation as a linear process.[1] This approach, sometimes called "straight-line theory,"[2] describes the process of forming a relationship between host societies and migrants as unidirectional, where minorities inevitably merge with the host society. Later, most scholars replaced this view of assimilation by the "two-dimensional theory."[3] This approach describes the cultures of migrants and host societies as independent from one another. It states that identification with one of these cultures influences the other to a small extent. Although the second theory of assimilation tends to consider the more complex nature of the researched phenomenon than "straight-line theory," in both cases ethnicity is treated as something real—as an entity that can be quantified and measured. Often the proponents of the "two-dimensional theory" claim that ethnicity changes with every new generation of migrants—it can weaken as well as revive and become

---

[1] For instance, see Robert Ezra Park, "Assimilation, Social," *Encyclopedia of the Social Sciences* 2 (1930), p. 281.

[2] See Neil C. Sandberg, *Ethnic Identity and Assimilation: The Polish-American Community Case Study of Metropolitan Los Angeles* (New York, 1974).

[3] For instance, see Judith R. Porter and Robert E. Washington, "Minority Identity and Self-Esteem," *Annual Review of Sociology* (1993), pp. 139–61.

stronger. This perspective depicts assimilation as moving along a spectrum that measures ethnicity as whole and complete on one end and completely dissolved into a host society on the other. The position of an individual or a group on this scale is often determined by what generation of migrants they belong to. I should add that usually ethnicity is treated as a more or less stable entity that is equal to itself within one generation. This approach does not necessarily state that ethnicity weakens with every new generation, but it tends to overestimate the role of time in the assimilation process, while the influence of the context that ethnicity functions in plays an auxiliary role.

Since the beginning of the 1980s, as the constructivist paradigm for understanding ethnicity became more popular, this approach has evolved. Scholars began to treat ethnicity as a perspective on the world rather than as a concrete entity or a stable set of markers. This new understanding moved the subjective feelings and expectations of *the ethnicity bearer* from the periphery of research attention to its center. Moreover, scholars began to treat ethnicity as a social identity—an identity that is produced and retained through social interaction and the stability of which depends both on the process of self-identification (counting oneself as a member of a group, practices of describing one's behavior and actions as a consequence of belonging to an ethnic group, etc.) and on creating and maintaining the image of an *ethnic alien*.[4] Nevertheless, within the tradition of migration studies there still remain works in which, for example, food preferences of migrants or church attendance are viewed as a sign of either their assimilation or of a revitalization of their ethnicity. I contend that it is not a transformation of practices that reflects the ethnicity shift, but rather a change of the perception of those practices.

Brief History and Current State of the Community

To begin, I will summarize the history of Armenians in St. Petersburg. The first historical sources to mention Armenians in St. Petersburg date from 1708, which is five years after the city itself was founded.[5] Notwithstanding the fact that Peter the Great declared favored treatment for Armenians in Russia, they could not build churches and conduct services in St. Petersburg according to

---

[4] For further details, see Fredrik, Barth, "Introduction" in F. Barth (ed.) *Ethnic Groups and Boundaries: the Social Organization and Cultural Differences* (Long Grove, Illinois: Waveland Press, 1998), pp. 9–38.

[5] Ruben Anghaladyan, "Armyanskiy Peterburg" [Armenian Petersburg], *21 vek* 4, no. 16 (2010), p. 94.

the traditions of the AAC. For more than 60 years Armenian churches did not exist in the capital of the Russian Empire. In 1770, Catherine the Great finally allowed Armenians to erect the Church of Saint Catherine on Nevskiĭ Prospect, the main street of St. Petersburg. This church opened in 1780, and in 1794 another Armenian church, the Church of the Resurrection, was built at the Armenian cemetery on Vasil'evskiĭ Island in St. Petersburg. During the eighteenth and nineteenth centuries the Armenian population in the city did not grow significantly: according to the 1897 Census, slightly over 850 Armenians lived in the city.[6] However, during the following two decades, this number increased dramatically. This was also a period when approximately 12 Armenian organizations appeared in St. Petersburg, including the Armyanskiĭ kruzhok (Armenian Circle), the Obshchestvo popechitel'stva nad armyanami (Organization of Patronage Over Armenians) and the Armyanskiĭ klub (Armenian Club).[7] Religious institutions were not created during this period, but the two previously mentioned Armenian churches served as religious centers for Armenians in St. Petersburg from the end of the eighteenth century on.

After the civil war in Russia, in the 1920s and 1930s, all the Armenian organizations in St. Petersburg (Petrograd from 1914 to 1924 and Leningrad from 1924 to 1991) were forced to close and their property was appropriated by the state. From the 1930s through the early 1980s all ethnic institutions were banned from St. Petersburg, and only the period of Perestroika made it possible for Armenians in Leningrad to begin a campaign to reclaim their rights to the buildings that used to belong to the Armenian community, including both of the churches. In 1988, by a resolution of the Leningrad Executive Committee, the Church of the Resurrection,[8] located at the Armenian cemetery, reopened its doors to parishioners.[9] Five years later, in 1993, the Church of St. Catherine on Nevskiĭ Prospect was also returned to the Armenian community.

After receiving the churches, the Armenian community of St. Petersburg formed its shape and structure, which have since changed little. The term "community" is used here in a narrow sense, not as encompassing all ethnic Armenians in the city, but referring to those who are actively involved and

---

[6] The results of the Russian Census of 1897 can be found at the Russian *Demoskop Weekly* journal, published by the Higher School of Economics: see Russian Census Results.

[7] Romanova, Nina, *National'nye obshchestva Sankt-Peterburga XVIII-XXI Vek* [National communities of St. Petersburg in 18–21 Centuries] (St. Petersburg: SPN, 2004).

[8] Before 1988, this church was used as a workshop for a Soviet sculptor.

[9] Avgustin Nikitin, "Armianskaya khristianskaya obshina v Peterburge" [Armenian Christian Community in St. Petersburg], *Neva* (2011), p. 199.

engaged in various community projects.[10] Nor do I mean by "community" a single formal association: it is rather an informal umbrella that includes a few registered groups that I will list below.

It is significant that the post-Soviet Armenian community in St. Petersburg is a new phenomenon. It has very little in common with pre-revolutionary Armenian organizations, although the members of the community refer to it as a centuries-old tradition. Approximately 30,000–35,000 Armenians live in St. Petersburg, while less than 1,000 of them are actually interested and take part in the life of the community. So, despite the fact that people know that during the Soviet period the community did not exist, they usually stress the venerable age of the community. This strategy of adding years to the age of a tradition is used to legitimize its existence—a practice that comes from the belief that the older a tradition is, the more valuable, righteous and attractive it is for its followers.[11]

Despite the fact that in the beginning of the 1990s organizations initiated by ethnic and political groups were created all over the USSR, the creation of the Armenian community in St. Petersburg had a few unique traits. First, unlike in most other cities,[12] the core of the Armenian community was constituted by the Church. The Armenian Church formed the foundation of the community and took a key position in it. Both priests and grassroots members agree that it was and still is the Armenian Church that glues the community together:

> In other cities they speak about 'church' and 'community' as separate entities. We don't have that here. When we mention the church, we imply the community as well. We can't imagine the community without the church. It is like a person without a soul and a soul without a body—they are supposed to be together.[13]

---

[10] The term "community" does not automatically include the entire Armenian population of the city. It refers exclusively to an organization with a high level of institutionalization, i.e., formalization of relationships between its members, the creation of an official or unofficial hierarchy of power, and a more or less coherent structure of communal subdivisions. This definition allows us to divide the Armenian population of St. Petersburg into two groups: members of the community and non-members. This is necessary because of the way in which the Church is perceived is specific to each group.

[11] For further details, see Eric Hobsbawm "Introduction: Inventing Tradition," in E. Hobsbawm and T. Ranger (eds), *Invention of Tradition* (Cambridge: Cambridge University Press, 1983).

[12] In cities like Krasnoyarsk and Novosibirsk, communities were organized by ambitious and industrious people, and religious elements were brought later. Also, in Moscow the AAC and non-religious communal institutions function simultaneously and, to a great extent, independently.

[13] Informant, male, priest of the AAC, St. Petersburg.

… [If we did not have a church here,] I think we would not have a community either. People gather here. I like when I notice that young people come to church on holidays. They are interested in it. They will definitely pass it on to their children. So, as during our whole history, our faith saved our people.[14]

The second important characteristic that makes the Armenian community in St. Petersburg different from those in other cities is the Lazarev Brothers Educational Center (*Kulturno-prosvetitel'skiy tsentr brat'ev Lazarevyh*),[15] where students of various ages study the Armenian language, literature, history, folk art, and take Bible lessons. There is a library with books in Armenian, Russian, English and other languages. Other communities also have Sunday schools, but unlike in other cities, the school in St. Petersburg is located close to the Church of St. Catherine and other communal branches. This is intended to promote communal socialization for students and their parents. Furthermore, the religious component in teaching is exceptionally important. For example, every Sunday before classes, students and teachers gather in a hall and sing the national anthem of the Republic of Armenia and read the Lord's Prayer in Armenian. In addition to the church and the educational center, other key institutions in the Armenian community of St. Petersburg include the Council of Elders (*Sovet Stareîshin*),[16] a Women's Council (*Zhenskiî Sovet*)[17] and the Youth Union (Molodyozhniî Soyuz "Nor Serund").[18]

The Perceived Goals of the Community

The existence of the community has several purposes. The members are aware of some of them, while other purposes are implied and mostly remain unarticulated. One of the main goals for the community is to promote mono-ethnic marriages

---

[14] Informant, female, teacher of Sunday school, St. Petersburg.

[15] The Lazarevs was a family of merchants and patrons of the arts of Armenian descent who lived in the Russian Empire during the eighteenth and nineteenth centuries.

[16] This subdivision is a sort of opposition to Church authorities in the community. In other words, they represent the secular power that can be judicial towards the communal policy of the Church.

[17] This name is used by all community members, while the full title of the organization is *The Saint Petersburg Union of Armenian Women Named after Saint Rhipsime at the Armenian Apostolic Church*. The main goal of *The Council* is to organize and coordinate charity projects.

[18] The Organization of Armenian Youth is always in charge of organizing public events, such as April 24 demonstrations, sport and knowledge contests for community members, etc.

as a way to prevent or slow down the assimilation process. Most of the events that are organized by the Organization of Armenian Youth are regarded as a perfect way for young Armenians in search of starting a new family to find each other in a large cosmopolitan city:

> I think that a threat of assimilation exists when it comes to Russian-Armenian marriages. I have a son, and I'm worried about this. When you bring them up and invest a lot in them, you also want to find him a girl who has the same knowledge and skills. My daughter always says, 'There is no way I will marry a guy of another nationality.' My nephew dates a Russian girl—a very good girl. My daughter says, 'I do not understand it.' She has formed her position, but my son hasn't yet.[19]

The second goal of the community may be referred to as ethnic socialization. To analyze it, I have split the community members into several groups. The first group consists of migrants who came from Armenia or other parts of the former USSR. The members of this group grew up in surroundings where the principles and elements of Armenian culture (Armenian language, traditional Armenian rules of social interaction, etc.) dominated over patterns of other cultures. They identify themselves as Armenian people who are members of Armenian culture, and, most importantly, have a high level of cultural competence, which means that they know "how to be Armenian."

The second group includes those who were brought up in the community—in the particular narrow sense that I defined above—through such activities as attending Sunday school and playing with peers after lessons. In other words, this group includes those whose parents were ethnically oriented in their upbringing.

The third group is of most interest for my analysis because it embraces those who were raised outside of the community and whose ethnic identity had until a certain moment been of lesser importance (compared to gender or other identities), or for whom this had not been an object of reflection at all. At a certain moment, ethnic identity gets actualized and sometimes begins to play a primary role in reference to other identities. This shift can occur, though not necessarily, as a result of categorization from members of a host society. For instance, insulting nicknames ("*churka*," "*hachik*," "*cherniy*") that are based on one's phenotypic differences can cause actualization of identity with the Armenian ethnic group. In other words, ethnicity can be awakened by a recipient society, rather than by family or community.

---

[19] Informant, female, member of the community, St. Petersburg.

As a child I was constantly told that I was not Russian. It happens. They say, for example, 'In this skit Tanya will play the role of Snowflake because she has blue eyes and white hair, but Katya is not suitable here.' So, beautiful blond girls always played princesses, and I played the third maidservant or something.[20]

After a person identifies as a member of the Armenian community, he or she, in contrast to members of the first two groups, will raise the following question: "What does it mean to be Armenian?" In situations where this kind of knowledge has never been provided before (such as with a member of our third group), one needs a source of information to fill the gap. Among potential *enlighteners* I will name the two most significant in my opinion: self-education (reading books, watching films, etc.) and the community. In other words, besides the mission of finding a marriage partner, the community also plays the role of an ethno-socializing agent by fostering the acquisition of patterns and values of Armenian culture and teaching the markers of being Armenian.

The moment of joining the community is most important because new members are tacitly introduced and held to the *code of the ethnic club* (hereinafter "the code"), which is a set of unspoken rules and expectations that impose a responsibility on members of the community to preserve Armenian traditions and customs. This code prescribes members to do various practices and activities and labels these practices as part of the "Armenian tradition," despite the fact that some of these activities have never been practiced in Armenia or in other Armenian communities outside of Armenia.[21]

Good command of the Armenian language is one of the most important rules of this code. However, if newcomers do not speak Armenian, which is often the case, Russian can be used as a legitimate substitution, and the new member is supposed to learn the Armenian language and, most importantly, regard it as a value. Nevertheless, these expectations do not imply that they will ever practically speak the language. This means that, in order to satisfy the claims of the code, they must demonstrate a striving to acquire the language of their ancestors. In other words, speaking Armenian is not necessary, while regarding it as a value is an obligation. For instance, some leaders of the youth organization *Nor Serund* do not speak Armenian, but this does not cause any damage to their reputation or status in the community.

---

[20] Informant, female, member of the community, 32 years old.
[21] For example, the images of *masculinity* and *femininity* include dress-code requirements that cannot be found anywhere else but in St. Petersburg.

Belonging to the Church as a Core of the Identity Code

Another central obligation of the code is that members of the community visit church regularly:

> There was a librarian in the community—Sophia Ambartsumovna. She had a humpback. And they [the leaders of the community] let her work there. She was from Baku and her Armenian was very bad, because of which she developed an inferiority complex. She always said that they got very angry when she did not go to church, and her disability could not be used as an excuse. I want to say that it is thought that if the community is built around the Church, it is obligatory to go there.[22]

This statement by a community member allows us to conclude that members of the Armenian community in St. Petersburg exercise control over one another. In order to obtain and retain membership in this *club*, one is expected to be loyal to the rules—both articulated and non-articulated. This loyalty gives people the right to consider themselves as Armenian, or *true Armenians*, while disregarding the rules may cause a delegitimization of one's Armenianness,[23] or even *expulsion* from the organization. The rules of the code are seen by community members as characteristics of Armenianness that constitute the image of an Armenian. Consequently, if one obeys all the prescriptions, he or she has the right to consider his or herself a real Armenian. This image is so meaningful for members of the community that adherence to it is thought to grant the right to consider oneself more Armenian even than Armenians who live in Armenia:

> I am proud that when we speak on the phone all my relatives from Armenia become surprised that my kids speak proper Armenian, while their children only speak the vernacular language.[24]

There are several reasons why the community code includes an obligation to visit the AAC. The first was mentioned above—namely the placement of the Church at the core of the organization. In addition to this, people argue that there can be no Armenianness without the Armenian Church:

---

[22] Informant, female, member of the community, 43 years old.
[23] Non-adherence to the norms of a community often leads to the expulsion of the rule-breaker (see Russel Hardin, "Migration and Community," *Journal of Social Philosophy* 36, no. 2 (2005), pp. 273–87).
[24] Informant, female, member of the community, 47 years old.

> Everything would be different [if there was no Church]. As someone said, 'If two Armenians meet, they build a church, a school, and publish a newspaper.' And it is true because without language, school, and faith, Armenians would never survive.²⁵

> For centuries, the AAC has played the role of a mother for the Armenian people, both metaphorically and literally. I mean that, as a mother is important in every person's life, the 'Mother-Church' is significant in the life of the people.²⁶

It is normal for members of the community to think of Christianity as an inherent marker of Armenianness:

> I heard that many political leaders of Soviet Armenia, and of the rest of the Soviet Union in general, secretly visited churches. And if they weren't there when their children were baptized, their parents or grandparents did it. I mean, they knew what was happening and approved of it. What does this say to us? It says that national identity, Christian national identity, for Armenians in particular, became a part of us. Even those who lived in the Soviet Union managed to save it, sometimes even at the expense of life or liberty.²⁷

These words clearly show a correlation between belonging to the AAC and being or feeling Armenian. Any attempts to adhere to or represent the image of a "real Armenian" are considered unsuccessful without demonstrated affiliation with the national Church.²⁸ This rule does not necessarily imply a requirement for religious beliefs. It is attendance at church that is valued. Faith and religiosity, on the other hand, are often viewed as obvious consequences of either Armenianness or affiliation with the Church. Therefore, going to church is enough to think of oneself as a Christian, which is necessary for considering oneself to be a *true Armenian*. This correlation between church affiliation and Armenianness is a result of the policy of representation that the AAC has pursued for the past two decades.

---

²⁵ Informant, female, member of the community, 30 years old.
²⁶ Informant, male, priest of the AAC, St. Petersburg.
²⁷ Informant, male, member of the community, 30 years old.
²⁸ The AAC argues against the claims of proponents of new-paganism who say that Christianity is not native for Armenians, while paganism has always been the primordial and original religion of the Armenian people. These views are shared by very few Armenians. (For more details, see Antonyan "'Vossozdanie' religii: neoyazychestvo v Armenii" ["Reconstituting" Religion: Neo-Paganism in Armenia], *Laboratorium* 1 (2010), pp. 103–27).

During the Soviet period, the Armenian Church was controlled by the government, so it was unable to pursue its own independent policy. However, after the disintegration of the USSR, the Armenian Church faced a problem: it had to find a new role in a new world, and make others recognize this role. To promote self-image among both Armenians and non-Armenians, the AAC has chosen self-representation as the main defender of the Armenian people:

> *Interviewer*: Besides the support of the Church, what should the community and Armenians in general do to preserve language, literature …?
>
> *Informant*: In order to retain all of these things, the only thing we must do is save the Church. Why? History can help us find the answer to this question. For centuries, the Armenian people didn't hold statehood. And during all this time, the 'Mother-Church' played the role of the state, the role of heart and home, of Faith and of its people. If we look back in history, we'll see that the Armenian language, as well as culture, first appeared in the Church. I mean, the art of miniature, the language, and, most importantly, the alphabet was created by Mesrop Mashtots. Almost all schools were located in monasteries. If we take all these facts into account, we will understand that the Church saved our faith, language, and culture.[29]

The AAC tends to highlight its impact on the preservation of the Armenian people as significant, and often more significant, than that of the state. In other words, the AAC can be compared with the Ministry of both Foreign and Domestic Affairs. In the Republic of Armenia, the AAC strives to take control over education, cultural diversity, religious policy, etc. Outside of Armenia, the Armenian Church usually establishes close ties with other churches that are considered *traditional* for these countries. The AAC recognizes some Christian denominations as "Sister-Churches":

> We recognize the Catholic Church … We call it the Sister-Church … The Russian Orthodox Church is also our Sister-Church,[30] so we accept all its sacraments.[31]

---

[29] Informant, male, priest of the AAC, St. Petersburg.

[30] While officially there is no Eucharist communion between the Russian Orthodox and Armenian Apostolic churches, Armenian priests pay very little, if any, attention to this fact in practice and allow the members of the ROC to receive sacraments. They, for instance, do not require both a bride and groom to be members of the AAC for them to take the Ordinance of Marriage.

[31] Informant, male, priest of the AAC, Krasnoyarsk.

Through this definition of "Sister-Church," the Armenian Church acknowledges the legitimacy of the rituals and theology of these other churches.[32] In ecclesiastical terms, the Armenian Church agrees that these churches are also bestowed with God's grace. This implies that followers of these "Sister-Churches" have the same chances as members of the AAC to save their souls from sin, which is one of the central tenets of Christianity. It also means that Etchmiadzin has almost reached the peak of the ecumenical movement, meaning that it agrees that other churches can be as close to God as the AAC. By pursuing this accepting policy towards other Christian denominations, the Armenian Church demonstrates loyalty to host societies on behalf of all Armenians.

The fact that the AAC recognizes other churches' dogmatic and ritual systems as righteous practically means sacrificing its own theology to ecumenism. But the fact that the AAC does not provide the only way for salvation does not make the AAC less appealing to its followers. Rather, the AAC attracts followers by means of argumentation that does not concern salvation; the AAC claims that it is unique not because of its theology, but because of the particularities of its rituals, which can be traced back to the First Apostles, as well as because of its being the first Christian Church to be named an official state Church in the world's history (which occurred in 301, according to tradition), and because of passages in the Bible that mention Armenia. Moreover, the Armenian Church argues that all this constitutes the core of Armenian culture and Armenianness. Therefore, following the AAC—a source or citadel of Armenianness—is the only mechanism by which Armenians can remain themselves and prevent their dissolution into the modern global world. Turning back to the Armenian community in St. Petersburg, that is why the obligation to attend church is seen as an inevitable part of belonging to the community; members of the community regard attending the AAC as the only efficient way to avoid assimilation with the host society. So, from this point of view, failure to obey the prescription that members of the community attend the Armenian church every week can lead to a loss of Armenianness.

However, the perception of Christian affiliation can sometimes be ambiguous, as in the following conversation:

> *Informant*: Tell me, please, who the heck is Armenian? Since we are talking about Armenians ... Armenians who believe in Islam—are they Armenians, or

---

[32] The list of recognized churches usually includes Chalcedonian Orthodox churches, Roman Catholic churches and churches that did not recognize the 4th Ecumenical Council in Chalcedon.

scoundrels or villains? I will tell you—they are Armenians. I mean that the most important thing is to feel Armenian, to respect Armenian history, to understand Armenian traditional values. That's it. Whether they believe in Buddha or in some Australian idol is their personal business. But for most Armenians, our Church is the foundation of Armenianness. But those who choose Buddha—the Armenian Church, even if it wants to, can never say to them, 'Listen, you believe in this pillar? Go away, you are not Armenian.'

Interviewer: So, this does not make Armenians less Armenian, right?

Informant: No ... Our Church should do everything to return its 'children.' A lot of them belong to other churches, but this does not mean that we should renounce them.[33]

This kind of conflicting interpretation is widely spread among the members of the community. On the one hand, the belief that following the AAC is the only way to retain Armenianness is very popular and never questioned openly. On the other hand, in the context that is set by the question "Do you think that Armenians outside of the AAC lose their Armenianness?" community members often claim that it is possible to remain Armenian without being affiliated with the AAC. This claim is usually followed by a list of other requirements that must be fulfilled, such as respecting Armenian history, feeling Armenian, etc. In this context, the mentioned requirements are considered more important for the image of "true Armenianness" than is attending the Armenian Church. Hence, members of the community evaluate the AAC's role as savior of the Armenian people differently in different contexts.

Thus, in general discourse, affiliation with the Armenian Church is seen as necessary to prevent assimilation, but a direct question about the correlation between attending the AAC and being Armenian brings the opposite opinion. In everyday life, members of the community understand the meaning of ethnicity in general, and Armenianness in particular, in two mutually exclusive contexts. On the one hand, the community imposes the markers of "true Armenianness" on its members, and affiliation with the AAC is among those markers. On the other hand, they cannot help but notice that some Armenians successfully retain their Armenianness outside of the community and without attending the AAC. Both standpoints have valid examples from real life experience that can be used as a proof. Using one of them usually helps escape facing the contradiction. Hence,

---

[33] Informant, male, member of the community, 57 years old.

switching between different kinds of experience helps avoid the contradiction and allow people to make a decision that makes more sense in a certain situation, i.e. to claim that the Church is necessary for retaining Armenianness in one context while denying this rule in other contexts.

According to the code that regulates the image of "the real Armenian," Armenians who prefer the Russian Church over the Armenian Church are more likely to be absorbed by the host society because they do not have access to the central *source of Armenianness*, meaning the AAC. However, the code does not impose a complete taboo on visits to the ROC. In the event of an *emergency*, when one feels a need to communicate with God,[34] the Russian Church can be an acceptable substitution for the Armenian Church. Besides that, members of the community use cases when Armenians visit the ROC to highlight the good relationship between Russians and Armenians.[35] But permanent affiliation with this other Church can threaten a person's Armenianness.

Russian Orthodox Armenians: A Partial Substitution

Armenians who rarely or never visit the community have a different perception of their ethnicity. Armenians who are not members of the community either belong to another religious movement or are indifferent to all religious activity. In order to illustrate the situation fully, I will describe the features of a group of Armenians who attend the Russian Orthodox Church.

Outside of the community, the choice of which Church to attend is frequently made based on factors other than ethnicity: personal preference, geographical location, etc. So, maintaining a strong connection between affiliation with a Church and ethnicity—the basic idea of the community code—becomes irrelevant outside of the community. Thus, attending the Russian Orthodox Church can bear no connotations with ethnic identity.

Both the ROC and the AAC strive to represent themselves as protectors of *their peoples*. However, the ROC's policy toward theological disputes with other churches is completely different from that of the AAC. It is theological correctness and purity that the Russian Church stresses as its advantage over the Armenian Church and as the reason why people should follow Orthodoxy. Nevertheless, this position does not imply that just anyone can become

---

[34] To pray for success in work or business, to light a candle, etc.
[35] "We have no problems [in our relationship with Russians]. I know many Russians, I have Russian friends, I sometimes go to Russian churches." Informant, female, member of the community, 30 years old.

Orthodox. The ethno-religious discourse[36] (actively formulated and supported by both churches) describes ethnic groups as primordially attached to a certain religious tradition. Hence, all members of an ethnic group from the very first day of their lives are thought to belong to *their church*. This widespread opinion plays into the hands of both churches, as it makes people think that their membership in a Church is not a matter of choice, but of heritage and ethnicity. Thereby, the ROC is considered the Church of Russians, or the *Church of Russia*,[37] while the AAC is the Church of Armenians. In other words, neither the ROC nor the AAC strive to attract members of each other's flock. Rather it is much more important for them to display themselves as guardians of their people.[38]

There are several reasons why Armenians go to the *ethnically alien* Russian Church. First, many Armenians who came to St. Petersburg from regions of the former USSR other than Armenia (Azerbaijan, Georgia or Central Asia, for instance) often have a low competency in Armenian culture, meaning that they speak Armenian poorly or do not speak the language at all and do not eat or prepare Armenian food, among other factors. These factors sometimes make them fear that their desire to join the Armenian community would not be legitimized. For instance:

> My brother goes to the Armenian Church, but his spouse (who is also Armenian) goes to the Russian Church. It is easy—she was born in Ashkhabad [Central Asia] and she speaks no Armenian at all. So, she is afraid to go to our Church

---

[36] Below, I provide an example of the position of the ROC concerning the correlation of ethnicity and belonging to the Church. It is an excerpt from "The Foundations of the Social Conception of the ROC," published on the website of the Patriarchate of Moscow: "Christian patriotism is patriotism to the nation, where the nation is both an ethnic group and a group of citizens. Orthodox Christians should love their motherland, which can be measured territorially, and their blood-brothers all around the world. This kind of love is one of the ways to obey the commandment to 'love thy neighbor as thyself.' It includes love to one's family and compatriots." www.patriarchia.ru/db/text/141422.html, accessed August 5, 2012.

[37] In this case "Russia" includes territories outside the Russian Federation, for example Ukraine, Belarus, Moldova, and the rest of so-called "canonical territory" claimed by Russian Orthodox ecclesiology.

[38] Sometimes when the priests of the ROC learn about the Armenianness of potential parishioners they refuse to officiate. For example: "We wanted to baptize a girl in the Orthodox Church. Her parents were Georgians and her Godfather was Armenian. When a priest was told this he said, 'Are you Armenian? The ritual cannot be done.' Though another priest from the same church agreed." Informant, female, member of the community, 51 years old.

because she knows you need to know Armenian here. Generally speaking, she says that she feels better in the Russian Church.[39]

This quote provides an example of how a person's inability to satisfy the expectations of members of the Armenian community can determine his or her choice in favor of the ROC. On the other hand, there are Armenians who, unlike members of the community, often do not feel the need to breathe new life into their ethnicity. At the same time, they may feel a need to attend church to realize their religious feelings. Affiliation with the Armenian Church often results in joining the community where, besides visiting the church, one is usually encouraged to follow all other rules. Unwillingness to obey these rules often excludes the option of attending the AAC. Therefore, reluctance or inability to restore and retain Armenianness, which is the central aim of the community, discourages them from attending the AAC.

Another reason why Armenians often affiliate with the ROC is the notion that their Armenianness is dissolved in a mixture of other ethnicities. Often the only connection with Armenianness is based on Armenian descent. For such "nominal" Armenians, having Armenian ancestors—parents, grandparents or great grandparents—on the one hand, prevents them from completely renouncing their Armenianness, but, on the other hand, cannot be sufficient enough for them to consider themselves Armenians.

> *Informant*: My grandfather was Armenian. That's it. So, I don't think I'm an Armenian. I can call myself Ukrainian. I don't know anything about Armenians or about the Armenian Church—I never found it interesting. I think I am Russian.[40]

> *Informant*: It is hard for me to decide which ethnic group I belong to ... My family is a mixture of different nationalities. So, genetically, my father is half-Armenian and half-Ukrainian. He doesn't look like an Armenian though. My mother is half-Kazakh and half-Tatar ... So, for me it is hard to consider myself one of those.[41]

Identification with a group of non-Armenians does not necessarily imply identification with Russians, as demonstrated in the first of the last two quotes. Indeed, *deactivated* Armenianness can also mean that, in everyday life, one's identification with an ethnic group can remain optional and unnecessary. The

---

[39] Informant, female, member of the community, 30 years old.
[40] Informant, male, priest of the ROC, 47 years old.
[41] Informant, female, Orthodox church-goer, 51 years old.

second of the last two quotes clearly demonstrates how the informant denied her belonging to any ethnic group, being unable to describe a coherent *ethnic history* for her ancestors. This situation cannot be explained in terms of assimilation theory because ethnic identity does not change or drift toward another identity. What we see is *deactivation* of any ethnic identity at all. In other words, ethnicity does not change in quantity, but it does change in quality.

Conclusion

Armenians who belong to the Armenian community—in the narrow sense that I have defined in this chapter—regard the Armenian Apostolic Church as the foundation of Armenianness and as an inevitable part of their image of a *true Armenian*. Thus, the task of retaining Armenianness becomes impossible without attending the Armenian Church. This attitude toward the Armenian Church can be characterized as pragmatic and instrumental, i.e., the AAC is seen as the perfect "medicine" that can cure the assimilation disease. As noted above, within the community, the Armenian Church primarily serves, so to speak, as a savior of Armenianness, while its role in saving the souls of parishioners is much less significant.

As for the Russian Orthodox Church, it is considered an adequate substitution for the AAC in cases when one has an urgent need to speak to God, but permanent affiliation with the ROC is regarded as a sign of assimilation and a loss of Armenianness.

Russian Orthodox Armenians do not take part in the life of the community. Some of them choose the Russian Church over the Armenian Church because they do not want to accept the responsibilities of obeying the rules of the Armenian community. They still value their Armenianness, but often they cannot accept the image of a *true Armenian* that is offered by the community. However, most often the decision to attend the Russian Church is not influenced by ethnic connotations or rationalizations. It is simply seen as a way to express one's religious feelings. Thus, in these situations, the problem of assimilation loses its relevance for church-goers because they do not consider losing ethnicity to be an important concern.

References

Anghaladyan, Ruben, "Armyanskiy Peterburg" [Armenian Petersburg], *21 vek*, no. 4 (2010): 91–108 (in Russian).

Antonyan, Yulia, "'Vossozdanie' religii: Neoyazychestvo v Armenii" ["Reconstituting" Religion: Neo-Paganism in Armenia], *Laboratorium* 1 (2010), pp. 103–27 (in Russian).

Barth, Fredrik, "Introduction" in F. Barth (ed.) *Ethnic Groups and Boundaries: the Social Organization and Cultural Differences* (Long Grove, Illinois: Waveland Press, 1998), pp. 9–38.

The Foundations of the Social Conception of the ROC (in Russian), http://www.patriarchia.ru/db/text/141422.html, accessed August 5, 2012.

Hardin, Russel, "Migration and Community," *Journal of Social Philosophy* 36 no. 2 (2005): 273–87.

Hobsbawm, Eric, "Introduction: Inventing Tradition," in E. Hobsbawm and T. Ranger (eds), *Invention of Tradition* (Cambridge: Cambridge University Press, 1983), 1–14.

Nikitin, Avgustin, "Armianskaya khristianskaya obshina v Peterburge" [Armenian Christian Community in St. Petersburg], *Neva* (2011): 191–237 (in Russian).

Park, Robert Ezra, "Assimilation, Social," *Encyclopedia of the Social Sciences* 2 (1930): 281.

Porter, Judith R. and Robert E. Washington, "Minority Identity and Self-Esteem," *Annual Review of Sociology* (1993): 139–61.

Romanova, Nina, *National'nye obshchestva Sankt-Peterburga XVIII–XXI Vek* [National Communities of St. Petersburg in 18–21 Centuries] (St. Petersburg: SPN, 2004) (in Russian).

Russian Census 1897, *Demoskop-weekly*, http://demoscope.ru/weekly/pril.php, accessed May 12, 2012.

Sandberg, Neil C., *Ethnic Identity and Assimilation: The Polish-American Community Case Study of Metropolitan Los Angeles* (New York: Praeger, 1974).

Chapter 11

Finger on the Pulse: Armenian Identity and Religiosity in Southern California

Dyron Daughrity and Nicholas Cumming

From 2009 to 2011, a study on Armenian identity and religion in the greater Los Angeles area took place involving several individuals from Pepperdine University.[1] The study is based on an anonymous survey for Armenians in Southern California; it was available in both English and Armenian. While the survey puts a "finger on the pulse" of Armenian cultural trends, the primary focus is to identify the role of religion in the lives of Southern California Armenians. Our conclusions are based on the results of 657 surveys.[2]

---

[1] Many thanks go to Lee Kats, Vice Provost for Research and Strategic Initiatives at Pepperdine, for funding this research project. The project began with a CDIUR grant enabling Levon Goukasian, Mike Sugimoto and Dyron Daughrity to work with several undergraduate students to create and distribute a survey and compile the results. The undergraduate students involved in this project were: Kristi Bansemer, Lilit Azizyan, Lida Manukyan, Gary Darakjian and Narine Adamova. Nicholas Cumming, the second author of this chapter, is a former graduate student/research assistant to Dyron Daughrity.

[2] A small body of specialized research on Armenian Americans exists, particularly on California's Armenians, although rarely does it focus on religion, as we have done. A few notable and somewhat recent works in this field are as follows: Anny Bakalian, *Armenian-Americans: From Being to Feeling Armenian* (New Brunswick, 1993); Matthew Jendian, *Becoming American, Remaining Ethnic: The Case of Armenian-Americans in Central California* (El Paso, 2008). Jendian's book focuses on ethnic identity and its relation to Armenian marriage trends. See also Stephane Dufoix, *Diasporas* (Berkeley, 2008) which discusses the Armenian diaspora in chapter two. There was some careful research done in the 1970s. See Jenny Phillips, *Symbol, Myth, and Rhetoric: The Politics of Culture in an Armenian-American Population*, PhD Diss. (Boston University, 1978). See also Randall Miller and Thomas Marzik (eds), *Immigrants and Religion in Urban America* (Philadelphia, 1977) which has a chapter on Armenian Orthodox and Armenian Protestants in America prior to 1915. For a cross-cultural analysis see Sheila Henry, *Cultural Persistence and Socio-Economic Mobility: A Comparative Study of Assimilation among Armenians and Japanese in Los Angeles* (San Francisco, 1978). Two older, but quite focused, works are Charles Mahakian, *History of the Armenians in California*, PhD Diss. (University of California-Berkeley, 1935), and Aram

One of the underlying questions motivating this study was whether Armenians tend to be secularizing (moving away from faith), keeping faith traditions alive in their communities, or coming back to faith after a period of time. The results were mixed, with, at times, paradoxical trends surfacing. For instance, the vast majority of responders considered their religion to be "very important" or "somewhat important," although it appears that a fair number are rather disengaged from local parish life. Results were surprising at times while some trends were expected. For example, respondents were more likely to view Muslims in a negative light than a positive one, and they believe the memory of the genocide causes increased religiosity. On a political note, respondents tend to believe the Soviet Union impacted their religion for the worse, but they may be wrong based on the current state of Armenian religiosity in Southern California.

Many of the issues we studied intersect with larger religious trends in the Western world, leading to important questions that warrant further investigation. For example, will younger Armenian-Americans follow the "nones" in disaffiliating from their churches?[3] Or will their unique history as descendants of genocide survivors impact their perception of religion and identity? It is a compelling dilemma. In other words, will Armenians follow their peers when it comes to religiosity or will they defy prevailing socio-cultural developments around them because of their unique Christian and cultural pedigree? Armenia's status as one of the earliest Christian societies makes this study even more compelling as scholars try to discern whether that illustrious Christian heritage can sustain itself against the seemingly "terminal decline" of Christianity in much of the West, especially Western Europe.[4]

This study sheds light on other factual data, such as who exactly *are* the Armenians living in Los Angeles? Do they speak Armenian, English, or both? How did they get to Southern California? Are their parents both Armenian? Or is there evidence to indicate that mixed marriages are relatively common in

---

Serkis Yeretzian, *A History of Armenian Immigration to America with Special Reference to Conditions in Los Angeles*, PhD Diss. (University of Southern California, 1923).

[3] "Religious nones" is an appellation in religious studies and sociological discourse given to those who claim to have no affiliation to religion. The religious "nones" category gained headlines in October 2012 after the Pew Forum on Religion and Public Life released a study dealing specifically with them. The study made bold claims, "The number of Americans who do not identify with any religion continues to grow at a rapid pace ... In the last five years alone, the unaffiliated have increased from just over 15% to just under 20% of all U.S. adults." See "Nones on the Rise," located at www.pewforum.org/Unaffiliated/nones-on-the-rise.aspx, accessed July 17, 2013.

[4] Callum Brown, *The Death of Christian Britain*, 2nd edn (New York, 2009), p. 30.

California's Armenian diaspora? How many children do Armenian American couples have? What level of education do they achieve? These and other questions were answered by our respondents, providing important insights on the state of Armenian identity in the cultural cornucopia that exists in Southern California today. At the heart of the study, however, is an interest in religion. Our expertise is in religion, and our conclusions attempt to understand religiosity trends in the lives of Armenian Americans in Southern California.

The state of Armenian Christianity in the United States is a complicated one. It is not exempt from the same influences, theological trends and social climate affecting all Christians in the United States; however, as we will see, social and theological trends can become more pronounced when applied to Armenian Americans. For example, in spite of the events of 9/11 and the turbulence since that fateful day, the more strident forms of Islam in the Middle East have impacted Armenians much more directly, and more profoundly, than they have most Americans. The Ottoman genocide against Armenians in the early twentieth century indelibly altered the state of Armenian Christianity all around the world as somewhere between 1 and 1.5 million Armenians were killed. The trauma of that event continues to reverberate in the cultural ethos of all Armenians, exacerbating tensions that have been present in the Armenian consciousness for well over a century.

Who Are Armenians in Southern California?

According to the findings of the US Census Bureau's 2011 American Community Survey, the United States of America contained 483,366 people of Armenian descent.[5] This number is routinely criticized as being too low, due largely to two factors: first, Armenian-Americans are more concentrated in certain regions of the United States, thereby skewing random social scientific surveys; and, second, since ethnic or national heritage is typically self-identified, there are likely individuals who do not report, whether due to ignorance or reluctance. Thus, while a precise accounting of Southern California's Armenian population is probably elusive, we *do* have the number of Armenians who self-identified to the US Census Bureau.

---

5   See "Total Ancestry Categories Tallied for People with One or More Ancestry Categories Reported: United States," located at http://ia601608.us.archive.org/26/items/2011AmericanCommunitySurveyAncestry/2011Acs.pdf, accessed July 12, 2013.

The 2011 American Community Survey found that 214,618 people in the Los Angeles metro area self-identified as being either fully or partly of Armenian heritage.[6] The number of Californians who claimed Armenian heritage in 2011 was 249,336.[7] The LA metro area is clearly an epicenter for Armenians, a fact that can be anecdotally established by visiting the city. For example, inside the Hollywood district of Los Angeles is a "Little Armenia" neighborhood wherein one can find all of the food and accoutrements to make a Yerevanian comfortable. Likewise, the cities of Glendale, Burbank and Pasadena all have significant Armenian-descendant populations.

Our study is based on the responses of 657 Armenians living in Southern California.[8] Those surveyed answered questions chiefly about their feelings toward religion, Armenian identity and interreligious issues. Clearly this research is not exhaustive of the Armenian American experience, but it does offer a snapshot of the Southern California Armenian American community, especially regarding religious issues.

Of those surveyed 268 (41 percent) were male and 381 (58 percent) were female; eight respondents chose to withhold their gender. We had a wide cross-section of ages who participated. About half (49 percent) were born between 1971 and 1994. Nearly 200 respondents (29 percent) were middle aged, being born in the 1950s and 1960s. Over a fifth (22 percent) of our respondents were seniors: born between 1916 and 1950. Indeed we had some very old respondents since one of our target areas was elderly person facilities.

Several questions were geared to help us understand the history and background of the respondents. While a large majority (78 percent) of our respondents hold US citizenship, over a quarter (27 percent) hold Armenian citizenship. Around 3 percent of respondents hold Russian citizenship, around 3 percent have Lebanese citizenship, and around 3 percent are Iranian citizens. Obviously some hold dual citizenship. While numerically insignificant, the remaining responses of citizenship illustrate the Armenian propensity to scatter

---

[6] See "Total Ancestry Categories Tallied for People with One or More Ancestry Categories Reported: Los Angeles-Long Beach-Santa Ana, CA Metro Area," located at http://ia601605.us.archive.org/13/items/LosAngeles-longBeach-santaanaCaMetroAreaAncestry2000/117073949-Aff-Reports.pdf, accessed July 12, 2013.

[7] See "Total Population: California," located at http://factfinder2.census.gov/rest/dnldController/deliver?_ts=391715283497, accessed July 12, 2013.

[8] The surveys were distributed to Armenian college students (primarily UCLA and Los Angeles Valley College), adult day care centers, and friends and family members—since five members of the research team are Armenian. Of the 657 survey participants, 245 of them completed it online while the remainder completed paper surveys.

to the ends of the earth: Estonia, Venezuela, Azerbaijan, Canada, the UK, Iraq, France, Sweden, Greece, Syria and Turkey.

Armenian Americans in California are polyglots. A large majority of our respondents speak English (73 percent), but even more speak Armenian (87 percent). A third (34 percent) of them can speak Russian. Twelve percent speak Spanish. Around 8 percent of respondents speak Turkish. After that, in descending order, they speak French (5 percent), Arabic (5 percent), Farsi (5 percent), German, Greek, Estonian, Georgian, Swedish, Ukrainian and Bulgarian.

One of the conclusions of our study is that Armenians tend to preserve their heritage by marrying other Armenians. While this topic is dealt with in more detail below, respondents did tell us that 92 percent of them are children of two Armenian parents. The small remainder has one Armenian parent.

On average, Eastern Europeans have fewer children than anywhere else in the world.[9] Armenians are part of this trend as Armenian Americans seem to prefer smaller families as well. Among our respondents, 41 percent have no children, 11 percent have one child, 29 percent have two children, 11 percent have three children and 4 percent have four children. As a rough comparison, we can look at the number of children born to Americans by the age of 44: 20 percent of them are childless, 17 percent have one child, 33 percent have two children and 31 percent have three or more.[10]

Our respondents are an educated lot: a total of 72 percent attended college and 21 percent of them have attended graduate school. As a comparison, around 63 percent of Americans have completed at least some college.[11]

"Survey Says"

When it comes to religion, the vast majority (82 percent) claimed membership in the "Armenian Apostolic" Church. Small percentages belong to the Russian

---

[9] For a discussion of fertility trends, see Dyron Daughrity, *The Changing World of Christianity: The Global History of a Borderless Religion* (New York, 2010), chapter three, "Eastern European Christianity."

[10] These statistics are from the year 2010. See the Centers for Disease Control and Prevention: "Key Statistics from the National Survey of Family Growth," located at www.cdc.gov/nchs/nsfg/abc_list_b.htm#birthexpectations, accessed August 20, 2013.

[11] See Pew Research Center, "American Adults Better Educated Than Ever Before," located at www.pewresearch.org/daily-number/american-adults-better-educated-than-ever-before, accessed August 20, 2013.

Orthodox Church (3 percent), Armenian Roman Catholic (1 percent) and Armenian Protestant/Pentecostal (3 percent) churches. The remainder claimed "other."

Church attendance is not a very accurate barometer for religiosity. Nevertheless, we did try to "put our finger on the pulse" of respondents' churchgoing habits by asking them how often they attend a "church related activity." Nearly a quarter of them (23 percent) reported that they "very rarely" attend. Over a third (34 percent) reported attending at "holidays and special services only." Thus, a majority (57 percent) of the respondents are rarely in church services. About 18 percent reported weekly attendance, and 16 percent reported attending once per month. Nearly a tenth (9 percent) are quite involved in church, reporting that they attend "more than once a week."

"How important is religion in your personal life?" This question takes us right to the core of religion in the Armenian American experience. Only 15.5 percent of all respondents (8 percent male, 7.5 percent female) said that religion is "not important" in their personal lives. Altogether this was only 104 of the 657 people surveyed. A full 80 percent of those surveyed responded that religion was either "somewhat important" or "very important" for them personally. Armenians value religion: almost half (47 percent) of those surveyed claimed religion was "very important" to them. These results do not contradict larger trends in the United States, however. For example, the 2007 Pew Religious Landscape Survey showed that 16.1 percent of all Americans considered themselves religiously "unaffiliated."[12] This is very similar to the 15.5 percent of our Armenian American respondents who deemed religion to be unimportant in their lives. Therefore, in a very broad sense, Armenian Americans in Southern California appear similar to other Americans when it comes to the importance of religion in everyday life.

When asked if they are more or less religious than their parents only 12 percent (5 percent males, 7 percent females) said they are more religious. More than twice that amount (30 percent) said they are less religious than their parents. However, a majority of respondents (53 percent) said they are equally religious.[13] While perception is different from reality, the responses to this question may provide a little evidence that religion among Armenians in California is fairly strong. Around 65 percent of respondents stated that they are either "more religious" or "equally as religious" as their parents. This data

---

[12] Located at http://religions.pewforum.org/reports, accessed May 20, 2013.

[13] For virtually every question there were people who opted not to answer. This fact accounts for there being less than 100 percent response to some questions.

might be encouraging for Armenian parents; their faith seems to be shaping the attitudes of the children. It is hard to tell if those who responded positively have parents who are active Christians, but these results—coupled with the results of the previous question—may show that religion is being passed effectively from parents to children. If there were statistics from earlier generations that also addressed these questions it would help to discern patterns, such as whether there is a slow downward trend between generations and religiosity. Nevertheless, a strong majority of our respondents believe themselves to be equally or more religious than their parents.

The results we received for the next question in our survey were somewhat surprising: "Are Armenian youth more or less religious than Armenian adults?" Very few (7 percent) of our respondents think Armenian youth are more religious than Armenian adults. A thin majority (56 percent) said Armenian youth are less religious than Armenian adults. About a third (34 percent) responded that Armenian youth are equally as religious as their adult counterparts. Therefore, our respondents seem to believe that the next generation is showing signs of diminished religiosity. These findings are curious in light of the previous question. A solid majority (65 percent) of respondents believe that they are equally or more religious than their parents. However, when we depersonalized the question—when we asked about "Armenian youth"—they responded that most young people are less religious than adults.

If we probe further, we see that among respondents born before 1950, 39 percent believe that Armenian youth are less religious than Armenian adults. This is significantly less than the overall percentage (56 percent). Fully 60 percent of those born before 1950 believe that Armenian youths are more (15 percent) or equally (45 percent) as religious as Armenian adults. Therefore, more elderly Armenians believe the youth to be at least as religious as the adults. It is a much different result for those born *after* 1950; nearly two-thirds of them (63 percent) believe that Armenian youth are less religious than Armenian adults. Of the post-1950 respondents, only 37 percent of them believe that Armenian youth are more (10 percent) or equally (27 percent) as religious as Armenian adults. The sample size of those born after 1950 is much larger than those born prior to 1950, but there is no doubt that the oldest generation perceives the younger generations to be more religious.

These results fly in the face of popular beliefs that seniors think the world is getting more godless all the time. It is possible that the experiences of the elder Armenian Americans cause them to have a grimmer view of society. We wondered if perhaps the pre-1950 group remembers a past that was darker than the optimism they encountered in the United States. For example, the pre-1950 respondents would have more vivid memories of the genocide, recollections of political upheaval, and remembrances of anti-Christian rhetoric—whether in Soviet or Muslim lands. Thus, in the perception of the elder Armenians, the youth might seem to display a much more Christian outlook than they remember from their own youth.

Of those who are 25 years old or younger (born after 1987) 68 percent believe that Armenian youth are less religious than Armenian adults. Only 2 percent of them believe that the youth are more religious than the adults. Therefore, it appears that younger Armenian Americans have a lower estimation of youth religiosity. These results could be due to the fact that seniors have a much longer and wider breadth of experience. For instance, seniors could see young people as being more faithful than the other generations they have been able to examine. This would make good sense for a person who lived in the Soviet Union. Those born after 1950 may not be able to see the more striking differences between the religiosity of various generations simply because their experience is limited. We must not miss the forest for the trees here, however: most of our respondents believe the current generation of Armenian youth is less religious than the adults. Those elderly people who think otherwise are in the minority.

When our respondents were asked to compare their religiosity to the religiosity of all Americans, 37 percent of them reported that they are more religious. The highest percentage (41 percent) believes that Armenian Americans are equally as religious as all Americans, while only 18 percent believe Armenians are less religious. Therefore, among all respondents, a large majority (78 percent) believes Armenian Americans are more religious or equally as religious as the total American population. This belief could be due to a strong religious identity within Armenian people. Perhaps, over time, religious customs became cultural customs. This certainly makes sense from an Armenian perspective. Armenian scholar Terenig Vartabed Poladian makes this point clear:

> In other churches religion may be concerned with individual life only, but in the Armenian Church religion is blended with the social and national life. In the mind of many an Armenian it is The Church that makes The Armenian an Armenian. Archbishop Ormanian, in his book *The Church of Armenia* says: 'The national Church (of Armenia) has been the sole bond which has united the scattered remnants of the race of Haik ... The nation has linked herself to her church as to an anchor of salvation.'[14]

---

[14] See Papken Catholicos Gulesserian, *The Armenian Church* (New York, 1939), trans. by Papken Catholicos Gulesserian. The quotation is from the translator's introduction,

Very few Americans would speak of their Church in this way. American religiosity has little to do with nationality. The Armenian experience is the polar opposite of Thomas Jefferson's "wall of separation" idea so prominent in the American consciousness. But being a member of the Armenian Church is a fairly important aspect of what makes a person Armenian.

When reflecting on the religiosity of Armenian Americans compared to the rest of the nation, we were struck by what our respondents said about marriage. Fully two-thirds (66 percent) of them stated it is important for Armenians to marry Armenians. Indeed, among our respondents, a full 92 percent of them were born to two Armenians and only 8 percent of them come from mixed (Armenian and non-Armenian) marriages. In other words, while most (66 percent) of our respondents *believe* it is important to marry an Armenian, an even higher percentage will likely marry an Armenian. As a result, unique Armenian customs are likely to get carried down through the generations. Marriage is one area where Armenians are rather predictable. Unlike Christians in other denominations that have intermarried and watered down their distinctive ideas and traditions, Armenian Americans may have preserved their unique religious traditions better due to the strong preference of an Armenian mate.[15]

One of our questions asked respondents to compare their American identity with their Armenian ethnicity. Well over a third (37 percent) of those surveyed said their Armenian ethnicity is "more important" than their American identity. Only 12 percent claimed their Armenian ethnicity was "less important" than their American identity. Nearly half (48 percent) said both identities are "equally important." Thus, 85 percent of those surveyed stated that their Armenian ethnicity is equally or more important than their American identity. This shows that Armenians hold very tightly to their cultural heritage. Coupled with the desire of Armenians to marry other Armenians, we may now gather why they believe they are rather religious when compared to the general American public. Though our statistics show that Armenians in Los Angeles have a nearly identical amount of "nones," Armenians in general still *believe* that they are more religious than the overall population. If their Church is an important part of their identity, and they tend to marry Armenians, then it should follow that each

---

pp. ix–x. See also Archbishop Malachia Ormanian, *The Church of Armenia*, 5th English edn (Burbank, 2004), trans. from French by G. Marcar Gregory.

[15] See, for example, Robert Putnam and David Campbell, *American Grace: How Religion Divides and Unites Us* (New York, 2010). Putnam and Campbell's claim is that America's "grace" (gift) is that it has "solved the puzzle of religious pluralism ... by creating a web of interlocking personal relationships among people of many different faiths." This quotation is found on p. 550.

Armenian generation will continue to acknowledge the importance of religion, even if it is derived mainly out of cultural obligation. Only time will tell whether the American context will cause Armenians to rethink these decisions, but for the time being, Armenian Americans place a high price on their religion (80 percent consider religion "somewhat" or "very" important) and an even higher price (85 percent) on their ethnicity. However, in the Armenian mind, there seems to be little separation between religion and ethnicity.

Our survey shows that Southern California's Armenians are highly—and perhaps equally—committed to faith and family. When asked what they think is "most important in being an Armenian Christian," about half (49 percent) responded that family ties are most important and about half (46 percent) made reference to faith. Around 17 percent chose "church participation" (weddings, funerals, baptisms, holidays) as their answer and 29 percent opted for "personal devotion" (prayers, devotional readings), making a combined total of 46 percent. Therefore, it appears that Armenians struggle to decide which is most important in being Christian—participation in church, commitment to family, or individual devotion apart from corporate church activity.

In all likelihood, Armenian Americans, like most Christian Americans, enmesh their faith with their family. American scholar Mary Eberstadt has shown that religiosity is directly tied to family commitment. If a family breaks up, or if a child is raised by a single parent, then there is a much greater likelihood that religiosity will diminish. Her thesis is that secularization in the Western world has occurred because of the breakdown of the family. Our respondents also linked faith and family, corroborating much of what Eberstadt has demonstrated.[16]

We were somewhat perplexed by the respondents' answers to the following question: "What is the most important thing that makes you feel Armenian while living in America?" We provided four answers from which to choose: attending church, family and friends, knowing the language, and cultural customs. Theoretically, the respondents were to check only one answer ("the most important thing") but in fact some circled more than one option, thus complicating our findings. In spite of some plural answers, the results did make it clear that church attendance was the *least* important aspect of feeling Armenian in America amongst the options we provided. Our study found that Armenians in California do not place a high priority on church attendance: well over half of them (57 percent) reported that they rarely attend church. Even still, over a quarter of both males (27 percent) and females (26 percent) indicated

---

[16] See Mary Eberstadt, *How the West Really Lost God* (West Conshohocken, 2013).

that attending church does make them feel Armenian in America. However, both men (63 percent) and women (58 percent) said family relationships and friendships are the "most important thing."

Thus it seems that the most conspicuous factor making Armenians feel Armenian while living in America is their connection to their families. Most people surveyed believe that Armenian Christianity is best maintained through family connections, and familial ties are also what help Armenian Americans feel Armenian. Together with the fact that Armenians prefer to marry other Armenians, it is clear that California's Armenians place a premium on keeping their heritage intact, chiefly through kinship. The Church provides another layer of connection to Armenian heritage as long as it unites the family and promotes Armenian customs and culture. These data confirm Eberstadt's conclusion that faith and family are linked together.

This emphasis on the family does not mean that most Armenian Americans prefer cultural insularity, however. Our results showed that 32 percent of respondents thought it was "very important" for Armenian children to develop friendships with non-Armenians; another 43 percent said that it was "somewhat important." However, a fairly substantial proportion (20 percent) did not believe it was important for their children to develop non-Armenian friendships. We are not entirely sure how to take this statistic, but it probably points toward maintaining the integrity of the Armenian heritage. Clearly, Armenians care about heritage and ancestry. If friendships and relationships are cultivated outside of the Armenian people then the likelihood of Armenians marrying non-Armenians will, naturally, rise. It is also clear, though, that the majority of our respondents endorse dialogue, interaction and relationships with non-Armenians.

In the last century or so, two of the most important impacts upon Armenians and Armenian Christianity have been conflicts with certain Muslim-majority nations, and the foundation/dissolution of the Soviet Union. Islam spread rapidly after Muhammad's death in AD 632, quickly encompassing areas near Armenia. It continued to knock on the door of Armenia for nearly a millennium and a half, sometimes violently, sometimes peacefully. But the catastrophes of the late nineteenth and early twentieth centuries in the Ottoman Empire crippled Armenia as a nation and a people. Like the Jewish Holocaust of World War II, the Armenian genocide evokes visceral reactions. The "Great Crime" seems to be an open wound within the Armenian consciousness, and it is hard to tell whether Armenians are able to discuss this topic openly, or answer survey questions about it freely.

When asked about whether Armenians and Muslims have good relations overall, 23 percent of all respondents said they do, and 38 percent said they do not. What surprised us was that 36 percent did not have an opinion on the matter. Could this result mean that Armenian Americans are not fully informed of the horrors of the Armenian genocide? Or does it indicate that many people simply do not want to answer this question for some reason? Could fear prevent them from having an opinion? Certainly apathy is not at play because Armenians, in our experience, generally do have an opinion—indeed strong opinions—on the "Great Crime." Our expectation was that only a *very* few people would express "no opinion" on Armenian–Muslim relations. Why would 36 percent not have an opinion on something so critical to Armenian history and identity? Our answer is this: Armenians in Southern California do not generally link Muslims around them to the horrors of the genocide. Most of them see the difference: Muslims in America had nothing to do with the Armenian Holocaust. The answers may have been more divisive if the question had instead addressed the Ottoman Empire or Turkey, rather than "Islam."

Whether a respondent was born inside or outside the United States had little impact on the assessment of Armenian–Muslim relations. For example, of the respondents who were born *inside* the United States, 28 percent believe Armenian–Muslim relations are good, 41 percent believe they are not good, and 27 percent hold "no opinion" on the matter. For those born *outside* of the United States (though many have become naturalized US citizens) the numbers are similar: 25 percent believe Armenian–Muslim relations to be good, 40 percent believe them to be not so good, and 31 percent hold no opinion. Armenian Americans in California seem largely in agreement when it comes to relations with Muslims, and, statistics show, there is a measure of distrust.

One of the most surprising pieces of data that surfaced from our survey was that among those who were born before 1950, around half (47 percent) believe that Muslims and Armenians have good relations. Thus, the seniors in this survey have a much more positive outlook on Muslim/Armenian relations than their younger counterparts. Our question was "Why?" It could be related to their broader, more nuanced understanding of Muslim/Armenian relations and how they have evolved since 1915. Some of the younger responders could have been reacting to the recent rise of Islamic radicalism, or to the Turkish government's refusal to acknowledge the tragedies. These considerations did not satisfy our curiosity however because the older respondents would be equally as informed—even more informed—of global developments. Our hypothesis is that elderly respondents, being closer in time to the events of the genocide, likely understand better that Muslims living today were not responsible for the crimes against their parents and grandparents. These findings may also be attributed to the idea that many Armenians do not view the genocide as an interreligious event. Again, our findings may have been different if respondents were asked about Armenian–Turkish relations.

In 1920 Armenia was annexed by the Soviet Union and remained part of it until 1991 when Armenian independence was declared. The Soviet Union was notoriously antagonistic toward religion although the Stalinist years (1922–53) were by far the worst. Two brief comments from Armenian scholars writing during Soviet times illustrate the challenges. In 1939, Papken Catholicos Gulesserian wrote:

> The serious events which took place during and after the Great War have had tragic repercussions on the lot of The Armenians and upset the organization of the Armenian Church ... The Soviet Regime, after having decreed the separation of the State from the Church, took a distinctly hostile position toward all religions. However, the Catholicossate of Etchmiadzin was able to oppose its moral authority against the revolutionary tempest and save at least the dignity of the Armenian Church, with the spirit of tolerance which is characteristic of her through the centuries. The see of the Catholicos of all the Armenians was stripped of all its possessions by the measures of secularization. Even the library of the Catholicossate was secularized.[17]

Another striking quote comes from Hagop Nersoyan, writing in 1963:

> The Turks resumed the war in 1920 and occupied Alexandropol (Leninakan) [today known as Gyumri] on November 7. Twenty-two days later the Communists took over. That was the beginning of the present Armenian S.S.R. where Etchmiadzin is located. Needless to say, all these circumstances were far from creating the best of atmospheres for the growth and progress of the Armenian church.[18]

Reading between the lines, one senses the precariousness of the context during which these quotations were written. Thoughtful Armenians knew they had to use restraint when discussing their Church under Soviet rule.

---

[17] Gulesserian, *The Armenian Church*, p. 55.
[18] Hagop Nersoyan, *The Armenian Church with Thirty-Five Stories*, 2nd edn (Burbank: Council for Religious Education Western Diocese of the Armenian Church of North America, 2006), p. 273. The first edition was published in 1963 by the Diocese of the Armenian Church of North America in New York.

When asked "Was the Soviet Union good for Armenian Christianity?" only 16 percent of all respondents said yes. Nearly half (45 percent) believe the Soviet Union had a negative impact on Armenian Christianity, and around one-third (36 percent) held no opinion. For respondents born *inside* the United States, only 8 percent said the Soviet Union had a positive impact, a small majority (57 percent) said it had a negative impact, and 35 percent held no opinion. While these results are somewhat similar, being born inside the United States did tend to make respondents slightly more negative toward the Soviet Union's impact on the Armenian Church. We were surprised by these results since—intuitively— those born *outside* the United States would have witnessed the full force of the USSR in a way those born in America did not.

We were even more surprised that 28 percent of respondents with *Armenian* citizenship said the Soviet Union was good for Armenian Christianity. Most (51 percent) of them agreed the Soviet Union was not good for the Church, and only 18 percent expressed no opinion. Therefore, only a slight majority of Armenian citizens view the Soviet Union's impact as being negative on their Church, a statistic that does not deviate much from the overall findings (45 percent). It seems, then, that the Soviet Union's legacy among Armenian citizens is unclear. We anticipated respondents to be more united on this question. Historians typically paint the Soviet era as being destructive of churches. For example, one Armenian historian describes the earliest days of Armenia's independence in 1991, when "His Holiness Vasken I, the Catholicos of All Armenians, lent his moral force to the actions of the new Armenian government":

> He began opening defunct churches, and authorized numerous, public occasions for the people of Armenia to express their long-stifled religious faith. Where once the sacrament of Christian baptism had been performed only quietly and in the greatest secrecy, now huge crowds of people were turning out all over Armenia, to be baptized into their ancestral Church.[19]

Our respondents from Armenia, however, are somewhat divided over whether the Soviet Union positively or negatively impacted their Church. Perhaps more analysis is needed, and certainly more history needs to be written. But few historians would argue that the Soviet Union was actually beneficial for the Armenian Church. One problem might be education—perhaps due to propaganda some Armenian citizens never knew the full extent of the

---

[19] Fr. Arten Ashjian, *The Torch Was Passed: The Centennial History of the Armenian Church of America*, ed. Christopher Hagop Zakian (New York, 1998), p. 139.

persecution against their churches and clergy during the Soviet experiment. Alternatively, it could be the case that some Armenian respondents believe the Church's health today has been propelled by the oppression of the twentieth century. In other words, what doesn't kill you makes you stronger.

The new atheism of the twenty-first century has placed the problem of evil at the forefront of the argument against God. Why would God, who is omnibenevolent and omnipotent, allow suffering? Armenians suffered greatly during the "Great Crime" and our survey offered a chance to answer the question "Did the Armenian Genocide make Armenians more or less religious?" Well over half (58 percent) responded that the genocide made Armenians *more* religious. Only 11 percent said the genocide had a negative impact on Armenian religiosity. This is a striking blow against the idea that suffering has an adverse effect on a person's faith. There is no doubt that Armenians faced great adversity during the twentieth century; both the Soviet Union and the Armenian genocide were tragic for them. Despite these events, Armenians have a tendency to allow suffering to bring them closer to God, evinced in the masterful writings of Armenia's national lamenter and poet, Grigor Narekatsi:

> And here, severed, torn off is the thread of hope for life ... My flesh has been exhausted, and is already dead for God ... The roads of life have closed very tightly; The comfort vanished ... I am engulfed into the flame of hell ... The chains of slavery enforced ... Lord Jesus Christ, the son of the living God, Creator of the earth and heaven ... Receive me, heavy sinner, having redeemed and cleansed me from sins ... So that I ... would firmly merge with you ... to you, your Father, and the Holy Spirit; the trinity of persons in one substance in the single deity. Amen.[20]

Only Narekatsi can capture the Armenian sorrow and resolve, both then and now, so precisely.

Where will Armenian Americans go from here? Will they cleave to the traditions of their ancestors or tread an entirely new path? Will the Church find a middle way that preserves the traditions and remains relevant? To whom will the younger generations listen?

Our survey asked the respondents to tell us "What is the most important influence in the lives of those under 30 years old?" Many respondents chose more than one option, complicating our findings. Nevertheless, some interpretations

---

[20] Grigor Narekatsi, *The Book of Sadness*, trans. by Hachatoor Hachatoorian (Yerevan, 2007), pp. 111–13. Narekatsi lived AD 951–1003 and is a canonized saint in the Armenian Church.

can be drawn. Around half (48 percent) of all surveyed answered with "parents," easily the top answer. In second place was "friends" at 27 percent. "Media" (television, Internet, movies) was third: 25 percent of all who were surveyed chose this answer. Respondents believe young people are influenced almost as much by media as they are by their friends. Only 15 percent acknowledged that school was an influence on people under 30—a full 10 percent less than the perceived influence of the media. Our respondents believe teachers, principals and classes are having less of an impact on young people than Internet and movies. In last place was "Church leaders" with a mere 6 percent. Only 1.5 percent of men surveyed said that Church leaders were the most important influence among the youth. Of the 657 surveyed only 40 men and women perceive Church leaders to be of primary influence on the youth. However, the data could be a little deceiving here. After all, respondents believe people under 30 are most influenced by their parents, and parents have the option of raising their children to be religious. These results may provide hope to parents—they are probably more influential than they realize.

Do Armenian Americans in California support their churches? If so, then how? Around 62 percent of all respondents said they contribute financially to the work of their church. A high percentage (79 percent) of those who contribute buy candles to light in the church. In second place (73 percent), respondents claim to give "individual contributions during the service." In third place (19 percent) was contributing through "special church services" such as weddings, funerals, and baptisms. A tenth of the givers donate money for special dinners and fundraisers.

Therefore, we may reason that while overall influence of Church leaders seems very low, as is church attendance, the amount of people investing in the Church is fairly high. Three-fourths (76 percent) of respondents born before 1950 contribute financially to the Church; 60 percent of those born after 1950 contribute. The older the respondents, the more likely they were to contribute financially. For example, among those aged 30 or younger, 47 percent reported giving to the Church while 46 percent said they do not. Of course it makes sense that the youth do not have the financial means to contribute financially. However, if there is a downward trend in both the Church's influence and in the amount donated by subsequent generations, then these findings could signal a decline in giving in the future.

Conclusion

Armenian Christianity has a long, storied, global history. As Armenians continue to immigrate to other countries, the impact upon the historic Armenian churches will change according to context. California offers an important snapshot of global Armenian Christianity since its members come from diverse backgrounds: Middle Easterners, former Soviet citizens, Russians, New Yorkers, Europeans, and third- or fourth-generation families from Fresno. One adjective that aptly describes Armenians is resilient. They have persevered and survived, preserving their illustrious Church during that time.

What may be a challenge for religious Armenians in California is the declining influence of the Church. Our findings show that the youth are not strongly influenced by their Church leaders. Without the influence of clergy on younger generations, Armenian faith may lose momentum, similar to what has happened to Western Europe's national churches. This may also mean that more personal, individualized forms of faith will emerge among younger generations, as has occurred in Western Europe. Armenian Christian leaders will likely monitor this trend and find ways to engage the youth. One approach will be to impact family units, as Armenians seem to treasure family deeply. Another approach would be for Armenian churches to adapt their historic model of Church in order to better satisfy the American hunger for relevance. That being said, however, Armenian Christianity is ancient, its traditions established. Churches with over 1,700 years of tradition do not change overnight. It will be fascinating to see how the Armenian churches adapt to the globalized, quickly changing culture of Southern California.

An important challenge that Armenian Americans will have to face is the "melting pot" mentality of American society. Our data shows that Armenians prefer to keep their families Armenian through marriage and other social relationships. However, American society promotes and celebrates diversity, plural ethnicities and the radical freedom of religion. Therefore, the question becomes, how should Armenian Americans hold onto their proud heritage and identity while assimilating into American culture? One answer is the Church. For instance, Putnam and Campbell's influential study *American Grace* found that Americans who have strong religious impulses are more active in civic society. Religious Americans are more generous, trusting and willing to partake in public life. These are some of the perceived strengths of being religious in America, and Armenians should take note. Armenians have a historic Christian faith that promotes community. Putnam and Campbell's findings show that simultaneously embracing religiosity and community leads to more robust civic engagement.

Armenian American religiosity, however, appears to be quite similar to the general religious landscape of America. Our findings were nearly identical to the findings of the Pew Research survey of religion when it came to the percentage of people who identify as non-religious (about 16 percent). It appears, then, that Armenian Americans are on a somewhat familiar path as Americans in general. Will more universal and pluralistic beliefs continue to emerge in the Armenian community or will the community become more insulated in order to preserve its historic beliefs and practices? If the Pew research and Putnam and Campbell's conclusions are indications of how Americans think, then perhaps Armenian Americans will continue to embrace tolerance and plurality. With the rise of the religious "nones" and America's history of religious diversity and pluralism, one may assume that Armenians will follow suit. However, Armenians still place the family unit in such high regard that they may resist this trend longer than other American demographics. In other words, since many Armenians are relatively new to the Western religious context and they prefer to keep their families Armenian, it may take longer for American pluralism to impact their communities.

Armenian Christianity has not only survived the calamities of its history, it is today an inspiring example of tenacious faith. Against staggering odds, it has remained true to its core theological convictions as articulated by Armenia's most beloved historian, Yeghisheh. Writing around the year AD 460, he described the AD 451 Battle of Avarair—against the Zoroastrian Sassanid Persians—leading to Armenia's treasured religious freedom:

> But we—who have been redeemed by the might of God and confirmed with a faith in the hope of Christ Who came and assumed a body like ours in the Holy Virgin, formed an indissoluble union with His divinity, suffered on His flesh the tortures of our sins, was crucified and buried, and after resurrection appeared to many, and in the presence of His disciples ascended to His Father and sat at the right of the Almighty—believe Him as the true God and we expect Him to come again with the glory and the power of His Father, to raise all the dead, to give new life to the creatures and to sit in eternal judgment between the righteous and the wicked.[21]

---

[21] *Yeghisheh* (New York: The Delphic Press, 1952), p. 101. The book was authored by Armenian historian Yeghisheh between the years AD 458–464 and was originally called *The History of Vartan and the Armenian War*.

References

Ashjian, Arten, *The Torch Was Passed: The Centennial History of the Armenian Church of America*, ed. Christopher Hagop Zakian (New York: St. Vartan Press, 1998).

Bakalian, Anny, *Armenian-Americans: From Being to Feeling Armenian* (New Brunswick: Transaction Publishers, 1993).

Brown, Callum, *The Death of Christian Britain*, 2nd edn (New York: Routledge, 2009).

Daughrity, Dyron, *The Changing World of Christianity: The Global History of a Borderless Religion* (New York: Peter Lang, 2010).

Dufoix, Stephane, *Diasporas* (Berkeley: University of California Press, 2008).

Eberstadt, Mary, *How the West Really Lost God* (West Conshohocken: Templeton Press, 2013).

Gulesserian, Papken Catholicos, *The Armenian Church* (New York: The Gotchnag Press, 1939).

Henry, Sheila, *Cultural Persistence and Socio-Economic Mobility: A Comparative Study of Assimilation among Armenians and Japanese in Los Angeles* (San Francisco, CA: R & E Research Associates, 1978).

Jendian, Matthew, *Becoming American, Remaining Ethnic: The Case of Armenian-Americans in Central California* (El Paso: LFB Scholarly Publishing, 2008).

Mahakian, Charles, *History of the Armenians in California*, PhD Diss. (University of California-Berkeley, 1935).

Miller, Randall and Thomas Marzik (eds), *Immigrants and Religion in Urban America* (Philadelphia: Temple University Press, 1977).

Narekatsi, Grigor, *The Book of Sadness*, trans. Hachatoor Hachatoorian (Yerevan: Nairi, 2007).

Nersoyan, Hagop, *The Armenian Church with Thirty-Five Stories*, 2nd edn (Burbank: Council for Religious Education Western Diocese of the Armenian Church of North America, 2006).

Ormanian, Malachia, *The Church of Armenia*, 5th English edn, trans. G. Marcar Gregory (Burbank: The Armenian Church of North America Western Diocese, 2004).

Phillips, Jenny, *Symbol, Myth, and Rhetoric: The Politics of Culture in an Armenian-American Population*, PhD Diss. (Boston University, 1978).

Putnam, Robert and David Campbell, *American Grace: How Religion Divides and Unites Us* (New York: Simon & Schuster, 2010).

Yeghisheh, *Yeghisheh* (New York: The Delphic Press, 1952).

Yeretzian, Aram Serkis, *A History of Armenian Immigration to America with Special Reference to Conditions in Los Angeles*, PhD Diss. (University of Southern California, 1923).

Chapter 12

Sanctuary, Community or Museum? The Apostolic Church in the Life-Worlds of a Sample of American Armenians

Sara Kärkkäinen Terian

Introduction

For a large portion of Armenians in the United States as elsewhere in the diaspora, the national Orthodox Apostolic Church is an anchor for common identity and culture. As Cowe observes, however, it is not "the sole institution" today as it was in ancient Armenia.[1] Many other spheres of modern life crowd out the overarching role of the Church of ancient times. Though most American Armenians are not actively involved in the Church,[2] even for them the Church plays a significant role in their life-worlds—unless they have totally assimilated in the dominant culture. For example, Jendian's research on Armenians in Central California shows that religious affiliation is "*the* explanatory variable in predicting the extent of ... assimilation and of retention of ethnicity."[3] The "Armenianness" of American Armenians' life-worlds appears to be quite strongly tied with the Church, an example of religion as the "major foundation"

---

[1] S. Peter Cowe, "Church and Diaspora: The Case of the Armenians," in Michael Angold (ed.), *Eastern Christianity*, The Cambridge History of Christianity, vol. 5 (Cambridge, 2006), p. 430.

[2] According to a survey conducted by Garbis Der-Yeghiayan ("The Armenian Community: An Opinion Survey" (Mashdots College, Glendale, 2005)), only 12 percent had attended church more than once during the previous month, and 21 percent had attended once.

[3] Matthew A. Jendian, *Becoming American, Remaining Ethnic: The Case of Armenian-Americans in Central California* (New York, 2008), p. 153.

of ethnicity.⁴ As Suni asserts, particularly in the diaspora "the church maintained the culture of its people."⁵

The term "life-world" is a central phenomenological concept. It refers to the lived, taken-for-granted, "pre-given" world that people experience, with its perceptual, personal, social, material and non-material dimensions. The concept (*Lebenswelt*) originates in the writings of Edmund Husserl⁶ who acknowledges the ambiguity of the idea of such pre-given world but defines it as follows: "It is the spatiotemporal world of things as we experience them in our pre- and extrascientific life and as we know them to be experienceable beyond what is [actually] experienced."⁷ It includes physical and social entities, thus it is not only the world of our personal experience but also a cultural world with its ideas, worldviews and interpretations that shape our personal orientations.

Although the task of phenomenology is to show the pure essence of the life-world, the structures of it that are universal, experiencing it is subjectively relative. In other words, the way people experience their worlds differs, even when outwardly everything looks the same. Husserl points out that the "objective" or "true" world is in fact "a theoretical-logical abstraction" because it is not actually experienceable.⁸ Furthermore, the life-world has parts or spheres—Husserl calls them vocations "whose universal subject matter is called the 'life-world.'"⁹ The world of work, civic and social life, family life and church are such spheres. Thus the church is only one sphere of the life-worlds of today's people in the Western world, and the perceptions of its role in their lives vary.

Implicit in Husserl's discussion of the life-world are different levels of it. His focus is on mathematical science which he contrasts with the "pre-given,"

---

⁴ Peter Kivisto, "Rethinking the Relationship between Ethnicity and Religion," in James A. Beckford and N.J. Demerath III (eds), *The SAGE Handbook of the Sociology of Religion* (Los Angeles, 2007), p. 493, citing Harold Abramson, "Religion," in Stephan Thernstrom, Ann Orlov and Oscar Handlin (eds), *Harvard Encyclopedia of American Ethnic Groups* (Cambridge, MA, 1980), p. 869.

⁵ Ronald Grigor Suny, *Looking Toward Ararat: Armenia in Modern History* (Bloomington and Indianapolis, 1993), p. 11.

⁶ David Carr, "Husserl's Problematic Concept of the Life-World," in Frederick Elliston and Peter McCormick (eds), *Husserl: Expositions and Appraisals* (Notre Dame, IN, 1977), p. 203.

⁷ Edmund Husserl, *The Crisis of European Sciences and Transcendental Phenomenology*, translated by David Carr (Evanston, IL, 1970), pp. 122, 138. According to Carr, Husserl considered this final version of *The Crisis* to be the definitive statement of the life-world concept.

⁸ Husserl, *The Crisis*, p. 127.

⁹ Husserl, *The Crisis*, p. 136.

pre-scientific, perceptual world of everyday experience that science presupposes. While he also acknowledges the cultural world, he does not adequately distinguish it from the natural world of immediate experience. In his criticism of Husserl's unclear exposition of these levels, Carr organizes them into three distinct strata: (1) the pre-scientific, taken-for-granted world of immediate experience; (2) the cultural world with its social groupings and interpretations; and (3) the scientific world that is built on the other two. While the first two are both taken for granted, they cannot be equated as one.[10] Alfred Schutz, who also emphasizes the social and cultural nature of the life-world that includes interpersonal relationships, institutions, customs and habits, sees it as "the sedimentation of all of man's previous experiences," knowledge and meaning.[11] Thus he points out that the life-world is heavily influenced by the historical tradition of the group.

History is the bedrock of Armenian identity in the twenty-first-century United States, as it is in the fatherland and perhaps everywhere in the Armenian diaspora. Historical studies of the Armenian diaspora abound,[12] though this orientation is not unique to Armenians.[13] Studies of contemporary Armenian communities likewise often show the historical orientation of Armenians' self-understanding; "History becomes the raison d'être, a mythical charter for the nation."[14] This is evident also for Armenians in the United States. The Church, though "both a unifying and divisive factor in Armenian life," plays an integral if not defining role in the history of the nation.[15] Even if the Church is merely a

---

[10] Carr, "Husserl's Problematic."

[11] Alfred Schutz, *On Phenomenology and Social Relations: Selected Writings*, ed. Helmut R. Wagner (Chicago, 1970), pp. 72–6.

[12] See, for example, Cowe, "Church and Diaspora"; Richard G. Hovannissian and David N. Myers (eds), *Enlightenment and Diaspora: The Armenian and Jewish Cases* (Atlanta: Scholars Press, 1999); Waltraud Kokot, Khachig Tölölyan and Carolin Alfonso (eds), *Diaspora, Identity, and Religion: New Directions in Theory and Research* (London and New York: Routledge, 2004); V. Diatlov and E. Melkonian, *Armianskaia diaspora: ocherki sotsiokul'turnoi tipologii* [Armenian Diaspora: Essays of sociocultural typology] (Yerevan: Caucasus Institute, 2009).

[13] See, for example, Astrid Wonneberger, "The Invention of History in the Irish-American Diaspora: Myths of the Great Famine," in Kokot et al., *Diaspora, Identity and Religion*, pp. 117–29.

[14] Susan Paul Pattie, *Faith in History: Armenians Rebuilding Community* (Washington, DC, 1997), p. 236.

[15] Suny, *Looking Toward Ararat*, p. 10.

distant memory, associated with one's grandmother, it is still a foundational part of what being Armenian means, "a vital marker of the groups' identity."[16]

Another central tenet of phenomenology is the notion that experiential worlds are socially constructed and maintained. As Peter Berger has observed, such worlds are "inherently precarious" and need an ongoing process of legitimation to help people accept the social order with its institutional authority. Though other institutions are also involved in such legitimation, religion has always been the most effective instrument of it. Religious rituals serve to remind and "make present" to the participants "the fundamental reality definitions and their appropriate legitimations." They thus "serve to 'recall' the traditional meanings embodied in the culture and its major institutions."[17]

In new circumstances, such as life in a diaspora,[18] there is an urgent need for legitimation of the old practices that help provide continuity and collective identity.[19] The life-worlds of twenty-first-century Armenians—at least in the United States of America—are quite different from those of fourth-century Armenians in the ancient world at the time the Church's rituals and practices were first established. Furthermore, religion has now been relegated to only one dimension of life—Husserl's "vocation." Adding to that situation the cultural differences brought about by the passage of time and geographical movement has resulted in fundamentally different "spatiotemporal" life-worlds. Yet the ancient Church has provided an anchor in the sea of change and appears to be a major vehicle for maintaining the Armenian identity and culture by its legitimating function.

This chapter presents a new analysis of the findings of a qualitative sociological study sponsored by the Eastern Diocese of the Armenian Church in America and carried out in 2006.[20] At that time I personally conducted in-depth interviews

---

[16] Martin Baumann, "A Diachronic View of Diaspora, the Significance of Religion and Hindu Trinidadians," in Kokot et al., *Diaspora, Identity and Religion*, p. 170. For Armenians, the Genocide of 1915 is another important ethnic marker.

[17] Peter L. Berger, *The Sacred Canopy: Elements of a Sociological Theory of Religion* (New York, 1967), pp. 29, 32–3, 40.

[18] The word "diaspora" is here used in its traditional and commonly understood meaning as "dispersion."

[19] Levon Abrahamian, *Armenian Identity in a Changing World* (Costa Mesa, 2006), pp. 111–17.

[20] Sara Kärkkäinen Terian, "Hidden Treasure: The Armenian Apostolic Church in America (Eastern Diocese) as Seen by a Sample of Its Constituents" (Armenian Church in America, Eastern Diocese, 2006). Data from this study are used by permission of the Primate. The Eastern Diocese encompasses the entire Eastern half of the United States, from the Atlantic coast through the Midwest.

(average one hour in length) with 56 individuals of various ages (ranging from 19 to 84) within the Diocese—six priests and nine non-Armenians who attend the Armenian Apostolic Church were included in the interviews. In addition, I conducted seven focus group interviews: five with Armenian students in various universities, one with a group of non-Armenians attending a specific Armenian church, and one with a group of young professionals in a major city. Altogether, a total of 90 individuals participated in the study.[21]

The purpose of the original study was to gain insight into the feelings and desires that members of the Armenian community have regarding their Apostolic Church. Responses to this key question explored in the interviews lend themselves well to the new, phenomenological analysis of this chapter.[22] While this analysis does not negate the previous interpretations, it provides further insights into the feelings that Armenians in the sample had about their Church.

The expressed feelings fall easily in the above-described three strata of life-world as articulated by Carr's theoretical exposition,[23] and they form the body of this chapter: the Church as (1) a sanctuary for a fresh, immediate, spiritual experience; (2) a community center where the lived culture is shared; or (3) a detached, "scientific" repository for the cultural heritage of the group, i.e., a museum. The feelings of some interviewees fit more strongly in one of the layers, while those of others include dimensions of the other two; thus they are not discrete categories. Altogether, the three strata of life-world incorporate all the feelings expressed by the participants toward the Church as it relates to their life-worlds.

Although space limitations preclude a full phenomenological analysis of all interview data in this chapter, the themes are derived from all the interviews.[24] Repeated listening to the taped interviews and reading of the transcripts provided a comprehensive idea of the prevalent concerns and feelings of the research participants, which then were organized within the framework

---

[21] The Diocese asked me to conduct the study not only because of my qualifications as a sociologist but also because I am not an Armenian but am married to an Armenian. Having attended the Armenian Church but not joined as a member, I personally had both an insider's and outsider's view of the Church.

[22] The report submitted to the Diocese merely described the findings without a theoretical analysis.

[23] Carr, "Husserl's Problematic."

[24] The model for this later analysis is what Clark Moustakas (*Phenomenological Research Methods* (Thousand Oaks, 1994)) calls "composite textural and structural synthesis."

of the life-world concept. Quotations from the interviews are used to illustrate these themes.[25]

Stratum 1: Church as Sanctuary

Husserl considers spiritual experiences as part of the first, "pre-scientific," taken-for-granted world of immediate experience.[26] For many of the interviewees, especially for immigrants, the Church provided a sanctuary, a setting for rich spiritual experiences. "I feel closer to God when I go into Church," Liza, a 57-year-old immigrant from Lebanon, stated. "And especially when I sing in the choir, it's um, kind of like a hypnotic state for me." She continued talking about the symbolic elements, the altar, pictures of Christ and the Virgin Mary, and the beauty of the hymns. Another middle-aged woman, SB, an immigrant from Syria, described how she "gets goose bumps" every time she sings in the choir. For her, the liturgy was a "heavenly experience." The priests also emphasized the spiritual core of the worship experience. It appeared that participation was the key to a fuller experience of the spiritual dimension, though Lorig, a 56-year-old non-Armenian, seemed to provide an exception: "Actually, when I was sitting in the pew, I had more of a spiritual feeling than I do in the choir," she stated.

Several of the young people in group interviews on university campuses also felt that the liturgy was spiritual, but one must remember that their very participation in the group interview was due to their interest and participation in the Church, thus there was a self-selection bias.[27] Sonia, a 20-year-old participant in a three-person group on an elite university campus, vividly described her experience of attending two churches:

> So for me going to church here is purely a religious base, to learn more and more about God. That's what keeps me going back. And that's also why I go to another church, an Armenian church and a non-Armenian church, because like I mentioned before I feel like both dimensions both like building a faith based on prayers and just like praying through the whole divine liturgy, prayers and prayers. I feel that Armenian religion is very very much faith-based and prayer-based, and I feel that more American Christianity is more textual and understanding the Bible. So for me personally it works to have both of those together ... Like when

---

[25] The pseudonyms used are self-chosen by the respondents.
[26] Carr, "Husserl's Problematic."
[27] Out of the scores of Armenian students on major university campuses, only 3–5 came to participate in each group interview, though all were invited.

you walk out of the church sometimes after a service, I don't feel, I feel I've been close to God because I've been praying for the past two hours and what not. But sometimes when I've come out of the other Christian church I feel that I've learned something.

For numerous evangelically minded Armenians and non-Armenians from Protestant backgrounds, spirituality meant to hear the Word of God. Many, like 53-year-old non-Armenian Candle, married to an Armenian, felt they are not getting it in the Armenian Church. For her, spiritual nourishment is the most important; "I go [to church] to be fed," she explained. Phyllis, another middle-aged non-Armenian wife of an Armenian, acknowledged the spiritual nature of the liturgy but missed singing hymns in English. She felt that the spirituality of the Armenian services is tied with the history and identity of the Armenian nation, and therefore she could not fully participate. Elsa, an elderly American-born Armenian, loved singing in the choir and the spiritual richness of Easter week, but felt that there should be more emphasis on spreading the Word of God. According to Krikor, an Armenian who attended a non-Armenian church for his wife's sake, in the Armenian Church "you get a little bit of the Bible, and the rest of it is all ceremony." Even 83-year-old Angie, an American-born Armenian, described having concluded with her friends that their knowledge of the Bible came from other churches.

Many interviewees had a heartfelt longing for spirituality, and they felt the Church did not provide it for them. Laura, a 60-year-old American-born Armenian, asked: "Why do I have to go to all these churches?" And she continued: "It's like I'm searching for Church, and searching for something that says something to me. So apparently I'm not getting it in my church." Even in the young professionals' group there was a prevalent feeling that spirituality is missing in their Church. One participant, Hovsep—a 48-year-old Armenian surgeon—however, stated that "spirituality is there but you have to look for it." Obviously, different definitions of spirituality led to these different perceptions.

The aesthetic element was important for many. Though they didn't specify it as spiritual, like all art it no doubt provided a fresh, "pre-scientific" experience. Arie, a 32-year-old with graduate education, for example, went to church for "aesthetic reasons." Aram, a 31-year-old half-Armenian, planning for graduate studies in anthropology, similarly stated that he enjoys the church aesthetically, but "I find that I don't really have much need for the um, theo-, for the theological aspects of church ... at this time in my life." The immediate experience is intensified by the fact that Orthodox worship involves all the senses: seeing the altar, the artifacts and the vestments, hearing the music, smelling the incense, tasting the Eucharistic bread dipped in wine, and touching one another (originally) with the "kiss of peace" and kissing the Gospel at the end.[28] Overall, the "spiritual-aesthetical element is very strong in Orthodoxy."[29]

For several interviewees, what Krikor called "ceremony" includes the mystery of the sacraments, and for them that is exactly the spiritual meaning of the liturgy. A married priest described his non-Armenian fiancée's first visit to the Armenian Church: "She saw a priest raising a chalice, holding the body of Christ, and then distributing it. And to her that was, that was enough." From that time on she felt at home in the Armenian Church. Ann, a 67-year-old non-Armenian from Catholic background, described how the sacrament of communion "makes me whole." The ancient language added to the mystery that made the service meaningful; she liked the Latin in the Catholic Church of her youth and now liked the classical Armenian used in the Armenian services. Lorig expressed the same sentiment, as did other non-Armenians from Catholic backgrounds. Several priests expressed these sentiments as well. One priest described a kit for home Eucharist that he was preparing, complete with a CD of Armenian prayers and incense to be burned at home, to bring the mystery to homes. While priests and non-Armenian ex-Catholics focused on the Eucharist as the center of their spiritual experience, most Armenian lay members did not appear to share this feeling.

All in all, 16 of the 50 non-clergy individual respondents emphasized the spiritual dimension, and seven of them were non-Armenians. Obviously for the latter group, the ethnic dimension was not important, as it was for the majority of Armenians in the sample. Thus their reason for attending the Armenian Church would be spiritual—unless it was merely loyalty to a spouse. Even among the Armenians who emphasized the spiritual dimension, ethnicity did not seem as important as simply being a Christian. For them, the Armenian Church should merely provide an ethnic context for the universal Christian message. Many participants longed for that dimension in their life-worlds.

This first, foundational level of the life-world most explicitly involves the direct, non-mediated, fresh and immediate experience, and that involves the role of the senses, the "organs of perception."[30] Different definitions and expectations regarding spirituality seemed to color the perceptions; for some it was being fed

---

[28] See Amy Frykholm, "Smells and Bells: Turning to Orthodoxy," *The Christian Century*, December 28, 2004, pp. 18–20, for a story of a convert to Orthodoxy and her orientation to this sensory experience.

[29] Lev Gillet (A Monk of the Eastern Church), *Orthodox Spirituality: An Outline of the Orthodox Ascetical and Mystical Tradition*, 2nd edn (Crestwood, 1996), p. 12.

[30] Husserl, *The Crisis*, p. 106.

by the Word or longing for it, for others the beauty of the hymns, for yet others the classical language that they didn't expect to understand, and for many the art and symbolism of the artifacts. Through these various forms, the Church did provide a pre-scientific, mystical or sensory experience for many participants.

Stratum 2: Church as Community

The second level of the life-world, according to Carr's analysis of the concept, is the cultural world, shared in a community. This refers to the world of lived culture with its customs, institutions and relationships. Language, literature, art, norms, values and worldviews also belong to this sphere. This level is taken for granted as well since members have internalized their culture since childhood. The second level presupposes the first level and is built on it. However, the perceptual level also is mediated through the cultural level since every perception necessarily involves interpretation, and the tools needed for interpretation are given by culture. Thus together these two levels constitute the pre-given, natural attitude of the life-world.

Language is an integral part of culture, and the language of worship is a contentious issue in the Armenian diaspora. In the interviews, I did not specifically ask about the language, but almost everyone brought it up in some context. Many wish for greater use of English, while others defend the continued use of the classical Armenian language. This controversy, of course, is not unique to the Armenian Church. In an insightful qualitative study, Woods describes language issues in seven Christian denominations in Australia.[31] She distinguished between sacred language, community language and English, and asked to what extent language was a "core value" for each denomination. She found that the attitude toward language depended on each Church's theological orientation:

> At one extreme, God may be viewed as so special that only a special language or variety of language ... may be used to communicate with or about God. At the other extreme, the emphasis on having a personal relationship with God results in the promotion of the vernacular as appropriate for worship. In other words, churches which feel that God needs to be directly accessible might consider

---

[31] Anya Woods, *Medium or Message? Language and Faith in Ethnic Churches* (Clevedon, Buffalo, Toronto and Sidney, 2004). The denominations she studied are Anglican, Baptist, Catholic, Lutheran, Orthodox, Reformed, and Uniting (Methodist, Congregational and Presbyterian).

'ordinary language' appropriate, while churches which hold a view of God which places Him at greater distance may consider that only a 'sacred' language admits them into His presence.[32]

Generally, Protestant denominations focus on a personal relationship with a God who is near, and at least traditionally Catholic and Orthodox churches have emphasized God's holiness that implies distance. In a diaspora, this dichotomy comes to the fore because of interaction with members of other churches, and because of cultural influences outside the Church that affect worldviews. In the old world, Orthodox societies were more homogeneous. In the American context any church, Orthodox or any other, is one among many possible churches people can attend. As Peter, a priest, observed, people may pass 20 other churches on their way to their own ethnic church. Desire to worship in the context of their own culture attracts them to the Armenian Church, but not understanding the language may make them wonder if it is worth the effort.

As briefly indicated earlier, ex-Catholic members of the Armenian community emphasized the mystery of the Eucharist and thus saw the language of worship less important or saw the ancient language as an integral part of the mystery. Theirs seemed to be a distant, holy God. It appears that those who longed to be fed by the Word desired a closer encounter with a personal God for which they needed a language that they could understand. A comment by Laura was echoed by many: "The service is all Armenian … so I don't get anything out of [it]."

Not understanding the language also complicates the feeling of community. Hye, a 67-year-old American-born Armenian whose parents were from Turkey, described how someone had said to him, "Whoever cannot speak Armenian is not an Armenian." He sighed, "And that, that hurt … Like someone stuck a knife in my back, that really hurt." He decided from then on not to come back to that church because he didn't feel at home there. The issue here, of course, was modern, spoken Armenian. Knowing only Turkish and English, he longed to participate in the Armenian community but did not feel accepted. On the other hand, the shared language of worship all over the world helps maintain the global community of Armenians. Prapeon, a 30-year-old graduate student in a major university, explained this function of the classical language:

> It's my opinion that it's one of the coolest things of being an Armenian that no matter where you go, no matter if it's a Prelacy church or Diocese church or a

---

[32] Woods, *Medium or Message?* p. 41.

Catholic church, the Badarak [Mass] is basically the same. And when you feel that kind of continuity across space it also reminds you of the continuity across time. And that's something that's very special I think about the Armenian Mass.

Cultural and social activities, such as lectures, dances, food and music, were a highly valued drawing point for most interviewees, particularly those who showed little or no interest in religion. As Prapeon said, "In the end, people are not going to the Armenian Church to find God; they're going there to be Armenian. And I think that if the Church can provide people with God, culture, and language, they would be doing a great job." The more educated research participants emphasized the need for lectures, tutoring programs for children, poetry readings, and the like. Fifty-year-old Jerry expressed the desires of many others. He had no interest in the Church except for social reasons, "to meet somebody." His wish was for more activities, dances and all kinds of social events, "coffee and cake"—a wish that he kept repeating. It is a well-known fact in the American Armenian community that social events bring large crowds together, whereas the more intellectual or religious events do not. Jerry thus stated explicitly what multitudes of Armenians show implicitly with their attendance patterns.

The wish for moral guidance was prevalent in the responses of several of the young professionals. Scott, a 36-year-old lawyer, expressed frustration: "Young professionals don't know what the Church believes; more honest discussion would make them go." He wished that priests and bishops would frankly admit when they don't know the answer to an ethical question, for example, rather than skirting around the question as he felt they often do. He especially appreciated a good sermon: "In the Episcopal Church," he said, "they have good speakers, scholars, ethicists, etc., and the sermons are intellectual." Marina, a 33-year-old professional woman, expressed similar frustration in a group discussion: "Listening to an Armenian sermon, you can't relate to it; can't take it with you into a week and have it inspire you. You can't relate to it and then you feel unfed because you haven't shared anything or taken anything from the church service that you can relate to." Also, she was disappointed at the lack of social welcome in the large church she attended, a feeling that was shared by most members of the group.

Several young people in the group interviews expressed a wish to have social programs sponsored by the church and directed to the larger world, beyond the Armenian community. Some members of the young professionals' group had made a proposal to start a soup kitchen, but "nobody followed up" so it never materialized. They had, however, put together a "One-world Festival" that was successful. There was a desire for encouragement, support and resources to continue such outreach.

The central mission of the Church, for most interviewees, was "to bring Armenians together," to help provide "continuity, the Armenian religion, or the Armenian language," as Victor, an active elderly deacon, explained and continued: "the spirituality is not necessarily ... the governing, uh, point ... I mean, the use of religion as a vehicle, but, uh, the real thing happening is our maintenance of our culture as we can." Religion, to him, had only a secondary role. Yet at the end he admitted that he found comfort in the Church; "you grow comfort from it when you are in bad need," he concluded.

Thus even for those not so religiously inclined, the Church with its rituals provides the opportunity for gathering. This was evident in the statement of Shushi, a 39-year-old American-born Armenian in the young professionals' group: "You have ritualistic activities, so that you don't feel weird being in the church, that it should be a natural." She seemed to say that a young, educated person would perhaps not want to be seen in church, but engaging in ritualistic activities that have to do with Armenian tradition and identity makes it "natural"—rituals thus served a "legitimating" function. Personally, she was active in Armenian cultural programs; her response was to someone who talked about "saving souls."

The role of the Armenian Church in providing a community and celebrating the Armenian culture and identity was vividly expressed by Chica, a 49-year-old non-Armenian who had participated in the local Armenian Church in a large city ever since getting married to an Armenian over 20 years earlier:

> And I think now the Armenian Church is not only the Christianity but to show the Armenians that they belong someplace. Because they didn't have a country for a long, long time. So the people that grew up in different countries, the only way that they could become Armenian: from the Armenian Church. So it's uh, it's like a country; it's like having a ship at sea around them. When they see an Armenian church, even though they are American, even though they are born Armenian, they have a place where they can really be Armenians ... So, you can understand, it is little Armenia, okay.

For those Armenians who have not fully assimilated to the dominant culture, the Armenian community is the center of their life-worlds, and the Apostolic Church is the nexus of that community. The Armenian culture, lived and celebrated in the context of the Church, together with the fresh sensory and spiritual experiences that the Church provides or is wished to provide, form the ground, the taken-for-granted foundation of the life-worlds of Armenians in this sample. Historical heritage informs this level of the life-world but is not its focal point.

Stratum 3: Church as Museum

The third level of the life-world that Husserl discusses at length, in fact what he criticizes as the sole preoccupation of Kant and other "rationalists," is that of science. His point is that science, however objective it may be, cannot ignore the pre-given world that people experience in their daily lives. This pre-given life-world is "the constant ground of validity," and "the sciences build upon [this] life-world."[33] As Carr states in his analysis and clarification of Husserl's theory, Husserl combines the cultural and pre-given levels; "the scientific level constitutes a *tertiary* stratum built on the second or cultural level."[34]

But what does science have to do with our examination of the Armenian Church and culture? Husserl and Carr focus on pure, "hard" science, but softer sciences are also part of the scientific enterprise. In its objectification, the scientific attitude places the observer outside the scene, as it were.[35] Whereas culture as lived culture is a taken-for-granted, internalized, more or less subconscious way of living, culture that has become an object of study and reflection has in effect become a science. Customs, artifacts, language, worship practices and all human actions take on a different character when they are simply lived than when they are put under the scrutiny of scientific analysis. Thus, when people work on maintaining their culture—as they often do in a diaspora—they have moved the concept from the lived, taken-for-granted level to the "exterior," scientific level which is the third level of the life-world. Zekiyan actually maintains that the Armenian culture developed "in places other than the land of Armenia—on foreign soils," i.e., in the diaspora,[36] and Braude credits the Enlightenment with

---

[33] Husserl, *The Crisis*, pp. 122, 125.
[34] Carr, "Husserl's Problematic," p. 210.
[35] Husserl, *The Crisis*, p. 113, discusses how "subjectivity objectifies itself as human subjectivity, as an element of the world" that is "exterior" and "grasps only 'externals,' objective entities."
[36] Boghos Levon Zekiyan, "The Armenian Way to Enlightenment: The Diaspora and Its Role," in Hovannissian and Myers, *Enlightenment and Diaspora*, p. 79.

"creating language, culture, and history as autonomous human spheres free from religious authority."[37] These are examples of the objectification of culture.

Museums are the repositories of culture that has been made into a science; they are objectifications of history. Re-enactments of historical events, customs or rituals to show the group's identity and heritage represent socially constructed legitimations of the social order.[38] While the responses quoted below illustrate how the historical heritage of the Armenian people informs their life-worlds today, they look at the Church and culture as if from a distance, as a subject in its own right rather than a subconscious way of living.

A detached attitude toward the Church, yet emphasizing its importance as an institution, was typical of the more educated, not-so-religious respondents. Vahan, a 65-year-old Iranian-born Armenian college professor, exemplified this attitude. By his own estimation, the last time he attended the Church was about 10 years earlier, and that was for a wedding. However, he asserted that "the Church is important for cultural identity, for Armenian identity. It's an institution that is there; it's reassuring that it is there." For Tamar, a 34-year-old Lebanese-born Armenian architect, the Church is "an institution that I should feel connected with, but attend? No!" While she described the Church as "our tie to God," she felt that it was for "the weak ones" who need religion. Personally, she had no need for it, though she sometimes went on Easter to hear the beautiful liturgy. The Church should be a spiritual and cultural pillar, though it was not for her. As an institution, it should never change, and it doesn't need to be relevant; "it has no positive power" or "influence," but some people ought to keep it up.

The cultural heritage was important also for most of the college students in the focus-group interviews. As from a distance, they appreciated the spiritual experience that the liturgy provides, and the community aspect—which they emphasized—was not the immediate, freshly felt experience since they left the church of their childhood. It was more a memory and a somewhat theoretical appreciation for family and community that they felt other churches do not emphasize as much. They appreciated the importance of their cultural heritage and felt that the Church should foster it. Some of them had even chosen Armenian studies or Middle-Eastern studies as their field of learning, or they were learning the Armenian language while in college. The Church, for them, was an institution that provided stability to their lives, a secure feeling that some

---

[37] Benjamin Braude, "The Nexus of Diaspora, Enlightenment, and Nation: Thoughts on Comparative History," in Hovannissian and Myers, *Enlightenment and Diaspora*, p. 44.

[38] Berger, *The Sacred Canopy*.

things do not change. Along with the Church, the culture was seen as "sacred," as Sophia, a 21-year-old half-Armenian, characterized it. Thus, culture was set apart, externalized.

In one small group at an elite university, two students had quite different opinions. While Sonia, quoted earlier, emphasized the spiritual aspect of the Armenian Church, Vartan strongly advocated its cultural mission. "It's not the responsibility of the Church to create better Christians," he remarked, "the Church should be there to create a cultural foundation to allow that process to occur." Then he gave an eloquent mini-lecture:

> From a historical perspective one of the bases for the Armenian Church was to preserve our Armenian uniqueness from the rest of the tribes and the cultures living in the same region at the time, and distance themselves from the Zoroastrian tradition that forced them to become part of the large Persian Empire that was controlling the region at the time. It's funny how the same situation is parallel with the United States right now, that a small group, small culture is trying to preserve its identity among the great large majority that has very different views and is directly or indirectly imposing the culture on the minority ... Christianity for the Armenian Church served as a buffer against absorbing the surrounding culture. And now it's acting in the same way, isn't it?

Along with the culture, the Armenian identity was very important to almost all of the participants in the five college groups, even those who were only partly Armenian.[39] They saw the Church as playing a vital role in maintaining and strengthening that identity, even when as individuals they did not actively participate in the Church. As 19-year-old Berj, who admitted being alienated from the Church, expressed it: "The Church is the center of being an Armenian." And Silencio wondered why "people have a hard time understanding that ethnicity and religion can be the same." One group agreed that the Armenian Mass is the event in which the rich heritage is made evident. Most felt that because of this cultural mission, non-Armenians would not feel at home in the Armenian Church. "For others," Charles explained, "it would have to be more theologically based or faith-based." This was an admission that the Church was "less about religion" than culture, as Emma expressed it. There was almost a missionary zeal about "spreading the word," educating other people about Armenian history, culture and language.

---

[39] Half-Armenian Denise observed that in a mixed family the Armenian culture and heritage tends to take over.

The point here is that when culture is thus explicitly advocated, it has moved to the sphere of science and thus belongs to the third stratum of the life-world. While this attitude may include participation in "cultural activities," these activities are practiced consciously rather than subconsciously. Culture has become an object "out there." This theoretical attitude is different from the simply lived culture. According to Husserl, it is "an attitude *above* the universal conscious life ... through which the world is 'there' for those naively absorbed in ongoing life, as unquestionably present."[40] Similarly, some of the theorizers of culture and Church in this sample implied if not expressed (as Tamar did) the idea that the Church is there for "the weak ones." Thus the "naive" attitude, including spiritual experiences in the Church, has become a phenomenon for study and analysis,[41] and culture has become an object of conscious effort to maintain the heritage and foster a collective identity in a multicultural world. Yet, as both Husserl and Carr indicate, the scientist and her science are part of the total life-world.[42] All in all, as an integral part of cultural identity, the Church is part of the life-worlds of Armenians in the United States like museums are part of the life-worlds of people everywhere, even when they are rarely visited. They are appreciated as storehouses of culture.

Discussion and Conclusion

The life-worlds of today's Armenians, at least in this sample, are in some way related to the Church, whether in opposition to it, in a constructively critical attitude toward it—the subject of endless conversations—or in various levels of involvement with it. The history and culture of the Armenian people and their Apostolic Church, inseparably intertwined,[43] together form the collective Armenian identity and a significant part of the life-worlds of Armenians in the diaspora. The three strata of life-world discussed above provide theoretical understanding of the prevalent attitudes toward the Church in this sample.

---

[40] Husserl, *The Crisis*, p. 150.
[41] Husserl, *The Crisis*, p. 152.
[42] Husserl, *The Crisis*, p. 126, states that "Einstein and every other researcher knows he is in as a human being, even throughout all his activity and research"; Carr, "Husserl's Problematic," p. 207, asserts that "both he [a scientist] and his picture belong within the 'real' world, which Husserl calls the life-world."
[43] See Abraham Terian, *Patriotism and Piety in Armenian Christianity: The Early Panegyrics on Saint Gregory* (Crestwood: St. Vladimir's Seminary Press, 2005).

One red line running through the experiences of the people in this sample is the dichotomy of continuity and change. Those who wished for the Church to continue its ancient practices basically represent three types of members of the Armenian community. First, elderly immigrants generally enjoyed the nostalgia of the familiar forms of worship, including the language and the ancient rituals and practices. The "heavenly experience" was closely related to feeling at home. They had experienced radical change in their lives by moving to another country; it was comforting to know that there is something that has not changed. The camaraderie of like-minded compatriots—even when arriving from different countries—added to the feeling of home by providing a community.[44]

Second, non-Armenian former Catholics who had moved to the Armenian Church, usually through marriage, drew comfort from the fact that, as Ann said, they basically "just moved from one building to another." The Eucharist was the center of their spiritual experience, and the classical Armenian language used in the liturgy was seen as an equivalent to the Latin Mass in the Catholic Church of their youth, necessary for the mystical experience. Some, in fact, were disappointed by the change in the Catholic Church and thus appreciated the continuity that the Armenian Church provided. While the intercultural marriage may have brought substantial change to their life-worlds, the Church represented an enduring dimension that brought stability.

Third, those who had been challenged by new ways of thinking, like college students and others with higher education, also looked to the Church for continuity. Even when they did not participate, knowing that the Church "is there," and hearing the familiar hymns if and when they did go, provided security and stability in a world of uncertainty. Perpetuating the culture as a precious heritage was seen by them as the primary mission of the Church. Even with the "theoretical attitude" of looking at the culture objectively as a historical memory, it gave them solid identity in the multicultural world of the United States.

Those who wished for change in the Apostolic Church were generally from evangelical backgrounds, or they had leanings in that direction. Generally American-born, they were no doubt influenced by the dominant culture of this country and perhaps assimilated to a greater extent than the traditionalists were. They wanted to worship in a language that they could understand, yet wished for

---

[44] This was by no means a universal feeling, as Armenians from different countries sometimes appear to have conflicts in the Church, as do immigrant Armenians in general with American-born Armenians. As Marc Nichanian remarks, Armenians "have interiorized their own dispersion, their own otherness to themselves" ("Prefatory Remarks" in Levon Abrahamian, *Armenian Identity*, p. xii).

a fresh spiritual experience in the context of their ethnic and cultural heritage. They could not see why that would not be possible. For them, language was not necessary for maintaining cultural identity; in fact, some felt the "foreign" (to them) Armenian language may drive them away from the community, thus adherence to the language may weaken the community, if not destroy it.

Whether as a sanctuary for an encounter with the Holy, a community with shared history and lived culture, or a museum for the preservation of cultural heritage, the Armenian Apostolic Church fills an integral part of the life-worlds of those American Armenians who want to preserve their cultural identity. And theoretically, the life-world concept provides a suitable framework for understanding the various shades of feeling that color the attitudes of American Armenians toward their Apostolic Church.

References

Abrahamian, Levon, *Armenian Identity in a Changing World* (Costa Mesa: Mazda Publishers, 2006).

Abramson, Harold, "Religion," in Stephan Thernstrom, Ann Orlov and Oscar Handlin (eds), *Harvard Encyclopedia of American Ethnic Groups* (Cambridge, MA: Harvard University Press, 1980), pp. 869–75.

Baumann, Martin, "A Diachronic View of Diaspora, the Significance of Religion and Hindu Trinidadians," in Waltraud Kokot, Khachig Tölölyan and Carolin Alfonso (eds), *Diaspora, Identity, and Religion: New Directions in Theory and Research* (London and New York: Routledge, 2004), pp. 170–188.

Berger, Peter L., *The Sacred Canopy: Elements of a Sociological Theory of Religion* (New York: Doubleday, 1967).

Braude, Benjamin, "The Nexus of Diaspora, Enlightenment, and Nation: Thoughts on Comparative History," in Richard G. Hovannissian and David N. Myers (eds), *Enlightenment and Diaspora: The Armenian and Jewish Cases* (Atlanta: Scholars Press, 1999), pp. 5–44.

Carr, David, "Husserl's Problematic Concept of the Life-World," in Frederick Elliston and Peter McCormick (eds), *Husserl: Expositions and Appraisals* (Notre Dame, IN: University of Notre Dame Press, 1977), pp. 202–12.

Cowe, Peter S., "Church and Diaspora: The Case of the Armenians," in Michael Angold (ed.), *Eastern Christianity*, The Cambridge History of Christianity, vol. 5 (Cambridge: Cambridge University Press, 2006), pp. 430–56.

Der-Yeghiayan, Garbis, "The Armenian Community: An Opinion Survey" (Mashdots College, Glendale, CA, 2005).

Diatlov, Viktor and Eduard Melkonian, *Armianskaia diaspora: ocherki sotsiokul'turnoi tipologii* [Armenian Diaspora: Essays of sociocultural typology] (Yerevan: Caucasus Institute, 2009).

Frykholm, Amy, "Smells and Bells: Turning to Orthodoxy," *The Christian Century* 28 (December 2004), pp. 18–20.

Gillet, Lev (A Monk of the Eastern Church), *Orthodox Spirituality: An Outline of the Orthodox Ascetical and Mystical Tradition*, 2nd edn (Crestwood: St. Vladimir's Seminary Press, 1996).

Hovannissian, Richard G. and David N. Myers (eds), *Enlightenment and Diaspora: The Armenian and Jewish Cases* (Atlanta: Scholars Press, 1999).

Husserl, Edmund, *The Crisis of European Sciences and Transcendental Phenomenology* (Original title *Die Krisis der europäischen Wissenschaften und die transzendentale Phänomenologische Philosophie*, edited by Walter Biemel, Matinus Nijhoff, 1954); trans. David Carr (Evanston, IL: Northwestern University Press, 1970).

Jendian, Matthew A., *Becoming American, Remaining Ethnic: The Case of Armenian-Americans in Central California* (New York: LFB Scholarly Publishing, 2008).

Kivisto, Peter, "Rethinking the Relationship between Ethnicity and Religion," in James A. Beckford and N.J. Demerath III (eds), *The SAGE Handbook of the Sociology of Religion* (Los Angeles: Sage Publications, 2007), pp. 490–510.

Kokot, Waltraud, Khachig Tölölyan and Carolin Alfonso (eds), *Diaspora, Identity, and Religion: New Directions in Theory and Research* (London and New York: Routledge, 2004).

Moustakas, Clark, *Phenomenological Research Methods* (Thousand Oaks: Sage Publications, 1994).

Nichanian, Mark, "Prefatory Remarks," in Levon Abrahamian, *Armenian Identity in a Changing World* (Costa Mesa: Mazda Publishers, 2006), ix–xiii.

Pattie, Susan Paul, *Faith in History: Armenians Rebuilding Community* (Washington, DC: Smithsonian Institution Press, 1997).

Schutz, Alfred, *On Phenomenology and Social Relations: Selected Writings*, ed. Helmut R. Wagner (Chicago: University of Chicago Press, 1970).

Suny, Ronald Grigor, *Looking Toward Ararat: Armenia in Modern History* (Bloomington and Indianapolis: Indiana University Press, 1993).

Terian, Abraham, *Patriotism and Piety in Armenian Christianity: The Early Panegyrics on Saint Gregory* (Crestwood: St. Vladimir's Seminary Press, 2005).

Terian, Sara Kärkkäinen, "Hidden Treasure: The Armenian Apostolic Church in America (Eastern Diocese) as Seen by a Sample of Its Constituents"

(Commissioned by the Eastern Diocese of the Armenian Church in America, 2006).

Wonneberger, Astrid, "The Invention of History in the Irish-American Diaspora: Myths of the Great Famine," in Waltraud Kokot, Khachig Tölölyan and Carolin Alfonso (eds), *Diaspora, Identity, and Religion: New Directions in Theory and Research* (London and New York: Routledge, 2004), pp. 117–29.

Woods, Anya, *Medium or Message? Language and Faith in Ethnic Churches* (Clevedon, Buffalo, Toronto and Sidney: Multilingual Matters Ltd., 2004).

Zekiyan, Boghos Levon, "The Armenian Way to Enlightenment: The Diaspora and Its Role," in Richard G. Hovannissian and David N. Myers (eds), *Enlightenment and Diaspora: The Armenian and Jewish Cases* (Atlanta: Scholars Press, 1999), pp. 45–85.

Index

Abgar, King of Edessa 15, 20
Abovyan, town 39, 40
Abrahamian, Levon 35, 51n, 107
Abrahamyan, Hovik 43
Adventist(s) 94, 116, 118, 121
Agatʻangeghos 15
aghandavor 84n; *see also* sects
Akori, village 38
Alaverdi, town 38
Alba Iulia, town 200n, 201, 209
Aleksanyan, Samvel 42
Aleppo, city 181–2
Alexandropol, *see* Gyumri
American, *see* United States
anamnesis 148–9
andastan (a prayer) 83, 84n
Ani, medieval city and kingdom 36n, 199
Antelias, Lebanon 4, 13n, 80n, 126, 128, 134, 137, 139, 160, 173–9, 186, 192
Arakelyan, Levon 39, 48, 51
Aram I, Catholicos 135–8, 140–41, 175–7
Ararat, bible translation 113
Ararat, Diocese of the Armenian Apostolic Church 82
Ararat, Mount (Masis) 13–15, 20, 22, 25, 107–8, 116
Ararat, town 76, 78n, 96
Ararat, valley 13
architecture, religious 35, 201
Ardzivian, Abraham 181–2
Argel, village 79
Arinj, village 42, 48, 51
Armenian Apostolic (Orthodox) Church 4, 37, 59–60, 72, 75, 85, 95, 100, 145–6, 172, 175–81, 199–200, 215, 237, 257
    construction of churches 35–55

    divided jurisdictions 125–33
    as foundation of identity 1, 9–30, 61, 66, 104–17, 230, 270
    main forms 74–5
    as related to other churches 76, 104, 110–13, 115–17, 203n, 224n
    traditional practices 146–68, 201–10
Armenian Catholics 1, 4, 24, 73, 95, 104, 108n, 153, 168
    in Lebanon 171, 174, 181–7, 191–3
    in Romania 197, 199–201, 206–9, 238, 260, 262
Armenian identity, *see* Armenianness
Armenian Protestants 1–4, 28, 36–7, 43, 50, 91–118, 153, 159, 167, 174n, 238, 259, 262
    in Lebanon 175, 187–93
Armenian Revolutionary Party, *see* Dashnaktsutyun
Armenianness 2, 5, 23, 36, 80, 88, 186, 205, 210, 222–30, 253; *see also* national identity; ethnic identity
Armenopolis, *see* Gherla
Arordiner, neo-pagans, Children of Ara 25n, 73, 116, 149, 223
Arpee, Leon 92, 100–101
Artashat, town 43
Artsakh, *see* Nagorno-Karabakh
Artsakh diocese 79
Askeran, town 43
assimilation 19n, 112, 117, 135, 155, 186, 198, 215–16, 226, 230
Ateşyan, Archbishop Aram 145n, 153, 164–6
atheism 2, 4, 247
atheist education 57–8
Avan, district 42

Avarayr, battle of 18, 26, 165
Azerbaijan 13, 78, 142–3, 228, 237

Bačau, town 208, 209n
Bakhtin, Mikhail 5, 198
Baku 96, 228
baptism, ritual 15, 16, 58, 103, 112, 127n, 140–42, 148
Baptist(s) 91–2, 94, 96–9, 102–6, 112–21, 261n
Bartholomew, Saint 14, 24
Batumi, town 96
Beirut 152n, 171–80, 83–93
Belgium 65
Berger, Peter 256
Bible 13n, 17, 20, 78, 80, 88, 102, 107, 110, 112, 157, 258–9
    as taught in schools 60–65
    biblical canon 113
Bible Society, Armenian 113
Bilal, Melissa 155, 163
Bourj Hammond, Beirut 173, 178–86
Braude, Benjamin 158n, 265
Brotherhood (*Yekhpairakts'ut'yun*) 4, 27, 71–89
Bucharest 197, 200, 205n, 208–9
Bucovina 199–204n
Budapest 202, 209
Bulgaria, Bulgarian 5, 23n, 237
Burbank, California 236
Byzantine 1, 99, 112

California 5, 145, 233–50, 253
Campbell, David 241n, 242, 249–50
Canada 135, 242, 249–50
canon, canonical 16, 37, 51n, 53n, 82, 84n, 85, 112, 137, 141, 157, 228n
canonization
    of genocide victims 18–20, 141, 162; *see also* genocide
    of saints 16, 20n, 147, 157–8, 161–2, 165, 247n; *see also* saints
Carr, David 254n, 255, 265, 268, 268n
Carruthers, Mary 4, 148–9, 154
Catherine the Great 217

Catholic(s), *see* Armenian Catholics; Armenian Catholics in Lebanon; Armenian Catholics in Romania; Mehitarists; Roman Catholic Church
Catholicos 15n, 16, 16n, 21–2, 22n, 26, 42–3, 45, 77, 77n, 78, 82, 85, 127–41, 158n, 159n, 162, 162n, 175–7, 183, 186, 192, 206n, 245–6; *see also* Etchmiadzin, Catholicosate of; Cilicia, Catholicosate of
Catholicosate, *see* Etchmiadzin, Catholicosate of; Cilicia, Catholicosate of
Ceaușescu, Nicolae 200, 204
Central Asia 96, 228, 228n
Charismatic(s) 91, 94, 96–9, 103, 106, 110–15, 117, 206–7
charismatic type of church 206–7
charity, charitable activity 42, 44, 46, 46n, 49, 55, 78, 189, 219n
Children of Ara, *see* neo-pagans
church construction 3, 35–55
Church of St. Catherine, Saint-Petersburg 217, 219
Cilicia, Armenian Catholic See of 182
Cilicia, Catholicosate (Patriarchate) of the Armenian Apostolic Church 4, 13n, 16n, 22n, 73, 74n, 76, 80, 80n, 81n, 125–43, 171, 175, 177, 180–83
Cilicia, Kingdom of 126n, 173, 191
Cilicia, province 76
Cluj-Napoca, city 197, 199n, 201, 209n
Cold War 128, 141, 192
communism 11n, 27, 73, 128, 134, 200, 204, 245; *see also* Soviet Union
Constantinople 92, 94, 95, 158, 173; *see also* Istanbul
Constantinople, Armenian Patriarchate of 126, 134, 139
Conybeare, Frederic 92, 99, 100, 100n
Cowe, S. Peter 253
creationism 4, 57, 62–8

Damascus 182
Darwinism 65–6; *see also* evolution
Dashnaktsutyun, Armenian Revolutionary Party 126–35, 140–43, 192
Der-Yeghiayan, Gabris 253n
diaspora, *Spyurkh* 1–5, 11, 14, 16n, 26, 40, 42, 45n, 46, 76, 80, 88, 93, 97, 109, 116, 125–43, 154, 171, 176–7, 183, 188, 197–201, 204–10, 233n, 235, 253–6, 261–2, 268
Dink, Hrant 145n, 152, 154, 159, 166–8
diversity 29, 63, 73, 103, 105, 115, 126, 171, 224, 249–50
Diyarbakır, town 151, 152, 152n, 154
donations to the church 3, 39–42, 45–7, 50, 53–4
dreams in religious practices 38–40, 48–52, 76, 102, 201; *see also* visions
Dumbrăveni, town 197, 201, 206–9
Durkheim, Emile 73, 210, 211n
Dwight, Henry O. 92, 95

Earpuz, Cilicia 76
earthquake (1988) 46, 78, 83, 127, 133, 135, 141
Eastern Europe 5, 96, 237
Eberstadt, Mary 242–3
Egypt 94
Eliade, Mircea 103
English, language used in the diaspora 104, 113, 172, 219, 233–4, 237, 261–2
English, translations of religious texts 14n, 146, 152–3, 156n, 259
Estonia, Estonian 237
Etchmiadzin, cathedral and religious center 15, 16n, 18n, 19–27, 81, 82, 113, 157, 159–62, 181, 206n, 225, 245
Etchmiadzin, Catholicosate (Patriarchate) of 4, 13n, 21n, 44, 73–4, 82, 100, 125–43, 158n, 159n, 161n, 180–81, 245
ethnic identity 155, 191, 215, 220, 227, 230, 233n; *see also* ethnicity
ethnic identity "code" 221–7

ethnicity 101, 105–7, 193, 215–16, 220, 226–30, 241–2, 253–4, 260, 267
ethos 116, 235
Evangelical(s) 5, 24n, 81, 83, 91–118, 171, 174–5, 186–93, 259, 269
evolution, theory of, subject in schools 4, 57, 63–7; *see also* Darwinism
Ezras, Archbishop 77n

Farnsley, Arthur 53
Farsi 172n, 237; *see also* Iran
Findikyan, Father Michael Daniel 148–9, 154, 156n
France, French 65, 172, 186, 237, 241n
Frumoasa, town 201, 207–8, 208n

Galstyan, Hambardzum 41
Gandzasar, monastery 38
Garegin I (Karekin I, Hovsepian), Catholicos of Cilicia 127
Garegin I (Karekin I, Sarkissian), Catholicos in Etchmiadzin 16n, 82, 127, 135–8, 141–2
Garegin II (Karekin II, Nersessyan), Catholicos of Etchmiadzin 16, 21, 22, 22n, 26, 82, 127, 133–5, 138–42
Gayanē, Saint 15
Gegharkunik, region 40
gender 84, 86, 113, 114, 117, 220, 236
genocide 2, 5, 11–12, 26, 45, 76, 93, 108, 108n, 116, 126n, 128–33, 135, 140–42, 154, 162n, 173, 177, 182, 186–7, 234–5, 240, 243–7, 256n; *see also* canonization of genocide victims; memory of genocide
Georgia, Georgian 2, 74n, 94, 96, 118, 228, 228n, 237
Germany, German 65, 237
Gevorgyan, Ruben 42
Gheorgheni, town 197, 201, 207–8, 209n
Gherla, town 197, 201, 206–10
Ghevond, Saint 18
Ghulyan, Artak 38–9
Glendale, California 236

globalization 113–14, 117
Godelier, Maurice 54
Gomidas, *see* Komitas
Goodel, William 92, 95
Goris, town 78
government of Armenia 58–9, 73, 96, 126, 134, 140, 246
Great House of Cilicia, *see* Cilicia, Catholicosate of
Greece, Greek 1, 2, 17, 65, 112n, 127n, 128, 175, 181, 200, 237
Greek Catholic Church 200
Gregory of Datev, *see* Grigor Tatevatsi
Gregory the Illuminator (Grigor Lusavorich), Saint 15, 16, 20, 45, 102, 139, 156, 177, 178, 197, 206–9
Grigor Narekatsi, Saint 110, 111, 247, 247n
Grigor Tatevatsi (Gregory of Datev), Saint 111, 146, 157
Gulesserian, Papken Catholicos 245
Gyumri (Alexandropol, Leninakan), city 76, 96, 98, 102, 117, 118, 245

Habermas, Jürgen 67, 148n
Hagigadar, monastery, feast 197, 201–6, 210
Haigazian University, Beirut 172, 174n, 189
Hayakaghak, *see* Gherla
Hayk 14
Hayrikyan, Paruir 41
Hemshins (Hemşins) 2, 152, 152n
Hervieu-Léger, Danièle 3, 9–10, 20, 71
History of Armenian Church (school subject) 59, 61–3, 66–7
Hollywood, California 236
Holocaust 243
Hovnanyan, Hrayr 46
Hrip'simē, Saint 15
Hungary, Hungarian 5, 197, 201, 206–10
Husserl, Edmund 5, 254–8, 265, 268, 268n

Iaşi, town 197, 209n
identity, *see* ethnic identity; national identity

Iorga, Nicolae 199
Iran 94, 126, 128, 236, 266; *see also* Farsi
Iraq 126, 237
Islam 2, 60, 152, 225, 235, 243–4
Istanbul 4, 5, 145–68, 182; *see also* Constantinople

Jefferson, Thomas 241
Jehovah's Witnesses 23, 25, 99, 99n, 116
Jendian, Matthew 233n, 253
Jerusalem 112n, 158–60
Jerusalem, Patriarchate of 13, 126, 134, 139, 158n, 161n, 176
Jesus Christ 149, 158, 247
Jews, Jewish 10, 95, 148–9, 243
John the Baptist (Surb Karapet) 49
John Scopes trial 64–5

Kant, Immanuel 265
Karabagh, *see* Nagorno-Karabakh
Karabagh Movement 78
Kara-Kala, village 96
Karpov, Viacheslav 67
Kars, town 96
khachkar (cross-stone) 17, 17n, 19, 43, 49
Khor Virap, monastery 15–16
Khorentsi, Movses 13, 13n, 15, 17, 24
Khrimian, Catholicos Mktrich (Khrimian Hayrig) 162, 162n, 165
Kirovokan, *see* Vanadzor
Kochetkov, Father Georgii 77n
Koghb, village 40–41
Köllner, Tobias 40, 48
Komitas (Gomidas, Soghomon Soghomonian) 19, 110, 111n, 121, 162
Koryun 17

Labashlyan, Elisabeth 76
Lazarev Brothers Education Center 219, 219n
Lebanon 4, 13n, 46, 46n, 76, 82n, 93, 126, 137, 171–93, 258
  Armenian Catholics, *see* Armenian Catholics

Armenian Orthodox Church Prelacy 139, 176–81, 192
Armenian Protestants, *see* Armenian Protestants in Lebanon
civil war 173–5, 178, 188–9, 193
Leipzig 202
Leninakan, *see* Gyumri
Levonyan, Rene 93, 96, 100, 104, 110
Little Armenia, Los Angeles 236, 264
liturgy, Armenian-Catholic rite 185, 201
liturgy (*Patarak, Badarak*), Armenian Apostolic 37, 43, 81n, 133, 148–9, 156, 156n, 157–63, 204–8, 258–60, 263, 266, 269
Lord's Prayer 58, 156n, 219
Los Angeles 118, 193, 233–4, 236, 236n, 241

madagh (*matagh*, sacrificial ritual) 49, 204–5
Malatya, district in Yerevan 38, 45
Malatya, town 151, 154
Mamikonyan, Vardan, *see* Vardan, Saint
Manoogian, Louise Simone 45
Mardakert, town 79–80, 83
Maronite(s) 181, 182n, 183n, 186, 192
Martiros, village 38, 47
martyr, martyrdom 12, 14, 15, 20, 20n, 36, 49, 133, 156; *see also* genocide
Mashtots, Mesrop 13, 17, 18, 20, 24, 75, 224
Masis, *see* Ararat, Mount
Matenadaran 18, 18n
matur (small shrine) 49–50; *see also* sanctuary
Mauss, Marcel 54
Mecca 19n, 208
Mekhitarists 24n, 184
memory, collective and historical 3, 4, 9–10, 14, 36–7, 40, 72, 86, 108, 146–50, 154, 156, 163–7, 256, 269
memory of genocide 5, 19, 20n, 116, 130, 133, 140–41, 155; *see also* genocide; canonization of genocide victims
Men, Father Alexander 77n

migration(s) 4, 44, 44n, 51, 93, 114, 127, 142, 174, 179–81, 188, 193, 198, 215–16
millet 2, 73n, 95, 153, 158n, 177
miracle 25, 38–40, 48, 51–2, 157, 207n
mission, missionaries (non-Armenian) 25, 79, 83, 91–6, 101–2, 115, 178n
mission, within Armenian Church 11, 50, 81, 85, 88, 183, 189, 207, 267
Moldavia (Moldova) 199, 203n, 228n
monasticism, monasteries 11, 16, 17n, 22n, 36, 38, 74, 74n, 160–61, 176–82, 197, 201–6, 210, 224
Moscow 77, 77n, 118, 218n
Mother of God, Surb Astvatsatsin 51, 177, 197, 201–4
Mother See of Holy Etchmiadzin, *see* Etchmiadzin, Catholicosate of
Mount Lebanon, Lebanon 176, 181–2, 186, 193
Moustakas, Clark 257n
Movses, village 40
Muhammad 243
Muron, Holy Muron (*surb miuron*) 127, 127n, 138
Muslim, *see* Islam
mythos 99, 100, 101–3, 107–10, 115

Nagorno-Karabakh 3, 16n, 21n, 25–6, 40, 43, 44n, 45–6, 73, 78–9, 83, 86, 95, 113, 133, 135, 142
national identity, in connection to religion 10–12, 21, 46, 66–7, 72, 74, 78, 86, 104–8, 112, 140, 155, 223
nationalism 2, 10–12, 19, 27, 72–3, 77, 86–7, 107–8, 140, 186, 206
nation-building 4, 66, 73, 86
neo-pagans, *see Arordiner*
Nersoyan, Hegop 245
New York 129, 249
Nichanian, Marc 269n
Noah, Noah's Arc 13–15, 20, 22, 52, 107, 116

oligarch 39–45, 53n, 54
Ōrats'oyts' (liturgical calendar) 157, 161n

Ormanian, Malachia, Patriarch 146, 162, 164–5, 240
Oshakan, town 17–18
Ottoman Empire 1–2, 11n, 19, 73n, 77, 91–2, 95, 100, 108, 112, 115, 129, 142, 145, 153–5, 158, 173, 181–2, 235, 243–4; *see also* Turkey

Panossian, Razmik 10, 11n
Pasadena, California 236
Paulician(s) 24n, 92, 99–101, 115; *see also* Tondrakian(s)
Pentecostal(s) 91–2, 94–9, 103–18, 238
Peter the Great 216
Pew Research Center 5, 234n, 238, 250
Poladian, Terenig Vartabed 240
post-secular 37, 67
post-Soviet (including post-Soviet religiosity) 3–4, 9, 23n, 25, 27, 39–40, 45n, 51–4, 65, 71–5, 87, 218, 224, 228
Protestant(s), *see* Armenian Protestants
Protestantism 73, 76, 82, 82–5; *see also* Armenian Protestants
public schools 3, 57–68
Putnam, Robert 241n, 249–50

Redgate, Ann Elisabeth 10
reform in Church 17n, 77, 85–7, 131, 137–8, 141
religion
 constructed 12, 35, 256, 266
 modernized 38, 83; *see also* religious modernity
 objectified 36, 72, 265–6
 vernacular 3, 17, 28, 38, 41, 74n, 80, 261
religiosity 2–5, 27, 36, 38, 42, 51, 71, 74–5, 80–82, 88, 150, 191, 223–5, 238–41, 250
religious identity 29, 60, 66, 88, 104–10, 115, 125, 240
religious modernity 71, 87–8
religious revival 2–3, 47, 58, 66, 74n, 75–81, 87, 96, 101–3, 185

Roman Catholic Church 146, 157, 203, 208n, 225n, 269
Romania, Romanian 5, 197–211
Rome 183–4, 199
Russia, Russian 1–5, 26, 40, 44, 48, 57, 65, 72, 96–8, 104, 114, 126, 131n, 142, 172, 176, 215–30, 236–7, 249
Russian Orthodox Church 2, 77n, 215, 224, 224n, 227–30

sacred 14, 17n, 18, 23–5, 36–8, 48–54, 71, 73, 82, 112, 148–9, 261–2, 267
sacred place (space) 36, 37, 51, 51n, 52, 112
sacredness 25, 36–8, 52
Saint-Petersburg 5, 65, 215–30
saints, veneration of 4, 147, 156, 161–8; *see also* canonization of saints
sanctuary 5, 51, 52, 203, 206; *see also matur*
Sardarapat, battle of 25
Sargsyan, Serzh 26, 104, 105n, 140
Sarkissian, Ani 25
Schutz, Alfred 255
sects, sectarian 4, 24, 24n, 28n, 59, 84, 84n, 100, 110, 116, 174–5, 188, 188n, 193; *see also aghandavor*
secular 1–5, 11–12, 16, 22–3, 28, 37–9, 42, 53, 55, 60, 66, 66n, 67, 131, 146–7, 154, 166–8, 219, 234, 245; *see also* secularization
secularization 11n, 14, 51, 54, 66, 67, 67n, 72
Shamakhi, village 95
sharagan (*sharakan*, hymn) 110–11, 159–60
Shnork Kaloustian, Patriarch 145–6, 163–8
Shoghakat, TV Channel 79
Shushi, town 95, 113, 264
Smith, Antony 10
Smith, Eli 92, 95
South America 94, 128
Soviet education 57–9, 66
Soviet impact on religion 4, 23, 28, 37–9, 47–9, 51n, 53–5, 72, 80–84, 224, 234, 240, 246–7

Soviet Union, Soviet, USSR 1, 2, 11, 11n, 12n, 23, 26, 29, 74–7, 82, 84n, 93, 96, 102–3, 115, 128–30, 141–2, 200, 218, 223, 240, 243–6, 249; *see also* post-Soviet
Spain, Spanish 65, 237
spirituality 2, 37–8, 77, 84n, 85, 259–60, 264
Spyurkh, *see* diaspora
Stalin, Stalinist 11n, 76, 245
Stavropol, town 44
Stepanavan, town 78n, 79
Suceava, town 197, 199, 201–6, 208
Sukhumi, town 96
Şumuleu, town 210
Sweden, Swedish 65, 237
Syria 46, 93, 126, 133, 172, 193, 237, 258
Syriac 1, 17, 182
Syuni, Vasak 18

Tavush, region 40
Terian, Abraham 10, 156n
Ter-Petrosyan, Levon 18, 136, 142
Thaddeus, Apostle 14–15, 24, 157
Tiflis, Tbilisi 96, 102
Tonavag (Tonavagian), Astvatsatur and Trakan, brothers 202
Tondrakian(s) 24n, 92–4, 99–101, 115; *see also* Paulician(s)
Tootikian, Vahan 93
tradition, religious 1–4, 13–18, 20–29, 35–8, 66–7, 71–6, 80–88, 91, 94, 97, 103–17, 146–8, 154–6, 167, 181, 199, 203–10, 217–20, 224–8, 234, 241, 247, 249, 255–6, 264, 267, 269
Transylvania 199–201, 206–10
Trdat III, Saint 15, 46
Tsarukyan, Gagik 39–42, 45, 53n
Tsitsernakaberd memorial 9n, 108
Turkey, Turkish 13, 26, 65, 77, 100, 104n, 109, 126n, 130n, 133, 140, 145n, 146–56, 163–8, 186, 200, 202n, 237, 244–5, 262; *see also* Ottoman Empire

ukht (vow) 85
Ukraine, Ukrainian 5, 201n, 228n, 229, 237
United Kingdom, British 65, 65n, 91, 93
United States, American 2, 5, 38–9, 46, 65, 91–2, 95, 101, 104, 125, 128, 131, 142, 145, 160–62, 200, 233–70
US Census Bureau 235
USSR, *see* Soviet Union

Vagharshapat, town 13n, 96
Vanadzor (Kirovakan) 76, 78n, 118
Vardan, Saint 18, 18n, 20, 20n, 26, 127
Vatican 182–4
Vazgen I (Vasken I), Catholicos 21n, 78, 82, 82n, 127–35, 141, 206n
Venezuela 237
Vienna 184, 202
visions, religious 15, 17, 22, 38, 48, 50–52, 76, 102–3, 111, 115, 202; *see also* dreams

Wallachia 199
Western Europe 234, 249
Woods, Anya 261

Yeghisheh 250
Yegiaian, Buzand 93
Yekhpairakts'ut'yun, *see* Brotherhood
Yerevan 4, 13n, 16, 18, 28n, 29, 38, 42, 45–8, 64, 76–80, 87n, 91, 96–9, 108–9, 114, 117–18, 152n, 181, 236
Yeritsian, Alexander 94

Zakharian, Hamlet 75, 77, 77n, 78, 80n, 81n, 82
Zamca, monastery 201–2, 205
Zekiyan, Boghos Levon 265
Zohrabyan, Grigor 113
Zoroastrian(s) 250, 267